TRACING BACK TH

KURODA INSTITUTE
Classics in East Asian Buddhism

The Record of Tung-shan
Translated by William F. Powell

Tracing Back the Radiance

CHINUL'S KOREAN WAY OF ZEN

Robert E. Buswell, Jr.

A Kuroda Institute Book
UNIVERSITY OF HAWAII PRESS • HONOLULU

Originally published as *The Korean Approach to Zen:
The Collected Works of Chinul.* © 1983 University of
Hawaii Press
Abridgment © 1991 Kuroda Institute
All Rights Reserved
Printed in the United States of America

01 00 99 98 97 96   6 5 4 3 2

Library of Congress Cataloging-in-Publication Data
Chinul, 1158–1210.
    [Works. English. 1992]
    Tracing back the radiance : Chinul's Korean way of Zen /
[translated with an introduction by] Robert E. Buswell, Jr.
        p.   cm. — (Classics in East Asian Buddhism)
    Abridged ed. of: The Korean approach to Zen.
    "A Kuroda Institute book."
    Includes bibliographical references (p.   ) and index.
    ISBN 0-8248-1427-4
    1.   Taehan Pulgyo Chogyejong—Early works to 1800. 2.   Zen
Buddhism—Korea—Early works to 1800. I.   Buswell, Robert E.
II.   Chinul, 1158–1210.   Korean approach to Zen. III.   Title.
IV.   Series.
    BQ9519.C454T7313   1992
    294.3'.927—dc20   91–28980
                                                   CIP

The Kuroda Institute for the Study of Buddhism and
Human Values is a non-profit, educational corporation,
founded in 1976. One of its primary objectives is to
promote scholarship on Buddhism in its historical,
philosophical, and cultural ramifications. The Institute
thus attempts to serve the scholarly community by
providing a forum in which scholars can gather at con-
ferences and colloquia. Conference volumes, as well as
individual monographs, are published in the Institute's
Studies in East Asian Buddhism series. To complement
these scholarly studies, the Institute also makes available reliable translations of some of the major classics
of East Asian Buddhism in the present series.

University of Hawai'i Press books are printed on acid-
free paper and meet the guidelines for permanence and
durability of the Council on Library Resources

To the Monks of Songgwang sa

Contents

Preface

CHINUL (1158–1210), the founder of the Korean tradition of Zen, provides one of the most lucid and accessible accounts of Zen practice to be found anywhere in East Asian literature. *Tracing Back the Radiance: Chinul's Korean Way of Zen* combines an extensive introduction to Chinul's life and thought with translations of three of his most representative works. Chinul's optimal regimen of Zen training starts with an initial sudden awakening to the mind's inherent enlightenment, followed by gradual cultivation of that awakening, so that one can learn to *act*, as well as *be*, enlightened. The principal means he proposes for catalyzing this initial awakening is through tracing the radiance emanating from the luminous core of the mind back to its source, restoring the mind to its natural enlightened state. Chinul was also the first Korean Buddhist to teach kōan meditation—the contemplation of Zen conundrums—as a supplementary technique for bringing about awakening. His distinctive explanation of the kōan technique provides real insight into the soteriological processes that govern this uniquely Zen form of meditation. Rather than the iconoclasm Westerners commonly presume to exemplify Zen, Chinul's works reveal the profound intellectual side of the tradition, where precise analysis of religious issues was welcomed, not denounced.

Tracing Back the Radiance is an abridgment of my book *The Korean Approach to Zen: The Collected Works of Chinul,* which the University of Hawaii Press published in 1983. *The Korean Approach to Zen* found a small, but I believe appreciative, audience of scholars of East Asian Buddhism as well as Western practitioners of Zen. By combining an extensive study of Chinul with annotated translations of most of his major works, I sought to provide a wider context for understanding Chinul's contributions to Korean Buddhism as well as make available to Westerners a substantive body of source materials on Korean Zen. Still, I always hoped that there would be a way to introduce a wider audience to Chinul and his Korean way of Zen.

Now that *The Korean Approach to Zen* has gone out of print, the University of Hawaii Press suggested reprinting the book in the Classics in East Asian Buddhism series the Press copublishes with the Kuroda Institute, a small association of Western Buddhist scholars. I broached with Peter Gregory, my good friend and executive director of the Institute, the possibility of doing instead a more accessible version of that book. *Tracing Back the Radiance* is the result, an abridgment that I hope will be of value to Westerners interested in Zen and useful in undergraduate courses in Buddhism, Zen, and Korean civilization. I also hope that this book may inspire readers who might at first have found the more comprehensive work, *The Korean Approach to Zen,* too daunting in size and technical in content.

In order to make this volume available in paperback at a reasonable price, it has not been possible to make any revisions of the material beyond correcting a few typographical errors. Readers wishing to explore how my own thinking on Chinul has evolved over the last eight years may want to consult the following relevant articles: (1) "Chinul's Ambivalent Critique of Radical Subitism in Korean Sŏn Buddhism," *Journal of the International Association of Buddhist Studies* 12-2 (1989): 20–44; (2) "Ch'an Hermeneutics: A Korean View," in *Buddhist Hermeneutics,* Studies in East Asian Buddhism, no. 6, ed. Donald S. Lopez, Jr. (Honolulu: University of Hawaii Press, 1988), pp. 231–256; (3) "The Short-Cut Approach of *K'an-hua* Meditation: The Evolution of a Practical Subitism in Chinese Ch'an Buddhism," in *Sudden and Gradual Approaches to Enlightenment in Chinese Thought,* Studies in East Asian Buddhism, no. 5, ed. Peter N. Gregory (Honolulu: University of Hawaii Press, 1987), pp. 321–377; and (4) "Chinul's Systematization of Chinese Meditative Techniques in Korean Sŏn Buddhism," in *Traditions of Meditation in Chinese Buddhism,* Studies in East Asian Buddhism, no. 4, ed. Peter N. Gregory (Honolulu: University of Hawaii Press, 1986), pp. 199–242.

Readers may also peruse Hee-Sung Keel's valuable *Chinul: The Founder of the Korean Sŏn Tradition,* Berkeley Buddhist Studies Series, vol. 6 (Berkeley: Center for South and Southeast Asian Studies, 1984). For background on Korean Zen prior to Chinul, see my recent *The Formation of Ch'an Ideology in China and Korea: The Vajrasamādhi-Sūtra, a Buddhist Apocryphon* (Princeton: Princeton University Press, 1989). And for Zen training in modern-day Korean monasteries, see my *Zen Monasticism: Buddhist Practice in Contemporary Korea* (Princeton: Princeton University Press, 1992).

Chinul's works are translated from the following editions: Pang Hanam, ed. and Kim T'anhŏ, trans., *Pojo pŏbŏ* (Chinul's Dharma Talks) (1937, reprinted, Chŏlla Namdo: Songgwang sa, 1975); and An Chinho, ed., *Pŏpchip pyŏrhaeng nok chŏryo pyŏngip sagi* (Excerpts from the *Dharma Col-*

lection and Special Practice Record with Personal Notes) (Seoul: Pŏmnyun sa, 1957). All of Chinul's works appear also in *Han'guk Pulgyo chŏnsŏ* (Complete Works of Korean Buddhism), vol. 4 (Seoul: Tongguk University Press, 1982). Other Buddhist classical works are cited in standard form from the *Taishō shinshū daizōkyō* and the *Dai-Nihon zokuzōkyō*. Modern works are as listed in the Bibliography. Daniel Altschuler helped me prepare the index.

I would like to express my thanks to Peter Gregory, general editor of the Kuroda Institute's series with the University of Hawaii Press, and all the members of the Institute's editorial board—Carl Bielefeldt, Robert Gimello, Luis Gómez, Donald Lopez, and Alan Sponberg—for generously backing this project. I am deeply grateful for the personal and professional ties we have all shared throughout the last decade.

Abbreviations

C	Chinese pronunciation.
CHT	*Chung-hua ch'uan-hsin-ti Ch'an-men shih-tzu ch'eng-hsi t'u* 中華傳心地禪門師資承襲圖. By Tsung-mi 宗密.
CTK	*Ch'eng-tao ko* 證道歌. By Yung-chia 永嘉.
CTL	*Ching-te ch'uan-teng lu* 景德傳燈錄. Compiled by Tao-yüan 道原.
CYC	*Ch'an-yüan chi* 禪源集. By Tsung-mi. Not extant.
CYCTH	*Ch'an-yüan chu-ch'üan chi tou-hsü* 禪源諸詮集都序. By Tsung-mi.
CYHJ	*Pŏpchip pyŏrhaeng nok sagi hwajok* 法集別行錄私記畫足. By Hoeam Chŏnghye 晦庵定慧.
CYKM	*Pŏpchip pyŏrhaeng nok chŏryo kwamok pyŏngip sagi* 法集別行錄節要科目並入私記. By Yŏndam Yuil 蓮潭有一.
DCSPR	Present English translation of Chinul's *Pŏpchip pyŏrhaeng nok chŏryo pyŏngip sagi* 法集別行錄節要並入私記.
FMC	*Ta-chi fa-men ching* [*Saṅgīti-sūtra*] 大集法門経. Translated by Dānapāla.
HHYCL	*Hsin Hua-yen ching lun* 新華嚴経論. By Li T'ung-hsüan 李通玄.
HTC	*Hsü tsang-ching*; Taiwanese reprint of the *Dainihon zokuzōkyō* 大日本續藏経. Kyoto, 1905–1912. Sequential number established according to listing in *Shōwa hōbō sōmokuroku* 昭和法寶總目錄, vol. 2.
HYC	*Ta-fang-kuang fo hua-yen ching* [*Avataṃsaka-sūtra*] 大方廣佛華嚴経. Translated by Śikṣānanda.

HYCb	*Ta-fang-kuang fo hua-yen ching* [*Avataṃsaka-sūtra*] 大方廣佛華嚴経. Translated by Buddhabhadra.
IBK	*Indogaku bukkyōgaku kenkyū* 印度學佛教學研究.
K	Korean pronunciation.
KJ	*Korea Journal.* Published by the Korean National Commission for Unesco.
KRS	*Koryŏ sa* 高麗史. Compiled by Chŏng In-ji 鄭麟趾 et al.
LCL	*Lin-chi lu* 臨濟錄. Recorded by Hui-jan 慧然.
LTTC	*Liu-tsu t'an ching* 六祖壇経. Compiled by Tsung-pao 宗寶.
PCPHN	*Pŏpchip pyŏrhaeng nok* 法集別行錄. By Tsung-mi.
PGHP	*Pulgyo hakpo* 佛教學報. Published by Tongguk Taehakkyo 東國大學校.
PKC	*Sungsan Pak Kil-chin paksa hwagap kinyŏm: Han'guk Pulgyo sasang sa* 崇山朴吉真博士華甲紀念：韓國佛教思想史.
PNP	*Po-na-pen erh-shih-ssu shih* 百衲本二十四史. *SPTK* ed.
PWYF	*P'ei-wen yün-fu* 佩文韻府. Compiled by Chang Yü-shu 張玉書.
SGYS	*Samguk yusa* 三國遺史. By Iryŏn 一然.
SPTK	*Ssu-pu ts'ung-k'an* 四部叢刊.
SSYN	*Shih-shih i-nien lu* 釋氏疑年錄. Compiled by Ch'en Yüan 陳垣.
T	*Taishō shinshū daizōkyō* 大正新修大藏経. Tokyo, 1924–1935.
TCCHL	*Ta-ch'eng ch'i-hsin lun* [*Mahāyānaśraddhôtpāda-śāstra*] 大乘起信論. Attributed to Aśvaghoṣa.
THYL	*Ta-hui yü-lu* 大慧語錄. Recorded by Wen-wen 蘊聞.
TYS	*Sinjŭng Tongguk yŏji sŭngnam* 新增東國輿地勝覽. Compiled by No Sa-sin 盧思慎 et al.
WH	*Wen-hsüan* 文選. Compiled by Li Shan 李善.
YCC	*Yüan-chüeh ching* 圓覺経. Translation attributed to Buddhatrāta.
YCCTSC	*Yüan-chüeh ching ta shu ch'ao* 圓覺経大疏鈔. By Tsung-mi.
ZZ	*Dainihon zokuzōkyō* 大日本續藏経. Revised edition (in progress), Tokyo, 1950–.

Introduction: The Life and Thought of Chinul

I. Korean Buddhism Before Chinul

CHARACTERISTICS OF THE KOREAN BUDDHIST TRADITION

When examining Korean Buddhism and the role played by exegetes like Chinul in the forging of that tradition, it is essential to remember that, its later "hermit kingdom" appellation notwithstanding, Korea was in no sense isolated from other areas of northeastern Asia. Descriptive and nativistic considerations aside, by ignoring the greater East Asian context in which Korean Buddhism developed and treating the tradition in splendid isolation, we stand more chance of distorting the tradition than clarifying it. In fact, there was an almost organic relationship between the Korean, Chinese, and, to a somewhat lesser extent, the Japanese Buddhist traditions. Korean Buddhist schools all have as their basis earlier doctrinal and soteriological innovations on the Chinese mainland. Although Korean scholars and adepts training at the mecca of the Chinese mainland participated personally in such achievements, and Koreans in their native land made signally important contributions in the development of East Asian Buddhist philosophy, China had closer ties, over the silk routes, with the older Buddhist traditions of India and Central Asia, and, in addition, its very size, both in territory and in population, allowed it to harbor a variety of Buddhist schools without undermining the vigor of the tradition as a whole. Both factors led to Chinese precedence in establishing trends within the religion. Early on, however, the Koreans, somewhat like the Sung dynasty Chinese Buddhists, found an important role for themselves as preservers and interpreters of the greater Buddhist tradition. By treating evenhandedly the vast quantity of earlier material produced by Chinese Buddhists, the Koreans formed what was in many respects the most ecumenical tradition in Asia. It is this feature which makes Korean Buddhism so fascinating today, for the tradition is a repository of many forgotten qualities of ancient Chinese Buddhism. And with the apparent obliteration of Buddhism from China, Korean Buddhism offers us a means of evaluating and, in certain cases, still experiencing directly some of the finest flowerings of Chinese Buddhist culture.

Paralleling early developments in the northern Chinese dynasties, Buddhism from its inception in Korea was a state religion enjoying the support of the crown and wielding immense ecclesiastical, political, and economic influence. Since the vulnerable geographical position of the country left it open to periodic foreign invasions, Korean tribal chiefs who aspired to hegemony during the political consolidation of the Three Kingdoms (first century B.C.–A.D. 668) relied heavily on the universalistic ethic of Buddhism to legitimize and empower their regimes. The responsive power of the Buddhas and bodhisattvas was considered to be not only an effective shield against the terrors of foreign invasion and natural disaster but also a unifying force among the populace at large. Thus the royal families gave enthusiastic and munificent support to the religion and encouraged its dissemination among the masses. Dynasties were won over to Buddhism not simply because of its profound philosophy, exotic rituals, or the promise of favorable rebirths in heaven for themselves and their ancestors; rather, they were as much concerned with the prosperity of their houses and the security of their kingdoms. Indeed, throughout Korean Buddhist history, many of the most visible accomplishments of the tradition, such as the woodblock carving of the Buddhist canon undertaken during the Koryŏ dynasty, were initiated as a means of national protection. This symbiotic relationship between Buddhism and the court—the court supporting the dissemination of the religion throughout the realm, the monks interceding on behalf of the court for the security of the kingdom—was vividly demonstrated during Hideyoshi's invasion of the Korean peninsula (1592–1598), when it was the monks' militia which first turned back the Japanese thrust. Even in modern-day Korea, the national Chogye Order, the officially recognized ecclesiastical body, has formed a Monks' Militia for National Defense (Hoguk Sŭngdan) in which all monks must participate.[1]

The need for social harmony dictated by the threats constantly lurking on all its borders soon was extended into a need for philosophical harmony as well. Korea could simply not support the large numbers of individual sects of Buddhism that were spawned on the Chinese mainland, and the syncretic vision which vivified the writings of many Chinese philosophers in the Chinese T'ien-t'ai (K. Ch'ŏnt'ae) and Hua-yen (K. Hwaŏm) schools soon inspired Korean thinkers as well. The intensely sectarian Buddhism of the medieval Chinese tradition was approached syncretically by almost all major Korean Buddhist thinkers. This syncretic focus of the tradition finds one of its finest exponents in Chinul, and it will be discussed in detail later.

As in China, indigenous religious and shamanistic beliefs were not abandoned by the people or the court upon their acceptance of Buddhism, and the religion in Korea was viewed through the veil of these native practices.[2] As Buddhism developed into a popular movement, it was seen as a miracle religion full of the bizarre and supernatural. Thaumaturgic elements which had been vital in the northern Chinese tradition became central in Korean Buddhism as well. Indeed, this contact was so intimate that some authors have gone so far as to say that the early tradition was a thoroughgoing amalgamation of Buddhism and native Korean shamanism.[3]

This popular orientation of early Buddhism in Korea led to a strong interest among the people in procuring present happiness rather than future salvation. The constant perils faced by the populace due to their geographic vulnerability made it only natural that the Koreans would place their greatest faith in peace, security, and physical well-being in this life, not the unknown quantities of the future. Indeed, it was the orientation of Buddhist piety toward present prosperity which made the religion so attractive on both an individual and a national level and led to its quick acceptance by the country.[4]

In evaluating Chinul's contributions to the development of Korean Buddhism, it will be well to keep these various features of the early tradition in mind: a need for harmony at all levels, close ties with the ruling families, an infusion of native and popular elements, and an emphasis on mundane benefits rather than spiritual achievement.

INTRODUCTION OF BUDDHISM INTO KOREA

By the latter half of the fourth century, approximately three centuries after the introduction of Buddhism into China, the tribal leagues which had ruled over Korean territory since the time of the early migrations into the peninsula had matured into full-fledged kingdoms.[5] Over the first centuries of the common era, the Koguryŏ clan, which was affiliated with the larger Puyŏ tribe,[6] conquered the neighboring tribal leagues of Okcho on the northeast coast, Tongye on the coast just south of Okcho, and finally the remaining Puyŏ tribes in central Manchuria. The Han colony of Hyŏnt'o (C. Hsüant'u) was overrun early in the second century, and in 313 Koguryŏ conquered the ancient Han colony of Nangnang (C. Lo-lang) and its southern extension Taebang (C. Tai-fang), ending four centuries of Chinese suzerainty in Korea. Thus was formed the earliest of the three kingdoms of ancient Korea: Koguryŏ,[7] which ruled over both the northern portions of the peninsula and south-central Manchuria.

Following soon upon Koguryŏ's lead, a tribal league in the old Mahan federation in the extreme south of the peninsula developed by the middle third century into the Paekche kingdom which came to rule the southwestern peninsula.[8] Somewhat later, by the middle of the fourth century, the Saro tribe centered near the southeastern coastline matured into the kingdom of Silla, the state which eventually unified the entire peninsula under a single banner.[9]

During the earliest period of its history, Korea was influenced most by the culture of the seminomadic tribes of Central and North Asia, with whom it shared racial and cultural affinities.[10] These contacts exerted a much stronger influence initially over Korean culture and society than did those with the Han race to the west. Indeed, Korean scholars remain fascinated with the idea that Buddhism in Korea traces from these early contacts with the Central Asian regions which had spawned Chinese Buddhism, if not from direct contacts with India itself.[11] By the time of the Warring States period (403–221 B.C.), when refugees from the northern Chinese states of Yen, Ch'i, and Chao immigrated into the state of Ancient Chosŏn during the Han unification wars, Chinese influence became all-pervasive.[12] With the advent of the Three Kingdoms came steadily increasing diplomatic and cultural exchanges with the Chinese dynasties of the mainland. Indeed, from the time of the Three Kingdoms, China's influence was so strong as to obscure entirely that coming from the Central Asian steppes.

Koguryŏ, the first tribal league to mature into a full-fledged kingdom, was continually challenged by neighboring tribes on both its northern and southern borders. Incursions from other Tungusic tribes in northwestern Manchuria and from the Paekche kingdom to the southwest ravaged Koguryŏ political and economic fortunes. In 342, the Hsien-pei[13] of the Former Yen state (349–370)[14] who had established themselves in the northeast of China, invaded Koguryŏ, took the capital, captured the queen and queen mother, and took fifty thousand men and women as slaves before withdrawing.[15] This northern threat was removed only in 370 when Yen was conquered by Fu Chien (r. 357–384), the third ruler of the Former Ch'in dynasty (351–394), a monarchy founded by the proto-Tibetan Ti people.[16] Ch'in's conquest of all northern China, as well as the Kansu corridor and the Indo-European petty kingdoms of the Tarim River Basin,[17] brought it control of the lucrative silk trade routes and put northern China in direct contact with Central Asian Buddhism.

Former Ch'in hegemony over eastern Turkestan allowed foreign influences to grow freely in northern China. The political, cultural, religious, and commercial fluidity and tolerance of Turkestan allowed Indian, Iranian, Hellenistic, and Chinese cultures to interact and enrich one another.[18] Hence the uniquely cosmopolitan atmosphere of the northern Chinese frontier regions provided a fertile ground in which a truly Sinified form of Buddhism could develop.

The victory of Fu Chien over the Yen encroachers brought close ties between him and his Koguryŏ contemporary, King Sosurim (r. 371–383). Through these contacts, Korea was opened to the cultural influences then current in the Ch'in state, including the northern Chinese variety of Buddhism.[19] Although our information on this period is scanty, we do know that the Buddhism was characterized by thaumaturgic elements, close church/state relations, Maitreya worship, and Sarvāstivādin/Mahāyāna scholastic investigations.[20] These features all became important elements in early Three Kingdoms Buddhism.

Buddhism is traditionally assumed to have been introduced into Korea by an official mission sent to Koguryŏ in 372 from the Former Ch'in dynasty. King Fu Chien dispatched the high priest Sundo (C. Shun-tao) as his personal envoy to the Koguryŏ court of King Sosurim (r. 371–384), together with Buddhist images and scriptures.[21] Soon afterward, in 384, the Serindian monk Maranant'a (*Mālānanda, *Kumāranandin)[22] arrived in Paekche by ship from Eastern Chin to an elaborate reception by the royal court.[23] The favorable receptions given Maranant'a in Paekche and Sundo in Koguryŏ, however, would seem to belie the fact that these were the first Korean contacts with Buddhism. The Liang *Biographies of Eminent Monks* record that the renowned Eastern Chin monk Chih-tun Tao-lin (314–366)[24] sent a letter to a Koguryŏ monk at least one decade before Sundo's mission.[25] That such communications were occurring even at that early date indicates a dialogue between Korea and China on Buddhist topics and certainly suggests more contact between the two regions than the extant evidence indicates.[26] At any rate, from this point on, Buddhism in Korea enjoyed remarkable success. Both the Koguryŏ and Paekche ruling houses established temples in their respective territories[27] and encouraged the faith among their subjects.[28] By 529, through the mythic efforts of Ado and the martyrdom of Ich'adon, the less-developed kingdom of early Silla, isolated on the east coast and the last of the three kingdoms to unify, had also converted.[29]

There is such a paucity of records concerning this earliest period of Korea's Buddhist history[30] that our assumptions about the nature of Three Kingdoms Buddhism must be tentative. The account of Sundo's mission to Koguryŏ tells us that he brought Buddhist images but it does not identify them. We do know, however, that Maitreya worship was widespread in Central Asia during this period and, clearly influenced by this fact, Fu Chien actively supported the dissemination of Maitreya images throughout his realm.[31] The visualization of images as a meditation device as well as a means of popularizing Buddhism among the masses was championed by the Ch'in ruler's spiritual advisor, Tao-an;[32] hence we can assume that the images first brought to Korea were those of Maitreya. The prevalence of Maitreya piety in the early Korean tradition also tends to support this hypothesis.[33]

The question of which scriptures Sundo presented to King Sosurim is more problematic. In China, the translation of Mahāyāna *sūtras* had begun as early as 179 with the first rendering of the *Aṣṭasāhasrikāprajñāpāramitā-sūtra* by Lokakṣema.[34] By the time of the transmission of Buddhism into Koguryŏ, many other important texts which would form the foundation of the Mahāyāna tradition in China had been translated, including the *Saddharmapuṇḍarīka-sūtra, Vimalakīrtinirdeśa-sūtra,* and *Daśabhūmika-sūtra.* As neither the *Āgama* texts nor the Sarvāstivādin Abhidharma canon were translated until after 383, we are safe in surmising that the scriptures which Sundo brought were texts from this early Mahāyāna corpus.[35]

In Paekche, in addition to this predominantly Mahāyāna material coming via China *Vinaya* texts also received an early introduction. The Paekche monk Kyŏmik (fl. sixth century) is said to have traveled to India via the southern sea route and studied Sanskrit, specializing in *Vinaya* studies. He returned to Paekche in 526, accompanied by the Indian monk Paedalta (*Vedatta), carrying five different recensions of the *Vinaya* as well as Abhidharma materials. As head of a translation bureau of twenty-eight monks established in the Paekche capital, Kyŏmik translated seventy-two fascicles of texts, and his disciples Tamuk and Hyerin wrote a thirty-six fascicle commentary to this new *Vinaya.* For this reason, Kyŏmik is considered the effective founder of the Vinaya school in Korea.[36]

Through the initiation of the courts of Koguryŏ and Paekche, most of the major scriptures and commentaries were imported from China and many monks were sent there to study the doctrines of the major schools of Chinese Buddhism and introduce their teachings into Korea. Among schools which flourished in these two kingdoms we have evidence for the existence of the schools of Samnon (C. San-lun), Sarvāstivādin Abhidharma, Nirvana, Ch'ŏnt'ae (C. T'ien-t'ai), and Satyasiddhi.[37] Simultaneous with the consolidation of the religion on the peninsula itself, Koguryŏ and Paekche began to send Buddhist missionary teams to Japan carrying scriptures and images. Paekche—a seafaring kingdom with well-developed sea lanes—made this propagation a national effort, and Buddhist iconographers, artisans, and architects were dispatched. Thus the rudiments of Chinese culture and civilization were transmitted to the Japanese and the foundations were laid for the rich Buddhist culture of the Asuka and Nara periods.[38]

UNIFIED SILLA DYNASTY (668–935)

The Silla conquest of the rival kingdoms of Paekche in 663 and Koguryŏ in 668 brought about the first political unification of the Korean peninsula[39] and ushered in a golden age of Buddhist scholasticism. Buddhist philosophical thought in Korea flourished to an extent never equaled again in its history. The strength of the dynasty and its staunch support of the church brought rapid development in both the scale and the profundity of Buddhist doctrinal investigations. A diversity of schools arose, and a number of great monks appeared who performed the creative work that sustained the tradition during later periods of weakness.

Most of the major approaches to doctrine which became the mainstays of the mature Korean tradition were developed during this period. The central scholastic teachings imported during the Three Kingdoms period were systematized into five main ideologies which became the orthodox schools of traditional scholastic Buddhism from the Silla period onward: the Kyeyul chong (Vinaya), Yŏlban chong (Nirvana), Pŏpsŏng chong, Wŏnyung chong (C. Yüan-jung; Avataṃsaka), and Pŏpsang chong *(Dharmalakṣaṇa, Yogā-cāra).*[40] (See Table 1.)

The Wŏnyung (Hwaŏm; C. Hua-yen) school enjoyed the widest and most enduring popularity during the Unified Silla dynasty and into the Koryŏ dynasty. The school was founded by Ŭisang (625–702), who studied in China under the second patriarch of the Chinese school, Chih-yen (602–668). Fa-tsang (643–712), the third Chinese patriarch and effective systematizer of the doctrines of the school, had great respect for Ŭisang's understanding and continued to correspond with him after the Silla monk's return to his native land.[41] Ŭisang's major work, the *Chart of the Avataṃsaka One-Vehicle Dharmadhātu (Hwaŏm ilsŭng pŏpkye to),*[42] written in 661 and presented to Chih-yen as the quintessence of his understanding of Hwaŏm doctrine, is one of the seminal works of extant Korean Buddhist literature and is quoted copiously by Chinul. Ŭisang returned to Korea in 670, and in 676 he founded Pusŏk sa, the head temple of the Hwaŏm sect.[43] Through the efforts of Ŭisang and his disciples, Hwaŏm theory became the foundation for most future Korean doctrinal developments and had the greatest influence of all the orthodox schools on the scholastic orientation of Korean Buddhism.[44]

The Pŏpsŏng (Dharma-nature) school, also known as the Haedong[45] school, deserves special mention as a uniquely Korean school of thought organized along syncretic lines. Its founder, the Korean monk Wŏnhyo (617–686), was a close friend of Ŭisang and probably the greatest scholar produced in the Korean Buddhist tradition. Wŏnhyo was the author of some 106 works on Buddhist topics, of which twenty are still extant;[46] his explications of the *Awakening of Faith* treatise in particular were a major influence in the development of Fa-tsang's thought—in fact, Wŏnhyo can be considered an important vaunt-courier in the Chinese Hua-yen school.[47] Wŏnhyo's commentaries on major *sūtras* were not intended simply to explicate terms and theories according to the dogma of a particular sect; rather, his approach was to demonstrate the relationship between those texts and the whole of Buddhism by examining them from the standpoint of an ideal,

Table 1. The Five Major Scholastic Schools of the Unified Silla Dynasty

School	Founder	Dates	Koryŏ Name	Main Monastery
Kyeyul chong (Vinaya) 戒律宗	Chajang 慈藏	608–686	Namsan chong 南山宗	T'ongdo sa 通度寺
Yŏlban chong (Nirvana) 涅槃宗	Podŏk 普德	fl. 650	Sihŭng chong 始興宗	Kyŏngbok sa 景福寺
Pŏpsŏng chong (Dharma Nature) 法性宗	Wŏnhyo 元曉	617–686	Chungdo chong 中道宗	Punhwang sa 芬皇寺
Wŏnyung chong (Avataṃsaka) 圓融宗	Ŭisang 義湘	625–702	Hwaŏm chong 華嚴宗	Pusŏk sa 浮石寺
Pŏpsang chong (Yogācāra) 法相宗	Chinp'yo 眞表	b. 718	Chaŭn chong 慈恩宗	Kŭmsan sa 金山寺

the one mind, which vivified each of them.[48] He also wrote outlines of the ideologies of the major Buddhist sects, again explaining them in ways which would lead to fraternal harmony, not sectarian controversy. In his treatise, the *Ten Approaches to the Reconciliation of Doctrinal Controversy* [*Simmun hwajaeng non*],[49] he proclaimed that his intent was to harmonize the differences between the various schools of canonical Buddhist thought and to explore avenues which would lead to an all-inclusive vision of those sects. Simultaneous with this philosophical development, Wŏnhyo preached and lived a popular form of Buddhism which had direct bearing on the everyday lives of ordinary followers. Wŏnhyo was the first major Korean Buddhist thinker to attempt, from the standpoint of the scholastic doctrine, a harmonization of the tenets of the major sects of Chinese Buddhist philosophy; his attempts inspired all future efforts of Korean thinkers, Chinul included.[50]

From the beginnings of Ch'an in China, Korean monks had been intimately involved with the tradition as disciples of the great masters and, in many cases, as leaders themselves.[51] Thus it received an early introduction into Korea, where it was known by its Korean pronunciation: Sŏn. The transmission proceeded at an accelerated pace throughout the Silla period until several different Sŏn lineages were established at separate mountain sites scattered throughout the peninsula; together they were known as the Nine Mountain Sŏn sect. (See Table 2.)[52]

According to traditional accounts, Sŏn was first brought to Korea by the Silla monk Pŏmnang (fl. 632–646), about whom little is known. After traveling to China, where he reputedly studied under the Fourth Patriarch of the Ch'an school, Tao-hsin (580–651), he returned to Korea in the latter half of the seventh century and passed his teachings on to the monk Sinhaeng (d. 779). Sinhaeng in turn traveled to China himself and studied under the monk Taejo Chigong (C. Ta-chao Chih-kung; 703–779), a fellow Korean who was a disciple of the second patriarch of the Northern school, P'u-chi (651–739). Sinhaeng's approach, which was a combination of his first teacher's transmission from the Fourth Patriarch and the so-called gradual teachings of the Northern school, continued to be passed on in Korea to Chunbŏm (n.d.) and Hyeŭn (n.d.) until it reached the monk Chisŏn Tohŏn (824–882). Chisŏn founded the Hŭiyang san school of Sŏn in 879—the oldest Sŏn lineage in Korea.[53]

Within a hundred-year period covering the eighth and ninth centuries, eight other mountain schools of Sŏn were started, all founded by Korean disciples of major Ch'an masters. Of these eight, seven were founded by disciples of first-generation successors of Ma-tsu Tao-i (709–788), founder of the iconoclastic Hung-chou school.[54] Only the last of the schools to

Table 2. *The Nine Mountains Sŏn Sect of the Unified Silla Dynasty*

Mountain	Temple	Founder	Teacher	Entered China	Returned Korea	Established Site	Site Extant?
Kaji san 迦智山	Porim sa 寶林寺	Toŭi (d. 825) 道義	Hsi-t'ang Chih-tsang (735–814) 西堂智藏	784	818	859	yes
Silsang san 實相山	Silsang sa 實相寺	Hongch'ŏk (fl. 826) 洪陟	Hsi-t'ang Chih-tsang	810	826	828	yes
Tongni san 桐裡山	T'aean sa 泰安寺	Hyech'ŏl (785–861) 慧哲 (徹)	Hsi-t'ang Chih-tsang	814	839	842	yes
Sagul san 闍崛山	Kulsan sa 崛山寺	Pŏmil (810–889) 梵日	Yen-kuan Ch'i-an (750?–842) 鹽官齊安	831	846	847	no
Pongnim san 鳳林山	Pongnim sa 鳳林寺	Hyŏnuk (787–869) 玄昱	Chang-ching Huai-hui (754–815) 章敬懷暉	824	837	897	no

Saja san 獅子山	Hŭngnyŏng sa 興寧寺	Toyun (797–868) 道允	Nan-ch'üan P'u-yüan (748–835) 南泉普願	825	847	850	no
Hŭiyang san 曦陽山	Pongam sa 鳳岩寺	Pŏmnang (fl. 632–646) 法朗	Tao-hsin (580–651) 道信	?	?	879	yes
		Chisŏn Tohŏn (824–882) 智詵道憲	Hyeŭn (n.d.) 惠隱				
Sŏngju san 聖住山	Sŏngju sa 聖住寺	Muyŏm (799–888) 無染	Ma-ku Pao-ch'e (b. 720?) 麻谷寶徹	821	845	847	no
Sumi san 須彌山	Kwangjo sa 廣照寺	Iŏm (869–936) 利嚴	Yün-chü Tao-ying (d. 902) 雲居道膺	895	911	931	no

form, the Sumi san school, belonged to a different lineage—that of Ch'ing-yüan Hsing-ssu (d. 740), which eventually matured into the Ts'ao-tung school of the mature Ch'an tradition. Hence, even in this earliest period of Sŏn in Korea, the so-called sudden teachings of the Southern school of Hung-chou, the precursor of the successful Lin-chi school of the later tradition, were already dominant—a position they retained from that time onward.

Deteriorating relations between the older scholastic schools of Buddhism in China and the new Ch'an schools produced a definite split in the church between these two streams of the tradition. Toŭi (d. 825), founder of the Kaji san school and the first Korean to return with the sudden teachings of Ch'an, stands out as a prime example of the devoted Sŏn adept willing to challenge the primacy of the scholastic schools. According to his memorial stele, Koreans of his time revered the scriptural teachings and did not place much faith in the new style of Sŏn.[55] Faced with a suspicious populace, Toŭi apparently adopted the confrontative tactics of some of his Chinese predecessors and advocated the inherent superiority of the Sŏn approach over those employed in the scholastic schools. An exchange between Toŭi and a Hwaŏm master sums up well his attitude toward the Sŏn/doctrinal controversy:

> The *Sŭngt'ong* Chiwŏn[56] asked National Master Toŭi, "What other *dharmadhātu* is there besides the four kinds of *dharmadhātu* of the Hwaŏm school? What other approach to dharma is there besides this progressive approach taught by the fifty-five wise advisors [during the pilgrimage of Sudhana in the *Gaṇḍavyūha* chapter of the *Avataṃsaka Sūtra*]? What do you have to say about this special way of patriarchal Sŏn which is separate from the doctrinal teachings?"
>
> Toŭi answered, "When the four kinds of *dharmadhātus* which you, the *Sŭngt'ong,* have brought up, are brought up straightaway in the school of the patriarchs, their correct principle is directly experienced, just like ice melting [on a hot furnace]. When the true principle of everything is brought up, the characteristics of those *dharmadhātus* cannot be found. In this Sŏn of the patriarchs' mind—the original wisdom which cannot be cultivated—even the characteristics of Mañjuśrī and Samantabhadra cannot be discovered. The progressive instructions of the fifty-five wise advisors are exactly like foam on water. The four wisdoms, *bodhi,* and all the rest are like ore [containing] the gold. Hence [the special transmission of the patriarchs] cannot be indiscriminately mixed with the scholastic teachings. For this reason, Master Kuei-tsung of the T'ang dynasty, when asked what was explained in the *Tripiṭaka,* merely raised his fist."[57]
>
> Chiwŏn asked again, "Then what is the purpose of belief, understanding, cultivation, and realization in regard to the principles and practices of the scholastic teachings? How can the fruition of Buddhahood be accomplished?"
>
> Toŭi answered, "The noumenal nature is believed, understood, cultivated, and

realized merely via thoughtlessness and noncultivation. The pointing to dharma in the school of the patriarchs cannot be understood by buddhas and sentient beings. It directly reveals the nature of the path. Hence, separate from the five scholastic teachings, there has been a special transmission of the dharma of the patriarchal mind-seal. For this reason, the display of the forms and figures of the Buddhas is intended for the faculties of those who have difficulty understanding the direct principle of the patriarchs—so provisionally [the Buddhas] manifest an expedient body. Even though one recites in succession the Buddhist *sūtras* for many years, if one intends thereby to realize the dharma of the mind-seal, for an infinitude of kalpas it will be difficult to attain."

Chiwŏn stood up, bowed, and said, "Until now, I had only heard the Buddha's ornate teachings and injunctions; I had never glimpsed the teaching of the Buddha's mind-seal."[58]

From this passage it is clear that Toŭi believed there were irreconcilable differences in the approaches of Sŏn and the scholastic teachings. For him, the question of which was superior was moot at best.

Perhaps the clearest battle lines in the conflict were drawn by the founder of the Sŏngju san school, Muyŏm (799–888), in his *Treatise on the Tongueless Realm:*

Question: What is the meaning of "tongued" and "tongueless"?
Answer: Yang-shan said,[59] "The tongued realm [the scholastic teaching] is the Buddha-realm. For this reason, it is the approach which responds to spiritual capacity. The tongueless realm is Sŏn; therefore, it is the approach of the correct transmission [from mind to mind]."
Question: What is the approach which responds to spiritual capacity?
Answer: To teach the dharma through intellectual knowledge, raising the eyebrows or twinkling the eyes—these are all approaches which respond to spiritual capacity. Therefore, they are tongued. This, of course, includes words as well.
Question: What is the tongueless realm?
Answer: This is the realm appropriate for people who have facility for Sŏn; it is without teachers or disciples.
Question: If this is the case, then why have the ancients referred to a transmission from master to disciple?
Answer: Chang-ching said,[60] "It is like empty space which has signlessness for its sign and nonaction for its function. The Sŏn transmission is also like this: it has nontransmission for its transmission; hence it is not transmitted and yet *is* transmitted."
Question: Concerning this tongueless realm in which there is found neither one who converts nor one who is converted: how is this any different from the explanation in the scholastic teachings where, in the *tathāgatas'* realization of mind, there is also found neither converter nor converted?
Answer: The ultimate in the scholastic teachings is the ocean-seal *samādhi,* which is the *tathāgatas'* realization of mind. In the three types of worlds, the dharma-seal manifests and yet is never understood. For this reason, it still has traces of

these three types of worlds. As far as the teachings of the patriarchal generations are concerned, in the mind of the equanimous, leisurely man of the way, the two weeds of purity or impurity never grow. As [the Sŏn teachings] are not overgrown by the weeds of the three types of worlds, they also have no traces of an exit or an entrance. Hence they are not the same [as the scholastic teachings]. When there is purity, [the mind-source becomes] the dharmas of true suchness and liberation. When there is impurity, it becomes the dharmas of birth/death and defilements. For this reason the ancients said, "The fountainhead of an adept's mind is like deep water where the two weeds of purity and impurity can never grow."

Furthermore, as far as the Buddha-realm is concerned, wearing the clothes of *samādhi* and *prajñā* one first enters the cave of glowing lamps; then, removing the clothes of *samādhi* and *prajñā,* one stands in the arcane land. Therefore, it still has traces. The realm of the patriarchs is originally free from liberation or bondage. There one does not wear even one strand of thread. Hence it is vastly different from the Buddha-realm.[61]

Here Muyŏm clarifies the attitude of the Sŏn schools of his time toward the scholastic teachings: doctrine (the tongued realm) is only expedient expression adapted to the capacities of (generally inferior) people; the direct mind-transmission of the Sŏn patriarchs (the tongueless realm) is the only true way. For Muyŏm, even the best words retain traces of dualistic thought and are, consequently, impure. In the special transmission of Sŏn, which is not dependent on even these best of words, there are no traces of purity or defilement. Hence Sŏn and doctrine are totally different from one another. The scholastic teachings are the provisional explanations of truth; Sŏn is truth itself.[62]

INITIAL ATTEMPTS AT SŎN/SCHOLASTIC RAPPROCHEMENT

It was in this atmosphere of increasingly strident controversy between the Sŏn and doctrinal schools that the first attempts were made to restore the spirit of harmony within the Saṃgha. Given the traditionally close ties between the aristocracy and the church, it seems only fair that this task was undertaken by Ŭich'ŏn (1055–1101), known posthumously as the National Master Taegak, who was the fourth son of the Koryŏ king Munjong (r. 1046–1083).

Ŭich'ŏn was one of the greatest scholars in Korean Buddhist history, a monk who had mastered not only the main currents of Buddhist philosophical thought but much of the Chinese classical literature as well. Ŭich'ŏn was quick to see the value of native East Asian Buddhist works and, an avid bibliophile and collector, resolved to gather a complete collection of all extant Buddhist literature. Against the wishes of his father, Ŭich'ŏn surreptitiously traveled to Sung China in 1085 at the age of thirty. Visiting there for fourteen months, he studied with renowned teachers in the Hua-yen, T'ien-t'ai,

Vinaya, Pure Land, and Ch'an sects and even tried his hand at Sanskrit.[63] Finally returning home at the behest of his father, he brought back more than three thousand fascicles of texts. In the meantime, he dispatched agents to scour China, Japan, and the realm of the Khitan Liao dynasty for texts.[64] In 1090 he published his catalog of this collection, the *Sinp'yŏn chejong kyojang ch'ongnok,*[65] which lists 1,010 titles in 4,740 fascicles. Fearing that these texts would be lost if not preserved in a compendium attached to the basic canon, Ŭich'ŏn had blocks carved for each of these titles and called them a supplement to the *Tripiṭaka.* This supplement was burned along with the first edition of the Korean *Tripiṭaka* during the Mongol invasion of 1231–1232; and, as Ŭich'ŏn feared, a change of editorial policy during the second carving of the canon omitted many of the texts and they are no longer extant.[66]

Ŭich'ŏn was not content with a purely scholastic role. Upon his return from Sung China, he attempted to unify the divided Saṃgha by merging the Sŏn schools and the traditional scholastic schools into an expanded and refurbished Ch'ŏnt'ae school. Ch'ŏnt'ae studies had by no means been neglected in Korea previous to Ŭich'ŏn, but they had never received the widespread recognition enjoyed by the five orthodox scholastic schools. During the Silla period, Hyŏn'gwang (fl. 539–575) traveled to China and studied with Nan-yüeh Hui-ssu (515–577), one of the two precursors of T'ien-t'ai thought in China and the teacher of the ultimate systematizer of the school, Chih-i (538–597). Hyŏn'gwang later returned to his native land and achieved renown as a teacher of the school.[67] Another Silla monk, Nangji (fl. 661–680), is reputed to have lectured widely on the *Lotus Sūtra,* the main scripture of the school, and gained a reputation as a thaumaturge.[68] Ŭich'ŏn himself attributes the inception of Ch'ŏnt'ae studies in Korea to Wŏnhyo, who wrote an outline of the sect, the *Pŏphwa chongyo,*[69] and to Ch'egwan, who traveled to China in 960 and became an important figure in the Chinese school, writing the *T'ien-t'ai ssu-chiao i.*[70] Faced with competition from the flourishing Hwaŏm and Sŏn schools, however, Ch'ŏnt'ae never achieved the status of an independent school.[71] Ŭich'ŏn was himself strongly influenced by Hwaŏm teachings,[72] but he saw the stress on meditation in the Ch'ŏnt'ae school—an emphasis which encouraged identification with Sŏn methods—as the ideal vehicle for accommodating the two major branches of Korean Buddhism.[73] It is because Ŭich'ŏn was able to revitalize its teachings and establish the school as a fully autonomous sect for the first time in Korea that he is generally considered the founder of the Korean Ch'ŏnt'ae school.[74]

According to Ŭich'ŏn's analysis of the Sŏn/doctrine problem, meditation had originally been an integral part of all Buddhist schools, including those oriented toward scriptural study and explication. Sectarian differences continued to grow through the centuries, however, until a noticeable rift developed between schools devoted primarily to meditation and those concerned mainly with doctrinal questions. The division led to a polarization of the approaches—the scholastic schools emphasizing theoretical studies at the expense of practice, the Sŏn schools abandoning scriptural knowledge in favor of meditation. Ŭich'ŏn deplored the sectarianism which had infected the Saṃgha and criticized both Sŏn adepts and doctrinal students for their intransigence.

> The dharma is devoid of words or appearances; but it is not separate from words and appearances. If you abandon words, you are subject to distorted views and defilements; if you grasp at words, you are deluded as to the truth. . . . Students of the scriptures often abandon their inner work and pursue externals; Sŏn adepts prefer to ignore worldly activity and simply look inward. Both positions are biases which are bound at the two extremes. They are like fighting over whether a rabbit's horns are long or short, or arguing over whether flowers in the sky are profuse or scarce.[75]

To mitigate sectarian attachments, Ŭich'ŏn advocated a comprehensive approach to doctrinal study in order to develop a well-rounded and balanced understanding of Buddhist theory:

> Without studying the *Abhidharmakośa-śāstra,* the explanations of the *Śrāvakayāna* cannot be understood. Without studying the *Vijñaptimātratāsiddhi-śāstra,* how can one perceive the meaning of the Mahāyāna inception doctrine? Without studying the *Awakening of Faith,* how can one understand the purport of the final and sudden teachings? Without studying the *Avataṃsaka Sūtra,* it is difficult to enter the gate of perfect interfusion.[76]

Nevertheless, although he recognized the utility of *sūtra* study in engendering a conceptual understanding of the goal of practice and the path to that goal, study alone was not enough for Ŭich'ŏn; meditation was necessary as well in order to produce personal realization of that goal.[77] Hence, according to Ŭich'ŏn both study and practice should complement one another; both internal and external pursuits should be in proper balance.[78]

As an exponent of the Ch'ŏnt'ae teachings, however, Ŭich'ŏn retained some of the traditional Ch'ŏnt'ae antipathy toward Sŏn and reserved the majority of his criticism for the Sŏn schools. Sŏn had been based firmly in the *sūtras;* indeed, it can be said that the original approach of the school was to perfect meditation practice while relying on the instructions and outlines of the scriptural teachings. It is recorded in the Sŏn texts themselves that Bodhidharma, legendary founder of the school, transmitted the *Laṅkāvatāra Sūtra* to his disciple Hui-k'o, and the traditional fifth and sixth patriarchs Hung-jen and Hui-neng both taught the *Prajñāpāramitāsūtras,* particularly the *Diamond Sūtra.* But Sŏn had veered toward an increasingly narrow interpretation of Bodhidharma's dictum, "not establishing words and letters," and had become intensely bibliophobic. Ŭich'ŏn noted:

> What was called Sŏn in the past was the approach which matured one's meditation while relying on the teaching. What is called Sŏn nowadays is to talk about Sŏn while abandoning the teaching. To speak about Sŏn nowadays is to grasp the name but to forget the core; to practice Sŏn is to base oneself on the scriptural explanations and realize their meaning.[79]

To Ŭich'ŏn, such an attitude bordered on heresy.[80] He felt it necessary to restore a right attitude toward the value and purpose of the *sūtra* teachings by ensuring the dominance of the scholastic schools in any accommodation with Sŏn.[81]

Ŭich'ŏn's efforts at merging the various schools of his time into an ecumenical Ch'ŏnt'ae school were sponsored by the royal family and given legitimacy by the wide respect he commanded from Buddhists of all persuasions. However, his early death at the age of forty-seven doomed his experiment to failure. Rather than bringing all the sects together, his pronounced anti-Sŏn bias only solidified the insularity of the Sŏn schools which survived him. He ended up merely adding one more school to the already crowded sectarian scene. But this first trial at merging Sŏn with the orthodox scholastic schools, and the various problems which resulted from Ŭich'ŏn's approach were important lessons for the similar attempt by Chinul one century later.[82]

II. The Life of Chinul

KORYŎ BUDDHISM AT THE TIME OF CHINUL

In the middle of the Koryŏ dynasty (937–1392), Buddhism was firmly entrenched in the political structure and social makeup of the kingdom. From the inception of the dynasty, the founder Wang Kŏn (T'aejo, r. 918–943) had correlated the fortunes of the kingdom with those of the religion and actively encouraged close relationships between court and ecclesia.[83] In 943, the year of his death, T'aejo promulgated ten admonitions to guide his successors in ruling the kingdom. His statement opens with the solemn caveat: "All the great enterprises of our kingdom depend upon the protective power of all the Buddhas."[84] To ensure that this protection would be forthcoming, the Koryŏ dynasty, like Silla before it, held numerous ceremonies and dharma assemblies to invoke the goodwill of the Buddhas and bodhisattvas[85] and lavished riches on the monasteries and monks.[86] The Buddhist church wielded immense economic influence throughout the country, controlling vast tracts of tax-exempt paddy and forest lands, presiding over armies of serfs to work that land, and possessing a fortune in precious metals cast as Buddhist images and artifacts. Massive amounts of government funds were expended in building projects, and the new capital of Kaesŏng itself became a thriving Buddhist metropolis. The monasteries were commercial centers in the rural regions of the country and were engaged in the distillation of spirits, noodle making, and tea production.[87] The monks themselves enjoyed exemption from corvée labor and military obligations. Monks were even brought into positions of secular power while remaining within the ecclesiastical ranks: a series of examinations modeled along the lines of the civil service tests enabled the conscientious student of either the Sŏn or scholastic schools to work his way to the very heights of the church hierarchy, making him eligible for appointment to the post of royal master *(wangsa)* or national master *(kuksa)* and placing him near the sources of secular authority.[88]

Almost inevitably, it was its very success which created the most problems for the church. Although the examination system for monks raised the general scholastic level of the Saṃgha as a whole, it emasculated the spiritual essence of Buddhism by bringing about a preoccupation with secular pursuits. Furthermore, officials in the civil bureaucracy who recognized the influence of the church over the higher echelons of government also used the religion for private gain. Korean Buddhism of the eleventh and twelfth centuries was increasingly exploited by people both inside and outside the church.

As the years progressed, the ranks of the monks were swelled by people pursuing wealth and position on the one hand and avoiding the hardships of the peasant life and the dangers of military service on the other. The influx of persons with less than the holiest of motivations added to the gradual decline of the religion and led to a backlash from the authorities. Beginning in 1059, during the reign of King Munjong, a series of restrictive measures were promulgated by the aristocratic leadership which limited the participation of commoners in ecclesiastical matters and diminished the influence of monks and their families in affairs of state. The first of these rules was that only one son in three could ordain, and then only after age fifteen.[89] Later, serfs and indigent persons were prohibited altogether from ordaining.[90] Nepotism in government was limited by prohibiting children of monks, born before a person's ordination, from taking the civil service examinations—effectively barring their participation in public life.[91] To keep the monks in monasteries where they belonged, they were forbidden to lodge overnight in villages.[92] These and other restrictions remained in effect for the rest of the Koryŏ period, but they were supplanted by even more severe restrictions imposed by the Confucian-oriented Yi dynasty administration.[93]

Along with the growing corruption of the Saṃgha, the level of scholarship in the scholastic sects and the intensity of practice in the Sŏn schools declined. Sŏn's initial disadvantage in its competition with the scholastic schools had been overcome during the opening decades of the Koryŏ period through the profound influence that the Sŏn Master Tosŏn (827–898), and the geomantic techniques he imported from China, allegedly wielded over the Koryŏ founder T'aejo.[94] Such influence, however, ended up becoming the Sŏn school's own nemesis, for it involved the monks in building projects and ceremonial observances rather than practice. Moreover, the examination system required monks to spend many years in study in order to prepare for the rigorous tests, which again involved them in pursuits antithetical to the best interests of the practice-oriented Sŏn school. Furthermore, Ŭich'ŏn's Ch'ŏnt'ae school had lured many of the best Sŏn masters away from their mountain sites, thereby devitalizing the traditional Nine Mountains schools. Hence, although the Sŏn school had expanded widely from scattered mountain sites until it could be found throughout the peninsula, it had in fact grown weaker.[95] It was during this period of severe degeneration of the Saṃgha that Chinul, a devoted Sŏn monk with pronounced sympathy for the doctrines of the scholastic sects, was born.

Chinul himself describes the corrupted motivations which had enervated the Saṃgha:

> When we examine the inclination of our conduct from dawn to dusk, we see that we rely on the Buddha-dharma while adorning ourselves with the signs of self and person. Infatuated with material welfare and submerged in secular concerns, we do not cultivate virtue but only waste food and clothing. Although we have left home, what merit does it have? How sad! We want to leave the triple world, but we do not practice freeing ourselves from sensual objects. Our male body is used in vain for we lack a man's will. From one standpoint we fail in the dharma's propagation; from another we are negligent in benefiting sentient beings; and between these two we turn our backs on our four benefactors [ruler, teachers, parents, friends]. This is indeed shameful! All this has made me lament since long ago.[96]

Chinul was to abandon all ties with the self-seeking church hierarchy and act as the exemplar in reestablishing a proper spiritual orientation among the clergy. His attempt to reform Buddhism from outside the established system came at a time when nearly all the progressive impetus in the religion was generated by the court and the court-sponsored church hierarchy. And his eventual success—even after Ŭich'ŏn with his royal ties had failed from within the system—restored the spirit of Korean Buddhism for the remainder of the Koryŏ period.[97]

Chinul was born during an extremely volatile period in Koryŏ political history. Khitan invasions in 993, 1010, and 1018 had wreaked havoc throughout the country and demoralized the political leadership, leading to a series of court intrigues which progressively undermined the power of the ruling house. Factional strife in the court immediately preceding the reign of the seventeenth Koryŏ monarch, Injong (r. 1122–1146), led to regional conflicts which further eroded political stability. Increasingly, the power of private families in the aristocracy rivaled, and occasionally even eclipsed, that of the king himself. The year 1126 saw an actual revolt against the royal family, coupled with a rebellion by members of the king's own coterie of advisors, including the Buddhist monk Myoch'ŏng (d. 1135). Although defeated in 1136, this rebellion only underscored the precarious position of the ruling house.

During the reign of Ŭijong (r. 1146–1170), military dissatisfaction with Koryŏ policies finally led to a coup d'état and, in 1170, King Ŭijong was captured and exiled by a general in his army. The king's younger brother (posthumous title, Myŏngjong, r. 1170–1197) was placed on the throne. For the next twenty-seven years the puppet ruler presided helplessly over a series of coup and countercoup. It was not until 1196 that another general, Ch'oe Ch'ung-hŏn, and his brother were finally able to consolidate control in the Ch'oe family's name. For the next sixty years, until the fourth family dictator, Ch'oe Ŭi, was assassinated in 1258, the Ch'oe family ruled Koryŏ in fact as well as in principle.[98]

According to his biographer, Kim Kun-su,[99] Chinul was born in 1158[100] in the Tongju district to the west of the Koryŏ capital of Kaesŏng.[101] His lay-surname was Chŏng, and he was born into a family of the gentry class. His father, Chŏng Kwangu, was an administrator in the royal academy.[102] From birth, the boy was of weak constitution and plagued by serious illnesses. After continued attempts to cure him through conventional medical therapy, his father in desperation decided to entreat the Buddha. He vowed that if his son was cured, he would have him ordained into the Buddhist order. Soon afterward, the illnesses are supposed to have vanished and, keeping his vow, Kwangu's child had his head shaved at the age of seven and received the precepts at the age of fifteen.[103] He was given the Buddhist name Chinul; later, he referred to himself as Moguja (The Oxherder).

Chinul's preceptor was Chonghwi, the Sŏn master at Kulsan sa on Sagul san, one of the sites of the Nine Mountain sect of Korean Sŏn. Chonghwi, about whom little is known, was the tenth-generation successor of Pŏmil

(810–889), the Silla Sŏn monk who traveled to China and received the transmission from Yen-kuan Ch'i-an (750–842) of the Hung-chou school. Hence, by ordination lineage, Chinul belonged to the Nan-yüeh line of the Southern school of Ch'an.[104]

The young monk's relationship with his preceptor does not seem to have been especially close, for his biographer states that he never had a permanent teacher.[105] Chinul's intellect and his natural inclination toward solitude and retreat had been noticeable since his youth; with the fractious climate of the church in his days, he probably felt more comfortable learning to get along on his own considerable talents in seclusion. From early on in his vocation Chinul made up for the lack of personal instruction by drawing inspiration from the Buddhist scriptures. In the spirit of self-reliance that is central to Buddhism, he took responsibility for his own spiritual development and followed the path of practice outlined in the scriptures and confirmed through his own Sŏn meditation. Chinul's progress in Buddhist practice was, therefore, based on using scriptural instructions to perfect formal Sŏn practice. This accommodating attitude toward the written teachings, unusual for Sŏn students in his time, and his simultaneous study of both *sūtras* and meditation, contrasted sharply with the strong sectarian climate of his age and anticipated the future trend of his thought.

THE VOW TO FORM A RETREAT SOCIETY

After nine years at his home monastery, in 1182 Chinul traveled to Poje sa in the capital to take the Sŏn Saṃgha examinations.[106] Although he passed his tests, he apparently became disgusted with the worldly climate surrounding them. His interest in joining the ecclesiastical hierarchy dampened, he aired his views about the corrupted state of the Saṃgha and the need to return to the proper pursuits of the monk's life. He seems to have struck a responsive chord among at least a few of his fellow adepts; together, they decided to gather at some future date to form a retreat society dedicated to the development of *samādhi* and *prajñā*. Chinul relates in his earliest work, *Encouragement to Practice,* composed in 1190:

> One day I made a pact with more than ten fellow meditators which said:
> "After the close of this convocation we will renounce fame and profit and remain in seclusion in the mountain forests. We will form a community designed to foster constant training in *samādhi* and *prajñā*. Through worship of the Buddha, recitation of *sūtras,* and even through common work, we will each discharge the duties to which we are assigned and nourish the self-nature in all situations. We vow to pass our whole lives free of entanglements and to follow the higher pursuits of accomplished and true men. Would this not be wonderful?"
> All those present who heard these words agreed with what was said, and vowed, "On another day we will consummate this agreement, live in seclusion in the for-

est, and be bound together as a community which should be named for *samādhi* and *prajñā.*"

Chinul seems to have been the first person to initiate the religious society *(kyŏlsa)* movement in Korea. Such religious societies had their antecedents in the Amitābha society of Hui-yüan (334–416) during the Eastern Chin dynasty; by the time of the Sung dynasty they were burgeoning throughout China, especially in the southern provinces. Most of these societies had close affiliations with the T'ien-t'ai, Hua-yen, and Pure Land schools and had become popular as the sectarian equivalent of the legendarily strict, but increasingly decadent, Ch'an temples.[107] In these societies, both lay and ordained adepts would train together intensively in their own sectarian pursuits. These groups seem to have found comfort in numbers. We read again and again in the compacts of the Pure Land groups that their goal was to assemble ten thousand people and cultivate everything together as a group —offerings, recitation, and vowing to be reborn in the Pure Land.[108] Chinul's motivations in forming such a society seem to parallel the reasons for the formation of such groups in China: first, both were attempting to counter the degenerative tendencies in the Saṃgha; second, both efforts were undertaken from outside the established order. Hence Chinul's adoption of this form of community as a means of reviving the debased Sŏn practice of his day was a particularly innovative use of an original Chinese development which had proved itself formidable on the mainland.[109]

Before Chinul could form his community, however, difficulties were encountered in the selection of the site and the attestants were scattered among many different monasteries. Although we have no indication what these problems might have been, it seems reasonable to surmise that they were political in nature, resulting from the antihierarchical sentiments implicit in the compact. Many monasteries would have been reluctant to harbor a community which seemed to threaten the power of the central ecclesiastical authorities. During this period of successive military coups, the countryside was in a state of turmoil and a series of peasant and slave revolts had shattered any sense of local security—another deterrent to the assembly of monks from around the country at an isolated rural or wilderness site. It was to be eight years before the monks saw the establishment of the Samādhi and Prajñā Community.

TO CH'ŎNGWON SA: FIRST AWAKENING

Faced with the delay in the formation of the proposed Samādhi and Prajñā Community, Chinul decided to leave the capital, traveling down the Korean peninsula. He finally "set down his walking staff" at Ch'ŏngwon sa in Ch'angp'yŏng in the far southwest,[110] the region of the ancient Paekche kingdom. Chinul's reason for traveling to this area of Korea becomes clear when we consider that it was the focus of flourishing trade relationships with the Southern Sung dynasty. The native Chinese Sung dynasty, having lost its territory in the northern plains to Chin forces in 1126, was firmly ensconced in the region south of the Yangtze River. During the Khitan invasions in the early eleventh century, the Koryŏ court had been obliged to sever all diplomatic ties with the Sung in order to placate the threat on its northern border; this move had not, however, interrupted unofficial commercial and cultural exchanges between Sung and Koryŏ via long-established routes on the Yellow Sea. Two major routes were frequented by Chinese, Korean, and occasionally even Arab merchants: an eastern route from Hwanghae to in the central portion of the Korean peninsula to Teng-chou and Mi-chou on the northern coast of the Shantung peninsula; and a southern route which traveled from Yesŏng kang and the many islands and ports along the west and southwest coast of Korea to Ming-chou, the present-day Ning-p'o in Chekiang province.[111] Relations were particularly strong with these Chinese coastal regions, where the religious society movement was strongest in China. Hence, by moving to the southwest, Chinul had placed himself in the best possible location for getting firsthand information about Sung Buddhism.

While Chinul was staying at Ch'ŏngwon sa, he had the first of a series of three awakenings which profoundly affected his attitude toward Buddhist cultivation. As his memorial stele relates:

> By chance one day in the study hall as he was looking through the *Platform Sūtra of the Sixth Patriarch,* he came across a passage which said, "The self-nature of suchness gives rise to thoughts. But even though the six sense-faculties see, hear, sense, and know, it is not tainted by the myriads of images. The true nature is constantly free and self-reliant." Astonished, he was overjoyed at gaining what he had never experienced before and, getting up, he walked around the hall, reflecting on the passage while continuing to recite it. His heart was satisfied. From that time on, his mind was averse to fame and profit; he desired only to dwell in seclusion in the mountain ravines. Bearing hardship joyfully, he aspired to the path; he was obsessed with this quest.[112]

This experience was Chinul's true initiation into Buddhism. In all his future writings, Chinul would stress the need for an initial awakening to the mind-nature to ensure the consistent development of practice. Subsequent readings of the *Platform Sūtra* as well as the influence of Tsung-mi's writings spelled out the need to support the initial awakening to the mind-nature with the simultaneous cultivation of *samādhi* and *prajñā,* and the concurrent development of alertness and calmness of mind. In works like *Secrets on Cultivating the Mind* and *Encouragement to Practice,* which concentrate on the fundamentals of Buddhist meditation, this sudden/gradual approach to Buddhist spiritual cultivation is emphasized. In one of his last works, *Excerpts from the Dharma Collection and Special Practice Record,* this approach forms the foundation of a systematic outline of Sŏn practice. For the rest of his life, the *Platform Sūtra* remained one of his favorite works; indeed, his esteem for the text was so high that, it is said, whenever he was asked to lecture, it was always his first preference.[113]

POMUN SA: SECOND AWAKENING

In 1185, Chinul again took up his staff and set off in search of a new environment in which to further his practice. In the autumn of that year he finally settled at Pomun sa on Haga Mountain in southeastern Korea.[114] Chinul seems to have been particularly concerned at that time with the continued split between the Sŏn and scholastic schools which was destroying the integrity of the Saṃgha. Taking as an example his own development in Buddhism—in which Sŏn practice was complemented with insights gleaned from the scriptures—Chinul became convinced that the discrepancies between the two streams of thought could be reconciled. Although his primary focus so far had been the special transmission of Sŏn, he was positive that the Sŏn approach could be confirmed in the *sūtras.* If he could find the evidence, the validity of both Sŏn and the scriptures would then be verified.

In the preface to his synopsis of Li T'ung-hsüan's commentary to the *Avataṃsaka Sūtra,* the *Excerpts from the Exposition of the Avataṃsaka Sūtra [Hwaŏmnon chŏryo],*[115] Chinul discusses the events leading to his discovery of a textual passage which confirmed the approach of the Sŏn school:

> In the autumn of [the Chin dynasty's] Great Stability era [1185], as I began living in retreat on Haga Mountain, I reflected constantly on the Sŏn adage "Mind is Buddha." I felt that if a person were not fortunate enough to meet with this approach, he would end up wasting many kalpas in vain and would never reach the domain of sanctity.
>
> I had always had doubts about the approach to entering into awakening in the Hwaŏm teachings: what, finally, did it involve? Accordingly, I decided to question a [Hwaŏm] lecturer. He replied, "You must contemplate the unimpeded interpenetration of all phenomena." He entreated me further: "If you merely contemplate your own mind and do not contemplate the unimpeded interfusion of all phenomena, you will never gain the perfect qualities of the fruition of Buddhahood."
>
> I did not answer, but thought silently to myself, "If you use the mind to contemplate phenomena, those phenomena will become impediments and you will have needlessly disturbed your own mind; when will there ever be an end to this situation? But if the mind is brightened and your wisdom purified, then one hair

and all the universe will be interfused for there is, perforce, nothing which is outside [the mind]." I then retired into the mountains and sat reading through the *Tripiṭaka* in search of a passage which would confirm the mind-doctrine [of Sŏn].

Three winters and summers passed before I came upon the simile about "one dust mote containing thousands of volumes of *sūtras*" in the "Appearance of the *Tathāgatas*" chapter of the *Avataṃsaka Sūtra*. Later [in the same passage] the summation said, "The wisdom of the *tathāgatas* is just like this: it is complete in the bodies of all sentient beings. It is merely all these ordinary, foolish people who are not aware of it and do not recognize it."[116] I put the *sūtra* volume on my head [in reverence] and, unwittingly, began to weep.

However, as I was still unclear about the initial access of faith which was appropriate for ordinary people of today, I reread the Elder Li T'ung-hsüan's explanation of the first level of the ten faiths in his *Exposition of the Avataṃsaka Sūtra*. It said, "Chief of Enlightenment Bodhisattva has three [realizations]. First, he realizes that his own body and mind are originally the *dharmadhātu* because they are immaculate, pure, and untainted. Second, he realizes that the discriminative nature of his own body and mind is originally free from the subject/object dichotomy and is originally the Buddha of Unmoving Wisdom. Third, he realizes that his own mind's sublime wisdom, which can distinguish the genuine from the distorted, is Mañjuśrī. He realizes these three things at the first level of faith and comes to be known as Chief of Enlightenment."[117] It says elsewhere, "The difficulties a person encounters in entering into the ten faiths from the ordinary state are due to the fact that he completely accepts that he is an ordinary man; he is unwilling to accept that his own mind is the Buddha of Unmoving Wisdom."[118] It also says, "The body is the reflection of wisdom. This world is the same. When wisdom is pure and its reflection clear, large and small merge with one another as in the realm of Indra's net."[119]

Thereupon I set aside the volume and, breathing a long sigh, said, "What the World Honored One said with his mouth are the teachings. What the patriarchs transmitted with their minds is Sŏn.[120] The mouth of the Buddha and the minds of the patriarchs can certainly not be contradictory. How can [students of both Sŏn and the scholastic schools] not plumb the fundamental source but instead, complacent in their own training, wrongly foment disputes and waste their time?" From that time on, I have continued to build my mind of faith and have cultivated diligently without being indolent; a number of years have already passed.

Chinul's realization of the fundamental unity of Sŏn and the scriptures led to his subsequent incorporation of Hwaŏm theory and Sŏn practice in two later treatises published posthumously: *The Complete and Sudden Attainment of Buddhahood* and *Resolving Doubts About Observing the Hwadu*. His experience at Pomun sa was thus the basis for a syncretic perspective toward Buddhist thought which could unify the contending sectarian elements within the church into an all-inclusive approach to Buddhist spiritual development.

THE RETREAT BEGINS

By 1188, it had been over eight years since the original decision to form the Samādhi and Prajñā Community, but the monks had still been unable to arrange for a site. While Chinul was staying at Pomun sa, however, he received a letter from one of the signatories, a Sŏn meditator named Tŭkchae,[121] who was staying at Kŏjo sa on Kong Mountain.[122] Tŭkchae had not forgotten their original pledge, and he entreated Chinul repeatedly to join him at Kŏjo sa and begin the formal retreat. Although at first reluctant to make the move, Chinul finally consented and, in the spring of 1188, together with his fellow meditator Hang,[123] he joined Tŭkchae.

After establishing himself at the monastery, he and Tŭkchae invited all the monks who had signed the initial agreement to join them at Kŏjo sa. Some of the monks had died; others were sick; still others had become entranced with the pursuit of fame and profit. Of the original group of over ten monks, only three or four were able to come. The retreat began formally in 1190 and, in commemoration of the occasion, Chinul composed his first major work, *Encouragement to Practice: The Compact of the Samādhi and Prajñā Community,* as a guide to the style of practice which he and his fellow meditators intended to emulate. In this work, Chinul chronicled the events and motivations which led up to the formal establishment of the community—which certainly must have attracted the attention of many monks for its explicit criticism of the corrupting influences in the Saṃgha.

Chinul welcomed people from all backgrounds into the community, as long as they were willing to renounce secular concerns and dwell in seclusion in the cultivation of *samādhi* and *prajñā.* He also actively enlisted fellow meditators into the retreat at Kŏjo sa and accepted these new recruits as full-fledged members of the society. As Chinul states explicitly in his *Encouragement to Practice:*

> I humbly hope that men of high moral standards who have grown tired of worldly affairs—regardless of whether they are adherents of Sŏn, the scholastic sects, Confucianism, or Taoism—will abandon the dusty domain of this world, soar high above all things, and devote themselves earnestly to the path of inner cultivation which is commensurate with this aim. Then, although they might have had no role in the formation of this project, I have allowed them to add their names at the end of the compact of this community.

There is at least one extant account of a monk who was encouraged by Chinul to join the retreat group at Kŏjo sa: Yose, the National Master Wŏnmyo (1163–1240).[124] Yose was a popular monk in the Ch'ŏnt'ae tradition whose life shows many parallels with Chinul's. He eventually became known as the revitalizer of the Koryŏ Ch'ŏnt'ae school by following Chinul's example and instituting a religious society structure for the Paengnyŏn Community he established in 1211.[125] Yose had traveled to the capital in the spring of 1198 for a dharma assembly convened at Kobong sa. In the autumn of the same year he left the capital with a group of more than ten monks to tour some of the famous mountain sites around the country. He eventually stopped at Changyŏn sa on Yŏngdong Mountain, where he began a retreat similar in approach to the one Chinul had begun at Kŏjo sa.[126] Chinul eventually heard of his popularity and decided that Yose was the kind of monk he wanted in the Samādhi and Prajñā Community. Chinul sent a poem to Yose, indirectly inviting him to join him in the practice of Sŏn:

> When the waves are choppy,
>   it is difficult for the moon to appear,
> Though the room is wide,
>   the lamp can fill it with light.
> I exhort you to clean your mind-vessel,
> Don't spill the sweet-dew sauce.[127]

Yose was moved by this entreaty and joined Chinul. They cooperated for a number of years and became close friends. Yose accompanied Chinul on the move to Kilsang sa before parting from him there; he eventually moved to Mandŏk san in the far southwest of the peninsula, where, after restoring an old monastery, he established Paengnyŏn sa and remained there for the rest of his life.

By 1197, seven years after its formation, the community at Kŏjo sa had achieved widespread renown and gained a large following among people from all social strata. Although Chinul was still concerned primarily with his personal practice, he had gradually attracted a large number of students —in fact, "those who were studying under him had become like a city."[128] The small size of the temple and the growing number of students made it impossible to continue with the retreat without expanding the monastery site. Since the limited area available at Kŏjo sa made expansion impossible, Chinul sent one of his disciples, Suu,[129] into the Kangnam region of the southwest peninsula to search for a site for a major meditation center.[130] After visiting a number of monasteries, Suu arrived at Songgwang Mountain, where he found the neglected remains of a small temple, Kilsang sa, which was no more than one hundred *kan*[131] in size and able to accommodate only thirty to forty people. Although it was much too small for the requirements of the retreat group, the area was ideal: "The site was outstanding and the land fertile; the springs were sweet and the forests abundant. It was truly a place which would be appropriate for cultivating the mind, nourishing the nature, gathering an assembly, and making merit."[132]

In 1197, together with his dharma-brothers Ch'ŏnjin and Kwakcho,[133] Suu commenced the reconstruction and expansion of the monastery. With a few dilapidated buildings as a beginning, they built the new quarters for the Samādhi and Prajñā Community and established thereby a monastery which, even down to the present day, has been one of the most important in all Korea.[134]

RESPITE AT SANGMUJU AM: FINAL AWAKENING

After receiving news that construction of the community's new facilities was progressing satisfactorily, Chinul prepared to move the society to its new site. In the spring of 1197 Chinul departed from Kŏjo sa with a few of his companions and set out for Kangnam.[135] On their way out of present Kyŏngsang pukto the monks climbed Mount Chiri, where they intended to spend time in intensive meditation before their final trek to Kilsang sa. Before reaching Kilsang sa where his responsibility as spiritual leader to a large and growing community would take up much of his time, Chinul apparently wanted some time to himself in order to consolidate his own practice.

Chinul and his companions made what appears to have been a premeditated stop at Sangmuju am, near the top of the Mount Chiri massif.[136] Sangmuju am was "isolated and quiet—first in all the kingdom as a peaceful place perfect for the practice of Sŏn."[137] The atmosphere was conducive to his meditation, and he made great progress. His stele relates that a number of miraculous occurrences took place at the time—so numerous that they could not be recorded in the inscription—which indicated to his companions that he had attained enlightenment.[138] Chinul himself relates the progress he made at Sangmuju am:

> Since I came from Pomun sa [to Kŏjo sa], more than ten years had passed. Although I was satisfied with the diligence of my cultivation and did not waste my time, I had not yet forsaken passions and views—it was as if my chest were blocked by something, or as if I were dwelling together with an enemy. I went to live on Mount Chiri and found [a passage in the] *Records* of the Sŏn Master Ta-hui P'u-chüeh which said, "Sŏn does not consist in quietude; it does not consist in bustle. It does not involve the activities of daily life; it does not involve logical discrimination. Nevertheless, it is of first importance not to investigate [Sŏn] while rejecting quietude or bustle, the activities of daily life, or logical discrimination. If your eyes suddenly open, then [Sŏn] is something which exists inside your very own home." I understood this passage. Naturally, nothing blocked my chest again and I never again dwelt together with an enemy. From then on I was at peace.[139]

Ta-hui Tsung-kao (1089–1163), disciple of Yüan-wu K'o-ch'in (1063–1135) and seventeenth-generation successor in the Lin-chi line of Ch'an, was the popularizer of the *hua-t'ou* (K. *hwadu*) method of Ch'an practice.

Chinul was the first Korean Sŏn teacher to be influenced by Ta-hui's approach, and Chinul's adoption of the *hwadu* method brought him into the mainstream of Ch'an development in China. That fact that Ta-hui and Chinul were only one generation apart has led some scholars to speculate that Chinul might first have heard tales of Ta-hui's renown during his earlier stay at Ch'ŏngwon sa and personally contracted with Sung or Koryŏ merchants to bring a copy of his records from China.[140] Regardless of how Chinul came upon Ta-hui's *Records,* he was profoundly affected by them. The "shortcut" approach they advocated figured prominently in Chinul's later works such as *Resolving Doubts About Observing the Hwadu,* published posthumously in 1215, and *Excerpts from the Dharma Collection and Special Practice Record with Personal Notes,* written in 1209, one year before his death. This stress on *hwadu* observation was even more heavily emphasized by Chinul's successor, Hyesim; since that time, *hwadu* practice has been the hallmark of the Korean Sŏn school and is widely practiced even today in Sŏn monasteries.

Chinul's three major spiritual experiences—first at Ch'ŏngwon sa, where he read the *Platform Sūtra;* next at Pomun sa, where he studied the *Avataṃsaka Sūtra* and its exposition by Li T'ung-hsüan; and finally the reading of Ta-hui's *Records* at Sangmuju am, which capped them all—guided his subsequent systematization of Buddhist doctrine. These experiences appear in his works as three major approaches to Buddhist practice: the concurrent development of *samādhi* and *prajñā,* the faith and understanding of the complete and sudden teachings, and the shortcut *hwadu* method. But perhaps as important as the influence of these three works in his formulations of doctrine is the fact that they were also the focus of his formal instructions to the community as well. His biographer tells us: "He would often encourage people to recite the *Diamond Sūtra.* When he lectured on dharma his preference was for the *Platform Sūtra of the Sixth Patriarch.* When he expanded on this, he used Li T'ung-hsüan's *Exposition of the Avataṃsaka Sūtra* and the *Records of Ta-hui,* which were like the two wings of a bird."[141] The use of the *Diamond Sūtra* in chanting shows the direct influence of the Sixth Patriarch, who had achieved his own enlightenment through hearing that text. And the interesting combination of two Sŏn texts with an abstruse scholastic composition shows that he brought all these scriptures into the realm of daily practice as well, thereby demonstrating their living meaning.

REESTABLISHMENT OF THE COMMUNITY AT KILSANG SA

After three years at Sangmuju am, Chinul left for the southwest along with Yose and his other companions. When he arrived at Kilsang sa in 1200, the site was still under construction—work which was to continue for the next

five years. Along with repairing the one hundred *kan* of dilapidated buildings, the workers added eighty *kan* of structures: shrine halls, dormitories, a
refectory, kitchen, and storehouses.[142] The construction was a group project
in which all members of the community as well as Buddhist believers from
the surrounding villages participated. Finally, after nine years of work, the
reconstruction was completed in 1205.

King Hŭijong (r. 1204–1211), whose ascension to the throne just preceded
completion of the reconstruction project, had respected Chinul even while
he was a prince. After the project was finished, the king issued a proclamation on the first day of the tenth month of 1205 (13 November 1205) calling
for one hundred and twenty days of celebration in honor of the occasion.
Lectures were held on the *Records of Ta-hui* and, during the evening, meditation was conducted.[143] In commemoration of the event, Chinul also wrote
an outline of the training rules to be followed by members of the society:
Admonitions to Beginning Students. This little work, comparable in moti-
vation and influence to the *Po-chang ch'ing-kuei* in China, helped to establish ethical observance as the basis of indigenous Korean Sŏn and eventually
came to be adopted as the standard of conduct for all Sŏn monasteries.

The transfer of the community to Kilsang sa resulted in some confusion,
for in the same district, about forty *i* to the northeast, was another temple
called Chŏnghye sa (Samādhi and Prajñā Monastery).[144] To resolve the
problem, the king ordered the name of the community changed to Susŏn sa,
the Sŏn Cultivation Community, and wrote the name-plaque in his own
hand. He also renamed the mountain on which Kilsang sa had been located
from Songgwang san to Chogye san, the same characters as the Ts'ao-ch'i
shan where the Sixth Patriarch Hui-neng had resided, presumably in honor
of Chinul's revival of Sŏn practice in Korea. Finally, as a special token of
his esteem for Chinul and the community, the king offered Chinul a special
embroidered robe.[145]

Chinul based himself at Susŏn sa until his death in 1210, although he
made numerous excursions to hermitages he had built in the surrounding
mountains.[146] The community grew rapidly in those years and attracted
people from a broad cross section of the population. As his stele relates: "It
was a large and magnificent assembly which included people who had abandoned fame and rank and left behind their wives and children [to become
monks]. . . . Also included were royalty, aristocrats, literati, and commoners; there were several hundred of them who had also abandoned fame to
enter the community."[147] Hence it is clear that Susŏn sa had gained the
respect of the government as well as the following of the local populace.

THE TRAINING OF A SUCCESSOR

Of the many disciples who gathered around Chinul, one stands out as the
master's favorite, the monk to whom he finally passed on his successorship:

Hyesim, the National Master Chin'gak (1178–1234). Hyesim, whose surname was Ch'oe, was born in the Hwasun district in the immediate vicinity of Susǒn sa. Early in his youth, Hyesim had asked his mother for permission to ordain as a monk, but her firm refusal had deterred him. Instead, he was compelled to study for the civil examinations following the standard lines of a Confucian education; nevertheless, throughout his conventional studies, he diligently read Buddhist *sūtras* and chanted Sanskrit *dhāraṇīs*. It was not until his mother's death when he was twenty-four that he was finally free to follow his own wishes. After making a funeral offering in his mother's name at Susǒn sa, he immediately asked Chinul's permission to shave his head and receive ordination. It was granted and he became Chinul's disciple.[148]

From the time of his ordination, Hyesim was vigorous in his practice. It is said that once, when he was meditating on Mount Chiri, snow piled up to his head while he was sitting outside without his noticing it. It was not until his companions roused him from his *samādhi* that he realized the danger he had been in.[149]

Chinul apparently took an early liking to Hyesim. References in Hyesim's stele describe meetings between the two in which Hyesim's spiritual abilities were recognized. These passages are especially important because there are no other extant records of Chinul's day-to-day relationships with his disciples to give us some perspective on his personal style of instruction. The collections in which such material might have been preserved, Chinul's formal dharma lectures *(Sangdang nok)* and his dharma talks, songs, and verses *(Pŏbŏ kasong),*[150] have been lost; hence, the few incidents recorded in Hyesim's memorial stele are invaluable. Although the incidents recorded there demonstrate Hyesim's ability to match the wisdom of Chinul—which is to be expected in an inscription dedicated to him—they do show us something as well of Chinul the man:[151]

In the autumn of 1205, National Master Chinul was staying at [Paegun am on] Ŏkpo Mountain. Master Hyesim went to pay respects to him along with a number of fellow meditators. While they were resting at the bottom of the mountain, still over a thousand steps from the hermitage, the master heard the national master call to his attendant. He then composed a *gāthā* which said, in brief:

> The sound of the call to the boy
>   falls as if it were Spanish moss mist.
> The fragrance of steeping tea
>   is carried by wind over the stony path.
> [A talented man at the bottom
>   of the road to Paegun Mountain
> Has already paid respects to the
>   venerable master in his hermitage.][152]

[After they had arrived at the hermitage] and paid their respects, Hyesim presented his verse. The national master accepted it and gave the fan that he was holding to the master. Hyesim then presented another *gāthā* which said:

> Before, the fan was in the venerable master's hand;
> Now it is in your disciple's.
> If you meet with burning haste and mad action,
> There is nothing wrong with cooling it
>   with a fresh breeze.

In another instance which is undated, but apparently occurred after this meeting, Hyesim's stele relates the following story:

> One day when Hyesim was traveling with the national master, the national master held up a pair of shoes which had been cast aside and said, "The shoes are here now; but where is the man?"
> Hyesim answered, "How is it that you did not see him then?"
> The national master was extremely pleased [with his answer].

A different exchange between master and disciple took place during a formal dharma lecture—the only record available of Chinul's teaching style:

> Once Chinul brought up Chao-chou's *hwadu*—a dog has no Buddha-nature—and questioned his students about the ten defects to its contemplation delineated by Ta-hui.[153] The assembly had no answer. But Hyesim replied, "A person with three kinds of defects can comprehend this meaning."
> The national master asked, "Where does a person with three kinds of defects breathe out?"
> Master Hyesim struck the window once with his hand. The national master laughed heartily.
> When he returned to the master's room, Chinul secretly called him, and spoke further with him. He joyfully said, "Since I have found you, I have had no apprehension about dying. You now have self-mastery in your use of the Buddha-dharma; do not go back on your original vow."

Chinul was obviously impressed with the progress of his young student. After only seven years, he had passed into advanced stages of Sŏn meditation and displayed an ability to use his understanding properly during Sŏn tests. By 1208, at the age of fifty, Chinul apparently had sufficient confidence in Hyesim's capacities to try to pass the successorship on to him, so that he could go into permanent retreat at Kyubong am, a small hermitage he had built in the vicinity of Susŏn sa.[154] Chinul's two major works were all but completed by that time—*Excerpts from the Exposition of the Avataṃsaka Sūtra* [*Hwaŏmnon chŏryo*] in 1207 and *Excerpts from the Dharma Collection and Special Practice Record,* finished in the summer of 1209, probably nearing final form—and Chinul perhaps felt that as the major part of his teaching had been transmitted, he could retire from an active teaching role and devote himself to his own practice in solitude. Whatever Chinul's own hopes might have been, however, Hyesim was reluctant to accept the post and ended up leaving the community to go into retreat on Mount Chiri. It was only with Chinul's death in 1210 that Hyesim was finally compelled by royal order to return to Susŏn sa as spiritual leader.[155]

CHINUL'S DEATH

Chinul's desire to pass the successorship to Hyesim might have been due in some measure to precognition of his early death. Although his stele and personal writings do not state directly that he was aware of his impending death, it is clear that at least one month in advance he anticipated the date. A detailed report of the events appears in his stele and indicates that his death was carefully orchestrated and occurred with Chinul in full control:

> During the spring of the second month of the second year of the [Chin dynasty's] Great Peace reign era [26 February—26 March 1210] the master held a dharma ceremony for the guidance of his departed mother's spirit which lasted for several weeks. At that time, he announced to the monks of the community, "I will not be staying much longer in this world to expound the dharma. Each of you should be vigorous in your practice." Suddenly, on the twentieth day of the third month [15 April 1210] he showed signs of illness and after eight days the end was near. He had known in advance.
>
> The night before, when he went to the bathhouse to bathe, his attendant asked for a *gāthā*. The master replied in a natural and easy manner. Late in the night, he retired to the master's room and engaged in questions and answers as before. Toward dawn he asked, "What day is it today?" Someone answered, "It is the twenty-seventh day of the third month [22 April 1210]." The master then washed and rinsed his mouth and, donning his ceremonial dharma robe, said, "These eyes are not the eyes of my ancestors; this nose is not the nose of my ancestors. This mouth is not the mouth born of my mother; this tongue is not the tongue born of my mother."
>
> He then ordered the monastery drum beaten to summon the monks of the community and, carrying his staff with six rings, he walked toward the dharma hall. There he lit incense, ascended the platform, and proceeded to perform all the usual formalities. He then struck his staff and, after mentioning the circumstances surrounding the questions and answers exchanged in his room the previous evening, said, "The miraculous efficaciousness of the Sŏn dharma is inconceivable. Today I have come here because I want to explain it fully to all of you in this assembly. If you ask me clear, unattached questions, this old man will give you clear, unattached answers." He looked to the right and left and, rubbing his chest with his hands, said, "The life of this mountain monk is now entirely in all of your hands. You are free to drag me aside or pull me down. Let anyone who has bones and tendons come forward."
>
> He then stretched his legs and, sitting on the seat, gave answers to the different questions put to him. His words were precise and the meaning detailed; his elocu-

tion was unimpaired. The events are recorded in the *Death Record* [*Imjong ki*].[156] Finally a monk asked, "I am not clear whether the past manifestation of illness by Vimalakīrti of Vaiśālī and today's sickness of Chogye's Moguja are the same or different."[157] The master replied, "You've only learned similarity and difference!" Then, picking up his staff, he struck it several times and said, "A thousand things and ten thousand objects are all right here." Finally, supported by his staff, he remained sitting immobile and quietly passed away.[158]

After Chinul's death, his disciples held the traditional prefuneral ceremonies, which lasted for seven days. It is said that, throughout this period, his complexion remained as if he were still alive and his beard and hair continued to grow. After the appropriate rituals, a cremation was held to dispose of the body. In the ashes, thirty large relics and innumerable smaller pieces were discovered. Moreover, the remaining bits of bone were multicolored. These relics were enshrined in a small stone stupa at the foot of the mountain north of the monastery.[159]

King Hŭijong was grieved by Chinul's passing. As a token of his respect, he conferred on the master the posthumous title National Master Puril Pojo ("Buddha-Sun Shining Universally") and named his stūpa the Kamno t'ap ("Sweet-Dew Reliquary").[160]

THE LEGACY OF SUSŎN SA

The efforts of Chinul and his successors at Susŏn sa over the next hundred and eighty years established the monastery as a major center of Korean Buddhism for the remainder of the Koryŏ period. Kim Kun-su mentions that even in Chinul's time the community numbered several hundred members, including those who had renounced royalty and high government positions in order to cultivate *samādhi* and *prajñā*.[161] It was during Hyesim's tenure, however, that Susŏn sa truly blossomed into an important center of the tradition wielding nationwide influence. A report by a renowned Korean literary and political figure, Yi Kyu-bo (1168–1241),[162] indicates Hyesim's success in establishing Chinul's syncretic vision in fact as well as theory:

> All those who have entered the community are cultivating diligently. Men of eminent practice, like Chin'gong [Ch'ŏnjin] and the rest,[163] have come. They have invited elder venerables in the remaining schools [of Sŏn, the old Nine Mountains sect], of whom none have not joined; they have assembled like the clouds. Such flourishing of a Sŏn convocation has not been known before in past or present. Pyŏn'gong [Hyesim] is leader of the covenant; Chin'gong is assistant director. They lecture on the *Platform Sūtra of the Sixth Patriarch* and the *Records* of Ching-shan [Ta-hui]. Each evening they discourse on emptiness. In general, this is the standard practice. In addition, great teachers from the five scholastic sects are also participating.[164]

Hyesim's stele also substantiates the claim that scholars from all five sects of traditional scholastic Buddhism had gathered at the monastery, and it adds that court officials ranging from the premier to the king himself regarded Hyesim as their teacher and bestowed special honors on him.[165] Indeed, the community had grown so much in size that a major expansion of the campus was ordered by Hŭijong's successor, Kangjong (r. 1212–1213).[166]

Although Hyesim was gratified at the flourishing community at Susŏn sa, he was at times melancholy that his master could not have witnessed it himself. Once, in the spring of 1231, Hyesim was visiting the room at Pomun sa where Chinul had stayed before forming the retreat at Kŏjo sa. A poem he wrote there tells of his sorrow that Chinul did not live to see the full success of his experiment:

> In this quiet room,
>   I think long on my old master.
> His cocoon remains in these mountains.
> I am still sorrowful that he died when not yet
>   even half a hundred,
>   robbed of his old age,
> And was unable to see the time when our path
>   would flourish.[167]

Hyesim's successors continued to build the Susŏn sa tradition. From Chinul to National Master Kobong (1350–1428), a series of sixteen national masters are reputed to have resided at Susŏn sa, indicating the important role the monastery played in the Buddhism of its time.[168] (See Table 3.) By the end of the Koryŏ dynasty, the tradition established at Susŏn sa—which was, by then, popularly known as Songgwang sa—was held in such wide esteem that the court of King Kongmin (r. 1352–1374) issued a proclamation declaring Songgwang sa to be "the finest large monastery in the East."[169] Due to the monastery's strong orientation toward practice, Songgwang sa has traditionally been regarded since the Yi dynasty as the temple representative of the Saṃgha-jewel in Korea.[170]

III. Chinul's Thought

SYNCRETISM

The first two centuries of Buddhism's development in its Indian homeland saw a fairly consistent approach to the original corpus of scripture. Although contending schools did flourish, they looked for inspiration to a common stratum of *Āgama* material and were distinguished as much by dif-

Table 3. Songgwang sa's Sixteen National Masters

Title	Dharma Name	Dates	Writings Extant?	Stele Extant?
1. Puril Pojo 佛日普照	Chinul 知訥	1158–1210	yes	yes
2. Chin'gak 真覺	Hyesim 慧諶	1178–1234	yes	yes
3. Ch'ŏngjin 清真	Mongyŏ 夢如	?–1252	no	yes
4. Chinmyŏng 真明	Hŏnwŏn 混元	1191–1271	no	yes
5. Chajin Wŏno 慈真圓悟	Ch'ŏnyŏng 天英	1215–1286	no	yes
6. Wŏn'gam 圓鑑	Ch'ungji 冲止	1226–1292	yes	yes
7. Chajŏng 慈靜 (精)	?	?	no	no
8. Chagak 慈覺	?	?	no	no
9. Tamdang 湛堂	?	?	no	no
10. Myomyŏng Hyegam 妙明慧鑑	Manhang 萬恒	1249–1319	no	yes
11. Myoŏm Chawon 妙嚴慈圓	?	?	no	no
12. Hyegak 慧覺	?	?	no	no
13. Kagŏm Kakchin 覺儼覺真	Pugu 復丘	1270–1355	no	yes
14. Puam Chŏnghye 復庵淨慧	?	?	no	no
15. Hungjin 弘真	?	?	no	no
16. Kobong Pŏpchang 高峰法藏	Ilmyŏng Chisung 一名志崇	1350–1428	no	yes

ferences in *Vinaya* interpretations as by controversies over the central issues of Buddhist practice and ideology.[171] After five hundred years, new *sūtras* began appearing in the south and northwest of the subcontinent which expanded upon and eventually challenged the authority of the early texts, fostering an increasing divergence in scriptural interpretation. The tenets of these new *sūtras,* which came to provide the foundation for Mahāyāna theology, were often difficult to reconcile with traditional doctrine and engendered considerable controversy between new progressive sects, which found their inspiration in these texts, and the conservative elements of the Saṃgha which regarded them as heterodox.

The Mahāyāna movement is commonly assumed to have developed out of the orientation, found in certain later schools of the early church, to minister to the needs of secular adherents of the religion rather than primarily to its monastic followers.[172] The proto-Mahāyāna progressive sects proved to be more adaptable in dealing with the individual needs of their followers, as well as more flexible in responding to differences in social conditions. These inclinations, coupled with the vast quantity of new scriptural material becoming available, made the Mahāyāna schools quite eclectic in their presentation of doctrine. They did not hesitate to incorporate elements of the folk traditions and popular religious rituals that they encountered, reinterpreting them always from a Buddhist perspective. Consequently, Mahāyāna Buddhism came to flourish over a wide area of India and demonstrated a unique ability to take root in new cultures where other religious traditions were already well established.

Over the centuries, the development of schools devoted to particular sections of this later canon, combined with the inherent eclecticism of the Mahāyāna ecclesia, led to a remarkable diversity in Buddhist thought as well as increased factionalism within Mahāyāna itself. The introduction of Buddhism into China corresponded with this period of sectarian development on the Indian subcontinent and in Central Asia, and China itself rapidly developed sectarian traditions. The vastness of the country and the large size of the Saṃgha allowed various sects to coexist on a scale probably unsurpassed even in India. In China, too, up through the middle of the T'ang dynasty, Buddhism was gradually reinterpreted in light of native religious perspectives.[173] This process of adaptation culminated in the development of Ch'an—a system of Buddhist thought and practice which molded the Indian worldview, still inherently alien to China, with Chinese modes of thought. For a people which found the intricate exegeses of the scholastic schools difficult to assimilate, the Ch'an school proposed a simple yet potent approach to Buddhism that eschewed theory in favor of practice. From the time of Ch'an's ascendency, Chinese Buddhism was repeatedly to exhibit a tendency toward two extremes: either excessive emphasis on scriptural research or rejection of the utility of the *sūtras* with emphasis on formal practice.

During the golden age of Buddhism in China, from the Sui dynasty to the Hui-ch'ang persecution of 842–845, this sectarian atmosphere prevailed and a broad diversity of doctrinal outlooks flourished. Even during this period, however, Chinese Buddhist theoreticians became increasingly concerned with finding some common denominators among the different schools of thought—that is, discovering an inclusive approach to harmonize the conflicting interpretations of these schools, as well as to reconcile the often incongruous tenets of the different strata of the *sūtras* themselves. Besides the need to introduce some consistency into the broad divergence of Mahāyāna doctrines, this new syncretic movement also responded to the vision of a unified church which had become fragmented during its cyclical periods of political disfavor and clerical degeneracy. Although syncretism had already been adumbrated in major Mahāyāna scriptures like the *Avataṃsaka Sūtra* and the *Saddharmapuṇḍarīka Sūtra,* the Indian preoccupation with religious polemics and sectarian debate had vitiated its systematic investigation as well as the application of the syncretic principle in practice. It was Chinese Buddhist philosophers who first developed the theoretical framework upon which syncretism could be realized. The writings of the T'ien-t'ai founder Chih-i (538–597), the Hua-yen systematizers Fa-tsang (643–712) and Ch'eng-kuan (738–840), and Ch'an theoreticians like Tsung-mi (780–841) and Yen-shou (904–975) all explored the harmonization of Buddhist doctrine and practice from the standpoint of their own sectarian proclivities. Ch'eng-kuan and Tsung-mi both made attempts to demonstrate the correspondences between Ch'an and Hua-yen—the representative schools of the two major approaches to Buddhism, practice and theory—but neither was able to go beyond the recognition of correspondences to an explicit effort to merge the two sects either doctrinally or practically.[174] Fa-yen Wen-i (885–958) and Yen-shou employed Hua-yen analogies to explicate the truths of Ch'an, and many Ch'an monks advocated the reconciliation of the Ch'an and scholastic schools,[175] but the dissociation of the two major schools was maintained up to the thirteenth century, when syncretism finally became the predominant tendency within most sectors of the Chinese Saṃgha.[176]

Korea was one of the last countries in East Asia to inherit the Buddhist teachings, and it received them in a highly developed and prolix form. The vast numbers of sects which formed in Chinese Buddhism led to attempts to find in these various approaches to dharma—each ostensibly Buddhist, yet each so different—some common denominator through which their disparate elements could be incorporated. The flourishing of Buddhism in Korea during the Unified Silla period coincided with a rapid acceleration of these investigations in China; ultimately, most major Korean Buddhist theoreticians were influenced by these efforts and their works established syncretism as the predominant theme of the Korean doctrinal outlook.

Certain circumstances peculiar to Korea also strengthened the tendency toward syncretism. The small size of both the country itself and its monk population simply did not allow a split into large numbers of contending factions. Furthermore, the continual threat of foreign invasion and the often unstable political atmosphere created the need for a unified, centrally controlled, ecclesiastical institution. Although the vision of a church unified both doctrinally and institutionally had inspired Buddhist theoreticians in China, the first establishment of the interdenominational Buddhism which had eluded the T'ang theoreticians and their confreres came in Korea with Chinul and his successors.

Living in the middle of the Koryŏ dynasty, Chinul was faced with a fully developed church showing serious signs of moral and spiritual decline. A major split had occurred between the scholastic and Sŏn sects, a split exacerbated by increasingly inflammatory and intransigent attitudes among adherents of both schools. Drawing inspiration from his vision of the basic unity of Sŏn and the *sūtras,*[177] Chinul developed an approach to Buddhism in which the theoretical aids of the scholastic doctrine—particularly as presented in Li T'ung-hsüan's interpretation of Hua-yen philosophy—could be used to support Sŏn epistemological and soteriological views, especially as outlined in the Ho-tse school of Ch'an. This unique combination can, with little exaggeration, be considered the most distinctive Korean contribution to Buddhist thought.[178]

There was also a personal consideration which prompted Chinul's accommodating attitude toward the scholastic schools. Chinul was first and foremost a Sŏn adherent,[179] but certainly not of the same pedigree as Ma-tsu Tao-i (709–788) or Lin-chi I-hsüan (d. 866). He was, of course, ordained into the Sŏn lineage of Sagul san, which was traditionally assumed to descend from the Nan-yüeh line of Southern Ch'an, and passed his Saṃgha entrance examinations in the Sŏn sector, not the *sūtras.* Nevertheless, Chinul did not study formally under a Sŏn master for any extended period of time and never received transmission from a recognized teacher in the tradition.[180] And as one of the few important Korean masters who was never stimulated by a pilgrimage to the Chinese mainland, he was compelled to look for his information and spiritual guidance to the only authentic source available to him: the *sūtras,* commentaries, and records of the Ch'an masters which were collected in the *tripiṭaka.* For this reason, from early on in his vocation he developed a natural eclecticism and did not hesitate to borrow from the teachings of the scriptures if he found them helpful.

Throughout his life, Chinul owed his progress and all of his enlightenment experiences to insights gained from passages in the canon. Indeed, it is difficult to conceive that he could have denied their value as a tool in spiritual cultivation.

CHINUL'S VIEW OF THE CH'AN SCHOOLS

Western accounts of Ch'an have been dominated by descriptions of the five schools into which the mature tradition of the late T'ang and early Sung dynasties was divided: Lin-chi, Ts'ao-tung, Yün-men, Fa-yen, and Kuei-yang.[181] It was through these schools that Ch'an emerged as a distinctly Chinese school of Buddhism with a viable doctrine and practice. Until this systematization of the Ch'an teachings, however, there was considerable experimentation among the immediate followers of the early teachers—experimentation concerning not only expedient methods of meditation but the underlying epistemological foundations of the Ch'an dharma itself. This is the period of Middle Ch'an,[182] dating roughly from the early eighth to middle ninth centuries. Although little literature remains from the teachers of this period, the traditionally recognized fifth patriarch of both the Hua-yen and Ho-tse schools, Kuei-feng Tsung-mi (780–841), has left a considerable amount of interpretative material concerning the various approaches to Ch'an in his day.[183] In his *Notes to the Great Commentary on the Complete Enlightenment Sūtra,* Tsung-mi discusses seven major schools which were popular during this period,[184] and there are passing references to still other schools in some of his other works.[185] Four of these schools, which are representative of the approaches current in other Ch'an schools, are singled out for detailed treatment in his *Portrayal of the Successorship in the Chinese Ch'an School Which Transmits the Mind-Ground:* the Northern school, the Niu-t'ou school, the Hung-chou school, and the Ho-tse school.[186] Chinul was greatly influenced by Tsung-mi's analyses of the various Ch'an schools, and he closely examined these same schools himself in his magnum opus, *Excerpts from the Dharma Collection and Special Practice Record with Personal Notes,* a commentary on the immediately preceding work of Tsung-mi, unknown as titled in China. His analysis, however, differs in several respects from Tsung-mi's. Tsung-mi was the last exponent in China of the Ho-tse school, and his critiques of the other schools were, consequently, distinctly colored by his sectarian affiliation. Although Chinul generally favors the Ho-tse approach, he is not nearly so critical of the other schools and finds something of value in each of them.

I will consider the details of their respective analyses later, but I would like first to examine the basic criteria employed in the judgments of Tsung-mi and Chinul. According to their analyses, the teachings of the Ho-tse school offer, uniquely, a balanced approach toward, first, dharma *(pŏp)*—

the nature of reality, covering the epistemological outlook of the Ch'an teaching—and, second, person *(in)*—the soteriological process followed in the spiritual development of the individual. Dharma refers to the two factors of immutability and adaptability; person includes the two aspects of sudden awakening and gradual cultivation. Through the sudden awakening to the mind-essence—the absolute, immutable aspect of dharma—a proper foundation is laid for the refinement of the phenomenal qualities innate to that essence via gradual cultivation of the myriads of bodhisattva practices. In such an approach, the absolute and phenomenal aspects of reality and the ultimate and conventional approaches to practice are kept in harmony, and consistent progress in spiritual development can be expected. Each school of Ch'an is weighed according to how well it emulates this ideal approach.[187]

It should be understood that Chinul's intent was not to give a historically valid description of the development of these four Ch'an schools or the philosophical influences which shaped them; indeed, in his day such an attempt would have been impossible. Instead, Chinul takes each of the schools to represent an idealized approach to Ch'an theory and practice. Hence his account does not deal with any of the multifaceted issues raised by the historical schools of the Middle Ch'an period; rather, he treats basic attitudes toward practice which can be found in any era and any group of practitioners, including the Sŏn adherents of his own time.

Our knowledge of the Middle Ch'an period is developing rapidly, and it would be presumptuous of me to attempt a comprehensive treatment of the era here. I will limit myself therefore to the briefest of historical descriptions in order to bring the schools into focus and then turn to Tsung-mi and Chinul's analysis of the virtues and weaknesses of their approaches to practice and enlightenment. In this way, we will gain some sense of the approach Chinul stresses in his own Sŏn synthesis.

The Northern school of Ch'an was founded by Shen-hsiu (606?–706), a prominent disciple of the Fifth Patriarch, Hung-jen (601–674). Shen-hsiu was a renowned Ch'an master of the seventh and eighth centuries and commanded a large following in both clerical and secular circles from the imperial capital at Lo-yang in the north of China. Although later he was criticized by proponents of Hui-neng's sudden teachings in the south, most early Ch'an works recognize him as the legitimate successor to the Fifth Patriarch.[188] The nature of his teachings have, in the main, to be ascertained from the admittedly biased accounts which appear in the polemical works of his opponents in the Southern school. Traditionally, Shen-hsiu is portrayed as having advocated a gradual approach to enlightenment modeled along the lines of the *sūtra* teachings.[189] All beings were considered to possess a luminous and monistic enlightened nature which, in the ordinary person, is obscured by passions and bifurcated by dualistic tendencies of thought. Enlightenment is to be achieved by gradually cleansing the mind of these passions and thoughts until that nature is rediscovered and its inherent qualities are again able to manifest.

After the ascension of the sudden approach to a position of orthodoxy in Ch'an, the gradual teachings of the Northern school were belittled by teachers in virtually all other schools of Ch'an. The critique of this school which is given by Tsung-mi[190] and accepted without reservation by Chinul in *DCSPR* is no exception. Because the gradual teachings center on the removal of essentially void passions and thoughts, its entire theory is compromised, for it substantiates the reality of conditionally arisen phenomena rather than recognizing that they come into existence through dependence on the absolute mind-ground. By ignoring the immutable aspect of dharmas, the Northern school is attached to adaptability—the mundane characteristics of phenomena. Hence, by trying to counteract the defilements, it deals with them on their own terms, which further enmeshes the practitioner in their net. Although the school's counteractive practices are used at the stage of gradual cultivation as outlined in the Ho-tse school and should, therefore, be acceptable, those practices are not based upon the initial sudden awakening which would assure a proper outlook on the practice. Consequently, the adept cannot know that, although the defilements must be counteracted, there is nothing in reality to be counteracted and no such practice to be performed. Finally, such relative practices only sustain the illusion that defilements do exist and must be counteracted and that there *is* a practice which accomplishes this. With a theory and practice which are both incorrect, right enlightenment is, accordingly, impossible to achieve through this approach.

Shen-hsiu's teachings attracted considerable attention during his lifetime and that of his principal disciple, P'u-chi. However, the virulent attacks of Shen-hui in the south, beginning in 732, severely undermined its influence. Finally, its location in the capital made it particularly vulnerable to political changes in the imperial court and led to its enervation during the An Lu-shan rebellion of 755–756 and its eventual demise during the Hui-ch'ang persecution of 842–845. Its influence on the later development of Ch'an both in China and in Korea was nil.

After the Fourth Patriarch, Tao-hsin (580–651), had handed down his patriarchate to Hung-jen, he was traveling, according to legend, in the vicinity of Niu-t'ou (Oxhead) Mountain, south of present-day Nanking in Kiangsu province. Supposing that adepts of outstanding potential were hidden in that austere and isolated environment, he climbed up and discovered the monk Fa-jung (594–657) practicing in a rock cave near Yu-hsi Monastery. After receiving instructions from Tao-hsin, Fa-jung was enlightened and received the transmission from the patriarch. Thus began one of the most successful of the early Ch'an schools—the Niu-t'ou or Oxhead school, which lasted for at least eight generations until the end of the eighth century.[191]

Before his conversion to Ch'an by Tao-hsin, Fa-jung had been an avid student of the *Prajñāpāramitā* texts, the tenets of which are centered on the ultimate voidness of all particularities. Even after the Fourth Patriarch had shown Fa-jung that the absolute mind-nature is originally enlightened and inherently endowed with all spiritual qualities, Fa-jung's approach to Ch'an still was influenced by this early exposure to the doctrine of voidness, as can be clearly seen in Tsung-mi's synopsis of his teachings.

The theory of the Niu-t'ou school was designed to point the way toward a vision of the essential voidness of all mundane and supramundane dharmas. Through this vision, the affairs of this world—which are commonly considered to be real—are exposed as the deluded hallucinations of the ignorant mind. It is by understanding the illusory nature of all affairs that the ability to abandon all attachments is gained. Once one realizes voidness, one can begin to overcome those defilements by relinquishing passions and desires and, eventually, transcend suffering.

Tsung-mi's critique of this approach is based upon the school's emphasis on the immutable aspect of dharmas: their voidness. Niu-t'ou simply recognizes that all qualities, whether mundane affairs or the supramundane experiences of nirvana or enlightenment, are essentially nonexistent. For Tsung-mi, this is not a particularly encouraging vision. The dharma-nature might be void, but it is also pure; it might be characterized by absolute immutability, but it also involves the adaptability of expedients. The Niu-t'ou teachings penetrate through falsity, but they do not reach the full realization in which the dharma-nature is seen to be the sum total of both immutability and adaptability. Consequently, as the school entirely neglects the positive role of the Buddha-nature in promoting spiritual progress, it reaches only halfway to the approach of sudden awakening found in the Ho-tse school. From the standpoint of the gradual cultivation after awakening, however, its approach is acceptable because it stresses the cultivation of techniques which clear away defilements and maintain the essential calmness of the mind.

Chinul is not quite so critical of Niu-t'ou and looks for another motive behind Tsung-mi's appraisal. Quoting a passage from Tsung-mi's *Preface to the Fountainhead of Ch'an Collection* which says that the Niu-t'ou idea that everything is simply an illusion is not the only dharma of this school, Chinul surmises that Tsung-mi's reason for criticizing the school is to ensure that Ch'an students do not grasp at this voidness as being the only truth but also move toward realization of the dynamic aspect of that void mind-essence: the numinous awareness *(yŏngji)* which is the original functioning of the self-nature. Hence Niu-t'ou's approach is a perfectly valid teaching which can be effective in enlightening people who obstinately grasp at dharmas as being real—the fault to which the Northern school was subject.[192] Furthermore, in combination with the positive teachings of the Hung-chou school, Niu-t'ou's negative approach becomes a perfectly valid path to enlightenment—one that counters the tendency toward unrestraint and "unlimited action" *(muae haeng)* which is a typical fault of the idealist teachings of Hung-chou. Hence, in Chinul's view, the Niu-t'ou approach is worthy of being retained as an expedient method of Sŏn practice.

Of the seven schools of Middle Ch'an covered by Tsung-mi in his *YCCTSC*, only one survived the T'ang dynasty: the school of Hung-chou. Although there are no reliable sources through which to trace the history of this school's lineage, it traditionally is considered to have been founded by Nan-yüeh Huai-jang (677–744), an obscure disciple of Hui-neng (638–713), the reputed Sixth Patriarch. The school was popularized, however, and its approach set, by Huai-jang's renowned successor Ma-tsu Tao-i (709–788), who was based at K'ai-yüan Monastery in Hung-chou, a district in present-day Kiangsi. Since Ma-tsu's disciple Po-chang Huai-hai (720–814), another important figure in the school's early history, lived on Po-chang Mountain in the same region, the school which grew up around them came to be known as the Hung-chou school.

Unlike the three other schools of Middle Ch'an covered in the *PCPHN*, the Hung-chou school was based in the south, far from the northern capitals of Lo-yang and Ch'ang-an. Because of its isolated rural location, it was able to avoid most of the periodic persecution suffered by all the schools based on the capitals. It was this school which developed the distinctive style of Ch'an practice that later became identified with Ch'an itself: the iconoclastic use of shouts, beatings, and paradox to give expression to the ultimate reality beyond all words and awaken its students into this state. Its teachings eventually branched into the Kuei-yang and Lin-chi schools of the mature tradition, and its Lin-chi lineage was the only direct transmission line of Ch'an to outlast the T'ang dynasty in China. Although its unique approach to Ch'an eventually became the hallmark of the Ch'an dharma, it should be remembered that at the time Tsung-mi was writing—the middle of the ninth century—it was still but one of many competing schools and its approach had gained anything but widespread acceptance.[193]

The Hung-chou's approach to dharma is portrayed by Tsung-mi as positive and idealist. It views all discriminative phenomena as manifestations of the nondual Buddha-nature. This Buddha-nature embraces fully the absolute, immutable characteristics of the mind, as well as its relative, adaptable properties. Ma-tsu's statement, "Mind is Buddha," signals this central conception.[194] Awakening in this school means simply the understanding that all thoughts and discriminative activities are nothing other than the Buddha-nature itself and, accordingly, are all equally real. Shouting and the use of paradoxical expressions are expedients designed to expose directly to the student the reality of that nature. The view that all phenomena are manifestations of the Buddha-nature allows the school to accept all things equally. But, while this understanding brings it close to the Ho-tse conception of sudden awakening, it ignores the differences between positive virtue and negative demerit and thus is not as precise a formulation as is found in Ho-tse.

Moreover, there is one major inconsistency in its description of practice which, for Tsung-mi, flaws the entire approach: it does not actively encourage further spiritual development after awakening but holds that practice involves nothing more than keeping the mind in a completely receptive state, free to act naturally and spontaneously. Hence, rather than cultivating positive qualities or counteracting defilements, the student is simply to release the mind from all artificially imposed restraints and let it return to its fundamentally pure state. Once the Buddha-mind is functioning freely, all the qualities and attributes which are inherently contained in that mind can then operate freely as well. The school represents, accordingly, a sudden awakening/sudden cultivation approach to practice, in contrast to the sudden/gradual approach of the Ho-tse school, which Tsung-mi considers to be most proper. As the Hung-chou school lacks any conception of gradual cultivation, it is inferior to the Ho-tse school. This controversy over sudden and gradual awakening and cultivation is discussed more fully below.

Chinul, writing nearly four centuries after Tsung-mi, is of course aware of the eventual success of the Nan-yüeh lineage in establishing Ch'an solidly in China; he is aware also of the extinction of the Ho-tse line immediately following its brief respite under Tsung-mi's leadership. He is, therefore, considerably more lenient with the Hung-chou approach. Although he, like Tsung-mi, supports the basic approach of the Ho-tse school, he finds that the Hung-chou school also presents a fully viable approach to Sŏn practice. Indeed, quoting from another of Tsung-mi's works, *Preface to the Fountainhead of Ch'an Collection,* he goes so far as to say that they are the same school—implying thereby that even though the Ho-tse lineage died out in China, its teachings lived on in the guise of the Hung-chou school. Chinul demonstrates that the Hung-chou teachings are an effective means for perfecting the ultimate instrument of any meditation practice: thoughtlessness, or no-mind. If, through thoughtlessness, the student can maintain the awareness that all things are void, he cannot be trapped by either good or evil dharmas; consequently, his practice and understanding will be irreproachable.[195]

Chinul assumes that the reason for Tsung-mi's criticism of this school stems not from the inherent inferiority of its approach but rather from two fears. First, adepts might become attached to an insouciant attitude encouraged by the school's idealist outlook. Since all things are innately true and are completely indistinguishable from the noumenal Buddha-nature, there is nothing which needs to be cultivated, for everything is perfected already. This assumption that everything is essentially the same could hinder the mental faculty which distinguishes the wholesome from the unwholesome. Second, students might end up grasping only at verbal descriptions of the Buddha-nature, effectively blocking their ability to awaken personally to that nature.

In Chinul's view, the Hung-chou teachings contain valuable expedients for the development of practice. Their positive character is, moreover, a perfect complement to the negative tendencies of the Niu-t'ou teachings. They ensure that the Ch'an student does not fall into the error of cessation —that is, taking all things as being nothing but voidness. Hence they are especially useful in dealing with a mistake all too common among Ch'an adepts: attachment to the mental calmness which comes with practice, rather than going forward to develop the dynamic qualities immanent in the mind.

Throughout the first quarter of the eighth century, the Northern school of Ch'an retained considerable spiritual and temporal influence in the northern T'ang capitals. In 732, however, a relatively unknown monk from the south of China launched a grand assault on the Ch'an of Shen-shiu's successor, P'u-chi. Advocating a sudden approach to Ch'an which supposedly derived from the truly orthodox transmission of the patriarchs, he eventually triumphed over all the other schools of his time and established his own as the legitimate lineage of the Ch'an patriarchs. It thus became the dominant school of Ch'an in the capitals.

The initiator of this new movement was the monk Shen-hui (670–762), a reputed disciple of Hui-neng, one of the Fifth Patriarch's eleven main disciples. Challenging the Northern school with the enthusiasm of the true prophet, Shen-hui made accusations about the Northern school's doctrine and the legitimacy of its lineage which sometimes approached hyperbole and fabrication. By retelling the history of the Ch'an transmission, he established his teacher Hui-neng as the Sixth Patriarch. And to confirm that the Northern school's gradual approach was a blatant misconstruction of the true teachings of Ch'an, he produced a collection of sermons by his teacher which vindicated the sudden doctrine of the patriarchal lineage. This sudden teaching assumed that, since the mind-nature is always complete and perfect in itself, systematic development of the mind prior to enlightenment through expedient methods of practice is utterly redundant. What is required instead is the sudden awakening to that nature, which automatically assures that its operation becomes unimpaired. Although there is no guarantee that a similar doctrine was not in fact advocated by the Northern school as well, its branding as an inferior "gradual" teaching which had usurped the rightful teachings of the patriarchs placed it immediately in a defensive position from which it never recovered.

By 745 Shen-hui had attracted enough attention to warrant an invitation to reside in a monastery within the precincts of Lo-yang itself. Undoubtedly, the wider audience there increased the tone of his invective. Unable to ignore the continued attacks of Shen-hui, coming then at such close range, the Northern school took action. Their political position, gained through long years of imperial favor, enabled them to convince important officials that Shen-hui's motives were subversive. In 753 he was exiled to the remote province of Kiangsi.

The exile was to be short-lived. The An Lu-shan rebellion of 755–756 created havoc in the capitals and placed considerable financial strain on the meager resources of the exiled government. To raise money for its military campaigns, the T'ang administration set up ordination platforms throughout the country at which monk's certificates were sold. After the capital was recovered, Shen-hui was called back to Lo-yang to assist in this money-raising campaign, and his efforts were so successful that the government was considerably strengthened. In recognition of his success, the government ordered that a Ch'an center be built for him on the site of Ho-tse Monastery in Lo-yang; accordingly, the school he founded is called the Ho-tse school. He remained there until his death in 762. The centers of the Northern school were seriously disrupted during the rebellion and were never able to recover their former stature. Shen-hui's Southern teachings had won the day.[196]

Although Shen-hui had been successful in his struggle with the Northern school, his followers were not nearly so adept in maintaining his teachings. He had many disciples, but none achieved the renown of their teacher, and the school fell into gradual decline. Apart from a brief respite under its fifth patriarch, Kuei-feng Tsung-mi, its influence continued to dwindle until it finally disappeared in China during the Hui-ch'ang persecution of 842–845.

Tsung-mi, the last patriarch of the Ho-tse school, was one of the most incisive theoreticians in the Ch'an tradition whose writings covered many areas of the scholastic teachings as well. His attempts to harmonize the views of the Ch'an and scholastic schools greatly influenced the future development of both Korean and Japanese Buddhism.[197] Ŭich'ŏn had been impressed by Tsung-mi's balanced appraisal of the two systems,[198] and Chinul incorporated Tsung-mi's thought—though not uncritically—in his own approach to the systematization of the teachings of Ch'an and the scholastic schools. Tsung-mi's presentation of the teachings of the Ho-tse school regards them as the basis of both the exoteric *sūtra* teachings and the esoteric mind-transmission of Sŏn: they are, consequently, uniquely capable of absorbing all limited perspectives toward dharma and practice held by schools of Buddhist thought.[199]

The theoretical suppositions of the Ho-tse school as they were interpreted by Tsung-mi center on the two aspects of the mind-nature: immutability and adaptability. The absolute basis of all dharmas is the void and calm mind. Although this mind is ultimately indescribable, it can be characterized from a relative standpoint through its original function—the inherent quality of numinous awareness. Whether the individual is enlightened or deluded, this awareness is unchanged either by the machinations of the discriminatory intellect or by the obscuring influence of external sense-objects. Nevertheless, as this awareness cannot be limited or defiled by either internal mental and emotional states or by external sensory contacts, it is free to adapt in an infinite variety of ways depending on the individual's state of mind. If a person is deluded and immersed in sensual pleasures, this awareness adapts in such a manner that it is displayed as ignorance, karmic action, and finally suffering. But if a person is awakened, this awareness manifests in its basic void and calm guise. Hence, in Ho-tse's approach, awakening implies an understanding of these two aspects of the mind: its immutable absolute character and its adaptive relative faculties. In contrast to the other schools of Ch'an discussed by Tsung-mi, only the Ho-tse approach is perfectly balanced between the immutable and adaptable aspects of dharma.

Through the sudden awakening to the void and calm mind-essence, awareness is revealed in its fundamental form—free of thoughts and void of all relative signs. To maintain this state of thoughtlessness is the primary practice of the Ho-tse school according to Tsung-mi, and it is by maintaining this state that the remainder of the bodhisattva practices are brought to consummation. Thoughtlessness keeps the mind in a pure, receptive state so that it can become gradually infused with the positive states of mind developed through various wholesome practices. It is through this gradual cultivation which follows upon awakening that the mind is filled with spiritual qualities which can be used for the student's own spiritual development as well as for instructing others. Accordingly, practice in the Ho-tse school cannot begin until there is sudden awakening to the mind and its immutable and adaptable functions. Through this awakening, the adept realizes that he is originally endowed with the nature which is no different from that of all

Buddhas—in short, that he is potentially a fully enlightened Buddha already. With the understanding gained through this awakening, the student gradually cultivates the full range of wholesome qualities until Buddhahood is achieved in its active form as well.

For full realization to occur, however, the symbiotic relationship between sudden awakening and gradual cultivation must be recognized and their respective qualities carefully balanced. The awakening to the numinous awareness exposes the voidness of all phenomena. Based on that awakening, the student continues to cultivate the whole range of wholesome qualities even though he has realized the essential voidness of those qualities. Thus he practices without believing there is really anything which is being practiced. Through continued cultivation, the obscuring operation of the defilements is overcome and birth and death are transcended. At that point the natural functioning of the numinous awareness is completely restored; the person is free to manifest in an infinite variety of ways the positive qualities which have thoroughly infused his mind in order to help sentient beings of all levels and capacities. This perfect combination—the absolute calmness achieved through sudden awakening, and the dynamic responses gained through gradual cultivation—is the state of Buddhahood and the goal of all Buddhist training. Hence the approach of sudden awakening/ gradual cultivation, the path which all the saints of the past have followed, is the optimum method for ensuring the ultimate attainment of Buddhahood for the ordinary Buddhist practitioner.

Sudden awakening/gradual cultivation is the hallmark of the Ho-tse school and the ideal which distinguished it from other schools of Ch'an. Sudden awakening/gradual cultivation is, as well, the approach which is most easily reconcilable with the teachings of the *Avataṃsaka Sūtra,* the pinnacle of the scholastic doctrine. There practice follows a process in which a sudden awakening to the Buddha-mind at the entrance onto the bodhisattva path is followed by gradual cultivation until that Buddha-mind is able to act freely, which is the final attainment of Buddhahood. By advocating sudden awakening/gradual cultivation in Ch'an as well, Tsung-mi found a bridge between the scholastic and Ch'an sects. The Ho-tse teachings emerge as an approach broad enough to embrace not only all other Ch'an schools, but all the scholastic sects as well. In Chinul's examination of the Ho-tse school, he demonstrates that a combination of the diametrically opposed teachings of Hung-chou and Niu-t'ou results in the Ho-tse outlook; eventually, through understanding that ultimate outlook, all limited views drop away and a full vision of the true import of Ch'an is achieved.

Tsung-mi's interpretation of Ho-tse practice places most of its stress on thoughtlessness. In Shen-hui's writings, however, there is an emphasis instead on the identity of *samādhi* and *prajñā*. *Samādhi,* the calm, absolute aspect of the mind, means the nonarising of thoughts and correlates with Tsung-mi's term "thoughtlessness." *Prajñā,* the dynamic, analytical processes of the mind, refers to constant awareness of this nonarising of thoughts and the voidness of all phenomena. In passages which recall and often parallel sections in the *Platform Sūtra* of Hui-neng, Shen-hui advocates that *samādhi* and *prajñā* are two aspects of the same nondual mind-nature which cannot be differentiated absolutely.[200] *Samādhi* is the essence of *prajñā; prajñā* is the function of *samādhi.* Hence these assimilative and dialectical abilities of the mind cannot be bifurcated, but should always operate in combination with one another. This theme receives detailed consideration in a number of Chinul's writings, especially *Secrets on Cultivating the Mind* and *Encouragement to Practice.*

The Ho-tse school did not last out the T'ang dynasty. Indeed, Tsung-mi's ecumenical approach which, to many Ch'an adepts, seemed to blur the distinctions between the scholastic teachings and the special transmissions of Ch'an gained him little but invective from Ch'an writers of later generations. The teachings which the Ho-tse school had emphasized—the syncretic spirit, the sudden awakening/gradual cultivation approach to practice, the balanced development of *samādhi* and *prajñā*—inspired no lasting following within the Ch'an sect and can be said to have exerted little influence over the further development of Ch'an in China. But four hundred years later, in Korea, Tsung-mi's writings found an ardent, though by no means uncritical, admirer in Chinul, who used them as the foundation upon which the epistemological suppositions of a uniquely Korean variety of Ch'an were constructed. It was this adoption of the teachings of an early school of Ch'an and their use in bringing about a reconciliation between the Sŏn and scholastic sects which augured the whole future development of Buddhism in Korea.[201] Chinul ensured that the Ho-tse approach became a truly ecumenical teaching, and he broadened its scope so that it could encompass not only the Niu-t'ou and Hung-chou approaches of the early Ch'an tradition but even the later Hua-yen and Lin-chi teachings, the culminating achievements of the scholastic and Ch'an sects. Chinul's debt to Tsung-mi is immense, and its ramifications will be brought out in the following pages.

THE HUA-YEN TEACHINGS OF LI T'UNG-HSÜAN AND
THE RAPPROCHEMENT WITH SŎN

The rapprochement Chinul brought about in Korea between the scholastic schools and Sŏn was based on his conviction that the message of the *sūtras* and the special transmission of Sŏn were essentially identical. To demonstrate this basic similarity Chinul relied on the description of Ch'an practice given in the Ho-tse school as outlined in the works of Tsung-mi; to bring the scholastic schools into focus, he used the approach to practice detailed in the *Avataṃsaka Sūtra*, especially in the explication of Hua-yen teachings appearing in the *Exposition of the Avataṃsaka Sūtra* by Li T'ung-hsüan (635–730).

The *Avataṃsaka Sūtra*,[202] a massive sourcebook of Mahāyāna Buddhism, was interpreted by its commentators in the Hua-yen school to give the most complete description of the bodhisattva path to Buddhahood appearing anywhere in the canon. Fifty-two separate stages in the bodhisattva's development are outlined: ten faiths,[203] ten abidings, ten practices, ten transferences, ten *bhūmis*, one equal enlightenment, and one sublime enlightenment. The account I give of them here is based on Li T'ung-hsüan's *Exposition*.[204]

The ten faiths are, in a sense, a preliminary level prior to the entrance onto the bodhisattva path proper at the abiding stage of the arousing of the *bodhicitta*. Essentially, they involve developing faith that the fundamental nature of every sentient being is the Buddha of Unmoving Wisdom and that this innate Buddhahood is endowed with two aspects: the noumenal essence and the phenomenal function. Although the bodhisattva's faith in these facts is strengthened at each of the ten separate levels of faith, it is still based on intellectual and emotional acceptance, not direct, personal experience. As Li says, "The stage of faith reveals the fruition-dharma and brings up cause and fruition simultaneously. But it merely catalyzes the arising of faith; it does not yet involve any real awakening."[205]

Direct experience of the reality of inherent Buddhahood is achieved through penetrating realization at the next stage: the ten abidings. At the time of the first arousal of the *bodhicitta*, or thought of enlightenment, which occurs at the initial abiding stage, the bodhisattva realizes that he "abides" in the "abiding-place" of the Buddhas and has their same wisdom-nature. This realization constitutes his formal initiation as a bodhisattva and the true beginning of the path toward Buddhahood. At this point, the noumenal wisdom—the wisdom based upon the suchness of the Buddha-nature's essence—is fully perfected, and the bodhisattva is endowed with all the qualities of Buddhahood in potential form.

Although he might have realized that he is essentially a Buddha, it still remains for the bodhisattva to put that potential into action and make it function in fact as well as theory. This development begins at the next stage: the ten practices. Based on the understanding that the original wisdom of Buddhahood is empty and simply "such," the bodhisattva begins to cultivate the myriads of wholesome practices without, however, giving rise to the thought that there is really something which is being practiced or someone who is practicing it. Consequently, he can bring to perfection all expedient means of practice without falling into subject/object dualism—which would only further entrap him in the perceptual distortions that character- ize the realm of *saṃsāra*. At this stage, the bodhisattva begins to develop his phenomenal wisdom: the wisdom which is able to adapt to the ordinary world and to employ the things in that world for the benefit of other senti- ent beings.

Up to this point on the path, there is still a dichotomy between the nou- menal wisdom of suchness and the phenomenal wisdom of expedients. To ensure that such a false dichotomy is not maintained, which could cause either of those aspects of wisdom to ossify, the bodhisattva continues on to the development of the ten transferences. At this level, the phenomenal practices developed in the stage of the ten practices are merged with the noumenal understanding gained at the ten abidings, bringing about the unimpeded interpenetration of noumenon and phenomenon. Through this merging, both the noumenal and phenomenal aspects of wisdom are free to operate independently and yet harmoniously. The culmination of the bodhi- sattva path is reached, and he enters the ten *bhūmis*.

The ten *bhūmis* are the original foundation of all dharmas. Here the bodhisattva pervades all dharmas, all directions, and all positions simulta- neously. Development before this stage involved some measure of effort and entailed as well the progressive development of meritorious practices. By the time the bodhisattva has reached the ten *bhūmis,* however, he has nothing left to practice and nothing left to achieve. It is a kind of "firming- up" stage at which all the qualities and achievements attained throughout the previous levels are matured and allowed to infuse his entire being. He merges with all dharmas without, however, losing his own identity in the process. This is the stage of the unimpeded interpenetration of all phe- nomena—the highest expression of spiritual attainment in the *Avataṃsaka Sūtra* and, by implication, in all the Buddhist scriptures.

Once the experience of this perfect interpenetration of all phenomena has been stabilized by passing through each of the ten separate *bhūmis,* the bodhisattva enters into Buddhahood itself at the equal enlightenment and sublime enlightenment stages. "Equal" connotes the noumenal perfection of Buddhahood; "sublime" implies the perfection of phenomenal qualities. Both together signify the ultimate stage of Buddhahood. Here the funda- mental wisdom of suchness and the discriminative wisdom of expedients are perfectly balanced; compassion and wisdom operate simultaneously and in tandem. As a Buddha, the adept becomes one with all beings—again with- out losing his own identity in the process—and is, accordingly, supremely able to adapt to the unique needs of each and every individual.

Li T'ung-hsüan is an obscure figure in the early history of the Hua-yen school. His hagiographies have little to say about his life, although it is stated that he was related to the T'ang imperial house.[206] In 709, toward the end of his life, it is said that he took up residence in a hermitage on Fang shan outside of Pei-ching[207] and devoted himself to writing a number of Hua-yen exegetical works, including his magnum opus, a forty-fascicle commentary to Śikṣānanda's translation of the *Avataṃsaka Sūtra*. Best known during his lifetime for his thaumaturgic talents, Li's works initially had little influence on the development of the Hua-yen philosophical stance.

Centuries after the orthodox Hua-yen school had ossified after the fifth and last of its patriarchs, Tsung-mi, Li's thought enjoyed the attention of teachers in other sects, particularly teachers in the Yang-ch'i lineage of the Sung Lin-chi school of Ch'an. Li's works, transmitted during this period to Korea and Japan, exerted immense influence on the Buddhist traditions of those countries. Chinul himself was profoundly affected by his reading of Li T'ung-hsüan's commentary, and through his advocacy Li's thought assumed a central place in forging the Korean Buddhist doctrinal outlook. In Japan, Chinul's contemporary Kōben, or Myōe Shōnin (1173–1232), was similarly impressed by Li T'ung-hsüan and Li became thereby an important influence in medieval Japanese Buddhist thought. And in China proper, Li enjoyed a resurgence of interest among both Ming and Ch'ing Buddhist scholars, including the major Ch'ing dynasty Hua-yen figure, P'eng Chi-ch'ing (1740–1796). Hence, from a position of all but total obscurity, Li T'ung-hsüan's reputation rose until it finally eclipsed that of the orthodox Hua-yen patriarchs themselves.[208]

Li's contemporary Fa-tsang, the systematizer of orthodox Hua-yen doctrine, took the *Avataṃsaka Sūtra*'s "Appearance of the *Tathāgatas*" chapter as the basis of his hermeneutical approach and interpreted the *sūtra* from a metaphysical standpoint: the philosophical implications of the *dharmadhātu* theory.[209] As such, his analyses of the *sūtra* converge on the ultimate realization of the unimpeded interpenetration of all phenomena in the *dharmadhātu*, also called the conditioned arising of the *dharmadhātu*.[210] Although it does not seem that Fa-tsang intended to commit himself inflexibly to a fixed temporal scheme as far as the development of practice is concerned, he does mention that, from a conventional standpoint, Buddhahood is attained through a process of learning, practice, and realization over a period of three lives.[211] This process eventually culminates in the achievement of the unimpeded interpenetration of all phenomena.

In contrast with this philosophical orientation, Li T'ung-hsüan presented an approach to Hua-yen thought which is strongly practice-oriented. Unlike Fa-tsang, who concentrated on a description of the state of enlightenment— the realm of reality or *dharmadhātu*—Li's interpretation of the *Avataṃsaka Sūtra* centers on Sudhana's personal realization of the *dharmadhātu*:[212] his pilgrimage in search of instruction so that he will be able to enter into the *dharmadhātu,* as explained in the Gaṇḍavyūha chapter of the *sūtra.*[213] Li eschewed both the classical Yogācāra computation, in which Buddhahood was achieved after arduous practice over three *asaṃkhyeya* kalpas,[214] as well as Fa-tsang's theory of the attainment of Buddhahood over a period of three lives; rather, he proposed the immediate achievement of Buddhahood in this very life,[215] at the preliminary level of the ten faiths.[216]

Li was able to justify this extraordinary claim by abandoning Fa-tsang's focus on the conditioned arising of the *dharmadhātu* in favor of an approach based on the theory of the conditioned arising from the nature, or nature origination.[217] In his *Treatise on the Complete and Sudden Attainment of Buddhahood,* Chinul's synopsis of Li T'ung-hsüan's Hua-yen thought, Chinul gives a thorough analysis of the strengths and weaknesses of the two theories and comes out solidly in favor of nature origination as well, because of its presumed efficacy in bringing about direct realization in Buddhist students.[218] Rather than working through a complicated series of theoretical instructions before attaining the final vision of the unimpeded interpenetration of all things, nature origination—in which all phenomena are seen to arise directly from the nondual true nature of suchness—provides the conceptual justification for Li's unique form of contemplation practice: the immediate vision of the identification of Buddhas and sentient beings. Li shows that the fundamental wisdom of Buddhahood and the ignorant, discriminative minds of sentient beings are originally of the same essence; it is only because of the arising of defilements and the processes of dualistic thought that a barrier has been erected between the two states. If a sentient being has a sudden awakening to the fact that his mind is innately free of defilement and is originally in full possession of the wisdom-nature, then his relative mind and the absolute mind of Buddhahood will merge and the fruition of Buddhahood, at that very instant, will be realized.[219] Hence, for Li T'ung-hsüan, Buddhahood is not something which results from the maturation of theoretical understanding: it is an inviolable fact which requires merely the presence of an appropriate catalyst to prompt its recognition.

Li T'ung-hsüan's interpretation of Hua-yen doctrine was well suited for Chinul's attempt to demonstrate the correspondences between the Sŏn and Hwaŏm systems. In *DCSPR* and later in *Complete and Sudden Attainment of Buddhahood* Chinul shows that the terse formulas of Sŏn—"Mind is Buddha" and "See the nature and achieve Buddhahood"—correspond respectively to Li's statements that the discriminative mind of sentient beings is the unmoving wisdom of the Buddha and that the fullness of Buddhahood can be achieved suddenly at the initial entrance onto the bodhisattva path. In this thinly disguised manner as well, Chinul correlates the Sŏn emphasis on the pure nature with Li's stress on nature origination. Through such an approach, the massive metaphysics of Hwaŏm philosophy was brought within the utilitarian outlook of the Korean Sŏn schools. This was an incorporation which strengthened the theological foundations of Sŏn while increasing the practical value of Hwaŏm philosophy.

Chinul also drew upon the terminology of the Hwaŏm school to defend Sŏn against the charges of heterodoxy made by the scholastic schools. He demonstrates in *Complete and Sudden Attainment of Buddhahood* that the awakening experience in Sŏn is what the Hwaŏm teachings term the sudden realization of the *dharmadhātu*. This awakening is not the mere passive vision of the self-nature, as might be implied in the formula "See the nature and achieve Buddhahood." Rather, it involves the dynamic application of all the qualities revealed through that awakening in one's interaction with the world. The realization of the nondual nature which is the essential ground of sentient beings and Buddhas exposes the two properties of that nature: the noumenal essence, which is the perfect, bright, and self-reliant foundation of the *dharmadhātu,* and the phenomenal function which manifests objects in the sensory realms in all their diversity. It is through these two properties that the true nature exhibits itself throughout the world and thus accomplishes the perfect, unimpeded interpenetration of all phenomena. The function of the self-nature is unimpeded during all activities and is never separate from the pure, enlightened nature; hence if a student looks back on the radiance of that enlightened nature, falsity is extinguished, the mind's activities are cleansed, and the myriads of phenomena are illuminated and shown to be in dynamic interaction with each other. Consequently, the ultimate state of the interpenetration of all phenomena is not distinct from the fundamental wisdom inherent in the self-nature of all sentient beings; if that nature is recognized through Sŏn practice, the ultimate goal of the Hwaŏm school is realized.

By the same token, Chinul countered the notion prevalent among many Sŏn adepts that the scholastic sects, Hwaŏm in particular, were simply involved in speculative philosophizing which had no bearing on actual practice. In *Encouragement to Practice,* Chinul shows that sudden awakening and cultivation are possible in the Hwaŏm sect as well, and he states explicitly that Sŏn students should never assume they have an exclusive claim on suddenness. Chinul points out elsewhere that the doctrinal explanations of Hwaŏm are intended to prompt students toward the attainment of Buddhahood, just as in Sŏn. The detailed analyses appearing in the scholastic descriptions—which disturbed the Sŏn adherents who preferred terse explanations—were actually designed for sentient beings of lesser capacity. For those incapable of going beyond the judgments and guidance of the relative mind, such descriptions provide a conceptual framework for approaching practice and a realistic account of the results to be expected. This approach encourages people who are less familiar with spiritual matters to start out themselves in Buddhist practice. Eventually, these relative descriptions will have to be abandoned for a direct realization of the true nature; but this is not to deny their conventional utility at a particular stage in spiritual development.

It should be clear that Sŏn and the scholastic schools have their own propensities, but these are not, however, necessarily contradictory. Indeed, a combination of the theoretical and practical stances which characterize these major branches of Buddhism can often be the most effective means for promoting enlightenment in the majority of practitioners. In the final formulation of Chinul's own approach to Sŏn, which was to become the standard for the Korean Sŏn tradition as a whole, these two branches are synthesized into an approach which is of the widest possible application. Because most individuals of normal and inferior spiritual capacity require the help of scriptural instruction in order to prompt enlightenment, the descriptions of dharma given in the Ho-tse school and in Li T'ung-hsüan's *Exposition* are used initially to clarify the absolute and relative aspects of the mind and the proper course of practice. Such an understanding gives the beginner a clear picture of the nature and purpose of Buddhist meditation. But the student cannot merely remain content with these conceptual descriptions, regardless of how strongly they encourage his cultivation. The student must learn to put that doctrine into practice and realize its validity directly. Once he understands the path of practice, he should abandon all relative descriptions of dharma and enter upon the living road of Sŏn practice: the way of *hwadu* investigation.[220]

It should not be assumed, however, that Chinul's syncretic stance compromises the practice orientation of the Korean Sŏn schools. Even when engaged in the theoretical study considered essential for the average student, the aspirant has been steeped in the transcendent outlook of Sŏn. Hence the student remains aware of the original sublimity of the nondual mind from which the discriminative theories he studies all emerge. With this understanding, the student will not grasp at the conceptual form of theories and take them as ultimate but will use them as guides pointing always to their source: the mind. Finally, after he has studied the doctrine and realized through Sŏn practice the highest expression of that doctrine—the unimpeded interpenetration of all phenomena—he will understand that, after all, everything is simply the operation of the fundamental wisdom of his own self-nature. I will come back to this question in the discussion of Chinul's methods of practice.

SUDDEN AWAKENING/GRADUAL CULTIVATION: CHINUL'S APPROACH
TO PRACTICE AND ENLIGHTENMENT

The varied descriptions of practice and enlightenment appearing in Buddhist scriptures fostered numbers of analytical studies by Buddhist theoreticians. Indeed, the many schools of Buddhism which arose in China each had their own approach to practice and enlightenment. As factionalism developed within the church, considerable controversy arose over the effectiveness and authenticity of these different approaches. Chinul, in his *DCSPR,* discusses a number of them and compares the analyses of Ch'eng-kuan, Tsung-mi, and Yen-shou. Tsung-mi had examined this question in some detail in various works and became a strong advocate of an approach consisting of initial sudden awakening followed by gradual cultivation. Such a course was, for him, the most comprehensive and accurate description of the process of practice; and since it could be shown to apply to all Buddhist cultivators, from beginners with little spiritual background to experienced meditators, it was the ideal teaching method. Furthermore, Tsung-mi saw sudden awakening/gradual cultivation as a perfect bridge between the practices of Ch'an and the scholastic schools, for Ho-tse's teachings and the approach to practice outlined in the Hua-yen school both followed a similar course. Due to the demise of the Ho-tse school after the death of Tsung-mi, this approach never gained widespread favor among Ch'an followers in China and the rival approach of sudden awakening/sudden cultivation, as advocated by masters in the Lin-chi line, reigned supreme. Chinul, however, was convinced by Tsung-mi's arguments in favor of sudden awakening/gradual cultivation and went into considerable depth in his own investigations of the question. Through his influence, the sudden awakening/gradual cultivation approach flourished in Korea and received at least tacit acceptance by most teachers in the later tradition. Even though it has had its detractors among Korean Sŏn teachers—especially those using the radical Imje (C. Lin-chi) methods—it is clearly the hallmark of the Korean tradition and is discussed sympathetically by such later Sŏn figures as T'aego Pou (1301–1382) and Sŏsan Hyujŏng (1520–1604). Chinul's attention to the question did not arise merely from theoretical interest. Rather, he feared that an improper understanding of spiritual development would hinder the progress of Buddhist students in either doctrinal or Sŏn schools—and indeed there is evidence in abundance that such a situation had developed in the Buddhism of his era. By giving a detailed description of sudden awakening/gradual cultivation and the reasons for favoring it over other alternatives, he hoped to present an approach to Buddhism which could serve his students as a practical guide to meditation.

Tsung-mi and Chinul give parallel accounts of the import of sudden awakening and gradual cultivation. The ordinary person generally assumes that his physical frame is his body and his thought processes are his mind. Someday, however, he might make the sudden discovery that, in their original forms, his body is actually the true dharma-body of all the Buddhas and his mind is actually the void and calm, numinous awareness of the true mind. He would then understand that he is inherently endowed with the Buddha-nature and that this nature is originally untainted by defilements of any sort and fully endowed with all the meritorious qualities of the Buddhas. This discovery is initial sudden awakening.

Although the student may then understand that he is essentially a Buddha, his actions are still, in large part, guided by the force of long-ingrained habits—habits which continue to involve him in defilements like greed, hatred, and delusion. For this reason, even after the inital awakening to his fundamental Buddhist-nature, the student must learn to apply his understanding in the ordinary world and transform his knowledge into useful and proper action. This requires that he train himself to counter the arising of defilements and to develop the whole range of positive spiritual qualities; then he will be a Buddha in fact as well as theory. This process is gradual cultivation. However, because he has already had the initial awakening to his mind-nature, which is eternally free of defilement and endowed innately with all these qualities, he counters defilements while knowing that there is actually nothing which is being counteracted and develops spiritual qualities while understanding that there is actually nothing which is being developed. His continued cultivation allows his initial understanding to infuse gradually all of his being until that absolute Buddha-wisdom and the relative positive qualities of Buddhahood have become an inexorable part of his patterns of thought and behavior. The person becomes a perfect saint in both understanding and conduct; Buddhahood is achieved; and he is able, as is no other individual, to help other living beings.[221]

In this approach the awakening to the noumenal essence of the mind is accomplished suddenly; however, the annihilation of falsity and the development of the positive qualities of sainthood are accomplished only gradually. Tsung-mi compares this process to human maturation: although a newborn infant possesses all its sense faculties and is endowed physically with all the organs and capacities of an adult, it takes years to reach its full adult potential. With Buddhist practice it is just the same: through sudden awakening, one is endowed with the same understanding and ability to help others as are all the Buddhas. It requires much supplementary training before that potential becomes fact in the everyday world, however.[222]

This necessity for gradual cultivation after awakening does not mean that the content of the awakening experience is altered in any way by its subsequent development. Rather, this practice involves the perfection of skill in means and the refinement of the discriminative faculties of wisdom which expand the ability to express one's enlightenment to others and help them realize it for themselves. Without this continued cultivation after awakening, the student loses vitality and, accordingly, humanity; and without humanity—that basic empathy of sentient being to sentient being which is the underlying force activating the bodhisattva's compassion—the entire purpose of practice, to ease the sufferings of all sentient beings and lead them along the road to enlightenment, is also lost.

In this outline, both awakening and cultivation have two distinct aspects which Chinul discusses in *DCSPR:* the initial understanding-awakening and the subsequent realization-awakening; and the cultivation of thoughtlessness and the cultivation which deals with all matters. The understanding-awakening is the initial awakening which precedes cultivation proper. It occurs as a result of the thorough understanding of the mental properties—that is, the nature and characteristics of the mind, as well as its essence and function. This is the relative awakening which allows one to enter into the ten faiths, the preliminary stage before starting out on the bodhisattva path. The subsequent realization-awakening, which occurs after cultivation has matured, is the ultimate awakening: the understanding gained through the initial awakening finally permeates one's entire being, and one truly enters onto the bodhisattva path at the initial abiding stage of the arousing of the *bodhicitta*.

The cultivation of thoughtlessness is the absolute aspect of cultivation in which the mind remains unified with the undifferentiated noumenal mind-nature. It is essentially passive—that is, the individual simply remains in a state of harmony with the essential suchness of the self-nature. The cultivation which deals with all matters is the relative aspect of cultivation that develops expedient practices to counter negative habits and nurture positive qualities. It is essentially dynamic—that is, it brings the noumenal calmness of thoughtlessness to bear on the manner of one's reaction to sense-objects, ensuring that those reactions are positive and beneficial. This cultivation does not involve the discriminative processes of mind. It is, rather, the activation of the noumenal nature, which is possible because of the principle that essence and function are nondual—that is, simply two complementary aspects of the mind.

The unique feature of the sudden awakening/gradual cultivation approach is that, unlike other styles of practice, the absolute and relative aspects of both awakening and cultivation are kept in careful balance so that each aspect supports the development of the other. The sudden awakening at the beginning of the student's practice assures a proper attitude toward cultivation: without this foundation, there is a constant danger that the student might find Buddhist practice intimidating. He might then assume that he lacks the capacity to develop all its many facets and therefore content himself with cultivating only relative practices—complacency which might make him neglect the goal of practice for the practice itself. Gradual cultivation ensures that awakening is kept dynamic. Through cultivation, awakening is applied in ordinary life, protecting the student from indifference to the sufferings of others and the compulsion to seek quietude and isolation which often characterizes ascetic hermits.

By the same token, the two aspects of cultivation are also kept in equilibrium, ensuring that cultivation develops with balanced stress on both the absolute and relative spheres. In an approach to practice based solely on thoughtlessness, the undifferentiated noumenal nature plays the central role in development. This could lead to a nihilistic attitude in which calmness and aloofness—concomitants of the noumenon—predominate. Conversely, developing wholesome qualities and countering unwholesome tendencies— the approach of the cultivation which deals with all matters—could lead the student to assume that there is actually something real which needs to be counteracted or developed. By accepting the separate reality of individual dharmas, he would find himself sinking deeper into the relative world of the phenomenal. Hence, rather than lessening his attachment to the things of the world and adverting to the mind-nature which is their source, he might end up hopelessly immersed in mundane affairs. By emphasizing the simultaneous practice of both aspects of cultivation, their unitary nature is clarified: thoughtlessness is the essence of the cultivation which deals with all matters; the cultivation which deals with all matters is the function of thoughtlessness. Hence both noumenal and phenomenal practices are developed equally in this approach.

At first glance, it might seem that an approach in which awakening precedes cultivation defies all the dictates of logic. Surely spiritual development through meditation, character training, and meritorious action is essential because it prepares the ground for awakening. While common sense might require that relative practices must be developed before the awakening into the absolute, Chinul and, indeed, almost all masters of both Sŏn and doctrine summarily dismiss this gradual cultivation/sudden awakening approach. It is fallacious because it relies on the development of relative practices which substantiate the reality of conditionally arisen phenomena —all of which are essentially illusory. Since these practices are not based on an understanding of one's innate Buddhahood, one's innate freedom from defilement, and one's innate endowment with all the qualities of sainthood, the student will be forced to undergo a long and bitter period of practice during which he will, unavoidably, be beset by spells of disillusionment and frustration. And this critique does not even mention the old question: how can conditioned practices produce the realization of the unconditioned realm? Because true practice begins with sudden awakening, the student's progress will be smooth and natural. Sudden awakening/gradual cultivation is, consequently, a practical approach that assures a greater likelihood of success than does gradual cultivation/sudden awakening.[223]

Sudden awakening/sudden cultivation, which became the Ch'an orthodoxy through the strong advocacy of the Lin-chi school, is also viewed with some suspicion by Chinul. This approach assumes that, since the mind-nature is fully endowed with all meritorious qualities, once it is fully revealed through a complete awakening, nothing remains to be cultivated because all the qualities of that nature are simultaneously revealed as well. Hence a sudden awakening to the mind-nature brings the instantaneous perfection of all meritorious qualities—"sudden" cultivation. While such an approach seems the ideal style of practice because it does not indulge in relative expedients, Chinul finds it deceptive. Certainly it leads too easily to a nihilistic attitude toward practice: since everyone is inherently endowed with the Buddha-nature and since all the defilements in the relative world are inherently void, there are really no wholesome qualities to be developed (they are all present naturally), no defilements to be counteracted (they are all void), no goal to be reached in the practice (Buddhahood is already achieved). It places excessive emphasis on the noumenal aspect of practice and neglects the development of the phenomenal qualities which allow that noumenon to manifest clearly in the ordinary world.[224]

The advocate of the sudden awakening/sudden cultivation approach can find many examples in Sŏn literature which seem to show that some people did gain perfect enlightenment instantly without having to continue with gradual cultivation. From the standpoint of this life, such examples apparently authenticate the sudden awakening/sudden cultivation approach; if past lives are taken into account, however, it is clear that sudden perfection in this life is based on long gradual development throughout many previous existences. These individuals have, at some past time, had a sudden awakening, begun their long-term gradual cultivation, and, in this life, seemingly without effort, completed their practice. Hence sudden awakening/sudden cultivation is actually only perfected sudden awakening/gradual cultivation —that is, the sudden awakening/gradual cultivation of people with advanced spiritual capacity. Sudden awakening/sudden cultivation only applies to cultivation matured during the life in which final enlightenment occurs; it is not valid throughout the whole process of spiritual training over many lives. As sudden awakening/gradual cultivation applies to any number of lives and to any stage of spiritual development, it is, accordingly, a more comprehensive description of the path of practice than is sudden awakening/sudden cultivation.[225]

Since sudden awakening/gradual cultivation is broad enough to encompass all other approaches to enlightenment, it acts again as an ideal vehicle for bringing together the Sŏn and scholastic schools.[226] Chinul demonstrates that the outline of sudden awakening/gradual cultivation in the Hotse school can be explicated just as clearly using Hwaŏm terminology. Through sudden awakening, the student realizes the undifferentiated noumenon—the Buddha of Unmoving Wisdom—and discovers that his karmic activities are all identical to those of the Buddhas and are all arisen according to conditions from the productionless self-nature. This realization commences his bodhisattva career. While understanding that he and others are all nonexistent, the bodhisattva still recognizes that sentient beings are immersed in suffering and, out of compassion, he decides to cultivate the vast vows and practices of Samantabhadra in order to rescue them. These myriads of practices are the stage of gradual cultivation and carry him through all the levels of the bodhisattva path until Buddhahood is finally attained. But the only reason that the bodhisattva is able to continue with his arduous practice over innumerable eons is because he has already realized his true nature through his initial sudden awakening.[227] As Chinul notes in *Encouragement to Practice,* where he discusses the fact that suddenness and gradualness in the scholastic teachings are more a matter of the individual's spiritual capacity than the inherent character of the teaching: "Even in the scholastic sects there appears the doctrine that sentient beings, in this wise, all belong to the Buddha's spiritual family and, in the land of birth and death, can suddenly awaken to the Buddha-vehicle in which realization and cultivation are simultaneous. So how is it that the Southern school alone involves a sudden approach?"

Lest this convoluted discussion leave the reader more bemused than enlightened, I might add that Chinul himself admits that all this controversy over the proper approach to Buddhist practice in somewhat tedious and overdrawn. Although the theoretical descriptions of awakening and cultivation may differ, for the truly ardent student they all come down to essentially the same thing. If awakening fully penetrates to the fundamental mind-nature, it cannot be obstructed by any sort of "relative" gradual cultivation. And, by the same token, if cultivation is done properly, it is associated with the understanding which only comes through awakening.[228] Hence in all cases, from beginners on the spiritual quest to those who have nearly perfected their practice, sudden awakening/gradual cultivation provides, in Chinul's view, the most complete and accurate description of the entire course of spiritual development.

CHINUL'S METHODS OF MEDITATION

Chinul's ecumenical attitude toward Buddhist philosophy led him to develop a remarkably eclectic approach toward meditation practice. While that approach remained fundamentally Sŏn in focus, he incorporated a number of techniques which would appeal to practitioners of differing capacities and needs. It was Chinul's accomplishment to demonstrate how these techniques, the characteristic practices of independent sects in China, could all work together to guide Buddhist students toward the same goal of liberation. Chinul regarded these methods as expedient devices designed to assist different types of people in their own spiritual development, and he insisted that all would eventually lead to the same result for the adept who cultivated with sincerity and vigor.

As his biographer, Kim Kun-su, first noted,[229] Chinul tailored three main styles of Sŏn practice which show the direct influences of his three enlightenment experiences: the balanced cultivation of *samādhi* and *prajñā,* deriving from the *Platform Sūtra;* faith and understanding according to the complete and sudden teachings of the Hwaŏm school, from Li T'ung-hsüan's *Exposition of the Avataṃsaka Sūtra;* and, finally, the shortcut approach of *hwadu* investigation, from the *Records of Ta-hui.* These styles were intended to instruct people of inferior, average, and superior spiritual capacities respectively. To supplement these three basic methods, Chinul taught two additional techniques for people of highest and lowest capacity: the approach of no-mind (thoughtlessness) and the recollection of the Buddha's name.[230] He explained that each method could be followed exclusively or a progression from the simpler techniques to the more difficult could be cultivated. The wide variety of approaches available in Chinul's system allowed people at all stages of spiritual ability to follow a path suited to their own unique needs and reach finally the goal of Buddhahood. Each of these five approaches to practice will be recounted briefly in the following pages.

In his early works like *Encouragement to Practice* and *Secrets on Cultivating the Mind,* Chinul places special emphasis on the need "to cultivate *samādhi* and *prajñā* in tandem" and "to maintain alertness and calmness equally"—both standard dictums which find application in nearly all methods of Buddhist practice. Buddhist spiritual culture traditionally involves three major forms of training: ethical restraint *(śīla),* mental absorption *(samādhi),* and transcendental wisdom *(prajñā).* At the beginning of his training, the Buddhist student is expected to learn to control his physical reactions to the objects in his environment by observing simple moral guides. This observance gradually brings under the sway of dharma the coarser manifestations of defilements through bodily actions and speech, and it weakens the normally exclusive interest in sense-related experiences. As the disentanglement from the senses accelerates, a new inner focus develops. Gradually, the mind learns through meditation to be content merely within itself; the mental processes are progressively calmed, and the student achieves absorption—pure mental concentration. Eventually, the concentrated power created through this absorption is turned toward an investigation of himself, his world, and the relationship between the two. This investigation develops wisdom, which teaches him about the processes of life and leads him to discover the true nature of himself and, indeed, of all things. Full development of such understanding turns back the power of ignorance which ordinarily impels the mind to take an interest in the senses. Simultaneously, the student breaks the inveterate tendency toward craving—the active aspect of ignorance which produces greed, hatred, and the whole range of defilements—and liberation is achieved.

The term Sŏn is the Korean pronunciation of the Chinese transliteration of the Sanskrit word *dhyāna,* which is equatable with *samādhi.* In the Sŏn school, however, the word carries a different connotation. As Tsung-mi explains, it is a comprehensive term for both *samādhi* and *prajñā,*[231] and Sŏn practice is intended to lead to the rediscovery of the original enlightened source of all sentient beings: the Buddha-nature, or mind-ground. The awakening to this source is called *prajñā;* the cultivation of this awakening is called *samādhi.* Chinul explains as well that *samādhi* and *prajñā* are also an abbreviation for the threefold training in *śīla, samādhi,* and *prajñā* just described. Consequently, Sŏn training involves the entire range of Buddhist spiritual endeavor from the beginning stages of morality to the highest stages of wisdom.

Two major interpretations of *samādhi* and *prajñā* are possible: a relative form, and an absolute form. Chinul discusses both at length in *Encouragement to Practice.* The relative type of *samādhi* and *prajñā,* taught in the gradual school, deals with objects in the conditioned realm in order to remove impurities; it is similar to the preceding description of *samādhi* and *prajñā. Samādhi,* in its guise of calmness, accords with the noumenal voidness; it is used to counter the tendency toward distraction. *Prajñā,* in its guise of alertness, accords with phenomenal plurality; it is used to stimulate the mind out of the occasional dullness which obscures its natural penetrative quality. In their relative form, *samādhi* and *prajñā* are instruments for counteracting ignorance and defilements; they are used until enlightenment is achieved.

Chinul followed the sudden approach to enlightenment in which awakening precedes cultivation, and his interpretation of *samādhi* and *prajñā* differs accordingly from this relative type. Chinul's approach, the second type of *samādhi* and *prajñā,* is the absolute form: the *samādhi* and *prajñā* of the self-nature. This new interpretation of *samādhi* and *prajñā* was first propounded in the Ch'an school by Shen-hui and is the major focus of the *Platform Sūtra of the Sixth Patriarch.* Here *samādhi* and *prajñā* are viewed as two aspects of the same self-nature; although each has its own specific role, they are not to be differentiated. *Samādhi* is the essence of the self-nature and is characterized by calmness; *prajñā* is the function of that self-nature and is characterized by alertness. Although the ways in which they manifest are distinguishable, both are based in the nondual self-nature; hence *samādhi* is actually the essence of *prajñā*, and *prajñā* is the functioning of *samādhi*. Because of this mutual identification, *samādhi* no longer implies detached absorption which is entirely removed from sense-experience; it is, rather, that same absorption during contact with sense-objects: a dynamic conception of *samādhi*. *Prajñā* is not simply a discriminative faculty which critically investigates phenomena and exposes their essential voidness; it carries the more passive sense of operating as the calm essence amid phenomena, and it manifests as radiance, or bare awareness. In this conception, both *samādhi* and *prajñā* are centered in the unmoving self-nature and are, consequently, always identified with this absolute nondual state. Even when the two faculties are operating as calmness or alertness in the conditioned sphere—activities which would seem to parallel those of the relative *samādhi* and *prajñā*—they never leave their unity in the unconditioned mind-nature.

Even after the sudden awakening to the self-nature reveals the identity of *samādhi* and *prajñā*, the power of habit will continue to immerse the student in defilements. These defilements can disturb the original harmony of the self-nature in such a way that one of its aspects of essence or function becomes distorted. If essence predominates, dullness might result from excessive calmness; if function is exaggerated, distraction might develop from excessive alertness. At such a time, it would be appropriate to use the relative practice of *samādhi* and *prajñā* in order to deal with the problem at hand. By employing the right countermeasure the mind is kept in harmony and rapid progress in overcoming residual habits can be expected. For this reason, Chinul stresses the need to keep both calmness and alertness in scrupulous balance so that the natural powers of the mind remain at optimum level.

At all stages in the student's development, *samādhi* and *prajñā* constitute an integral part of his practice. Although the designations might differ according to the level of his progress, the principles remain the same. Indeed, regardless of the method of meditation the student is practicing, he must always be attentive to the equilibrium between these two elements if the methods are to be brought to a successful conclusion.

As Chinul observes time and again throughout his writings, the success of any practice depends on a sudden awakening at the beginning of one's efforts to the fact of one's fundamental Buddhahood. Without the confidence that such experience brings, the long ages of struggle the bodhisattva contemplates would be unbearable for even the most enthusiastic of adepts. To induce this awakening is the purpose of "faith and understanding according to the complete and sudden teachings"—the practice, based on Hwaŏm theory, intended for the majority of students. The discussion which follows recapitulates the explication of Li T'ung-hsüan's thought given in Chinul's *Complete and Sudden Attainment of Buddhahood.*[232]

The unmoving wisdom of Buddhahood, otherwise known as the wisdom of universal brightness,[233] is the source of all dualistic phenomena including Buddhas and sentient beings. Through faith and understanding that this unmoving wisdom is identical to the discriminative thoughts of sentient beings, the individual realizes that even in his present deluded state he is, and indeed has always been, a perfect Buddha. By understanding this fact at the very beginning of the spiritual quest—at the first of the ten levels of faith—the student becomes fully endowed with the wisdom and compassion of Buddhahood in potential form. This accomplishment was usually assumed to occur only at the arousing of the *bodhicitta* stage of the ten abidings—and only after the adept had supposedly passed through all ten levels of faith for ten thousand kalpas. But through the knowledge of this fundamental wisdom nonretrogressive faith is established, assuring the student's continued progress on the bodhisattva path and perfecting the other constituents of the ten stages of faith. Accordingly, the student is able to enter the initial abiding stage directly. At that stage there is immediate experience of the fact that he is a Buddha, and the former tacit faith and understanding are confirmed. With the tremendous potential of the "great effortless functioning" inherent in Buddhahood, the subsequent stages of the bodhisattva path are instantly completed. Consequently, the wisdom of universal brightness is not simply the origin of sentient beings and Buddhas: every accomplishment along the bodhisattva path reveals the operation of that fundamental wisdom. Thus faith and understanding are enough to consummate the immediate and full attainment of Buddhahood even when the adept has progressed no further than the normal level of the ordinary sentient being. This is the essence of the complete and sudden approach.

Although Buddhas and sentient beings are originally only the phantom-like manifestations of the fundamental wisdom of universal brightness, the defilements of passion and discriminative thought have narrowed that wisdom and obscured its brightness. Even though the bodhisattva who realizes this fundamental wisdom is completely endowed with the compassion and wisdom of Buddhahood, his ability to display that wisdom through expedient means of expression and spiritual powers is still inchoate. Consequently, he must continue to cultivate the wide-ranging practices and vows which are developed on the remaining stages of the bodhisattva path. Any defiling actions which might arise from the inertial force of habit must also be corrected; his awakening has given him the ability to see through these habits, however, so he is free to employ appropriate methods during his progression along the path until they subside. Once his practice has been perfected, he will have arrived in fact, as well as potential, at the stage of Buddhahood. Nevertheless, throughout all his subsequent development, the bodhisattva has in fact never strayed from the fundamental unmoving wisdom which was realized upon the initial awakening at the first of the ten stages of faith. This fundamental wisdom of universal brightness is thus the cause for the attainment of Buddhahood as well as its fruition—hence its importance in Chinul's system of practice.

If practice is to be conducted successfully, the average student requires support from the teachings to explain the course and goal of practice and to encourage him along that course. At the higher reaches of spiritual development, however, such scriptural explanations can block further progress. As long as the student depends on secondhand descriptions of the enlightened state, he cannot progress to direct experience of that state itself. Although the two preceding methods of practice are excellent expedients, especially for beginning students, they still involve an element of conceptualization. Without the concepts of *samādhi, prajñā,* and self-nature, the method of cultivating *samādhi* and *prajñā* equally would be impossible to comprehend, let alone follow. Without the concepts of fundamental unmoving wisdom as well as sentient being and discriminative thought, the approach of faith and understanding would have little meaning, let alone utility. While those concepts are a great aid for the student at the inception of his practice, they can only take him to the limits of the operation of the relative mind. Mediation with the unconditioned realm itself is still required to effect the adept's crossing over to the "far shore" of liberation. The *hwadu* is designed to act as such a mediator. Thus Chinul's third approach to practice is the shortcut approach of observing the *hwadu,* in which all scriptural explanations and conceptual descriptions are avoided and pure Sŏn is entered.

Hwadu practice was the product of a long process of development in the later Ch'an schools of the middle T'ang period in China. Most of the Ch'an schools during the T'ang were characterized by a close master/disciple relationship in which the master's influence and charisma played a central role in inspiring the student, instructing him in his practice, and finally catalyzing the ultimate realization which is the goal of such practice. Many of the stories which were transmitted about the direct instructions of the early teachers were recorded in a burgeoning literature exclusive to the Ch'an school. As the creative drive of Ch'an waned after the mid-800s, later Ch'an masters began to draw upon these stories as teaching devices for their own students. Teachers in the Lin-chi school especially, among them Nan-yüan Hui-yung (d. 930), Fen-yang Shan-chao (947–1024), and Yüan-wu K'o-ch'in (1063–1135), used these stories as a systematic way of instructing their students, and began to collect them together in large anthologies. These stories came to be called *kung-an* (K. *kongan*), or "public case records," because they put an end to private understanding *(kung)* and are guaranteed to be in harmony with what the Buddhas and partriarchs would say *(an)*. [234]

In its earliest usage in Sŏn texts, *hwadu* (literally, "head of speech") meant simply "topic" and was parallel in function to the similar terms *hwaje* ("theme of speech"), *hwabyŏng* ("handle of speech"), and *hwach'ŭk* ("rule of speech"). [235] In this nontechnical sense, *hwadu* can be taken as the primary topic of the entire situation set out in a complete *kongan,* or test case. Take, for example, the popular *kongan* attributed to Chao-chou Ts'ung-shen (778–897): "Does a dog have Buddha-nature or not?" "No!" The entire exchange is the *kongan;* the *hwadu* is "dog has no Buddha-nature" or simply "no." Eventually the *hwadu*—the central point of the test case extracted as a concise summary of the entire *kongan* situation—became a topic or subject of meditation in its own right, closely connected with *kongan* investigation but clearly distinguishable.

Hwadu practice was popularized in China by Ta-hui Tsung-kao (1089–1163), a disciple of Yüan-wu K'o-ch'in in the Lin-chi lineage, who established the method as the formal technique of the Lin-chi school. It was through reading the *Records of Ta-hui* in which *hwadu* investigation was strongly advocated that Chinul attained his last, and final, awakening. From that point on, the use of *hwadu* played a major role in the whole ensemble of Chinul's thought. Only one generation removed from Ta-hui, Chinul was the first teacher in Korea to advocate the use of *hwadu* in its formalized sense and is, consequently, the forerunner of Korean masters in the late Koryŏ period who placed *hwadu* practice at the forefront of the various methods of Buddhist meditation. Today in Korea, *hwadu* is the predominant technique cultivated in meditation halls, and almost all masters advocate its use for students at all levels.

Hwadu, which means "head of speech," can best be taken metaphorically as the "apex of speech" or the "point beyond which speech exhausts itself." Since the mind is the initiator of speech, speech in this context includes all the discriminating tendencies of the mind itself in accordance with the classic Indian Abhidharma formula that speech is fundamentally intellection and imagination *(vācīsaṃskāra* equals *vitarkavicāra)*. [236] In leading to the very limit of speech, or more accurately thought, the *hwadu* acts as a purification device which sweeps the mind free of all its conceptualizing activities and leaves it clear, attentive, and calm—the ideal meditative state. Cessation of the discriminative processes of thought strips the mind of its interest in the sense-experiences of the ordinary world and renders it receptive to the influence of the unconditioned. Hence, as Chinul explains at length in *Resolving Doubts About Observing the Hwadu* and in *DCSPR,* the *hwadu* produces a "cleansing knowledge and understanding" which purifies the mind. As this approach allows none of the conventional supports for practice provided in the scriptural teachings and eschews conceptual understanding, it is obviously intended only for students of superior capacity, or for those who have first matured themselves through another technique.

The method of *hwadu* is considered a shortcut to realization because it proposes that enlightenment can be achieved without following the traditional pattern of Buddhist spiritual development through morality, concentration, and wisdom. By focusing the student's attention exclusively on the one thought of the *hwadu,* all the discriminative tendencies of the mind are brought to a halt. From this state of thoughtlessness, one more push is all that is needed to move from the ordinary world, governed by cause and effect, to the transcendental realm of the unconditioned. This push comes from the force of "doubt," which I will explain in a moment.

There are two ways to approach investigation of the *hwadu:* either via the meaning *(ch'amŭi)* or through the word itself *(ch'amgu).* In the case of the *hwadu* mentioned above, if the student investigates Chao-chou's motive for having said no, he is investigating the meaning; if he looks into the word "no" itself, he is investigating the word. At the beginning of practice it is often helpful to investigate the meaning, because this examination, being easier and more interesting, expedites the development of the practice. But because this investigation is concerned with the sense of the word "no" rather than the word itself, this is called investigating the "dead word" *(sagu).* Such investigation leaves the student vulnerable to the same defect which compromises most other meditation approaches, for it still retains conceptual interpretations. To overcome this defect, it becomes necessary to abandon the interpretative approach and investigate only the word itself. This "live word" *(hwalgu)* is the weapon which can destroy all the defects still present in approaches involving conceptualization. Investigation of the word alone allows no understanding through the intellect and is, consequently, more difficult to perform: there is nothing for the discriminative mind to latch onto for support. Because of this quality, it is sometimes called "tasteless" *(mumi).*

Throughout *hwadu* investigation the very nature of the question stumps the ability of the rational mind to fathom its significance. This perplexity, wonder, or spirit of inquiry is called "doubt." As doubt grows, the intensity of the investigation increases and ordinary dualistic trends of thought are disrupted. Eventually, the fundamental activating consciousness is revealed.[237] As the *Awakening of Faith* explains,[238] the activating consciousness is the origin of the deluded mind. It represents the point at which subject and object are bifurcated and dualistic patterns of thought are generated. This activating consciousness impels the individual toward ignorance and craving, and it is only through revealing it that the whole pastiche of defilements can be annihilated and the original unity of the enlightened mind restored. As the concentration of the mind intensifies through the power of the doubt, finally any catalyst—the shout of a master, the blow of his stick, a sudden sound—is enough to break through the activating consciousness, free the original enlightened mind, and display the unconditioned realm. Hence, through investigation of the *hwadu*, the student can bypass all the gradual stages of development and get to the very source of the problem. And because its investigation can be undertaken at two levels —either through the meaning or through the word itself—the *hwadu* method is broad enough to accommodate students at all stages of development. Chinul's emphasis in his later works on the shortcut practice of *hwadu* augured the stronger Imje orientation of his successor, Hyesim, who compiled in 1226 the first Korean collection of *kongan* stories: the *Sŏnmun yŏmsong chip*.[239] This posture of Korean Sŏn became more striking as the centuries passed, and it was particularly pronounced after the return from China of T'aego Pou (1301–1382), who brought the orthodox Chinese Linchi lineage to Korea.

Beyond the three basic approaches to Sŏn practice outlined above, Chinul taught another method for people well advanced in their practice. This is the cultivation of "no-mind which conforms with the path" *(musim hapto mun)*,[240] or thoughtlessness *(munyŏm)*, based on the ultimate teachings of the patriarchs of the Sŏn school.[241] Through copious quotations from the writings of major figures in Chinese Buddhism, Chinul demonstrates in Part II of his *DCSPR* that all practice entails a leaving behind of words and a severing of thought processes at the moment of realization. This severing of thought, or no-mind, is the culmination of all other approaches to practice. Since it is the form which practice takes only after all expedient supports have been dispensed with, it is suitable only for people of the highest spiritual capacity who can progress without the aid of set methods and conceptual explanations.

As the *Awakening of Faith* explains, the identity between the mind and undifferentiated suchness is destroyed through the operation of the activating consciousness, creating intellection and dualistic thought. A split is then felt between oneself and the objects in one's environment; through the inception of the succeeding evolving consciousness this differentiation proliferates throughout the sense-spheres as well. The continuation of that process gradually leads the by then utterly deluded individual to concretize those perceptions into concepts—that is, to generalize the sense contacts unique to a particular moment along lines which accord with his past experience and understanding. Those concepts are invested with a measure of reality because of their obvious utility in ordering the mass of sense-experience. Furthermore, because of the influence of conventional language governed by standardized vocabulary and grammatical rules, those concepts are endowed with an objectivity which is entirely consistent within the conceptual realm. Once those concepts are introduced into the processes of ideation, the whole of one's thought becomes crystallized. Finally, the concepts which had been employed for convenience now overwhelm the individual: all conscious activity and all sense-experience are now dominated by understanding which is rooted in those concepts. Even sense perception, otherwise a neutral process, is colored by conceptual understanding so that objective sense-awareness becomes impossible: pleasant objects become a focus for greed, unpleasant objects for hatred, and neither pleasant nor unpleasant objects for delusion.[242]

The only way out of this morass is through the complete demolition of the conceptual scaffolding upon which all mentation is constructed. This is precisely the function of thoughtlessness or no-mind practice. Thoughtlessness in no way implies an absence of conscious activity. To remain simply without thought is to grasp at blankness; it is little different from the insentience of rocks and plants. Thoughtlessness refers rather to the absence of defilements *during* conscious activity. The maintenance of this pure state of awareness frees the mind from the constraints produced by ignorance and defilement and restores the basic suchness of the mind. In this way, the original objectivity of sense-perception returns, the impulsion of the defilements during sense-contact ceases, and spontaneous interaction with the world becomes possible again.

In *Straight Talk on the True Mind,* Chinul describes ten ways of practicing no-mind: through blocking out attention to either sense-objects or the activities of thought, or through various combinations of the two. Once any of these ten methods is brought to perfection, all the others are perfected simultaneously and thoughtlessness—the noumenal purity of the mind—is achieved. This is possible because all these techniques break the discriminatory tendencies of the mind—which is, after all, the goal of every method of practice. The state of thoughtlessness so engendered is, finally, the element which enables penetration into the unconditioned sphere and is, consequently, a prime constituent of any approach to practice.

The difficulties inherent in Buddhist practice led many in China to despair at their ability to achieve progress or realization in their lifetime. Such people often found solace in Pure Land teachings, which claimed that by recollecting the name of the Buddha Amitābha, the disciple could gain entrance into Amitābha's Pure Land in his next life. The Pure Land, a transcendental sphere of existence created through a Buddha's vows, was said to offer ideal conditions for spiritual development; consequently, by recollecting the Buddha's name and gaining rebirth in that Buddha's Pure Land, great efforts to cultivate the path in this lifetime would be unnecessary.

Pure Land practice gained enormous popularity among lay adherents of Buddhism in China, but it was often scorned by followers of other schools. In his earliest work, *Encouragement to Practice,* Chinul too showed little sympathy for Pure Land beliefs. He assumed that they foster complacency by denying the need to cultivate *samādhi* and *prajñā* in this life and by holding out hopes of future reward without requiring present effort. In one of his later works, however, the *Essentials of Pure Land Practice,* Chinul takes a closer look at Pure Land practice and interprets it in such a way that it too can lead to the same goal as other forms of Buddhist practice.[243] This is Chinul's fifth approach to practice: recollection of the Buddha, which was intended for ordinary men with minimal ability in spiritual matters.

In this approach, Chinul outlines ten stages in the development of recollection. The influence of the Pure Land schemes of Ch'eng-kuan and Tsung-mi on Chinul's approach is readily apparent.[244] Beginning with simple verbal recitation, the practice eventually leads to recollection of the Buddha in thoughtlessness and finally in suchness. Hence it is a self-contained method which leads to realization of the one true *dharmadhātu,* the goal of both Sŏn and Hwaŏm practice, in this very life.

Although this approach is of minor importance in the full spectrum of Chinul's thought, the fact that he was willing to espouse it at all shows again his concern that people of all abilities and interests be able to find a method of practice suited to their own unique needs. By receiving proper direction in the use of that method, they should be able to achieve the same results as are forthcoming from all other types of Buddhist practice.

NOTES

1. Thanks in large part to government encouragement, as well as to the inherent importance of the subject in Korean history, there are many Korean studies on the role of Buddhism as an agent of national protection. Scriptural justification for the role comes from (1) the *Jen-wang po-jo po-lo-mi ching* 2, *T* 245.8.830a.1–20, and *Jen-wang hu-kuo po-jo po-lo-mi-to ching* 2, *T* 246.8.84a.11–19; and (2) the *Suvarnaprabhāsôttama-sūtra, Chin kuang-ming ching* 2, *T* 662.16.340c–341c, quoted in William de Bary, *Sources in Japanese Tradition,* vol. 1, pp. 100–101. For the textual background and its interpretation in Korea see: Rhi Ki-yong (Yi Ki-

yŏng), "*Inwang panya kyŏng* kwa hoguk sasang"; Matsunaga Yūkei, "Gokoku shisō no kigen," pp. 69–78; Peter Lee, *Lives of Eminent Korean Monks,* pp. 13–16; Kim Tong-hwa, *Pulgyo ŭi hoguk sasang;* idem, "Silla sidae ŭi Pulgyo sasang," pp. 31–41; Yi Ki-baek, "Samguk sidae Pulgyo chŏllae," p. 146 ff.; Hong Yun-sik, "Koryŏ Pulgyo ŭi sinang ŭirye," pp. 658–660.

2. For the social milieu into which Buddhism was introduced in Korea, see Kim Chŏng-bae, "Pulgyo chŏllipchŏn ŭi Han'guk sangdae sahoesang," especially pp. 14–20, and Yi Ki-baek, "Samguk sidae Pulgyo chŏllae."

3. See Yi Ki-baek, "Samguk sidae Pulgyo chŏllae," pp. 171–172; see also J. H. Kamstra, *Encounter or Syncretism,* pp. 146–184, 206–217.

4. See Roger Leverrier, "Buddhism and Ancestral Religious Beliefs in Korea," pp. 38–39, and Yi Ki-baek, "Samguk sidae Pulgyo chŏllae," pp. 171–172.

5. For the early tribal leagues see Yi Pyŏng-do and Kim Chae-won, *Han'guk sa* I, pp. 209–259 for the northern tribes and pp. 262–323 for the southern; Han Woo-keun, *History of Korea,* pp. 12–37; Takashi Hatada, *History of Korea,* pp. 8–13.

6. The Koguryŏ clan's native area was in the Tongga River basin, north of the central course of the Yalu River; Han Woo-keun, *History,* pp. 26–29.

7. Yi Pyŏng-do, *Han'guk sa* I, pp. 392–397, 406–429; Han Woo-keun, *History,* pp. 41–42.

8. Yi Pyŏng-do, *Han'guk sa* I, pp. 429–441; Han Woo-keun, *History,* pp. 42–43.

9. Yi Pyŏng-do, *Han'guk sa* I, pp. 397–406, 441–458; Han Woo-keun, *History,* pp. 44–45.

10. As Han Woo-keun notes (*History,* p. 9), early bronze techniques used in Korea were not those of China, but rather the Sytho-Siberian methods of North Asian tribes. Yi Pyŏng-do mentions (*Han'guk sa* I, p. 41) that early Korean earthenware belongs to the same northern variety found in Siberian river basin sites, a type which extends as far west as Scandinavia. See also the discussion in Takashi Hatada, *History,* pp. 1–2.

11. Such generally reliable scholars as Suh Kyung-soo (Sŏ Kyŏng-su) and Kim Chol-jun (Kim Ch'ŏl-chun) ("Korean Buddhism: A Historical Perspective," pp. 122, 277–278) state that Korean Buddhism first came directly from Central Asia, bypassing China. Kim Ch'ŏl-sun ("Han'guk misul," pp. 42–44) mentions that in the monastery history of Sŏnam sa in Cholla namdo there is a notice that according to a lost book on Korean history, the *Kyerim kogi* (Kim Tae-mun's *Kyerim chapki?*), Buddhism was transmitted to Korea by "sea" long before it was known in China. "Sea" here must refer to the sea of sand, the northern silk roads of Central Asia. He also notes that Koguryŏ mural paintings and relief tiles of the Three Kingdoms period show similarities with paintings preserved in the Tun-huang caves. The traditional style of Korean religious paintings, well exemplified in Yi dynasty Buddhist paintings, exhibits elements which parallel Central Asian styles detailed during the Pelliot and Stein expeditions. Finally, he mentions that Chinese critics of the Sung and Yüan dynasties advocated that Korean paintings showed peculiar features which exhibited closer connections with the style prevalent in Central Asian countries than with those of China. As romantic as such notions might be, the literary evidence for

such contact consists of a few tantalizing references in the *Samguk yusa,* references so legendary in character that Kim Pu-sik (1075–1151) does not even deign to mention them in his more conservative *Samguk sagi.*

The *Annals of the Karak Kingdom* (*Karak kuk ki,* not extant, portions preserved in *SGYS* 2, pp. 982b–985c; Ha Tae-hung and Grafton K. Mintz, *Legends and History of the Three Kingdoms,* pp. 158–172) record that the queen of King Suro, founder of Karak kuk, was sent to him through divine intervention from the Indian kingdom of Ayodhyā. (Ha and Mintz, *Legends,* p. 162, imply that this reference was in fact to the Thai capital of Ayuthia [Ayutthaya]; but this city was not founded until 1350 according to G. Coedès, *The Indianized States of Southeast Asia,* p. 76. Ayodhyā was the old capital of Kośala and was called Saketa in the Buddha's time; A. L. Basham, *The Wonder That Was India,* pp. 414, 200.) She was found on a mysterious ship at sea off the Kaya coast, and became queen in A.D. 48. (The cyclical number is wrong in the text, *SGYS* 2, p. 989c.28.) It is said that for protection on her long journey, she brought along a stone stūpa, the style, shape, and material of which were different from anything known in Korea. (For its description, see *SGYS* 2, p. 990a.9–11, Ha and Mintz, *Legends,* p. 204.) The stūpa was enshrined at Hogye sa in Kŭmgwan near modern Kimhae. For the story see *SGYS* 2, pp. 989c.25–990a.14; Ha and Mintz, *Legends,* pp. 203–204.

A Koguryŏ mission into the Liaotung peninsula in southern Manchuria, led by a King Sŏng, supposedly resulted in the discovery of a three-story earthen cairn, the top story of which was shaped like an inverted cauldron, much like the style of early Indian Buddhist reliquaries. Digging near the stūpa, the king discovered a stone inscription in Brahmā writing (*pŏmsŏ;* Prakrit/Sanskrit) which one of his ministers deciphered as stating that the stūpa had been erected by King Aśoka. Iryŏn notes that some commentators assumed King Sŏng refered to Tongmyŏng wang (r. 37–19 B.C.), founder of the Koguryŏ kingdom. He, however, says that this is impossible because it would have predated the introduction of Buddhism into China; he assumes that the event must have occurred sometime during the Hou Han period (A.D. 25–222). It is known that Koguryŏ invaded the Liaotung area in A.D. 121 (Han Woo-keun, *History,* p. 42) and the legend could date from that time. For the story see *SGYS* 3, p. 989b.28–c.24; Ha and Mintz, *Legends,* pp. 201–202.

In another reference, this time from the Silla period, a ship is alleged to have arrived in Silla in 553 carrying iron and gold, as well as images of one Buddha and two bodhisattvas. Supposedly King Aśoka intended to cast a giant image from the metals, but since Indian ironworkers lacked the skill, he was unable to carry out his plans. Consequently, he had the metals loaded onto the ship along with images to be used as models for casting the larger statue and commanded the captain to sail throughout the Buddhist world until he found a country capable of consummating the feat. King Chinhŭng (r. 539–575) ordered a sixteen-foot image cast from the metals which was completed in 574 and enshrined at Hwangnyŏng sa. There is a thousand-year gap between the time of Aśoka and that of Silla, but the captain of the ship supposedly returned to India and reported the completion of his mission to his king. See *SGYS* 3, p. 990a.23–c.1; Ha and Mintz, *Legends,* pp. 205–207.

Most of these legends derive from the reputation of King Aśoka as the great disseminator of Buddhism throughout the known world; they apparently represent Korean aspirations to include itself in that select sphere of civilized society. For detailed bibliographic references see Jean Przyluski, *La Légende de l'Empereur Aśoka;* for East Asian sources see Peter Lee, *Lives,* p. 24, n. 46.

12. Han Woo-keun, *History,* pp. 14–16.

13. René Grousset (*Empire of the Steppes,* p. 58) assumes that they were probably proto-Mongolian in stock. Michael Rogers (*Chronicle of Fu Chien,* p. 6) says simply that they were an Altaic tribe.

14. For the Former Yen state, see the synopsis in Rogers, *Fu Chien,* pp. 6–8. The definitive work on the dynasty is G. Schreiber's study, "The History of the Former Yen Dynasty."

15. Yi Pyŏng-do, *Han'guk sa* I, pp. 406–407; Han Woo-keun, *History,* pp. 42–43; Hatada, *History,* pp. 14–16.

16. See Rogers, *Fu Chien,* pp. 4–6, for the early history of the tribe.

17. See Grousset, *Steppes,* pp. 28–29, 39–41, for the most accessible account of these kingdoms. Edouard Chavannes, "Les Pays d'Occident," translates the Chinese records on the Tarim basin kingdoms from the *Hou Han shu.*

18. See Grousset, *Steppes,* pp. 48–53, for the culture of this region. For Central Asian Buddhism see Kshanika Saha, *Buddhism and Buddhist Literature in Central Asia,* and Hatani Ryōtai and Ho Ch'ang-ch'ün (trans.), *Hsi-yü chih Fo-chiao.*

19. See discussion in Kamstra, *Encounter,* p. 205, and Yi Pyŏng-do, *Han'guk sa* I, p. 407.

20. For general discussions of northern Chinese Buddhism in the post-Han period, see Tsukamoto Zenryū, *Hokuchō Bukkyōshi kenkyū;* Kamstra, *Encounter,* pp. 142–179, and especially pp. 179–186; Kenneth Ch'en, *Buddhism in China,* pp. 145–183. See also the important studies on Fo-t'u-teng (fl. 310–359) by Arthur F. Wright and on Tao-an (312–349) by Ui Hakuju, *Shaku Dōan kenkyū,* and Arthur Link, "The Biography of Shih Tao-an"; these two figures were predominant in shaping the early Buddhism of the north. See also Zürcher, *Buddhist Conquest of China,* pp. 180–239.

21. *Samguk sagi* 18, p. 303; *SGYS* 3, p. 86a; *Haedong kosŭng chŏn* 1, *T* 2065.50.1016a; Lee, *Lives,* pp. 30–32. As Rogers mentions (*Fu Chien,* pp. 228–229, n. 258), there is no information concerning the development of Buddhism in northern China or of this event in any of the Chinese histories. This does not necessarily cast suspicion on the veracity of this notice in Korean sources; the orthodox Chinese historians, all of whom were of Confucian persuasion, simply did not find Buddhist events to be sufficiently important to warrant mention.

22. See Lee, *Lives,* p. 26, n. 64, for the derivation of his name.

23. *Samguk sagi* 24, p. 407; *SGYS* 3, p. 986a; *Haedong kosŭng chŏn* 1, *T* 2065.50.1017b–c; Lee, *Lives,* pp. 45–49.

24. Chih-tun Tao-lin's biography appears in *Kao-seng chuan* 4, *T* 2059.50.348b–349c. See Ch'en, *Buddhism,* pp. 65–67; Zürcher, *Conquest,* pp. 116–130; Paul Demiéville, "La Pénétration du Bouddhisme dans la Tradition Philosophique Chinoise," pp. 26–28.

25. For this letter see: *Kao-seng chuan* 4, *T* 2059.50.348a.13–15; *Haedong kosŭng*

chŏn 1, *T* 2065.50.1016a.27–29; Lee, *Lives,* p. 33; Zürcher, *Conquest,* pp. 140, 360–361, n. 213.

26. See discussion in Yi Chae-ch'ang and Kim Yŏng-t'ae, *Pulgyo munhwa sa,* p. 66. Even the *Kosŭng chŏn* author, Kakhun (ca. thirteenth century), bewails the loss of records concerning early Buddhism in Korea: *Haedong kosŭng chŏn* 1, *T* 2065.50.1016b.2–9; Lee, *Lives,* pp. 33–34.

27. For Koguryŏ activities see *Samguk sagi* 18, p. 303 et passim; Kim Tong-hwa, "Koguryŏ sidae ŭi Pulgyo sasang," pp. 10–13. For Paekche, see *Samguk sagi* 24, p. 407; Kim Tong-hwa, "Paekche sidae ŭi Pulgyo sasang," pp. 60–61.

28. Both the Koguryŏ and Paekche ruling houses issued proclamations ordering their subjects to believe in Buddhism. For Koguryŏ, see *Samguk sagi* 18, p. 304 (given as the ninth year of King Kogugyang's reign); Kim Tong-hwa, "Koguryŏ Pulgyo," pp. 34–36, shows that this date must be taken as his sixth reign year, or 389. For Paekche, see *SGYS* 3, p. 986a.24; Hong Yun-sik, "Paekche Pulgyo," pp. 80–81.

29. For Ado, see *Samguk sagi* 2, p. 31; *SGYS* 3, pp. 986a–987b; *Haedong kosŭng chŏn* 1, *T* 2065.50.1017c–1018c; Lee, *Lives,* pp. 50–56. Ich'adon, also known as Pak Yŏmch'ok or Kŏch'adon, was a minister in the court of King Pŏphŭng (r. 514–540). For his martyrdom, see *SGYS* 3, p. 987b. ff.; *Haedong kosŭng chŏn* 1, *T* 2065.50.1018c.21–1019a.25; Lee, *Lives,* pp. 58–61. As Lee notes (*Lives,* p. 58, n. 261) the date for this event should be 527 or 528. For a critical discussion of the legends surrounding the foundation of Silla Buddhism, see Kim Tong-hwa, "Silla sidae ŭi Pulgyo sasang," pp. 6–10; for the different chronologies concerning the introduction of Buddhism into Silla, see Lee, *Lives,* p. 6, n. 29, Hong Chŏng-sik, "The Thought and Life of Wŏnhyo," p. 15.

30. See Kim Tong-Hwa, "Koguryŏ sidae," pp. 3–5, "Paekche sidae," pp. 57–58, and, for the early Silla period, "Silla sidae," pp. 1–2.

31. Kamstra, *Encounter,* p. 173; Zürcher, *Conquest,* p. 188.

32. Kamstra, *Encounter,* p. 173; Zürcher, *Conquest,* p. 223 ff.

33. Hong Yun-sik, "Paekche Pulgyo," pp. 83–86; An Kye-hyŏn ("Paekche Pulgyo," p. 198) notes, however, that Avalokiteśvara, Bhaiṣajyaguru, and Amitābha worship were also practiced. For a general survey of Maitreya worship in Korea, see Rhi Ki-yong and Hwang Su-yŏng (eds.), *Pŏpchu sa,* pp. 50–61; for the Silla period, see Sŏ Yun-gil, "Silla ŭi Mirŭk sasang." See also Kamstra, *Encounter,* pp. 168–184.

34. Lewis Lancaster, "An Analysis of the *Aṣṭasāhasrikāprajñāpāramitā-sūtra* from the Chinese Translations," p. 317 ff.; T'ang Yung-t'ung, *Han wei liang-chin nan-pei-ch'ao fo-chiao shih,* pp. 66–71.

35. Kim Tong-hwa, "Koguryŏ sidae," pp. 14–19.

36. Yi Nŭng-hwa, *Chosŏn Pulgyo t'ongsa* I, p. 33; Yi Chae-ch'ang and Kim Yŏng-t'ae, *Pulgyo munhwa sa,* p. 79; Kim Tong-hwa, "Paekche sidae," pp. 64–67; Hong Yun-sik, "Paekche Pulgyo," pp. 76–77; idem, "Samguk sidae ŭi Pulgyo sinang ŭirye," pp. 137–141.

37. Although most of our sources for the study of Koguryŏ Buddhism are passing references to Koguryŏ monks appearing in the biographies of other clerics, we can surmise from the available evidence that Samnon studies were particularly strong (Kim Tong-hwa, "Koguryŏ sidae," pp. 26–27). For the Koguryŏ monk Sŭngnang

(ca. 490), a disciple of Kumārajīva and important figure in the early development of the San-lun school in China, see the excellent treatment by Pak Chong-hong, *Han'guk sasang sa,* pp. 38–53; see also Yu Pyŏng-dŏk "Sŭngnang kwa Samnon sasang," Kim Hang-bae, "Sŭngnang ŭi hwa sasang," Kim Tong-hwa, "Koguryŏ sidae," pp. 27–29, 34, and *Kao-seng chuan* 8, *T* 2059.50.380c. Sarvāstivādin studies are represented primarily by the example of Chigwang (n.d.), who was well known even in China; see Kim Tong-hwa, "Koguryŏ sidae," pp. 37–38; Kim Yŏng-t'ae, "Koguryŏ Pulgyo sasang," p. 37; *Hsü Kao-seng chuan* 18, *T* 2060.50.572a. The Nirvana sect was founded in Koguryŏ by Sŏndŏk (n.d.); see Kim Tong-hwa, "Koguryŏ sidae," pp. 38–41. Ch'ŏnt'ae studies were pursued by the Koguryŏ monk P'ayak (562–613), a student of Chih-i; see Kim Tong-hwa, "Koguryŏ sidae," pp. 41–44, *Hsü kao-seng chuan* 17, *T* 2060.50.570c–571a.

Materials on Paekche Buddhism are even scarcer than for Koguryŏ. From the fact that Sŏng wang (r. 523–553) petitioned the Liang court in 541 for commentaries on the *Mahāparinirvāṇa-sūtra,* we can assume that the Nirvana school was strong at the time; see *Samguk sagi* 26, pp. 434, 437, and discussion at Kim Tong-hwa, "Paekche sidae," pp. 68–72. For Paekche Samnon studies, see Kim Tong-hwa, "Paekche sidae," pp. 72–75; for *Satyasiddhi-śāstra* studies, see Kim Tong-hwa, "Paekche sidae," pp. 75–78. Paekche *vinaya* studies have been referred to in the sources cited in note 36. See also Kim Tong-hwa, "Kudara jidai no Bukkyō shisō."

38. For early Korean influence on the development of Japanese culture see: Kim Tong-hwa, "Koguryŏ sidae," pp. 35–37; idem, "Paekche sidae," pp. 78–82; Yi Chae-ch'ang and Kim Yŏng-t'ae, *Pulgyo munhwa sa,* pp. 74–75, 78–80, 102; Enchō Tamura, "The Influence of Silla Buddhism on Japan"; Kamstra, *Encounter,* pp. 201–202.

39. Han Woo-keun, *History,* pp. 75–83; Yi Pyŏng-do, *Han'guk sa* I, pp. 500–527.

40. This is not to say that other sects were not operating during this period: as in the Three Kingdoms period, Sarvāstivādin Abhidharma, Samnon, and Satyasiddhi-śāstra schools were prevalent, and Tantric sects were introduced later; for an outline of these schools see Kim Tong-hwa, "Silla sidae," pp. 43–53, and Han Ki-du, *Han'guk Pulgyo sasang,* pp. 32–44. For Silla scholasticism in general see Cho Myŏng-gi's excellent article, "Silla Pulgyo ŭi kyohak," and Kim Tong-hwa, "Silla sidae ŭi Pulgyo sasang." For the five scholastic sects, see Yi Pyŏng-do, *Han'guk sa* I, p. 686, *Han'guk sa* II, p. 296; Yi Ki-baek, *Kuksa sillon,* p. 111; Cho Myŏng-gi, "Taegak kuksa," p. 931, n. 1, Kwon Sang-no, "Korean Buddhism," p. 10. For an outline of all the different sects of Silla scholastic Buddhism until their merger in the Yi dynasty, see Yi Sang-baek, *Han'guk sa* III, p. 711, n. 3, and Richard Gard, "Mādhyamika in Korea," p. 1173–1174, n. 62.

41. For the letter see *SGYS* 4, pp. 1006c.22–1007a.10; translated by Peter Lee, "Fa-tsang and Ŭisang," pp. 58–59.

42. *T* 1887A.45.711a–716a; and see Kim Chi-gyŏn, "*Kegon ichijō hokkaizu ni tsuite.*" There is an excellent Korean vernacular translation of this work and its exposition: see Rhi Ki-yong, *Segye sasang chŏnjip 11: Han'guk ŭi Pulgyo sasang,* pp. 243–332.

43. For Pusŏk sa and the other nine major temples of the Hwaŏm sect, see *SGYS*

4, 1007a.11–12; Lee, "Fa-tsang and Ŭisang," p. 57, nn. 16, 19; Rhi Ki-yong (ed.), *Pusŏk sa.*

44. For Hua-yen doctrine, I refer the reader to the following readily accessible Western scholarship: Francis Cook, *Hua-yen Buddhism: The Jewel Net of Indra;* Garma C. C. Chang, *The Buddhist Teaching of Totality,* Junjiro Takakusu, *The Essentials of Buddhist Philosophy,* pp. 108–125; Kenneth Ch'en, *Buddhism in China,* pp. 313–320; see also the subsequent sections on Chinul's thought in this introduction.

For Korean Hwaŏm thought see: Kim Ing-sŏk, *Hwaŏmhak kaeron,* pp. 17–96; Kim Yŏng-su, "Hwaŏm sasang ŭi yŏn'gu," pp. 14–25; Han Ki-du, *Han'guk Pulgyo sasang,* pp. 87–131; Kim Chi-gyŏn, "Silla Hwaŏmhak ŭi churyu ko" and "Silla Hwaŏmhak ŭi kyebo wa sasang."

For Ŭisang and his contributions to Korean and East Asian Hwaŏm thought see: *Sung Kao-seng chuan* 4, *T* 2061.50.729a–c, translated by Herbert Durt, "La Biographie du Moine Coréen Ŭisang d'après le Song Kao Seng Tchouan," pp. 415–422; Han Ki-du, *Han'guk Pulgyo sasang,* pp. 95–101; Chang Won-gyu, "Hwaŏm kyohak wansŭnggi," pp. 26–41; Cho Myŏng-gi, "Silla Pulgyo ŭi kyohak," pp. 14–15; Yi chae-ch'ang and Kim Yŏng-t'ae, *Pulgyo munhwa sa,* pp. 92–94; Yaotani Kōho, "Shiragi sō Gishō denkō." For his influence on Chinul's thought see Yi Chong-ik, "Chinul ŭi Hwaŏm sasang," pp. 539–540.

45. See *Excerpts from the Dharma Collection and Special Practice Record (DCSPR),* note 279.

46. For a summary of Wŏnhyo's extant writings see: Cho Myŏng-gi, "Silla Pulgyo ŭi kyohak," pp. 154–161; Yi Chong-ik, "Wŏnhyo ŭi saengae wa sasang," pp. 212–215; Rhi Ki-yong, "Wonhyo and His Thought," p. 6; Hong Chŏng-sik, "Thought and Life of Wonhyo," p. 24.

47. For Wŏnhyo's Hwaŏm thought see especially: Chang Won-gyu, "Hwaŏm kyohak wansŏnggi," pp. 11–26; Kim Hyŏng-hi, "Wŏnhyo ŭi *Hwaŏm kyŏng* kuan," pp. 32–78.

48. See *Kŭmgang sammae kyŏng non* 1, *T* 1730.34.964b.28–29; see discussion in Han Ki-du, *Han'guk Pulgyo sasang,* pp. 48–49; Rhi Ki-yong, "Wonhyo and His Thought," p. 6.

49. Only fragments are extant: see Cho Myŏng-gi, *Wŏnhyo taesa chŏnjip,* pp. 640–646. Yi Chong-ik has attempted to reconstruct the missing portions of the text in his *Wŏnhyo ŭi kŭnbon sasang: Simmun hwajaeng non yŏn'gu,* pp. 24–56.

50. Korean studies on Wŏnhyo are voluminous; I will mention only a few of the more important works. Pak Chong-hong, *Han'guk sasang sa,* pp. 85–127, gives an excellent description of his philosophy with copious selections from his writings. Rhi Ki-yong, the Korean expert on Wŏnhyo's thought, has made important contributions: his Korean vernacular translations of Wŏnhyo's commentaries on the *Awakening of Faith* and the *Vajrasamādhi-sūtra* in *Segye sasang chŏnjip,* pp. 29–137 and 138–240 respectively, are unsurpassed; see also his major work on Wŏnhyo, *Wŏnhyo sasang,* the first in his projected five-volume series on Wŏnhyo's thought. Sung-bae Park is probably the Western expert on Wŏnhyo; his dissertation, "Wŏnhyo's Commentaries on the *Awakening of Faith in Mahāyāna,*" is the best treatment yet on

Wŏnhyo in a Western language; Wŏnhyo's influence on Chinul is discussed at pp. 77–79. See also Yi Chong-ik, "Silla Pulgyo wa Wŏnhyo sasang" and "Wŏnhyo ŭi saengae wa sasang." For his pietistic popular stance, see An Kye-hyŏn, "Wŏnhyo ŭi Mirŭk chŏngt'o wangsaeng sasang"; Sŏ Yun-gil, "Silla ŭi Mirŭk sasang," pp. 292–295. For Wŏnhyo's syncretic focus, see especially: Kim Un-hak, "Wŏnhyo ŭi hwajaeng sasang"; Ko Ik-chin, "Wŏnhyo ŭi sasang ŭi silch'ŏn wŏlli," pp. 237–243; Yi Chong-ik, *Wŏnhyo ŭi kŭnbon sasang,* especially pp. 10–21.

51. Musang (684–762), also known as Kim Hwasang, is the perfect example of a Korean who became a successful teacher in China. He was the systematizer of an important school of the Chinese Middle Ch'an period, the second of seven early schools of Ch'an mentioned by Tsung-mi in his *Yüan-chüeh ching ta-shu ch'ao;* see *YCCTSC* 3b, p. 533c.11–15, translated by Jan Yün-hua in "Tsung-mi: His Analysis of Ch'an Buddhism," pp. 42–43. For Musang's biography and teachings see: *Li-tai fa-pao chi, T* 2075.51.184c–196b; *Sung Kao-seng chuan* 19, *T* 2061.50.832b–833a. Musang's success in China was well known to the Koreans: see the notice in *Hŭiyang san Chijŏng taesa t'ap pimyŏng,* in Yi Nŭng-hwa, *Chosŏn Pulgyo t'ongsa* I, p. 126.6, and *Chōsen kinseki sōran* I, p. 90.7. See also the treatment by Han Ki-du in his studies "Silla sidae ŭi Sŏn sasang," pp. 34–44, "Silla ŭi Sŏn sasang," pp. 346–348, *Han'guk Pulgyo sasang,* p. 52. Jan Yün-hua promises a major study on his life and thought. See also the list of Korean monks whose Sŏn exchanges appear in the *Ching-te ch'uan-teng lu,* culled by Han Ki-du in "Silla ŭi Sŏn sasang," pp. 368–372, and "Silla sidae ŭi Sŏn sasang," pp. 101–112.

52. Table 2 is adapted from Yi Chi-gwan, *Chogye chong sa,* p. 86, with some date changes based on Han Ki-du, "Silla sidae ŭi Sŏn sasang," pp. 45–100; see also Kwon Sang-no, "Han'guk Sŏnjong yaksa," pp. 267–274, who gives the modern addresses for the sites; Yi Pyŏng-do, *Han'guk sa* I, p. 687; Seo Kyung-bo, "A Study of Korean Zen Buddhism Approached Through the Chodangjip," pp. 78 ff., which must be used cautiously. Many of the dates listed in Table 2 are subject to dispute and should be considered tentative; our information for the early years of the Nine Mountains school is scanty at best. Kim Yŏng-t'ae of Tongguk University has even gone so far as to say that because there is no reference in the extant literature to any of these nine schools at such an early date, an early Koryŏ (tenth–eleventh century) foundation has to be assumed; see Kim Yŏng-t'ae, "Han'guk Pulgyo chongp'a sŏngnip e taehan chaegoch'al," p. 2; and the critique by Yi Chong-ik, "Ogyo Kusan ŭn Nadae e sŏngnip," p. 2.

Along with these nine teachers and their mountain sites, Han Ki-du would add two masters whose monasteries were at least as influential as the orthodox schools. The first is Hyeso (773–850), the National Master Chin'gam, who taught at Ssanggye sa on Chiri san; he was a disciple of Yen-kuan Ch'i-an. The second is Sunji (entered China 858), who taught at Yongŏm sa on Ogwan san; he was a disciple of Yang-shan Hui-chi (807–883). See Han Ki-du, "Silla sidae ŭi Sŏn sasang," pp. 82–88, 90–110; "Silla ŭi Sŏn sasang," pp. 362–368.

53. This information on Pŏmnang and his lineage appears in Chisŏn's memorial inscription, *Yu Tang Silla kuk ko Hŭiyang san Pongŏm sa kyo si Chijŏng taesa Chŏkcho chi t'ap pimyŏng,* in Yi Nŭng-hwa, *Chosŏn Pulgyo t'ongsa* I, p. 127.3–4,

Chōsen kinseki sōran I, pp. 90.15–91.1; written by the renowned Silla scholar Ch'oe Ch'i-won (b. 857).

54. The Hung-chou school is discussed in detail later in this introduction; see also *DCSPR,* Part II.

55. "People of his time only revered the teachings of the scriptures and cultivated contemplation methods which maintained the spirit [*chonsin*]; they could not understand the unconditioned school [of Sŏn] which is free in all situations." See *Silla kuk Muju Kaji san Porim sa si Pojo Sŏnsa yŏngt'ap pimyŏng,* in Yi Nŭng-hwa, *T'ongsa* I, pp. 120.13–121.1; see also *Chōsen kinseki sōran* I, p. 62.8–9, by Kim Wŏn (n.d.), his only extant composition.

56. *Sŭngt'ong* (roughly "Saṃgha overseer") was the highest rank attainable in the scholastic sects; see note 88 below. I have no information on this doctrinal master, who is presumably Korean; Seo ("A Study of Korean Zen Buddhism," p. 93, n. 1) proposes that it might be one of the Chinese Ch'an masters mentioned in *CTL,* but this seems doubtful.

57. Kuei-tsung Chih-ch'ang (n.d.), a disciple of Ma-tsu Tao-i; the story appears in *CTL* 7, p. 256b.13–14; *Chodang chip* 15, p. 97b.

58. From the *Sŏnmun pojang nok* 2, *HTC* 1261.113.997a–b; quoted with some differences in Han Ki-du, "Silla sidae ŭi Sŏn sasang," pp. 49–50; "Silla ŭi Sŏn sasang," pp. 349–350; I have no idea what text Seo Kyung-bo used for his translation of this exchange in his "Study of Korean Zen Buddhism," pp. 93–95. Some portions of this passage seem corrupted and are difficult to construe. The *Sŏnmun pojang nok* was compiled in three fascicles by the Korean Ch'ŏnch'aek (n.d.) in 1293; he notes that this story is from the *Haedong ch'iltae rok,* which is not extant.

59. Yang-shan Hui-chi (807–883). As Han Ki-du points out ("Silla sidae ŭi Sŏn sasang," pp. 64–65), the attribution of this quote to Yang-shan is doubtful; at any rate, it does not appear in the *CTL* or *Chodang chip* sections on Yang-shan.

60. Chang-ching Huai-hui, the teacher of Muyŏm's contemporary, Hyŏnuk; see Table 2. Han Ki-du doubts this attribution as well; the quote does not appear in the *CTL* or *Chodang chip* sections devoted to Chang-ching.

61. In *Sŏnmun pojang nok* 1, *HTC* 1261.113.990a.18–b.16; an earlier version appears in *Chodang chip* 17, p. 108a–b, translated by Seo Kyung-bo, "Korean Zen Buddhism," pp. 170–171; quoted, with misprints, in Han Ki-du, "Silla sidae ŭi Sŏn sasang," p. 63.

62. See the discussion in Han Ki-du, "Silla sidae ŭi Sŏn sasang," pp. 62–65; "Silla ŭi Sŏn sasang," pp. 355–356.

63. For a list of his teachers, see Cho Myŏng-gi, "Taegak kuksa ŭi Ch'ŏnt'ae ŭi sasang kwa sokchang ŭi ŏpchŏk," pp. 895–896.

64. *Koryŏ kuk Ogwan san ta Hwaŏm Yŏngt'ong sa chŭng si Taegak kuksa pimyŏng,* by Kim Pu-sik (1075–1151), author of the *Samguk sagi,* in Yi Nŭng-hwa, *Chosŏn Pulgyo t'ongsa* III, pp. 305–314; this statement is on p. 310.2.

65. *T* 2184.55.1166a–1178c; and see Cho Myŏng-gi, *Koryŏ Taegak kuksa wa Ch'ŏnt'ae sasang,* pp. 54–75.

66. For Ŭich'ŏn's role in compiling the supplement to the canon, see Lewis Lancaster and Sung-bae Park, *The Korean Buddhist Canon*, pp. xiii–xiv; Cho Myŏnggi, *Koryŏ Taegak kuksa*, pp. 78–103, and "Taegak kuksa ŭi Ch'ŏnt'ae ŭi sasang," pp. 911–917; Yi Chae-ch'ang and Kim Yŏng-t'ae, *Pulgyo munhwa sa*, pp. 118–120.

67. See Nukariya Kaiten, *Chōsen Zenkyōshi*, p. 231; Han Ki-du, *Han'guk Pulgyo sasang*, p. 135.

68. Cho Myŏng-gi, "Taegak kuksa ŭi Ch'ŏnt'ae ŭi sasang," p. 893.

69. *T* 1725.34.870c–875c.

70. *T* 1931.46.774c–780c. For Ch'egwan, see the biography in *Fo-tsu t'ung-chi* 10, *T* 2035.49.206a–b, quoted at Yi Nŭng-hwa, *Chosŏn Pulgyo t'ongsa* III, pp. 296–297; see also Nukariya Kaiten, *Chōsen Zenkyōshi*, pp. 206–207, Han Ki-du, *Han'guk Pulgyo sasang*, pp. 143–152. Ŭich'ŏn's reference to Wŏnhyo and Ch'egwan as his predecessors appears in his *Sinch'ang Kukch'ŏng sa kyegang sa*, in *Taegak kuksa munjip* 3, 1 changgyŏl.

Ch'egwan's work has been discussed in David Chappell, "Introduction to the *T'ien-t'ai ssu-chiao i*," pp. 72–86.

71. Cho Myŏng-gi, "Taegak kuksa ŭi Ch'ŏnt'ae ŭi sasang," p. 893.

72. Ŭich'ŏn went so far as to correlate the Hwaŏm taxonomy of the teachings with that used in the Ch'ŏnt'ae school; see Ko Ik-chin, "Wŏnmyo Yose ŭi Paengnyŏn kyŏlsa wa kŭ sasangjŏk tonggi," p. 120, quoting Ŭich'ŏn, *Taesong Ch'ŏnt'ae t'apha ch'inch'am parwŏn so*, in *Taegak kuksa munjip* 14, 3–4 changgyŏl; Ko wrongly cites fasc. 16.

73. Ko Ik-chin, "Wŏnmyo Yose," p. 120.

74. See Yi Nŭng-hwa, *Chosŏn Pulgyo t'ongsa* III, pp. 297–299; Han Ki-du, *Han'guk Pulgyo sasang*, p. 152 ff.; Nukariya Kaiten, *Chōsen Zenkyōshi*, p. 232; *Koryŏ kuk Ogwan san ta Hwaŏm Yŏngt'ong sa chŭng si Taegak kuksa pimyŏng*, in *Chosŏn Pulgyo t'ongsa* III, pp. 310–311, and especially p. 310.11–12.

75. *Kang Wŏn'gak kyŏng palsa*, in *Taegak kuksa munjip* 3.

76. *Kanjŏng Sŭng yusing non tan kwa sŏ*, in *Taegak kuksa munjip* 1.

77. As Ŭich'ŏn says, "Those who transmit [the teachings of] the great sutra [the *Avataṃsaka Sūtra*] and yet do not train in contemplation—although they are called 'lecturers,' I have no faith in them." *Si sinch'am hakto ch'isu*, in *Taegak kuksa munjip* 16.

78. See the excellent discussion in Pak Chong-hong, *Han'guk sasang sa*, pp. 148–166; and see Yi Yŏng-ja, "Ŭich'ŏn ŭi Ch'ŏnt'ae hoet'ong sasang," pp. 222–233.

79. Postface to *Pieh-ch'uan-hsin fa i*, *HTC* 949.101.323.

80. When the Liao king Tao-tsung (r. 1056–1100) decreed that the *Platform Sūtra*, the *Ching-te ch'uan-teng lu*, and other Sŏn texts should be burned as spurious texts, Ŭich'ŏn approved and said, "The words and phrases of the Sŏn sect contain many heresies." Postface to *Pieh-ch'uan-hsin fa i*.

81. Ŭich'ŏn's strong anti-Sŏn stance should explain as well the reason why he entirely omitted Sŏn writings from his catalog of Buddhist literature; cf. Lancaster and Park, *Korean Buddhist Canon*, p. xiv.

82. For further information on Ŭich'ŏn see Yi Pyŏng-do, *Han'guk sa* II, pp. 276–

284; Cho Myong-gi, "Prominent Buddhist Leaders and Their Doctrines," pp. 18–20; Han Woo-keun, *History of Korea,* pp. 147–148; Hong Chŏng-sik, "Koryŏ Ch'ŏnt'ae chong kaerip kwa Ŭich'ŏn."

83. For T'aejo's attitude toward Buddhism see Yi Pyŏng-do, *Han'guk sa* II, pp. 77–78; Kim Sang-gi, *Koryŏ sidae sa,* pp. 42–43; Han Woo-keun, *History of Korea,* p. 125.

84. *Koryŏ sa (KRS)* 2.15a.2. For a discussion of the ten admonitions see: Yi Pyŏng-do, *Han'guk sa* II, pp. 79–87; Kim Sang-gi, *Koryŏ sidae sa,* pp. 43–46; Han Ki-du, *Han'guk Pulgyo sasang,* pp. 62–63.

85. For Koryŏ national protection ceremonies see Yi Pyŏng-do, *Han'guk sa* II, p. 289 ff.; for such references from *KRS* see Hong Yun-sik, "Koryŏ Pulgyo ŭi sinang ŭirye," pp. 657 and 694. In dharma assemblies convened during the Koryŏ, the following sutras were most commonly used: *Jen-wang po-lo po-lo-mi ching* (107 times), *Suvarṇaprabhāsôttama-sūtra* (22 times), *Mahāprajñāpāramitā-sūtra* (14 times), *Avataṃsaka Sūtra* (12 times), *Bhaiṣajyagurupūrvapraṇidhāna-sūtra* (3 times), *Śūraṅgama Sūtra* (1 time); see the list culled from the *KRS,* in Hong Yun-sik, "Koryŏ Pulgyo," p. 662. The predominance of the first two *sūtras* shows the role played by national protection Buddhism under the Koryŏ.

86. For the close relationship between Buddhism and the Koryŏ court and the latter's support of the religion, see Yi Pyŏng-do, *Han'guk sa* II, pp. 271–276.

87. For the economic role of Buddhist monasteries in Koryŏ society see: Yi Chae-ch'ang, *Koryŏ sawŏn kyŏngje ŭi yŏn'gu;* Yu Kyo-sŏng, "Koryŏ sawon kyŏngje ŭi sŏnggyŏk," pp. 607–626; Yi Pyŏng-do, *Han'guk sa* II, pp. 298–302; Yi Sang-baek, *Han'guk sa* III, pp. 708–709; Han Woo-keun, *History,* pp. 146–147; Moon Sang-hee, "History Survey of Korean Religion," pp. 18–19. For the economic activities of Chinese Buddhist monasteries, which have many parallels with those in Korea, see the bibliography in Kenneth Ch'en, *Buddhism in China,* pp. 523–526.

88. The Koryŏ bureaucratic examination system began in 958, the ninth year of Kwangjong's reign (*KRS* 2.27b). It is uncertain when the Saṃgha examinations began, but most scholars think they probably began simultaneous with, or immediately following, the institution of the bureaucratic examinations; Yi Chae-ch'ang, "Koryŏ Pulgyo ŭi sŭnggwa sŭngnoksa chedo," p. 434; Yi Chae-ch'ang and Kim Yŏng-t'ae, *Pulgyo munhwa sa,* pp. 112–113; Nukariya Kaiten, *Chōsen Zenkyōshi,* pp. 206–207. The examinations were held once every three years, usually at the two chief temples of the Sŏn and scholastic sects in the capital of Kaesŏng: Kwangmyŏng sa for Sŏn and Wangnyun sa for the scholastic schools; Yi Chae-ch'ang, "Koryŏ sŭnggwa," p. 436. The Sŏn exams covered material in the *Ching-te ch'uan-teng lu,* and later, Chinul's disciple Chin'gak Hyesim's *Sŏnmun yŏmsong chip;* the scholastic schools' examination covered the *Avataṃsaka Sūtra* and the *Daśabhūmikasūtra-śāstra.* The ranking system for the two major sects was as follows: Sŏn—Taedŏk, Taesa, Chung taesa, Samjung taesa, Sŏnsa, Taesŏnsa; scholastic schools—Taedŏk, Taesa, Chung taesa, Samjung taesa, Sujwa, Sŭngt'ong. See Yi Chae-ch'ang, "Koryŏ sŭnggwa," pp. 436–437; Yi Chae-ch'ang and Kim Yŏng-t'ae, *Pulgyo munhwa sa,* p. 113. Monks at the two highest ranks of either Sŏn or the scholastic schools could be appointed by royal proclamation to the position of royal master or national master,

which were more government posts than religious ranks; see Lee, *Lives,* p. 28, n. 78, and Yi Chae-ch'ang, "Koryŏ sŭnggwa," p. 437, n. 32. For the Saṃgha administration, see Yi Chae-ch'ang, "Koryŏ sŭnggwa," p. 441. The strictness of this system abated somewhat later. Any of the examination ranks conferred by examination could be gained through royal appointment and were often conferred posthumously on monks who had distinguished themselves. Chinul's successor Chin'gak Hyesim was apparently the first monk to receive the appellation Sŏnsa or Taesŏnsa without taking the examination; see *Chin'gak kuksa pimyŏng, Chosŏn Pulgyo t'ongsa* III, p. 354.1.

89. *KRS* 8.14c.34.

90. *KRS* 85.6a.7–8.

91. See *KRS* 11.33a.8–b.1.

92. *KRS* 85.6a.9. See Yi Pyŏng-do, *Han'guk sa* II, p. 298 ff., for further details on these restrictive measures.

93. See Yi Sang-baek, *Han'guk sa* III, pp. 52–59 and 707–721, for the intensely anti-Buddhist stance of the Yi dynasty; see also Han Chong-man, "Nyŏmal Choch'o ŭi paebul hobul sasang," pp. 717–737.

94. For Tosŏn and his alleged influence on T'aejo see Han Ki-du, *Han'guk Pulgyo sasang,* p. 61; Nukariya Kaiten, *Chōsen Zenkyōshi,* pp. 182–185; Han Woo-keun, *History,* p. 106.

95. See Kwon Sang-no, "Han'guk Sŏnjong yaksa," pp. 274–275.

96. From *Encouragement to Practice.*

97. For this contrast between Ŭich'ŏn and Chinul see Chang Won-gyu, "Chogye chong ŭi sŏngnip kwa palchŏn e taehan koch'al," p. 348.

98. For the Ch'oe takeover of the Koryŏ government see the excellent accounts in Kim Sang-gi, *Koryŏ sidae sa,* pp. 413–453, and Han Woo-keun, *History,* pp. 154–169.

99. Kim Kun-su (fl. 1216–1220) was the son of Kim Ton-jung (d. 1170), grandson of the *Samguk sagi* author Kim Pu-sik, and a famous mid-Koryŏ literary figure in his own right; his biography appears at *KRS* 98.21b–22a. Much of the information on Chinul's life given here is drawn from the memorial inscription composed by Kim Kun-su upon royal command in 1211: the *Sŭngp'yŏng pu Chogye san Susŏn sa Puril Pojo kuksa pimyŏng,* in Pang Han-am (ed.), *Pojo pŏbŏ,* fol. 139a–143a; Yi Nŭng-hwa, *Chosŏn Pulgyo t'ongsa* III, pp. 337–342; Chōsen sōtokufu, *Chōsen kinseki sōran* II, pp. 949–953. Page numbers will be cited from the *t'ongsa* edition.

100. A Yi dynasty source gives an exact date for Chinul's birth: the third month, seventeenth day, twenty-eighth year of the Shao-hsing reign era of the Southern Sung emperor Kao-tsung (17 April 1158); *Ko Sŭngju Chŏnghye sa sajŏk,* in Im Sŏk-chin (ed.), *Chogye san Songgwang sa sago,* pp. 397–398. Due to the late date of this inscription and because its information is not verified in earlier records, its data must be taken with caution.

101. The present Sŏhŭng kun, Hwanghae to, North Korea; the district is known from Kogoryŏ times. For a thorough description of the region see *TYS* 41, fol. 21a–27a, pp. 729–732. There is a map of the region in Yi Pyŏng-do, *Han'guk sa* II, pp. 212–213.

102. Chinul's father does not appear in the *Koryŏ sa*. The position he held in the National Academy, that of *Hakchŏng (recto magnifico)*, was a ninth-rank position, the highest rank in the Koryŏ bureaucracy; *KRS* 76.30b, 31a. Fu-jui Chang translates the title as "Charge d'exécuter les règlements de l'école," the director of the Sons of the State Academy (K. *Kukcha kam;* C. *Kuo-tzu chien*); Fu-jui Chang, *Les Fonctionnaires des Song,* p. 58. The Kukhak (here translated "National Academy") was the common name for the Koryŏ Sons of the State Academy, the name it formally received in the first year of Ch'ungnyŏl wang's reign (1274); *KRS* 76.30b. In the first year of Ch'ungsŏn wang's reign (1308), the academy changed names again, this time to the appellation under which it has been known to the present day: the Sŏnggyun'gwan. For the development of the Sŏnggyun'gwan, see *TYS* 4, fol. 15a–17a, pp. 95a–96a; for the foundation of the academy and the daily life of its students, see Kim Chong-guk, "Some Notes on the Songgyun'gwan," pp. 69–91.

103. Kim Kun-su seems to contradict himself in his biographical inscription when he says (*Pojo kuksa pimyŏng,* p. 337.12) that Chinul shaved his head and received the full *Prātimokṣa* precepts at age eight (seven in Western age) and, later (p. 340.13), that he had been a monk for thirty-six years at the time of his death, making him ordained at age sixteen (age fifteen in Western years). The statements are puzzling and we can only assume that Chinul spent several years as a novice monk or lay practitioner in the temple before receiving full ordination later at age fifteen.

104. The successorship at Kulsan sa is somewhat questionable. The only record concerning its transmission line appears in a postscript to a Taehŭng sa edition of the *Records of Ta-hui,* written sometime in the middle fourteenth century by Yi Saek (1328–1396) and seen by Yi Chong-ik. According to this postscript, in the *Sŏn'ga chongp'a to* (not extant), written by Yi Chang-yong (1201–1272), an important mid-Koryŏ classical scholar and literary figure, the Kulsan sa lineage was transmitted as follows: Pŏmil; Pohyŏn Kaech'ŏng; Odae Sin'gyŏng; Taeŭn Tojang; Saja Chihyu; Chŏnghak Tojam; Tut'a Ŭngjin; Tansok Chihyŏn; Changsu Tamjin; Ch'ŏnch'uk Nŭngin; Sin'gwang Chonghwi; Pojo Chinul. Noted in Yi Chong-ik, *Chogye chong chunghŭng non,* pp. 93–94. Yi Chi-gwan (*Han'guk Pulgyo soŭi kyŏngjŏn yŏn'gu,* p. 29) identifies Chonghwi as an eighth-generation successor of Pŏmil but does not provide a source for his information. Kulsan sa was located in the present-day Kangnŭng district of Kangwon to; only the foundations remain.

105. *Pojo kuksa pimyŏng,* p. 377.12. This was a fairly common characterization of monks who made considerable progress through their own studies; see, for example, the parallel in *Taegak kuksa pimyŏng, Chosŏn Pulgyo t'ongsa* III, p. 306.6.

106. Poje sa, later known as Yŏnbok sa, was a major center of the Sŏn sect during the Koryŏ period. Han Ki-du (*Han'guk Pulgyo sasang,* p. 168) locates the temple inside the T'aean mun in the southern section of the capital of Kaesŏng. The *Tongguk yŏji sŭngnam* says simply that it was located in central Kaesŏng. For a description of the temple see *TYS* 4, fol. 21a–23a, pp. 98a–99a.

107. Suzuki Chūsei, "Sōdai Bukkyō kessha no kenkyū," pp. 76–97, gives an excellent outline of these fraternal societies during the Sung period; for their T'ang dynasty antecedents see the study by Naba Toshisada, "Tōdai no shayū ni tsuite." Hua-yen societies began to develop in China during the fifth century and were wide-

spread throughout the country by the ninth century; see Kamata Shigeo, *Chūgoku Kegon shisōshi no kenkyū,* pp. 42–47 and pp. 235–248; for the religious climate in China leading to the formation of Hua-yen societies, see the admirable discussion in Peter Gregory, "Tsung-mi's *Inquiry into the Origin of Man:* A Study of Chinese Buddhist Hermeneutics," pp. 69–91; references to Hua-yen and Samantabhadra societies are noted also in Yamazaki Hiroshi, *Shina chūsei bukkyō no tenkai,* pp. 804 and 811.

108. For examples of the compacts of some of these groups see Suzuki Chūsei, "Kessha no kenkyū," pp. 216–217.

109. For the *kyŏlsa* movement in Koryŏ Buddhism, see Han Ki-du, "Koryŏ Pulgyo ŭi kyŏlsa undong," pp. 551–583, and Ko Ik-chin, "Wŏnmyo Yose ŭi Paengnyŏn kyŏlsa wa kŭ sasangjŏk tonggi," pp. 109–120. Han (p. 552) lists fourteen separate *kyŏlsa* sites, mentioned in Koryŏ sources, which were located from Kangwon to to Chŏlla namdo.

110. There is no record of Ch'ŏngwŏn sa in any of the Korean geographical treatises. Ch'angp'yŏng too is somewhat problematic. Ch'angp'yŏng hyŏn was a district located in present-day Chŏlla namdo near Naju; known as Kulchi hyŏn during the Paekche period and Kiyang hyŏn during the Silla, it received the name Ch'angp'yŏng during the Koryŏ. *TYS* 39, fol. 26, p. 687. There was, however, a stream named Ch'angp'yŏng, located in Kwangsan hyŏn, which merged with the T'amyang and flowed west as the Ch'ilch'ŏn into the Naju area; *TYS* 35, fol. 18, p. 623. For geomantic as well as practical reasons, temples often were built along a river (and even on an island in the river), and Ch'ŏngwon sa might have been such a temple. At any rate, we can place it in the locale of present-day Naju, which is near the southwest coastal port of Mokp'o. Im Sŏk-chin (*Taesŭng Sŏnjong Chogye san Songgwang sa chi,* p. 57) assumes the temple was located near modern Ch'angp'yŏngsi in Tamyang kun, Chŏlla namdo. Unlike other scholars, Yi Chi-gwan (*Han'guk Pulgyo soŭi kyŏngjŏn,* p. 29) places the temple in Kyŏnggi to, at Ansŏng kun, Won'gok myŏn; he unfortunately provides no reference for his information.

111. For Koryŏ/Sung sea routes, see Yi Pyŏng-do, *Han'guk sa* II, p. 390. Establishing the location of Yesŏng kang, probably the main port for the overseas trade, has been problematic; the most plausible location seems to have been in Hwanghae to near present-day Inch'ŏn. See Yi Pyŏng-do, pp. 314–317. Important information on these sea routes can also be found in the *Kao-li t'u-ching* 39, pp. 93–95, and the Koryŏ section of the *Sung History, Sung-shih* 487.1–21, *PNP* 30, pp. 24734–24744. For Ming-chou, see Edwin Reischauer, *Ennin's Diary,* p. 43, n. 185.

112. *Pojo kuksa pimyŏng,* p. 338.1–3. For the *Platform Sūtra* quotation see *LTTC,* p. 353b.4–5.

113. *Pojo kuksa pimyŏng,* p. 339.4.

114. In Kyŏngsang pukto, Yech'ŏn kun, Pomun myŏn, Haga san; see *TYS* 24, fol. 4, p. 411, for Haga Mountain.

115. The *Hwaŏmnon chŏryo* is Chinul's three-fascicle summary of Li T'unghsüan's forty-fascicle *Hsin Hua-yen ching lun, T* 1739.36.721a–1008b. Chinul wrote the summary in 1207, but it was lost early on in Korea. It was rediscovered only in 1941 at the Kanazawa Bunko, one of the oldest libraries in Japan, by Yi Chong-ik;

for a firsthand account of these events see Yi Chong-ik, "Chinul ŭi Hwaŏm sasang," p. 526. The passage from the preface immediately following is taken from Kim Chi-gyŏn's reprint volume, *Hwaŏmnon chŏryo*, pp. 1–3.

116. *HYC* 51, p. 272c.23–25; the *sūtra*-volume simile appears at p. 272c.7–17.

117. *HHYCL* 14, p. 815a.3–8.

118. *HHYCL* 15, p. 819a.29–b.2.

119. *HHYCL* 21, p. 862a.7–8.

120. Chinul alludes here to a statement by Tsung-mi in his *Preface to the Complete Explanations on the Fountainhead of Ch'an Collection* [*Ch'an-yüan chu-ch'üan chi tou-hsü, CYCTH*]: "The *sūtras* are the Buddha's words. Sŏn is the Buddha's mind." *CYCTH* 1, p. 400b.10–11.

121. Tŭkchae (n.d.) is mentioned in the list of important members of the Samādhi and Prajñā Community found at *Taesŭng Sŏnjong Chogye san Susŏn sa chungch'ang ki, Chosŏn Pulgyo t'ongsa* III, p. 348.6; nothing more is known about him. The *Susŏn sa chungch'ang ki* was written by Ch'oe Sŏn (d. 1209); this is his only extant composition.

122. Kong Mountain is also known as P'algong san; Kŏjo sa is also called Ch'ŏngnyang kul; located in Kyŏngsang pukto, Yŏngch'ŏn kun, Ch'ŏngt'ong myŏn, Sinwon tong, Ŭnhae sa, Kŏjo am. For Kŏjo sa see *TYS* 22, fol. 25, p. 383; for Kong san, see *TYS* 22, fol. 21, p. 381. Kong san was obviously a burgeoning practice site at that time; *TYS* lists six different temples located on the mountain. Kŏjo am is well known today for the figurines of the five hundred arhants on display inside its main shrine hall.

123. Yi Chong-ik ("Pojo kuksa ŭi sasang ch'egye," p. 267) identifies Hang with Mongsŏn (n.d.), one of Chinul's more prominent students; he is mentioned in *Encouragement to Practice* and appears in the list of important members of the community which is found in the *Susŏn sa chungch'ang ki, Chosŏn Pulgyo t'ongsa* III, p. 348.5.

124. Yose's memorial stele, *Mandŏk san Paengnyŏn sa Wonmyo kuksa pi,* appears at *Chōsen kinseki sōran* I, pp. 590–593; *Chosŏn Pulgyo t'ongsa* III, pp. 319–323; page numbers will be quoted from the *t'ongsa* edition. The stele was written by Ch'oe Cha (1188–1260), a close associate of Yi Kyu-bo, in 1245. For Yose's life and thought see Ko Ik-chin, "Wŏnmyo Yose ŭi Paengnyŏn kyŏlsa wa kŭ sasangjŏk tonggi," pp. 109–120; Han Ki-du, "Koryŏ Pulgyo ŭi kyŏlsa undong," pp. 573–578; Nukariya Kaiten, *Chōsen Zenkyōshi*, pp. 278–280.

125. Paengnyŏn sa is located on Mandŏk san, Kangjin kun, Chŏlla namdo, to the southwest of Kilsang sa, the eventual permanent site of the Samādhi and Prajñā Community; for Paengnyŏn sa see *TYS* 37, fol. 17a–18a, p. 656; for Mandŏk san see *TYS* 37, fol. 14b, p. 654. Yose moved there in 1211 to found the *Pŏphwa kyŏlsa* and spent the next five years repairing the eighty units (K. *kan,* C. *chien;* a standard room measurement, approximately six feet square) of dilapidated buildings and expanding the site to accommodate a larger number of adepts; eventually, three hundred people are reputed to have been living and practicing there. See Ko Ik-chin, "Wŏnmyo Yose," p. 110; Han Ki-du, "Koryŏ Pulgyo ŭi kyŏlsa undong," pp. 574–575. (Han gives the date of his move to Paengnyŏn sa as 1230, which is incorrect; see *Wŏnmyo kuksa pimyŏng, t'ongsa* III, p. 321.6, which gives the 1211 date.)

126. I have been unable to locate any reference to a Kobong sa situated inside Kaesŏng, as is implied in the stele account; the only likely entry in the Korean geographical reference works is to a Kobong sa which was located in present P'yŏngan to, Chunghwa kun, on Haeap san, in the vicinity of the Koryŏ western capital, P'yŏngyang; see *TYS* 52, fol. 3a, p. 941. Yose's next stop, Changyŏn sa on Yŏngdong san, is even more problematic; I am unable to make any plausible identification based on the information in Korean geographical works and reserve judgment on its location.

127. "Sweet-dew sauce" *(amṛta)*: the elixir of immortality. Quoted in *Wŏnmyo kuksa pi, t'ongsa* III, p. 320.8.

128. *Susŏn sa chungch'ang ki, t'ongsa* III, p. 347.7–8.

129. Nothing more is known about Suu; he appears in the *Susŏn sa chungch'ang ki, t'ongsa* III, p. 347.8.

130. Kangnam includes all of modern Chŏlla namdo and Chŏlla pukto provinces.

131. See note 125.

132. *Susŏn sa chungch'ang ki, t'ongsa* III, p. 347.9–10.

133. Ch'ŏnjin (n.d.) was a prominent disciple of Chinul. Upon the succession of Chinul's disciple Hyesim to leadership at Susŏn sa after Chinul's death in 1210, Ch'ŏnjin was appointed the assistant director; he was an accomplished lecturer and rivaled even Hyesim as an interpreter of Buddhism. See the *Ch'angbok sa tamsŏn pang* in the *Tongguk Yi sangguk chip* 25, p. 268a; this is the literary collection of the important mid-Koryŏ writer and political figure Yi Kyu-bo (1168–1241). Ch'ŏnjin also appears frequently in Hyesim's *Records;* see, for example, *Chin'gak kuksa ŏrok,* in Kim Tal-chin (trans.), *Han'guk ŭi sasang tae chŏnjip* II, p. 242–470. Nothing more is known about Kwakcho.

134. This account appears at *Susŏn sa chungch'ang ki,* p. 347.4–7. Very little is known about the early history of Kilsang sa; only a few scattered and relatively late records remain concerning its foundation and history prior to Chinul's occupancy. These agree that the temple was built in the latter part of the Silla dynasty by a certain Sŏn master named Hyerin, who is otherwise unknown. As the *Sŭngp'yŏng sokchi* says, "Songgwang sa was constructed by the Sŏn Master Hyerin in the latter period of the Silla dynasty, and was called Kilsang sa. The buildings did not exceed one hundred *kan* in area, and there were no more than thirty to forty monks residing there." (Quoted in Rhi Ki-yong, ed., *Songgwang sa,* p. 20.) The *Sŭngp'yŏng pu Chogye san Songgwang sa sawon sajŏk pi,* written by Cho Chong-jŏ (1631–1690) in 1678, states also that Hyerin founded the monastery and "built a small hermitage and lived in it." (Quoted in *Chosŏn Pulgyo t'ongsa* III, p. 349.12.) Both these records are simply following the earlier account in the *Susŏn sa chungch'ang ki,* which was composed in 1207. No further information is available about the reputed founder, which has led some scholars to suspect that he is only a legendary figure invented later to account for the fact that the site was developed before Chinul's arrival (Rhi Ki-yong, *Songgwang sa,* p. 21). In the absence of contrary information, we have little choice but to accept tacitly the authenticity of this account. Over the centuries, time took its toll on the monastery; by the Koryŏ period, all the original buildings had fallen into ruins. Sometime during Injong's reign in Koryŏ (1123–1146), the mountain monk Sŏkcho (otherwise unknown) decided to rebuild the temple on the

scale of a large monastery. He gathered an army of workers and materials, but died before the work was completed. For lack of a director, work came to a halt and his renovations too fell into ruins (*Susŏn sa chungch'ang ki,* p. 347.6). Probably little remained when Suu first came upon the site. For popular accounts of Songgwang sa history, see Rhi Ki-yong, *Songgwang sa,* pp. 17–39; Im Sŏk-chin, *Songgwang sa chi,* p. 3 ff. Excerpts from all extant literature pertaining to the temple have been compiled in the massive sourcework *Chogye san Songgwang sa sago,* completed in 1932 by Im Sŏk-chin during his tenure as abbot of Songgwang sa during the Japanese occupation. Songgwang sa is located in Chŏlla namdo, at Sŭngju kun, Songgwang myŏn, Sinp'yŏng ni.

135. It is unclear exactly how many of Chinul's community accompanied him to Chiri san. Yose's companionship is recorded (*Wŏnmyo kuksa pi, Pulgyo t'ongsa* III, p. 320.9-10); Mongsŏn, who had accompanied Chinul from Pomun sa to Kŏjo sa, probably went along also. Doubtless there were a few others. Im Sŏk-chin (*Songgwang sa chi,* p. 12) assumes two or three others went along.

136. Chiri san is one of the largest mountains in Korea, measuring over eight hundred *i* (C. *li;* about 320 kilometers) in girth. The southernmost point in the Sobaek san range, it forms the natural border between Chŏlla and Kyŏngsang provinces. It is delimited by the towns of Kurye, Namwon, Hadong, Sanch'ŏng, and Hamyang. See Rhi Ki-yong (ed.), *Hwaŏm sa,* pp. 15–18, for legends associated with the mountain. Sangmuju am, also known simply as Muju am, is located on the Hamyang side of the mountain; see *TYS* 31, fol. 5b, p. 529.

137. *Pojo kuksa pimyŏng, Pulgyo t'ongsa* III, p. 338.7–8.

138. Ibid., p. 338.8.

139. Ibid., p. 338.9-12. The quotation from Ta-hui appears at *THYL* 19, pp. 893c–894a.

140. Yi Chong-ik, *Chogye chong chunghŭng non,* p. 83.

141. *Pojo kuksa pimyŏng, Pulgyo t'ongsa* III, p. 339.3–4.

142. *Susŏn sa chungch'ang ki, Pulgyo t'ongsa* III, p. 347.11.

143. Ibid., p. 347.12-13.

144. Chŏnghye sa is located on Kyejok san, in Chŏlla namdo, Sŭngju kun, Ch'ŏngso ri; Im Sŏk-chin, *Songgwang sa chi,* p. 13. See *TYS* 40, fol. 7a, p. 702a, for the temple and fol. 2b, p. 699a, for the mountain.

145. *Pojo kuksa pimyŏng, Pulgyo t'ongsa* III, p. 339.8.

146. These included Paegun am and Chŏkch'wi am on Ŏkpo san (the present Paegun san in Chŏlla namdo, Kwangyang kun) and Kyubong am and Chowol am on Sŏsŏk san (the present Mudŭng san in Chŏlla namdo, Kwangsan kun); these hermitages are all within one or two days' walk of Susŏn sa and still function today; *Pojo kuksa pimyŏng, Pulgyo t'ongsa* III, p. 339.6–7. Chinul is also reputed to have built Pojo am on Chogye Mountain near the monastery itself, but there is no evidence to support this tradition; the first record of any building on that site dates from 1725; see Rhi Ki-yong (ed.), *Songgwang sa,* p. 116. With so many retreat sites available, Chinul was apparently content in his old age to take more time in solitude for his own practice, rather than devote himself predominantly to running the community.

147. *Pojo kuksa pimyŏng, Pulgyo t'ongsa* III, p. 339.1–2.

148. Hyesim's memorial stele, *Chogye san cheise ko Tansok sa chuji Susŏn saju chŭng si Chin'gak kuksa pimyŏng*, appears in *Chosŏn Pulgyo t'ong-sa* III, pp. 351–355, and in *Chōsen kinseki sōran* I, pp. 460–464. The inscription was written in 1235 by the renowned Koryŏ literary figure and prominent Buddhist layperson Yi Kyu-bo (1168–1241), who was a close personal friend of Hyesim; his biography appears at *KRS* 102.3a–5a. For Yi Kyu-bo's role in Koryŏ Buddhism, see Sŏ Kyŏng-su, "Koryŏ ŭi kŏsa Pulgyo," pp. 587–594. These events appear in *Chin'gak kuksa pimyŏng, Pulgyo t'ongsa* III, p. 352.3–7.

There is surprisingly little secondary material on Hyesim, whose role in the development of *hwadu* study in Sŏn Buddhism is only beginning to become clear: see Nukariya Kaiten, *Chōsen Zenkyōshi*, pp. 292–305; Han Ki-du, *Han'guk Pulgyo sasang*, pp. 217–242. The *Chogye Chin'gak kuksa ŏrok* has been translated by Kim Tal-chin in *Han'guk ŭi sasang taechŏnjip 2*, pp. 205–375; the Chinese text is included (pp. 461–499).

149. *Chin'gak kuksa pimyŏng, Pulgyo t'ongsa* III, p. 352.10–11.

150. These works are listed by Kim Kun-su in Chinul's stele, *Pojo kuksa pimyŏng, Pulgyo t'ongsa* III, p. 340.13; both were in one fascicle. Another lost work, the *Death Record [Imjong ki]* is also mentioned at p. 340.8.

151. The following incidents all appear in *Chin'gak kuksa pimyŏng, Pulgyo t'ongsa* III, pp. 352.11–353.5. For Kyubong am see note 146 above.

152. The final two lines of this *gāthā* are added from Im Sŏk-chin, *Songgwang sa chi*, p. 78.

153. For Ta-hui's ten defects see *DCSPR*, Part III, The Live Word ("Practice of the *Mu Hwadu*" section); see also *Resolving Doubts About Observing the Hwadu*.

154. See note 146 above.

155. *Chin'gak kuksa pimyŏng, Pulgyo t'ongsa* III, p. 353.5–7.

156. See note 150 above.

157. Alluding to a chapter in the *Vimalakīrtinirdeśa-sūtra* in which the layman Vimalakīrti uses illness as an expedient means of teaching an assembly of bodhisattvas the dharma; see *Wei-mo-chieh so-shuo ching* 1, *T* 475.14.539c. ff.

158. *Pojo kuksa pimyŏng, Pulgyo t'ongsa* III, pp. 339.13–340.10.

159. *Pojo kuksa pimyŏng, Pulgyo t'ongsa* III, p. 340.10–12.

160. Ibid., p. 340.12. The year after Chinul's death, his successor, Hyesim, petitioned the court to prepare a memorial stele to preserve the master's achievements for all posterity and presented the king with a detailed account of his life to aid in its preparation. In a memorial issued in the twelfth month of Hŭijong's seventh year (1211), King Hŭijong ordered Kim Kun-su to compose the inscription, Yu Sin to write the calligraphy, and Po Ch'ang to supervise production of the memorial. Due to the detailed work involved in such a stone stele, the memorial was not completed until the last year (1213) of Hŭijong's successor, Kangjong (r. 1212–1213). On the tenth day of the fourth month of that year (2 May 1213), Kangjong ordered Kim Chin to erect the stone. The stele was set at the top of the front steps to the former lecture hall. Subsequently moved to various locations around the monastery, the stele was finally destroyed during the Hideyoshi invasion of 1597; later it was reproduced and placed at its original position. It is now located at Pudo chŏn in a Śarī-

radhātu-stūpa field just north of the main campus of Songgwang sa. See Im Sŏk-chin, *Songgwang sa chi,* pp. 60–61.

161. *Pojo kuksa pimyŏng, Pulgyo t'ongsa* III, p. 339.1–2.

162. See note 148 above.

163. See note 133 above.

164. *Tongguk Yi sangguk chip* 25, *Ch'angbok sa tamsŏn pang,* p. 268a; by Yi Kyu-bo.

165. *Chin'gak kuksa pimyŏng, Pulgyo t'ongsa* III, pp. 353–354.

166. Ibid., p. 353.8. A record remains of an inspection tour of Susŏn sa conducted during Hyesim's tenure, dated to within four or five years of A.D. 1221 (Im Ch'ang-sun, "Songgwang sa ŭi Koryŏ munsŏ," p. 48). In this survey, conducted by an astronomical officer *(sajin)* and a calendrical official *(saryŏk)* from the Bureau of Astronomy and Meteorology *(Sach'ŏnt'ae),* a census of the monastery population is given, along with a detailed list of the structures within the monastery compound, their arrangement, and respective sizes. It records as well the texts of the *Susŏn sa chungch'ang ki* and the *Pojo kuksa pimyŏng* and includes an account of the total assets of the monastery.

The first section of this report (pp. 40–43) gives a detailed account of the location of each building within the monastery precincts along with a description of the size and area of each structure. Although many lines in this section are obliterated and a number of characters are missing, there is mention of at least fourteen structures, including shrine halls, warehouses, gates, a bridge, toilet, bathhouse, mill, and granary. At the time of the inspection, it is recounted that there were forty-seven monks in attendance during dharma assemblies; the full assembly amounted to ninety-six individuals. This number is considerably less than the "several hundreds" Kim Kun-su mentions in his biography (see note 161 above); I assume that here we are seeing the difference between a sober official document and an enthusiastic account of Buddhist achievements. The final section includes a detailed accounting of the total assets of the monastery as well as a listing of the various donations offered to the monastery as part of funeral charges and other dharma offerings (see pp. 43–48 for text and detailed analysis). The donors involved in these merit-making activities reveal the community's deep influence both locally and nationally: the list includes prestigious figures in the Koryŏ bureaucracy, as well as high generals in the military and wives of major officials. (See pp. 44–45 for an examination of these donors and the implicit influence of Susŏn sa on Koryŏ society which their patronage shows.) Further expansions and reconstructions took place in 1212, 1400, 1420, 1601, 1609, 1660–1720, 1842, 1924–1928, and 1955. By 1631, the temple had expanded to more than 2,152 *kan* of structures; see Rhi Ki-yong (ed.), *Songgwang sa,* pp. 36–42, for discussion. Songgwang sa appears at *TYS* 40, fol. 7b, p. 702a.

167. From the *Chin'gak kuksa si chip,* quoted in Yi Chong-ik, *Chogye chong chunghŭng non,* p. 77; I have been unable to obtain a copy of the *Si chip* to check the reference. This work is discussed by Nukariya Kaiten, *Chōsen Zenkyōshi,* pp. 300–305.

168. The historicity of many of these masters—especially numbers seven through nine—has been questioned by several scholars. See: Han Ki-du, "Koryŏ Pulgyo ŭi

kyŏlsa undong," pp. 560–570; Rhi Ki-yong (ed.), *Songgwang sa,* pp. 77–98, for the most accessible treatment of these teachers; Nukariya Kaiten, *Chōsen Zenkyōshi,* p. 264. The sixteen national masters are listed in the *Sŭngp'yŏng pu Songgwang sa sajŏk pi, Pulgyo t'ongsa* III, p. 350.4–5. Table 3 is a composite of information culled from all these sources.

169. Quoted by Im Sŏk-chin, *Songgwang sa chi,* p. 161.

170. T'ongdo sa, where Buddha-*śarīra* are enshrined, is the Buddha-jewel temple; Haein sa, where the woodblocks of the Korean *Tripiṭaka* are stored, is the Dharma-jewel temple. Both temples are treated in the *Han'guk ŭi sach'al* series edited by Rhi Ki-yong and Hwang Su-yŏng.

171. See Ankul C. Banerjee, *Sarvāstivāda Literature,* p. 30; Charles Prebish and Janine Nattier, "*Mahāsāmghika* Origins: The Beginnings of Buddhist Sectarianism," pp. 237–272; Nalinaksha Dutt, *Buddhist Sects in India,* p. 32. This is not to minimize the ideological conflicts visible in the eighteen schools of the early church; their controversies do, however, pale when compared with the dissension which racked the later tradition.

172. See discussion in Edward Conze, *Buddhist Thought in India,* pp. 195–204; Lalmani Joshi, *Studies in the Buddhistic Culture of India,* p. 5.

173. For an excellent summary of this process, see Arthur F. Wright, *Buddhism in Chinese History,* pp. 42–64; for a general discussion of this adaptation see Kenneth Ch'en, *The Chinese Transformation of Buddhism.*

174. For background on Ch'an/Hua-yen rapprochement, see Kamata Shigeo, *Chūgoku Kegon shisōshi no kenkyū,* p. 476 ff.; Takamine Ryōshū, *Kegon to Zen to no tsūro,* pp. 67–124. See Yi Chong-ik, "Pojo kuksa ŭi Sŏn'gyogwan," pp. 76–78, for the rapprochement in Korea.

175. U Chŏng-sang ("Sŏsan taesa ŭi Sŏn'gyogwan e taehayŏ," p. 475, n. 12) gives extensive information and references to the following Ch'an monks, all of whom advocated a rapprochement between Ch'an and the scholastic schools: the Sixth Patriarch's disciple, Nan-yang Hui-chung (d. 775); Ch'ang-sha Ching-ts'en (n.d.); Fa-yen Wen-i (885–958); Yung-ming Yen-shou (904–975); and Yün-feng Miao-kao (1219–1293).

176. See the discussion in Chang Chung-yüan, *The Original Teachings of Ch'an Buddhism,* pp. xiii and 229–237; and compare Sung-peng Hsu, *A Buddhist Leader in Ming China: The Life and Thought of Han-shan Te-ch'ing,* pp. 36–52.

177. See the passage translated above in the "Pomun sa: Second Awakening" section.

178. This is the judgment of two modern Korean Buddhologists: Pak Chong-hong (*Han'guk sasang sa,* p. 193) and Yi Chong-ik (*Chogye chong chunghŭng non,* p. 90). Yi Chong-ik (p. 108) even goes so far as to state that Chinul succeeded in merging the scholastic penchant of the core Indian tradition with the uniquely Chinese Ch'an sect and the remaining schools of the heavily sectarian Chinese tradition, thereby establishing the ecumenical Buddhism of Korea. This claim is somewhat polemical, but it does show the high esteem in which Chinul is held by many Korean scholars.

179. Chinul explicitly states in *DCSPR,* Part III, Radical Analysis and Compre-

hensive Assimilation ("Vindicating the Sŏn Approach" section) that Sŏn might employ the scholastic teachings to explicate the principles of practice and enlightenment, but unlike the doctrinal schools it is not limited to those expressions. Hence, for Chinul, the scholastic teachings have their function but Sŏn is the superior approach.

180. In conversations I have had with contemporary Sŏn masters in Korea, including the Haein sa master Sŏngch'ŏl and his probable successor Ilt'a, this lack of a legitimate transmission as well as the fact that Chinul did not leave the incumbent enlightenment poem (included in Chinul's lost *Pŏbŏ kasong?*) are often mentioned when doubts about the validity of Chinul's approach are raised. Hence Sŏn advocates often consider T'aego Pou (1301–1382), whose Lin-chi credentials are impeccable, to be the ancestor of the Korean Sŏn lineage. Nevertheless, I believe it is clear that, all questions of lineage aside, Sŏn *thought* certainly finds its source in Chinul. See the definitive study by Sŏk Sŏngch'ŏl, *Han'guk Pulgyo ŭi pŏmmaek,* for all discussion on the Korean Chogye lineage; no other modern Korean scholar can claim his wide knowledge of scriptural and epigraphical materials. For T'aego Pou's life and thought see Han Ki-du, "Koryŏ hogi ŭi Sŏn sasang," 597–613, and his *Han'guk Pulgyo sasang,* pp. 243–273.

181. For accounts of these five schools based on traditional materials see: Chung-yüan Chang, *Original Teachings of Ch'an Buddhism;* Kuan-yü Lu, *Ch'an and Zen Teachings,* vol. 2, pp. 57–228; and Heinrich Dumoulin, *A History of Zen Buddhism,* pp. 106–122.

182. A useful term, coined by Jan Yün-hua, to refer to the period following the six orthodox patriarchs of the Ch'an tradition but before the systematization of the school into five major sects; see Jan, "Tsung-mi: His Analysis of Ch'an Buddhism," p. 4.

183. Information on Tsung-mi's life and thought and his syncretic attitude toward the Ch'an schools of his time can be found in a useful series of articles by Jan Yün-hua: "Tsung-mi: His Analysis of Ch'an Buddhism"; "Conflict and Harmony in Ch'an and Buddhism"; *"K'an Hui* or the 'Comparative Investigation': The Key Concept in Tsung-mi's Thought"; "Antagonism Among the Religious Sects and the Problem of Buddhist Tolerance"; "Tsung-mi's Questions Regarding the Confucian Absolute." Also worth consulting are the dissertations by Jeffrey Broughton, "Kuei-feng Tsung-mi: The Convergence of Ch'an and the Teachings," and Peter Gregory, "Tsung-mi's *Inquiry into the Origin of Man:* A Study of Chinese Buddhist Hermeneutics." In Japanese, Kamata Shigeo's work, *Shūmitsu kyōgaku no shisōshi teki kenkyū,* is in a class by itself; useful information on Tsung-mi's syncretic attitudes can also be found in Takamine Ryōshū's *Kegon to Zen to no tsūro,* pp. 22–35.

184. *Yüan-chüeh ching ta-shu ch'ao (YCCTSC)* 3b, pp. 532c–535b. See also the partial translation in Jan Yün-hua, "Tsung-mi," pp. 41–50.

185. As an example of the important Ch'an lineages which Tsung-mi does not mention in *YCCTSC,* the school of Ch'ing-yüan Hsing-ssu (d. 740), which evolved into the later Ts'ao-tung, Yün-men, and Fa-yen schools, can be given. As Yampolsky observes, (*Platform Sutra,* p. 54), its origins are obscure. Tsung-mi's *Ch'an-yüan chu-ch'üan-chi tou-hsü (CYCTH* 1, p. 400b–c) states that the body of the book

would cover one hundred masters divided into ten major schools; unfortunately, everything except the preface has been lost. I agree with the conclusions reached by Jan Yün-hua, following the lead of Sekiguchi Shindai, which support traditional claims for the existence of the hundred-fascicle main body of this work; see his article, "Two Problems Concerning Tsung-mi's Compilation of *Ch'an-tsang,*" pp. 37–47.

186. *CHT* parallels passages from the *PCPHN* text of Tsung-mi's included in Chinul's *Excerpts;* it is translated in full elsewhere in this book. For schematic charts comparing the treatment of the schools in the *CHT* and *PCPHN* with the different classifications in Tsung-mi's *CYCTH* and *YCCTSC,* see Kamata, *Shūmitsu kyō-gaku,* p. 296, and Kim Ing-sŏk, "Puril Pojo kuksa," p. 32.

187. These two important concepts are discussed at length in *DCSPR,* especially in these sections: "The Approaches of Dharma and Person"; "Recapitulation of the Main Ideas in the *Special Practice Record*"; and "Awareness Is Only an Expedient Explanation." See also Tsung-mi's explanations in *CHT,* p. 872a.10–14; Yŏndam Yuil's descriptions in *CYKM,* fol. 1a.4–5; and *Sŏnwon chip tosŏ so,* in Kamada, *Shūmitsu kyōgaku,* p. 277. The terms ultimately derive from the *Chao-lun* (see translation in Walter Liebenthal, *Chao Lun: the Treatises of Seng-chao,* pp. 106–107) and thence from the *Lao-tzu* (ibid., pp. 17–18).

188. See discussion in Yampolsky, *Platform Sutra,* p. 15.

189. Traditional views concerning the doctrines of the Northern school have been dramatically altered by the discovery of original documents in the Tun-huang caves. Scholarship in both Japan and the West on this school has burgeoned over the last several years and is rapidly filling in many details of the Northern school's perspective on Ch'an practice. At any rate, the school's doctrines appear not to have been merely gradual and not confined solely to the *Laṅkāvatāra-sūtra.* Rather, the Northern school apparently advocated a sophisticated approach to Buddhism involving both Hua-yen and *Prajñāpāramitā* teachings. There is evidence too that Shen-hsiu also used a sudden approach, reserving his gradual teachings for beginners; see Yampolsky, *Platform Sutra,* pp. 34–35. For the Northern school's Hua-yen connections, see Takamine Ryōshū, *Kegon to Zen to no tsūro,* pp. 67–75; Robert Zeuschner has contributed much to our understanding of the school in his excellent dissertation, "An Analysis of the Philosophical Criticisms of Northern Ch'an Buddhism."

190. *YCCTSC* 3b, p. 534c; partially quoted in Jan, "Tsung-mi," pp. 47–48.

191. Niu-t'ou Fa-jung's biography appears in Chang, *Original Teachings,* pp. 17–26; for the development of the school see John McRae's essay, "The Ox-head School of Ch'an Buddhism: From Early Ch'an to the Golden Age."

192. For Tsung-mi and Chinul's discussion of the Niu-t'ou school, see *DCSPR,* Part II, Review of the Four Sŏn Schools.

193. See Ishikawa Rikizan's article, "Baso kyōdan no tenkai to sono shijisha tachi," pp. 160–173, for an outline of the early development of the school. It is worth noting that the only other Ch'an school to survive the T'ang—the lineage which traces itself from Ch'ing-yüan Hsing-ssu—is of equally obscure origins. Its founder is virtually unknown, and whether such a monk even studied under Hui-neng cannot be verified. This school was based in Hunan, also deep in the country-

side. Indeed, the early isolation of these two schools probably contributed as much to their survival as any inherent superiority in their teachings; see Yampolsky, *Platform Sutra,* p. 54.

194. *CTL* 6, p. 246a.5.

195. See *DCSPR,* Part II, Review of the Four Sŏn Schools ("Chinul's Exposition" section) for the discussion; the *Preface* quotation which is relevant here appears in *CYCTH* 2, pp. 402c–403a.

196. See Ch'en, *Buddhism in China,* pp. 353–355, and Yampolsky, *Platform Sutra,* pp. 23–38, for details.

197. See Kamata Shigeo, "Chōsen oyobi Nihon Bukkyō ni oyoboshita Shūmitsu no eikyō," pp. 28–37, for a discussion.

198. See the notice in Ŭich'ŏn's *Kang Wŏn'gak kyŏng palsa,* in *Taegak kuksa munjip* 3.

199. See *CHT,* p. 871b; translated partially in Jan, "Tsung-mi," p. 50. For the following discussion, see *DCSPR,* Part II.

200. For example, at *Shen-hui ho-shang i-chi,* pp. 128–129, translated partially by Yampolsky, *Platform Sutra,* p. 33.

201. Tsung-mi's *CYCTH* is one of the works included in the *Sajip* collection, the basic textbook of the Korean monastic educational system even today. Since Chinul's *DCSPR,* which is an exposition of another of Tsung-mi's writings, is included in the same collection, fully half the fundamental texts of the Korean Buddhist doctrinal structure derive from Tsung-mi.

202. For outlines of the *Avataṃsaka Sūtra* see: Yutsugu Ryōei, *Kegon taikei,* pp. 155–161; Li T'ung-hsüan's *Ta-fang-kuang Fo Hua-yen ching-chung chüan-chüan ta-i lüeh-hsü, T* 1740.36.1008c–1011b, for a fascicle-by-fascicle summary of the eighty-*chüan* edition of the text; Nakamura Hajime, "A Critical Survey of Mahāyāna and Esoteric Buddhism Chiefly Based on Japanese Studies," pp. 36–42; D. T. Suzuki, *Essays in Zen Buddhism,* vol. 3, pp. 70–221, who also discusses the major philosophical issues of the *sūtra,* especially as they relate to Zen practice.

203. The ten faiths, although not an explicit stage in the account of the path of practice found in the *Avataṃsaka Sūtra* proper, were added to the Hua-yen school's explication of the path by Fa-tsang (643–712), who adopted the scheme from the *She ta-ch'eng lun (Mahāyānasaṅgraha);* see Nakamura Hajime and Kawada Kumatarō (eds.), *Kegon shisō,* p. 28. Kuan-ting notes (*T'ien-t'ai pa-chiao ta-i, T* 1930.46.771b.8–9) that the ten faiths first appear as the initial level of the seven stages of the path outlined in the *P'u-sa ying-lo pen-ye ching;* see *T* 1485.24.1011c.4–7. See the insightful discussion in Jae Ryong Shim, "The Philosophical Foundation of Korean Zen Buddhism: The Integration of *Sŏn* and *Kyo* by Chinul," pp. 28–34.

204. *HHYCL* 7, pp. 763c–764a; see also Chinul's *Hwaŏmnon chŏryo,* pp. 224–229. For a descriptive account of these five stages of the path see Chang Won-gyu, "Hwaŏm kyŏng ŭi sasang ch'egye wa kŭ chŏn'gae," pp. 35–40.

205. *HHYCL* 5, p. 752c.2–3; *Hwaŏmnon chŏryo,* p. 167.

206. See the account in the preface to Li's *Hsin Hua-yen ching hsiu-hsing ts'e-ti chüeh-i lun, T* 1741.36.1011c.

207. Pei-ching is the name which T'ai-yüan fu in Shansi province received in 742; *Ta-ch'ing chia-ch'ing ch'ung-hsiu i-t'ung-chih,* fasc. 136, T'ai-yüan fu 1.2a. Fang shan was located in Yang-ch'ü hsien, T'ai-yüan fu (fasc. 136, T'ai-yüan fu 1.8b).

208. Despite Li T'ung-hsüan's importance in the history of post-T'ang East Asian Buddhism, he has been surprisingly neglected by modern scholars. For short exegeses of his life and thought, see: Kim Ing-sŏk, *Hwaŏmhak kaeron,* pp. 131–146; Takamine Ryōshū, *Kegon ronshū,* pp. 403–426; idem, *Kegon shisōshi,* pp. 200–208; idem, *Kegon to Zen to no tsūro,* pp. 131–146, which is the best treatment of his significance for the later development of Ch'an thought; Chang Won-gyu, "Hwaŏm kyohak wansŏnggi ŭi sasang yon'gu," pp. 41–43; Yi Chong-ik, "Chinul ŭi Hwaŏm sasang," pp. 528–532, for his importance in Chinul's thought. Robert Gimello of the University of Arizona is the Western scholar who has paid the most attention to Li's thought in recounting the later development of East Asian Buddhist philosophy. For Li's traditional biography see *Sung kao-seng chuan* 23, *T* 2061.50.853c.3–854b.

209. Kim Ing-sŏk, *Hwaŏmhak kaeron,* p. 133.

210. For the theory of the conditioned arising of the *dharmadhātu,* see Kim Ing-sŏk, *Hwaŏmhak kaeron,* pp. 192–213.

211. In his *Hua-yen i-ch'eng chiao-i fen-ch'i chang* 2, *T* 1866.45.489c.4–15. Discussed also in Jae Ryong Shim, "Philosophical Foundation of Korean Zen Buddhism," pp. 30–32.

212. Kim Ing-sŏk, *Hwaŏmhak kaeron,* p. 133. This fact is noted also at Jae Ryong Shim, "Philosophical Foundation of Korean Zen Buddhism," p. 42.

213. See the discussion in Yi Chong-ik, "Chinul ŭi Hwaŏm sasang," pp. 4–5. For Sudhana's pilgrimage and its implications for East Asian Buddhist thought see Jan Fontein's work, *The Pilgrimage of Sudhana.*

214. Tsung-mi identifies this theory with the approach of the Mahāyāna inception teachings; see his *Yüan-chüeh ching lüeh shu chu* 2, *T* 1795.39.546c, and compare *She ta-ch'eng lun* 3, *T* 1593.31.126c.

215. *HHYCL* 7, p. 761b.13 ff.; *Hwaŏmnon chŏryo,* p. 210. Noted by Jae Ryong Shim, "Philosophical Foundation of Korean Zen Buddhism," p. 43.

216. See *Complete and Sudden Attainment of Buddhahood;* and *HHYCL* 14, p. 809b.

217. For the theory of nature origination see: Kamata Shigeo, "Shōki shisō no seiritsu," pp. 195–198; Sakamoto Yukio, "Shōki shisō to aku ni tsuite," pp. 469–477; Endō Kōjirō, "Kegon shōki ronkō," pp. 214–216 and 523–527; and for an adequate general discussion, see Kim Ing-sŏk, *Hwaŏmhak kaeron,* pp. 213–230. See also Whalen Lai, "Chinese Buddhist Causation Theories," pp. 249–259.

218. See Chinul's discussion in *Complete and Sudden Attainment of Buddhahood* and *DCSPR,* Part III, Radical Analysis and Comprehensive Assimilation. For the correlation between the two theories of conditioned origination and nature origination see Kim Ing-sŏk, *Hwaŏmhak kaeron,* pp. 230–239. Jae Ryong Shim has written an excellent account of Chinul's interpretation of nature origination in Li T'unghsüan's thought and its ramifications for Chinul's reconciliation of the Sŏn and scholastic schools; see his dissertation, "The Philosophical Foundation of Korean Zen Buddhism" pp. 28–48, 62–70, which I, unfortunately, did not learn about until

after the completion of my own work. Shim's thesis should be consulted for a more thorough explication of the Hwaŏm aspects of Chinul's thought than I am able to give here in this brief outline.

219. *HHYCL* 32, p. 941b.

220. *DCSPR,* Part III, Radical Analysis and Comprehensive Assimilation ("Vindicating the Sŏn approach" section).

221. For this account see especially *Secrets on Cultivating the Mind,* and *DCSPR,* Part II, Sudden Awakening and Gradual Cultivation ("Sudden awakening" section); see *CHT,* p. 874a–b.

222. See *Secrets on Cultivating the Mind; DCSPR,* Part III, The Patriarchs' Assessments of Sudden and Gradual ("Sudden and Gradual as Related to Spiritual Capacity: Gradualness" section). See also Tsung-mi, *CYCTH* 3, p. 407c; *YCCTSC* 3b, p. 535c.

223. *DCSPR,* Part III, The Patriarchs' Assessments of Sudden and Gradual ("Ch'eng-kuan's *Chen-yüan Commentary*" section).

224. *DCSPR,* Part III, The Patriarchs' Assessments of Sudden and Gradual ("Chinul's Critique of Suddenness" section).

225. *DCSPR,* Part III, The Patriarchs' Assessments of Sudden and Gradual ("Problems in Tsung-mi's Statements About Gradualness" section).

226. *DCSPR,* Part III, The Patriarchs' Assessments of Sudden and Gradual ("Yen-shou's Assessment of Sudden and Gradual" section).

227. *DCSPR,* Part III, The Patriarch's Assessments of Sudden and Gradual ("Problems in Tsung-mi's Statements About Gradualness" section).

228. *DCSPR,* Part III, The Patriarchs' Assessments of Sudden and Gradual ("Ch'eng-kuan's Divisions of Sudden and Gradual" section).

229. *Pojo kuksa pimyŏng, Chosŏn Pulgyo t'ongsa* III, p. 339.4–5.

230. Noted by Yi Chong-ik, *Chogye chong chunghŭng non,* p. 89.

231. *CYCTH* 1, p. 399a.

232. For accounts of the development and practices of Hwaŏm meditation see Kobayashi Jitsugen, "Kegonshū kangyō no tenkai ni tsuite," pp. 653–655, and Teitatsu Unno, "The Dimensions of Practice in Hua-yen Thought," p. 53 ff.

233. For the significance of this term in Li T'ung-hsüan's thought see Takamine Ryōshū, *Kegon to Zen to no tsūro,* pp. 101–102.

234. According to the explanation given by Chung-feng Ming-pen (1263–1323), translated in Miura and Sasaki, *Zen Dust,* p. 6. For the historical development of *k'ung-an* practice in Ch'an Buddhism, see *Zen Dust,* pp. 3–16; idem, *The Zen Koan,* pp. 3–16; Heinrich Dumoulin, *A History of Zen Buddhism,* pp. 127–129.

235. See, for example, *LCL,* p. 506b.8; *CTL* 19, p. 358c.14; *Pi-yen lu* 1, case 2, *T* 2003.48.141c.6; 5, case 49, p. 184c.14; 6, case 60, p. 192b.5.

236. See discussion in P. S. Jaini, *Abhidharmadīpa,* p. 84.

237. See Yüan-wu's commentary in *Pi-yen lu* 10, case 99, *T* 2003.48.222c.18, where he states that Ch'an exchanges—and by extension the *hwadus* which develop from them—break up the activating consciousness [*karmajāti(lakṣaṇa)vijñāna*].

238. *TCCHL,* p. 577b; Hakeda, *Faith,* pp. 47–48.

239. The *Sŏnmun yŏmsong chip* was an anthology of 1,125 *kongans* in thirty fas-

cicles, compiled by Hyesim in 1226. Beginning with stories concerning Śākyamuni Buddha, the work includes *sūtra* extracts, cases involving the twenty-eight traditional Indian patriarchs and their six Chinese successors, and accounts of episodes in the lives of subsequent Ch'an masters. To each case are appended descriptive verses by Hyesim himself and other Ch'an teachers. The first edition of the text was burned by the Mongols and the revised editions of 1244 and 1248 added 347 new cases, making a total of 1,472 *kongans.* For a brief description of the work and its different editions, see Pulgyo munhwa yŏn'guso, *Han'guk Pulgyo ch'ansul munhŏn ch'ongnok,* pp. 123–124.

240. See *DCSPR,* note 101, for this term and its development.

241. For the theory of no-mind and its development in Sŏn and its significance to Chinul's thought, see Yi Chong-ik, "Chosasŏn e issŏsŏ ŭi musim sasang," pp. 239–243; Suzuki, *The Zen Doctrine of No-mind;* and Yampolsky, *Platform Sutra,* pp. 137–138, n. 69.

242. For further information on this process, see the fascinating discussions in Bhikkhu Ñāṇananda, *Concept and Reality,* pp. 2–22, and *Magic of the Mind,* pp. 57–67.

243. See the preface to my translation for discussion of problems surrounding Chinul's authorship of the text. The work has been treated by Ono Gemmyō in *Bukkyō no bijutsu to rekishi,* p. 1213 ff., and by Minamoto Hiroyuki in "Kōrai jidai ni okeru Jōdokyō no kenkyū: Chitotsu no *Nembutsu yōmon* no tsuite," pp. 90–94.

244. For the schemes of Ch'eng-kuan and Tsung-mi, see Mochizuki Shinkō, *Shina Jōdo kyōrishi,* pp. 306–314.

Secrets on Cultivating the Mind

SUSIM KYŎL

SECRETS ON CULTIVATING THE MIND, an outline of basic Sŏn practices, was written by Chinul between 1203 and 1205 to instruct the throngs coming to the newly completed Susŏn sa. A seminal text of the Sŏn school, *Secrets* presents simple yet cogent descriptions of two important elements of Chinul's thought—sudden awakening/gradual cultivation and the simultaneous practice of *samādhi* and *prajñā*—interspersed with edifying words to encourage Buddhist students in their practice. Although *Secrets* was lost in Korea after the destruction wrought by the Mongol invasions two decades after Chinul's death, it was preserved in the Northern Ming edition of the *tripiṭaka,* produced in the early fifteenth century. Reintroduced into Korea around that time, it was translated in 1467 into the Korean vernacular language using the newly invented *han'gŭl* alphabet. It remains one of the most popular Sŏn texts in Korea today.

The triple world is blazing in defilement as if it were a house on fire.[1] How can you bear to tarry here and complacently undergo such long suffering? If you wish to avoid wandering in *saṃsāra* there is no better way than to seek Buddhahood. If you want to become a Buddha, understand that Buddha is the mind. How can you search for the mind in the far distance? It is not outside the body. The physical body is a phantom, for it is subject to birth and death; the true mind is like space, for it neither ends nor changes. Therefore it is said, "These hundred bones will crumble and return to fire and wind. But One Thing is eternally numinous and covers heaven and earth."[2]

It is tragic. People have been deluded for so long. They do not recognize that their own minds are the true Buddhas. They do not recognize that their own natures are the true dharma. They want to search for the dharma, yet they still look far away for holy ones. They want to search for the Buddha, yet they will not observe their own minds. If they aspire to the path of Buddhahood while obstinately holding to their feeling that the Buddha is outside the mind or the dharma is outside the nature, then, even though they pass through kalpas as numerous as dust motes, burning their bodies, charring their arms, crushing their bones and exposing their marrow, or else write *sūtras* with their own blood, never lying down to sleep, eating only one offering a day at the hour of the Hare [5 to 7 A.M.], or even studying through the entire *tripiṭaka* and cultivating all sorts of ascetic practices, it is like trying to make rice by boiling sand—it will only add to their tribulation.[3] If they would only understand their own minds, then, without searching, approaches to dharma as numerous as the sands of the Ganges and uncountable sublime meanings would all be understood. As the World Honored One said, "I see that all sentient beings everywhere are endowed with a *tathāgata*'s wisdom and virtue."[4] He also said, "All the illusory guises in which sentient beings appear take shape in the sublime mind of the *tathāgata*'s complete enlightenment."[5] Consequently, you should know that outside this mind there is no Buddhahood which can be attained. All the Buddhas of the past were merely persons who understood their minds. All the sages and saints of the present are likewise merely persons who have cultivated their minds. All future meditators should rely on this dharma as well.

I hope that you who cultivate the path will never search outside. The nature of the mind is unstained; it is originally whole and complete in itself. If you will only leave behind false conditioning, you will be "such" like the Buddha.[6]

Question: If you say that the Buddha-nature exists in the body right now, then, since it is in the body, it is not separate from us ordinary men. So why can we not see this Buddha-nature now? Please explain this further to enlighten us on this point.

Chinul: It is in your body, but you do not see it. Ultimately, what is that thing which during the twelve periods of the day knows hunger and thirst, cold and heat, anger and joy? This physical body is a synthesis of four conditions: earth, water, fire, and wind. Since matter is passive and insentient, how can it see, hear, sense, and know? That which is able to see, hear, sense, and know is perforce your Buddha-nature. For this reason, Lin-chi said, "The four great elements do not know how to expound dharma or listen to dharma. Empty space does not know how to expound dharma or listen to dharma. It is only that formless thing before your eyes, clear and bright of itself, which knows how to expound dharma or listen to dharma."[7] This "formless thing" is the dharma-seal of all the Buddhas; it is your original mind. Since this Buddha-nature exists in your body right now, why do you vainly search for it outside?

In case you cannot accept this, I will mention some of the events surrounding a few of the ancient saints' entrance onto the path. These should allow you to resolve your doubts. Listen carefully and try to believe.

Once long ago, a king who believed in a heterodox doctrine asked the Venerable Bharati:

"What is the Buddha?"
The venerable answered, "Seeing the nature is Buddha."
The king asked, "Has the master seen the nature yet, or not?"
The venerable answered, "Yes, I have seen the Buddha-nature."
"Where is the Buddha-nature?"
"This nature is present during the performance of actions."
"During what performance of action? I can't see it now."
"It appears in this present performance of action; your majesty just doesn't see it."
"But do I have it too, or not?"
"If your majesty performs actions, there are none in which it is not present. If your majesty were not acting, its essence would be very difficult to see."
"But when one acts, at how many places does it appear?"
"It appears in eight different places."
"Would you describe these eight places?"
"In the womb it is called a fetus. On being born it is called a person. In the eyes it is called seeing and in the ears it is called hearing. In the nose it smells, in the tongue it talks, in the hands it grasps, and in the feet it runs. When it is expanded, it contains worlds as numerous as grains of sand. When it is compressed, it exists within one minute particle of dust. Those who have recognized it know that it is the Buddha-nature; those who have not call it soul or spirit."
As the king listened, his mind opened into awakening.[8]

In another case, a monk asked the master Kuei-tsung:

"What is the Buddha?"
The master answered, "I will tell you, but I'm afraid you won't believe me."
"How could I dare not believe the sincere words of the master?"
The master said, "It's you!"
"How can you prove it?"
"If there is one eyelash in your eye, flowers in the sky will fall everywhere."
The monk heard this and understood.[9]

These stories I have just told about the saints of old entering the path are clear and simple; they do not strain the powers of comprehension. If you gain some faith and understanding from these two *kongan,* you will walk hand in hand with the saints of old.

Question: You talked about seeing the nature. But when there is true seeing of the nature, the person becomes an enlightened saint and should be able to perform magic and miracles—he would be different from other people. How is it, then, that among those who cultivate the mind nowadays, not one can display these spiritual powers and transformation bodies?

Chinul: You should not utter absurdities lightly; to be unable to differentiate the perverse from the noble is to be deluded and confused. Nowadays, you people who are training on the path chat about truth with your mouth, but in your minds you only shrink from it and end up falling into the error of underestimating yourselves by thinking that you do not share in the Buddha-nature. This is all that you are doubting. You train on the path but do not know the proper sequence of practice. You talk about truth but do not distinguish the root from the branches. This is called wrong view; it is not called cultivation. You are not only deceiving yourselves; you are deceiving others too. How can you not be on your guard against this?

Now, there are many approaches to the path, but essentially they are included in the twofold approach of sudden awakening and gradual cultivation. Although sudden awakening/sudden cultivation has been advocated, this is the entrance for people of the highest faculties. If you were to probe their pasts, you would see that their cultivation has been based for many lives on the insights gained in a previous awakening. Now, in this life, after gradual permeation, these people hear the dharma and awaken: in one instant their practice is brought to a sudden conclusion. But if we try to explain this according to the facts, then sudden awakening/sudden cultivation is also the result of an initial awakening and its subsequent cultivation. Consequently, this twofold approach of sudden awakening and gradual cultivation is the track followed by thousands of saints. Hence, of all the saints of old, there were none who did not first have an awakening, subsequently cultivate it, and finally, because of their cultivation, gain realization.

The so-called magic and miracles you mentioned manifest because of the gradual permeation of cultivation based on an initial awakening; it should not be said that they appear simultaneous with that awakening. As it is said in the *sūtras,* "The noumenon is awakened to suddenly, and is forged in accordance with this awakening. Phenomena cannot be removed suddenly; they are brought to an end step by step."[10] For this reason, Kuei-feng, in a profound explanation of the meaning of initial awakening/subsequent cultivation, said,

> Although we know that a frozen pond is entirely water, the sun's heat is necessary to melt it. Although we awaken to the fact that an ordinary man is Buddha, the power of dharma is necessary to make it permeate our cultivation. When that pond has melted, the water flows freely and can be used for irrigation and cleaning. When falsity is extinguished, the mind will be numinous and dynamic and then its function of penetrating brightness will manifest.[11]

These quotations should make it clear that the ability to perform magic and miracles in the phenomenal sphere cannot be perfected in a day: it will manifest only after gradual permeation.

Moreover, in the case of accomplished men, phenomenal spiritual powers are like an eerie apparition; they are only a minor concern of the saints. Although they might perform them, they do not give them undue emphasis. Nowadays, deluded and ignorant people wrongly assume that in the one moment of awakening, incalculable sublime functions, as well as magic and miracles, manifest in tandem. This is the sort of understanding I was referring to when I said that you did not know the proper sequence of practice and did not distinguish the root from the branches. To seek the path to Buddhahood while not knowing the proper sequence of practice or the root and the branches is like trying to put a square peg into a round hole. Can this be anything but a grave mistake? Because such people do not know of any expedients, they hesitate as if they were facing a steep precipice and end up backsliding. Alas, many have broken their ties with the spiritual family of the Buddha in this manner. Since they neither understand for themselves nor believe that others have had an understanding-awakening, when they see someone without spiritual powers they act insolently, ridiculing the sages and insulting the saints. This is really quite pitiful!

Question: You have said that this twofold approach of sudden awakening/ gradual cultivation is the track followed by thousands of saints. But if awakening is really sudden awakening, what need is there for gradual cultivation? And if cultivation means gradual cultivation, how can you speak of sudden awakening? We hope that you will expound further on these two ideas of sudden and gradual and resolve our remaining doubts.

Chinul: First let us take sudden awakening. When the ordinary man is deluded, he assumes that the four great elements are his body and the false thoughts are his mind. He does not know that his own nature is the true dharma-body; he does not know that his own numinous awareness is the true Buddha. He looks for the Buddha outside his mind. While he is thus wandering aimlessly, the entrance to the road might by chance be pointed out by a wise advisor. If in one thought he then follows back the light [of his mind to its source] and sees his own original nature, he will discover that the ground of this nature is innately free of defilement, and that he himself is originally endowed with the non-outflow wisdom-nature which is not a hair's breadth different from that of all the Buddhas. Hence it is called sudden awakening.

Next let us consider gradual cultivation. Although he has awakened to the fact that his original nature is no different from that of the Buddhas, the beginningless habit-energies are extremely difficult to remove suddenly and so he must continue to cultivate while relying on this awakening. Through this gradual permeation, his endeavors reach completion. He constantly nurtures the sacred embryo,[12] and after a long time he becomes a saint. Hence it is called gradual cultivation.

This process can be compared to the maturation of a child. From the day of its birth, a baby is endowed with all the sense organs just like everyone else, but its strength is not yet fully developed. It is only after many months and years that it will finally become an adult.

Question: Through what expedients is it possible to trace back the radiance of one's sense-faculties in one thought and awaken to the self-nature?

Chinul: The self-nature is just your own mind. What other expedients do you need? If you ask for expedients to seek understanding, you are like a person who, because he does not see his own eyes, assumes that he has no eyes and decides to find some way to see. But since he does have eyes, how else is he supposed to see? If he realizes that in fact he has never lost his eyes, this is the same as seeing his eyes, and no longer would he waste his time trying to find a way to see. How then could he have any thoughts that he could not see? Your own numinous awareness is exactly the same. Since this awareness is your own mind, how else are you going to understand? If you seek some other way to understand, you will never understand. Simply by knowing that there is no other way to understand, you are seeing the nature.

Question: When the superior man hears dharma, he understands easily. Average and inferior men, however, are not without doubt and confusion. Could you describe some expedients so that the deluded too can enter into enlightenment?

Chinul: The path is not related to knowing or not knowing.[13] You should get rid of the mind which clings to its delusion and looks forward to enlightenment, and listen to me.

Since all dharmas are like dreams or phantoms, deluded thoughts are originally calm and the sense-spheres are originally void. At the point where all dharmas are void, the numinous awareness is not obscured. That is to say, this mind of void and calm, numinous awareness is your original face. It is also the dharma-seal transmitted without a break by all the Buddhas of the three time periods, the successive generations of patriarchs, and the wise advisors of this world. If you awaken to this mind, then this is truly what is called not following the rungs of a ladder: you climb straight to the stage of Buddhahood, and each step transcends the triple world. Returning home, your doubts will be instantly resolved and you will become the teacher of men and gods. Endowed with compassion and wisdom and complete in the twofold benefit, you will be worthy of receiving the offerings of men and gods. Day after day you can use ten thousand taels of gold without incurring debt. If you can do this, you will be a truly great man who has indeed finished the tasks of this life.

Question: In our case, what is this mind of void and calm, numinous awareness?

Chinul: What has just asked me this question is precisely your mind of void and calm, numinous awareness. Why not trace back its radiance rather than search for it outside? For your benefit I will now point straight to your original mind so that you can awaken to it. Clear your minds and listen to my words.

From morning to evening, throughout the twelve periods of the day, during all your actions and activities—whether seeing, hearing, laughing, talking, whether angry or happy, whether doing good or evil—ultimately who is it that is able to perform all these actions? Speak! If you say that it is the physical body which is acting, then at the moment when a man's life comes to an end, even though the body has not yet decayed, how is it that the eyes cannot see, the ears cannot hear, the nose cannot smell, the tongue cannot talk, the body cannot move, the hands cannot grasp, and the feet cannot run? You should know that what is capable of seeing, hearing, moving, and acting has to be your original mind; it is not your physical body. Furthermore, the four elements which make up the physical body are by nature void; they are like images in a mirror or the moon's reflection in water. How can they be clear and constantly aware, always bright and never obscured— and, upon activation, be able to put into operation sublime functions as numerous as the sands of the Ganges? For this reason it is said, "Drawing water and carrying firewood are spiritual powers and sublime functions."[14]

There are many points at which to enter the noumenon.[15] I will indicate one approach which will allow you to return to the source.

Chinul: Do you hear the sounds of that crow cawing and that magpie calling?

Student: Yes.

Chinul: Trace them back and listen to your hearing-nature. Do you hear any sounds?

Student: At that place, sounds and discriminations do not obtain.

Chinul: Marvelous! Marvelous! This is Avalokiteśvara's method for entering the noumenon.[16] Let me ask you again. You said that sounds and discriminations do not obtain at that place. But since they do not obtain, isn't the hearing-nature just empty space at such a time?

Student: Originally it is not empty. It is always bright and never obscured.

Chinul: What is this essence which is not empty?

Student: As it has no former shape, words cannot describe it.

This is the life force of all the Buddhas and patriarchs—have no further doubts about that. Since it has no former shape, how can it be large or small? Since it cannot be large or small, how can it have limitations? Since it has no limitations, it cannot have inside or outside. Since there is no inside or outside, there is no far or near. As there is no far or near, there is no here or there. As there is no here or there, there is no coming or going. As there is no coming or going, there is no birth or death. As there is no birth or death, there is no past or present. As there is no past or present, there is no delusion or awakening. As there is no delusion or awakening, there is no ordinary man or saint. As there is no ordinary man or saint, there is no purity or impurity. Since there is no impurity or purity, there is no right or wrong. Since there is no right or wrong, names and words do not apply to it. Since none of these concepts apply, all sense-bases and sense-objects, all deluded thoughts, even forms and shapes and names and words are all inapplicable. Hence how can it be anything but originally void and calm and originally no-thing?

Nevertheless, at that point where all dharmas are empty, the numinous awareness is not obscured. It is not the same as insentience, for its nature is spiritually deft. This is your pure mind-essence of void and calm, numinous awareness. This pure, void, and calm mind is that mind of outstanding purity and brilliance of all the Buddhas of the three time periods; it is that enlightened nature which is the original source of all sentient beings. One who awakens to it and safeguards that awakening will then abide in the unitary, "such" and unmoving liberation. One who is deluded and turns his back on it passes between the six destinies, wandering in *saṃsāra* for vast numbers of kalpas. As it is said, "One who is confused about the one mind and passes between the six destinies, goes and takes action. But one who awakens to the *dharmadhātu* and returns to the one mind, arrives and is still."[17] Although there is this distinction between delusion and awakening, in their basic source they are one. As it is said, "The word 'dharma' means the mind of the sentient being."[18] But as there is neither more of this void and calm mind in the saint, nor less of it in the ordinary man, it is also said, "In the wisdom of the saint it is no brighter; hidden in the mind of the ordinary man it is no darker." Since there is neither more of it in the saint nor less of it in the ordinary man, how are the Buddhas and patriarchs any different from other men? The only thing that makes them different is that they can protect their minds and thoughts—nothing more.

If you believe me to the point where you can suddenly extinguish your doubt, show the will of a great man and give rise to authentic vision and understanding, if you know its taste for yourself, arrive at the stage of self-affirmation and gain understanding of your true nature, then this is the understanding-awakening achieved by those who have cultivated the mind. Since no further steps are involved, it is called sudden. Therefore it is said, "When in the cause of faith one meshes without the slightest de-

gree of error with all the qualities of the fruition of Buddhahood, faith is
achieved."[19]

Question: Once the noumenon is awakened to, no further steps are
involved. Why then do you posit subsequent cultivation, gradual permeation, and gradual perfection?

Chinul: Earlier the meaning of gradual cultivation subsequent to awakening was fully explained. But since your feeling of doubt persists, it seems
that I will have to explain it again. Clear your minds and listen carefully!

For innumerable kalpas without beginning, up to the present time, ordinary men have passed between the five destinies, coming and going between
birth and death. They obstinately cling to "self" and, over a long period of
time, their natures have become thoroughly permeated by false thoughts,
inverted views, ignorance, and the habit-energies. Although, coming into
this life, they might suddenly awaken to the fact that their self-nature is
originally void and calm and no different from that of the Buddhas, these
old habits are difficult to eliminate completely. Consequently, when they
come into contact with either favorable or adverse objects, then anger and
happiness or propriety or impropriety blaze forth: their adventitious defilements are no different from before. If they do not increase their efforts and
apply their power through the help of *prajñā,* how will they ever be able to
counteract ignorance and reach the place of great rest and repose? As it is
said, "Although the person who has suddenly awakened is the same as the
Buddhas, the habit-energies which have built up over many lives are deep-
rooted. The wind ceases, but the waves still surge; the noumenon manifests,
but thoughts still invade." Sŏn Master Ta-hui Tsung-kao said:

> Often gifted people can break through this affair and achieve sudden awakening
> without expending a lot of strength. Then they relax and do not try to counteract
> the habit-energies and deluded thoughts. Finally, after the passage of many days
> and months, they simply wander on as before and are unable to avoid *saṃsāra.*[20]

So how could you neglect subsequent cultivation simply because of one
moment of awakening? After awakening, you must be constantly on your
guard. If deluded thoughts suddenly appear, do not follow after them—
reduce them and reduce them again until you reach the unconditioned.[21]
Then and only then will your practice reach completion. This is the practice
of herding the ox which all wise advisors in the world have practiced after
awakening.

Nevertheless, although you must cultivate further, you have already
awakened suddenly to the fact that deluded thoughts are originally void and
the mind-nature is originally pure. Thus you eliminate evil, but you eliminate without actually eliminating anything; you cultivate the wholesome,

but you cultivate without really cultivating anything either. This is true culti-vation and true elimination. For this reason it is said, "Although one pre-pares to cultivate the manifold supplementary practices, thoughtlessness is the origin of them all."[22] Kuei-feng summed up the distinction between the ideas of initial awakening and subsequent cultivation when he said:

> He has the sudden awakening to the fact that his nature is originally free of defile-ment and he is originally in full possession of the non-outflow wisdom-nature which is no different from that of the Buddhas. To cultivate while relying on this awakening is called supreme vehicle Sŏn, or the pure Sŏn of the *tathāgatas*. If thought-moment after thought-moment he continues to develop his training, then naturally he will gradually attain to hundreds of thousands of *samādhis*. This is the Sŏn which has been transmitted successively in the school of Bodhidharma.[23]

Hence sudden awakening and gradual cultivation are like the two wheels of a cart: neither one can be missing.

Some people do not realize that the nature of good and evil is void; they sit rigidly without moving and, like a rock crushing grass, repress both body and mind. To regard this as cultivation of the mind is a great delusion. For this reason it is said, "*Śrāvakas* cut off delusion thought after thought, but the thought which does this cutting is a brigand."[24] If they could see that killing, stealing, sexual misconduct, and lying all arise from the nature, then their arising would be the same as their nonarising. At their source they are calm; why must they be cut off? As it is said, "Do not fear the arising of thoughts: only be concerned lest your awareness of them be tardy."[25] It is also said, "If we are aware of a thought at the moment it arises, then through that awareness it will vanish."[26]

In the case of a person who has had an awakening, although he still has adventitious defilements, these have all been purified into cream. If he merely reflects on the fact that confusion is without basis, then all the flow-ers in the sky of this triple world are like smoke swirling in the wind and the six phantom sense-objects are like ice melting in hot water. If thought-moment after thought-moment he continues to train in this manner, does not neglect to maintain his training, and keeps *samādhi* and *prajñā* equally balanced, then lust and hatred will naturally fade away and compassion and wisdom will naturally increase in brightness; unwholesome actions will nat-urally cease and meritorious practices will naturally multiply. When defile-ments are exhausted, birth and death cease. When the subtle streams of defilement are forever cut off, the great wisdom of complete enlightenment exists brilliantly of itself. Then he will be able to manifest billions of trans-formation-bodies in all the worlds of the ten directions following his inspi-ration and responding to the faculties of sentient beings. Like the moon in the nine empyrean which reflects in ten thousand pools of water, there is no limit to his responsiveness. He will be able to ferry across all sentient beings with whom he has affinities. He will be happy and free of worry. Such a person is called a Great Enlightened World Honored One.

Question: In the approach of subsequent cultivation, we really do not yet understand the meaning of maintaining *samādhi* and *prajñā* equally. Could you expound on this point in detail, so that we can free ourselves of our delusion? Please lead us through the entrance to liberation.

Chinul: Suppose we consider these two dharmas and their attributes. Of the thousands of approaches to enter the noumenon there are none which do not involve *samādhi* and *prajñā*. Taking only the essential outline into account, from the standpoint of the self-nature they are characterized as essence and function—what I have called the void and the calm, numinous awareness. *Samādhi* is the essence; *prajñā* is the function. Since *prajñā* is the functioning of the essence, it is not separate from *samādhi*. Since *samādhi* is the essence of the function, it is not separate from *prajñā*. Since in *samādhi* there is *prajñā*, *samādhi* is calm yet constantly aware. Since in *prajñā* there is *samādhi*, *prajñā* is aware yet constantly calm. As Ts'ao-ch'i [the Sixth Patriarch Hui-neng] said, "The mind-ground which is without disturbance is the *samādhi* of the self-nature. The mind-ground which is without delusion is the *prajñā* of the self-nature."[27] If you have this sort of understanding, you can be calm and aware naturally in all situations. When enveloping and reflecting—the characteristics of *samādhi* and *prajñā* respectively—are not two, this is the sudden school's cultivation of *samādhi* and *prajñā* as a pair.

The practice of *samādhi* and *prajñā* intended for those of inferior faculties in the gradual school initially controls the thinking processes with calmness and subsequently controls dullness with alertness; finally, these initial and subsequent counteracting techniques subdue both the dull and the agitated mind in order to enter into stillness. Although this approach also holds that alertness and calmness should be maintained equally, its practice cannot avoid clinging to stillness. Hence how will it allow those who would understand the matter of birth and death never to leave the fundamental calm and fundamental awareness and cultivate *samādhi* and *prajñā* as a pair naturally in all situations? As Ts'ao-ch'i said, "The practice of self-awakening has nothing to do with arguing. If you argue about first and last, you are deluded."[28]

For an accomplished man, maintaining *samādhi* and *prajñā* equally does not involve endeavor, for he is always spontaneous and unconcerned about time or place. When seeing forms or hearing sounds, he is "just so." When wearing clothes or eating food, he is "just so." When defecating or urinating, he is "just so." When talking with people, he is "just so." At all times, whether speaking or keeping silent, whether joyful or angry, he is "just so." Like an empty boat riding on the waves which follows the crests and troughs, or like a torrent flowing through the mountains which follows the bends and straights, in his mind he is without intellection. Today, he is at peace naturally in all conditions without destruction or hindrance. Tomorrow, in all situations, he is naturally at peace. He follows all conditions without destruction or hindrance. He neither eliminates the unwholesome nor cultivates the wholesome. His character is straightforward and without deception. His seeing and hearing return to normal and there are no sense-objects to come in contact with [which could cause new defilements to arise]. Why should he have to bother with efforts at effacement? Since he has not a single thought which creates passion, he need not make an effort to forget all conditioning.

But hindrances are formidable and habits are deeply ingrained. Contemplation is weak and the mind drifts. The power of ignorance is great, but the power of *prajñā* is small. He still cannot avoid being alternately unmoved and upset when he comes in contact with wholesome and unwholesome sense-objects. When the mind is not tranquil and content, he cannot but work both at forgetting all conditioning and at effacement. As it is said, "When the six sense-bases absorb the sense-spheres and the mind no longer responds to the environment, this is called *samādhi.* When the mind and the sense-spheres are both void and the mirror of the mind shines without obscuration, this is called *prajñā.*" Even though this is the relative approach to *samādhi* and *prajñā* which adapts to signs as practiced by those of inferior faculties in the gradual school, it cannot be neglected as a counteractive technique. If restlessness and agitation are blazing forth, then first, through *samādhi,* use the noumenon to absorb the distraction. For when the mind does not respond to the environment it will be in conformity with original calmness. If dullness and torpor are especially heavy, use *prajñā* to investigate dharmas critically and contemplate their voidness, and allow the mirror of the mind to shine without disturbance in conformity with the original awareness. Control distracting thoughts with *samādhi.* Control blankness with *prajñā.*

When both activity and stillness disappear, the act of counteraction is no longer necessary. Then, even though there is contact with sense-objects, thought after thought returns to the source; regardless of the conditions he meets, every mental state is in conformity with the path. Naturally *samādhi* and *prajñā* are cultivated as a pair in all situations until finally the student becomes a person with no concerns. When this is so, one is truly maintaining *samādhi* and *prajñā* equally. One has clearly seen the Buddha-nature.

Question: According to your assessment, there are two types of *samādhi* and *prajñā* which are maintained equally during cultivation after awakening: first, the *samādhi* and *prajñā* of the self-nature; second, the relative *samādhi* and *prajñā* which adapts to signs.

The self-nature type means to be calm yet aware in all circumstances. Since the person who has awakened to the self-nature is always spontaneous and free from attachment to objects, why does he need to trouble with effacing the defilements? Since there is not even one thought which creates passion, there is no need to make vain efforts at forgetting all conditioning. Your assessment was that this approach is the sudden school's equal maintenance of *samādhi* and *prajñā* which never leaves the self-nature.

The relative type which follows signs means either to absorb distraction by according with the noumenon or to investigate dharmas critically and contemplate their voidness. One controls both dullness and agitation and thereby enters the unconditioned. But your assessment was that this practice is for those of inferior faculties in the gradual school. We are not yet free of doubts about the *samādhi* and *prajñā* of these two different approaches. Would you say that one should first rely on the self-nature type and then, after cultivating *samādhi* and *prajñā* concurrently, make further use of the countermeasures or the relative approach? Or should one first rely on the relative type so that after controlling dullness and agitation, he can enter into the self-nature type? If, after initially using the *samādhi* and *prajñā* of the self-nature, he is able to remain calm and aware naturally in all situations, thus rendering the counteractive measures unnecessary, why would he subsequently have to apply the relative type of *samādhi* and *prajñā*? It is like a piece of white jade: if it is engraved, its natural quality will be destroyed. On the other hand, after the initial application of the relative type of *samādhi* and *prajñā,* if the work of counteraction is brought to a close and he then progresses to the self-nature type, this would be merely gradual development prior to awakening as practiced by those of inferior faculties in the gradual school. Then how would you be able to say that the sudden school's approach of initial awakening and subsequent cultivation makes use of the effortless effort?

If these two types can both be practiced in the one time that has no past or future [via sudden awakening/sudden cultivation], there would have to be a difference between the respective suddenness and gradualness of these two types of *samādhi* and *prajñā*—so how could they both be cultivated at once? The sudden school adept relies on the self-nature type and eschews effort by remaining natural in all situations. Students of inferior capacity in the gradual school tend toward the relative type and exert themselves applying countermeasures. The suddenness and gradualness of these two types of practices are not identical; their respective superiority and inferiority is obvious. So, in the approach of initial awakening and subsequent cultivation, why is it explained that there are two ways to maintain *samādhi* and *prajñā* equally? Could you help us to understand this and eliminate our doubts?

Chinul: The explanation is obvious. Your doubts only come from yourselves! If you try to understand by merely following the words, you will, on the contrary, only give rise to doubt and confusion. It is best to forget the words; do not bother with detailed scrutiny of them. Now let us go on to my assessment of the cultivation of these two types of practice.

Cultivation of the *samādhi* and *prajñā* of the self-nature involves the use of the sudden school's effortless effort in which both are put into practice and both are calmed; oneself cultivates the self-nature, and oneself completes the path to Buddhahood. Cultivation of the relative *samādhi* and *prajñā* which adapts to signs involves the use of the counteractive measures which are cultivated prior to awakening by those of inferior faculties in the gradual school. Thought-moment after thought-moment, confusion is eliminated; it is a practice which clings to stillness. These two types are different: one is sudden and the other gradual; they should not be combined haphazardly.

Although the approach involving cultivation after awakening does discuss the counteractive measures of the relative approach which adapts to signs, it does not employ the practices of those of inferior faculties in the gradual school in their entirety. It uses its expedients, but only as a temporary measure.[29] And why is this? In the sudden school too there are those whose faculties are superior and those whose faculties are inferior; their "baggage" [their backgrounds and abilities] cannot be weighed according to the same standard.

If a person's defilements are weak and insipid, and his body and mind are light and at ease; if in the good he leaves the good and in the bad he leaves the bad; if he is unmoving in the eight worldly winds; if the three types of feeling are calmed—then he can rely on the *samādhi* and *prajñā* of the self-nature and cultivate them concurrently in all situations naturally. He is impeccable and passive; whether in action or at rest he is always absorbed in Sŏn and perfects the principle of naturalness. What need is there for him to borrow the relative approach's counteractive measures? If one is not sick, there is no need to look for medicine.

On the other hand, even though a person might initially have had a sudden awakening, if the defilements are engrossing and the habit-energies deeply engrained; if the mind becomes passionate whenever it is in contact with sense-objects; if he is always involved in confrontations with the situations he meets; if he is always beset by dullness and agitation; or if he loses the constancy of calmness and awareness—then he should borrow the relative *samādhi* and *prajñā* which adapts to signs and not forget the counteractive measures which control both dullness and agitation. Thereby he will enter the unconditioned: this is what is proper here. But even though he borrows the countermeasures in order to bring the habit-energies under temporary control, he has had a sudden awakening to the fact that the mind-nature is fundamentally pure and the defilements fundamentally empty. Hence he does not fall into the corrupt practice of those of inferior faculties in the gradual school. And why is this? Although during cultivation prior to awakening a person following the gradual approach does not forget to be diligent and thought-moment after thought-moment permeates his cultivation, he still gives rise to doubts everywhere and cannot free himself from obstacles. It is as if he had something stuck in his chest: he is always uncomfortable. After many days and months, as the work of counteraction matures, the adventitious defilements of body and mind might then appear to weaken. Although they seem lighter, the root of doubt is not yet severed. He is like a rock which is crushing grass: he still cannot be self-reliant in the realm of birth and death. Therefore, it is said, "Cultivation prior to awakening is not true cultivation."[30]

In the case of a man who has awakened, although he employs expedients, moment to moment he is free of doubts and does not become polluted. After many days and months he naturally conforms with the impeccable, sublime nature. Naturally he is calm and aware in all situations. Moment by moment, as he becomes involved in sensory experience in all the sense-realms, thought after thought he always severs defilements, for he never leaves the self-nature. By maintaining *samādhi* and *prajñā* equally, he perfects supreme *bodhi* and is no longer any different from those of superior faculties mentioned previously. Thus, although the relative *samādhi* and *prajñā* is a practice for those of inferior faculties in the gradual school, for the man who has had an awakening it can be said that "iron has been transmuted into gold."[31]

If you understand this, how can you have such doubts—doubts like the discriminative view that a sequence or progression is involved in the practice of these two types of *samādhi* and *prajñā*? I hope that all cultivators of the path will study these words carefully; extinguish your doubts or you will end up backsliding. If you have the will of a great man and seek supreme *bodhi*, what will you do if you discard this approach? Do not grasp at the words, but try to understand the meaning directly. Stay focused on the definitive teaching, return to yourselves, and merge with the original guiding principle. Then the wisdom which cannot be obtained from any master will naturally manifest. The impeccable noumenon will be clear and unobscured. The perfection of the wisdom-body does not come from any other awakening.[32] And yet, although this sublime truth applies to everyone, unless the omniscient wisdom of *prajñā*—the basis of the Mahāyāna—is started early, you will not be able to produce right faith in a single thought. And how can this merely result in a lack of faith? You will also end up slandering the three treasures and will finally invite punishment in the Interminable Hell. This happens frequently! But even though you are not yet able to accept this truth in faith, if it passes through your ears just once and you feel affinity with it for even a moment, the merit will be incalculable. As it says in *Secrets on Mind-Only*, "Hearing the dharma but not believing is still cause for the fruition of the seed of Buddhahood. Training on the Buddhist path but not completing it is still merit surpassing that of men and gods."[33] But he who does not lose the right cause for the attainment of Buddhahood and who, moreover, listens and believes, trains and completes his training, and guards his achievement without forgetting it, how can his merit be calculated?

If we consider our actions in our past wanderings in *saṃsāra,* we have no way of knowing for how many thousands of kalpas we have fallen into the darkness or entered the Interminable Hell and endured all kinds of suffering.[34] Nor can we know how many times we have aspired to the path to Buddhahood but, because we did not meet with wise advisors, remained submerged in the sea of birth and death for long kalpas, dark and unenlightened, performing all sorts of evil actions. Though we may reflect on this once in a while, we cannot imagine the duration of our misery. How can we relax and suffer again the same calamities as before? Furthermore, what allowed us to be born this time as human beings—the guiding spirits of all the ten thousand things—who are clear about the right road of cultivation? Truly, a human birth is as difficult to ensure as "a blind turtle putting its head through a hole in a piece of wood floating on the ocean"[35] or "a mustard seed falling onto the point of a needle." How can we possibly express how fortunate we are?

Whenever we become discouraged or indolent, we should always look to the future. In one instant we might happen to lose our lives and fall back into the evil bourns where we would have to undergo unspeakable suffering and pain. At that time, although we might want to hear one phrase of the Buddha-dharma, and would be willing to receive and keep it with faithful devotion to ease our misfortune, how would we ever encounter it there? On the point of death, remorse is of no use whatsoever. I hope that all of you who are cultivating the path will not be heedless and will not indulge in greed and lust. Do not forget to reflect upon this as if you were trying to save your head from burning. Death is fast closing in. The body is like the morning dew.[36] Life is like the twilight in the west. Although we are alive today, there is no assurance about tomorrow. Bear this in mind! You must bear this in mind!

By relying on worldly conditioned, wholesome actions we will avoid the suffering of *saṃsāra* in the three evil bourns. We will obtain the favorable karmic reward of rebirth among gods or men where we will receive abundant joy and happiness. But if we give rise to faith in this most profound approach to dharma of the supreme vehicle for only a moment, no metaphor can describe even the smallest portion of the merit we will achieve. As it is said in the *sūtras:*

> If one takes all the seven jewels in all the world systems of this trichiliocosm and offers them to all the sentient beings of those worlds until they are completely satisfied; or, furthermore, if one instructs all the sentient beings of those worlds and causes them to realize the four fruitions, the merit so gained will be immeasurable and boundless. But it is not as great as the merit gained from the first recollection of this dharma for the period of one meal.[37]

Therefore, we should know that our approach to dharma is the holiest and most precious of all; its merit is incomparable. As the *sūtras* say:

> One thought of purity of mind is a *bodhimaṇḍa,*
> And is better than building seven-jeweled stupas as numerous as the sands
> of the Ganges.
> Those jeweled stupas will finally be reduced to dust,
> But one thought of purity of mind produces right enlightenment.[38]

I hope that all of you who are cultivating the path will study these words carefully and keep them always in mind. If this body is not ferried across to the other shore in this lifetime, then for which life are you going to wait? If you do not cultivate now, you will go off in the wrong direction for ten thousand kalpas. But if you practice assiduously now, practices which are difficult to cultivate will gradually become easier until, finally, meritorious practice will advance of itself.

Alas! When starving people are given princely delicacies nowadays, they do not even know enough to put them in their mouths. When they are sick they meet the king of doctors but do not even know enough to take the medicine. If no one says, "What shall I do? What shall I do?" then what shall I do for him?[39]

Although the character of mundane, conditioned activities can be seen and its effect experienced, if a person succeeds in one affair, everyone praises the rarity of it. The source of our minds has neither shape to be observed nor form to be seen; the way of words and speech is cut off there. Since the activities of mind are ended, *māras* and heretics have no way to revile us. Even the praises of Indra, Brahmā, and all the gods will not reach it; so how can the mind be fathomed by the shallow understanding of ordinary men? How pitiful! How can a frog in a well know the vastness of the sea?[40] How can a fox roar like a lion?[41]

Hence we know that in this degenerate dharma age, a person who is able to hear this approach to dharma, realize its rarity, and receive and keep it with faithful devotion has for innumerable kalpas served all the saints, planted all the roots of goodness, and fully formed the right cause of *prajñā* —he has the most proficiency. As the *Diamond Sūtra* says, "If there is a person who can have faith in these words, it should be known that this man has planted all the roots of goodness in front of incalculable numbers of Buddhas."[42] It also says, "This is spoken in order to produce the great vehicle; this is spoken in order to produce the supreme vehicle."[43] I hope that those of you who are aspiring to the path will not be cowardly. You must display your ardor. Good causes made in past kalpas cannot be known. If you do not believe in your superiority and, complacently resigning yourself to being inferior, you decide that you will not practice now because it is too difficult, then even though you might have good roots from past lives, you sever them now. The difficulty will keep growing and you will move farther from the goal. Since you have now arrived at the treasure house, how can you return empty-handed? Once you lose a human body, for ten thousand kalpas it will be difficult to recover. Be careful. Knowing that there is a treasure house, how can a wise person turn back and not look for it—and yet continue to resent bitterly his destitution and poverty? If you want the treasure you must throw away this skin-bag.

NOTES

1. Chinul is alluding here to the famous Parable of the Burning House from the *Lotus Sūtra*. See *Miao-fa lien-hua ching* 2, *T* 262.9.12c–13c; Leon Hurvitz, *Lotus*, pp. 58–62. See also *LCL*, p. 497b.17, and Wŏnhyo's *Palsim suhaeng chang*, in Cho Myŏng-gi (ed.), *Wŏnhyo taesa chŏnjip*, p. 605.

2. By Tan-hsia Tzu-ch'un (1064–1117), in the Ts'ao-tung lineage; from his verse, the *Wan chu-yin*, appearing in *CTL* 30, p. 463b–c. This passage is quoted also at *THYL* 8, p. 843b. "Hundred bones" (K. *paekhae*; C. *po-hai*): an allusion to *Chuang-tzu* 1, Ch'i wu lun sec. 2, p. 8.

3. Adapted from Wŏnhyo's *Palsim suhaeng chang*: "The practice of persons who have wisdom is to steam rice grains to prepare rice; the practice of persons without wisdom is to steam sand to prepare rice." In Cho Myŏng-gi (ed.), *Wŏnhyo taesa chŏnjip*, p. 605.

4. *Avataṃsaka Sūtra*, "Appearance of the *Tathāgatas*" chapter *(Ju-lai ch'u-hsien p'in)*, *HYC* 51, p. 272c.

5. In the *Complete Enlightenment Sūtra*, *YCC*, p. 914a.

6. Adapted from Ku-ling Shen-tsan (n.d.), disciple of Po-chang Huai-hai (720–814); in *Chodang chip* 16, p. 104c.25–26.

7. *LCL*, p. 497b.26–29.

8. *CTL* 3, p. 218b; quoted also in *THYL* 5, p. 829c. Korean *Igyŏn* (C. *yi-chien*) is a common designation for devotees of non-Buddhist Indian religious sects; compare

K. *osip igyŏn paramun nyŏ,* C. *wu-shih yi-chien p'o-lo-men nü,* "fifty heterodox Brahmin women," in *P'u-sa pen-sheng-man lun* 4, *T* 160.3.341c.18–19. Such sects were "heterodox" because they did not accept such basic Buddhist teachings as rebirth or karmic cause and effect; for a listing, see *Ch'ang A-han ching* 7, *T* 1.1.42c.1–3. Bharati was a prime exponent of the signless teaching *(musang chong)* —one of the six major divisions of the Indian Buddhist tradition reputedly current in Bodhidharma's time (*CTL* 3, p. 217b.3–5). Bharati was sent by Bodhidharma to reconvert the South Indian kings who had reverted to heterodox beliefs and were reviling the three treasures; see *CTL* 3, p. 218a–b.

9. Kuei-tsung Ts'e-chen (?–979), also known as Hui-ch'ao, was a disciple of Fa-yen Wen-i (885–958), founder of the Fa-yen school of the mature Ch'an tradition. For Kuei-tsung's biography, see *CTL* 25, p. 417a.3–22. A similar exchange in which Kuei-tsung asks the question and receives the same reply from Fa-yen constitutes case 7 in the *Blue Cliff Records;* see *Pi-yen lu* 1, *T* 2003.48.147a.

10. This quotation appears in *THYL* 26, p. 920a.12–13; Ta-hui does not cite his source, however, a not unusual occurrence in Ch'an texts.

11. The fourth answer to a series of ten questions asked by Kuei-feng Tsung-mi by the mountain man Shih; see *CTL* 13, p. 307b.16–19.

12. Adapted from Ma-tsu Tao-i; *Ma-tsu yü-lu, HTC* 1304.119.811a.10.

13. Adapted from Nan-ch'üan P'u-yüan (748–835) in *CTL* 10, p. 276c; see *Straight Talk on the True Mind,* note 1.

14. By P'ang Yün (740–808), lay disciple of Ma-tsu Tao-i; quoted in *CTL* 8, p. 263b.

15. One of the two major approaches to practice attributed to Bodhidharma.

16. Avalokiteśvara's method for tracing hearing to its source in the mind was praised by Śākyamuni Buddha as the ideal practice for people in a degenerate age; see *Śūraṅgama Sūtra, Leng-yen ching* 6, *T* 945.19.128b–129c.

17. By Ch'eng-kuan (738–840), the fourth Hua-yen patriarch, in his *Ta-fang-kuang Fo hua-yen ching sui-shu yen-i ch'ao* 1, *T* 1736.36.1b.

18. In the *Awakening of Faith, TCCHL,* p. 575c.

19. By Li T'ung-hsüan in his *Exposition of the Avataṃsaka Sūtra, HHYCL* 14, p. 809b; also quoted in Chinul's *Hwaŏmnon chŏryo,* p. 268.

20. *THYL* 26, p. 920a.

21. Adapted from *Lao-tzu* 48.

22. By Kuei-feng Tsung-mi; see *CYCTH* 2, p. 403a. This quote is attributed to Ho-tse Shen-hui in Tsung-mi's *DCSPR,* Part II, "the view of the Ho-tse school" section; see also *CHT,* p. 872a.

23. *CYCTH* 1, p. 399b.

24. By Pao-chih in his *Gāthā in Praise of the Mahāyāna (Ta-ch'eng tsan), CTL* 29, p. 450a.1.

25. Yung-ming Yen-shou in his *Mirror of the Source Record, Tsung-ching lu* 38, *T* 2016.48.638a.

26. By Kuei-feng Tsung-mi in *CYCTH* 2, p. 403a.5; see also *DCSPR* and *CHT,* p. 872a.4.

27. *LTTC,* p. 358c.

28. *LTTC,* p. 352c.19–20.

29. Literally, "it only borrows their way and boards at their house." For this allusion, see *Chuang-tzu* 4, T'ien-yün sec. 14, p. 84.

30. Kuei-feng Tsung-mi in *CYCTH* 3, p. 407c; see also *DCSPR.*

31. From Yung-ming Yen-shou's *Mirror of the Source Record, Tsung-ching lu* 1, *T* 2016.48.419c.24.

32. Adapted from the *Avataṃsaka Sūtra,* "Brahmacarya" chapter *(Fan-hsing p'in), HYC* 17, p. 89a, and *HYCb* 8, p. 449c.15.

33. *Wei-hsin chüeh, T* 2018.48.996c.

34. "Fallen into darkness" can refer to hell—as in the *Ti-tsang ching,* where it is said that the T'ieh-wei Mountains (Cakravāḍaparvata), which form the perimeter of hell, "are dark and devoid of any light from the sun or moon" (*Ti-tsang p'u-sa pen-yüan ching* 1, *T* 412.13.782a.4–5). The phrase can also refer to a spirit realm, however—"the ghosts of darkness" (see *Fo pen-hsing chi ching* 41, *T* 190.3.845b.4). The former alternative is probably intended here.

35. For this simile, see *Tsa A-han ching* 16, *T* 99.2.108c.

36. See *Ku shih, WH* 249.29.6b; compare Ts'ao Tzu-chien's *Sung Ying shih shih, WH* 82.20.32a.

37. cf. *Chin-kang ching, T* 235.8.749b.18–23.

38. Shih Wu-chu's verse in *Sung Biographies of Eminent Monks;* see *Sung Kao-seng chuan* 20, *T* 2061.50.837a.17–19.

39. Adapted from the *Lun-yü* 15.15.

40. An allusion to *Chuang-tzu* 4, Ch'iu shui sec. 17, p. 91; see also *Tsung-ching lu* 1, *T* 2016.48.420b.10.

41. See *Tsung-ching lu* 1, *T* 2016.48.420b.11, for this allusion; see also *PWYF* 587.2.

42. *Chin-kang ching, T* 235.8.749a–b.

43. *Chin-kang ching, T* 235.8.750c.

Straight Talk on the True Mind

CHINSIM CHIKSŎL

STRAIGHT TALK ON THE TRUE MIND is probably Chinul's most accessible exposition of the Sŏn meditation techniques practiced in his era. Chinul tackles the problem of correlating all the apparently conflicting descriptions of the absolute given in different strata of Buddhist texts. Tracing all these descriptions back to the true mind, he then describes the different attributes of this absolute sphere. Chinul's discussion leads into a consideration of ten different ways of cultivating thoughtlessness, or "no-mind," the fundamental approach for revealing the effulgence of the true mind.

The precise date of composition is unknown; it was probably written about the same time as *Secrets,* around 1205. *Straight Talk on the True Mind* represents a median stage in the development of Chinul's thought. Here he moves away from the basic practice of balancing *samādhi* and *prajñā,* the primary method explored in his early work *Encouragement to Practice,* and investigates the more sophisticated cultivation of no-mind. At this stage, however, he has yet to progress into an examination of the exclusively Sŏn technique of *hwadu* investigation which will characterize his late works. *Straight Talk* suffered the same fate as *Secrets:* lost in Korea during the Mongol invasions, it was reintroduced into Korea in the fifteenth century via the Northern Ming edition of the *Tripiṭaka.*

Chinul's Preface

Question: Can the sublime path of the patriarchs be known?

Chinul: Hasn't this already been explained by the ancients? "The path is not related to knowing or not knowing. Knowing is a false thought; not knowing is blankness. If you have truly penetrated to that realm which is free of doubt and as vast and spacious as the immensity of space, how could you bother to make such discriminations?"[1]

Question: But does this mean that sentient beings do not benefit from the patriarchs' appearance in the world?

Chinul: When the Buddhas and patriarchs "showed their heads" they had no teachings to offer men. They only wanted sentient beings to see their original nature for themselves. The *Avataṃsaka Sūtra* says, "You should know that all dharmas are the own-nature of the mind. The perfection of the wisdom-body does not come from any other awakening."[2] For this reason, the Buddhas and patriarchs did not let people get snared in words and letters; they only wanted them to put deluded thought to rest and see the original mind. This is why when people entered Te-shan's room he struck them with his staff,[3] or when people entered Lin-chi's room he shouted.[4] We have all groped too long for our heads; why should we set up more words and language?[5]

Question: We have heard that in the past Aśvaghoṣa wrote the *Awakening of Faith,*[6] the Sixth Patriarch expounded the *Platform Sūtra,*[7] and Huang-mei transmitted the *Prajñāpāramitā* texts;[8] all these efforts involved a gradual, sequential approach for the sake of men. How can it be right that you alone have no expedients regarding the dharma?

Chinul: At the summit of Mount Sumeru ratiocination has been forbidden for ages; but at the top of the second peak all the patriarchs have tolerated verbal understanding.[9]

Question: From the summit of this second peak, could you possibly bestow on us a few simple expedients?

Chinul: Your words are correct. And yet the great path is mysterious and vast; it neither exists nor does it not exist. The true mind is arcane and subtle; it is free from thought and abstraction. Hence people who have not yet entered into this state could peruse the teachings of five thousand volumes of the *tripiṭaka* but it would not be enough. But if those who have perceived the true mind say merely one word in allusion to it, it is already surplus dharma. Today, without fearing for my eyebrows,[10] I have modestly written a few passages to shed light on the true mind, in the hope that they will serve as a basis and program for entering the path. This will do by way of introduction.

Right Faith in the True Mind

Chinul: In the *Avataṃsaka Sūtra* it is stated:

> Faith is the fountainhead of the path
> and the mother of all meritorious qualities.
> It nourishes all good roots.[11]

Moreover, the Consciousness-only texts say, "Faith is like a water-purifying gem which can purify cloudy water."[12] It is clear that faith takes the lead in the development of the myriads of wholesome qualities. For this reason the Buddhist *sūtras* always begin with "Thus I have heard . . . ," an expression intended to arouse faith.

Question: What difference is there between faith in the patriarchal Sŏn and scholastic sects?

Chinul: There are many differences. The scholastic sects encourage men and gods to have faith in the law of karmic cause and effect. Those who desire the pleasures which come from merit must have faith that the ten wholesome actions are the sublime cause and that human or deva rebirth is the pleasurable result. Those who feel drawn to the void-calmness of nirvana must have faith that its primary cause is the understanding of the cause and conditions of arising and ceasing and that its holy fruition is the understanding of the four noble truths: suffering, its origin, its extinction, and the path leading to its extinction. Those who would delight in the fruition of Buddhahood should have faith that the practice of the six *pāramitās* over three *asaṃkhyeya* kalpas is its major cause and *bodhi* and nirvana are its right fruition.

Right faith in the patriarchal sect is different. It does not believe in conditioned causes or effects. Rather, it stresses faith that everyone is originally a Buddha, that everyone possesses the impeccable self-nature, and that the sublime essence of nirvana is complete in everyone. There is no need to search elsewhere; since time immemorial, it has been innate in everyone. As the Third Patriarch said:

> The mind is full like all of space,
> Without deficiency or excess.
> It is due mostly to grasping and rejecting
> That it is not so now.[13]

Chih-kung said:

> The signless body exists within the body which has signs,
> The road to the unborn is found along the road of ignorance.[14]

Yung-chia said:

> The true nature of ignorance is the Buddha-nature.
> The void, phantom body is the dharma-body.[15]

Hence we know that sentient beings are originally Buddhas.

Once we have given rise to right faith, we must add understanding to it. As Yung-ming [Yen-shou] said, "To have faith but no understanding increases ignorance; to have understanding but no faith increases wrong views." Consequently, we know that once faith and understanding are merged, entrance onto the path will be swift.

Question: Is there any benefit which accrues solely from the initial arousing of faith even though we are not yet able to enter the path?
    Chinul: The *Awakening of Faith* says:

> If a person hears this dharma without feeling fainthearted, it should be known that this man will surely perpetuate the spiritual family of the Buddha and receive prediction of his future Buddhahood from all the Buddhas. Even if there were a man who could convert all the sentient beings throughout the world systems of this trichiliocosm and induce them to practice the ten wholesome actions, he would not be as good as a man who can rightly consider this dharma for a period the length of one meal. It is beyond analogy just how much it exceeds the previous merit.[16]

Furthermore, it is said in the *Prajñāpāramitā sūtras:* "And if they give rise to one thought of pure faith, the *tathāgata* fully knows and sees this; through this faith, all sentient beings gain incalculable merit."[17] We know that if we want to travel for a thousand *i* it is essential that the first step be right; if the first step is off, we will be off for the entire thousand *i*. To enter the unconditioned kingdom, it is essential that our initial faith be right, for if that initial faith is wrong, we will move away from the myriads of good qualities. The Third Patriarch said, "One iota of difference, and heaven and earth are rent asunder."[18] This is the principle we are discussing here.

Different Names for the True Mind

Question: We have already given rise to right faith, but we are still uncertain what is meant by "true mind."
    Chinul: To leave behind the false is called "true." The numinous speculum is called "mind." The *Śūraṅgama Sūtra* sheds light on this mind.[19]

Question: Is it only named true mind or does it also have other appellations?
    Chinul: The names given to it in the teachings of the Buddha and in the teachings of the patriarchs are not the same. First let us explore the teachings of the Buddha. In the *Bodhisattvaśīla Sūtra* it is called the "mind-ground" because it produces the myriads of good dharmas.[20] In the *Prajñā-pāramitā sūtras* it is referred to as *"bodhi"* because enlightenment is its essence.[21] The *Avataṃsaka Sūtra* names it the *"dharmadhātu"* because it interpenetrates and infuses all dharmas.[22] In the *Diamond Sūtra* it is called

"tathāgata" because it does not come from anywhere.[23] In the *Prajñāpāramitā sūtras* it is also referred to as "nirvana" because it is the sanctuary of all the saints.[24] In the *Golden Light Sūtra* it is said to be "suchness" because it is true, permanent, and immutable.[25] In the *Pure Name Sūtra* it is named the "dharma-body" because it is the support for the reward and transformation bodies.[26] In the *Awakening of Faith* it is termed "true suchness" because it neither arises nor ceases.[27] In the *Mahāparinirvāṇa Sūtra* it is referred to as "Buddha-nature" because it is the fundamental essence of the three bodies.[28] In the *Complete Enlightenment Sūtra* it is called *"dhāraṇī"* because all meritorious qualities flow from it.[29] In the *Śrīmālādevīsiṃhanāda Sūtra* it is named *"tathāgatagarbha"* because it conceals and contains all dharmas.[30] In the definitive *sūtra* [the *Complete Enlightenment Sūtra*] it is named "complete enlightenment" because it destroys darkness and shines solitarily of itself.[31] As Sŏn Master Yen-shou's *Secrets on Mind-Only* says, "The one dharma has a thousand names: its appellations are each given in response to different conditions."[32] The true mind appears in all the *sūtras,* but I cannot cite all the references.

Question: We now know what true mind means in the teachings of the Buddha, but what about the teachings of the patriarchs?

Chinul: In the school of the patriarchs all names and words are severed; not even one name is sanctioned, let alone many. In response to stimuli and according to faculties, however, its names are also many. Sometimes it is referred to as "oneself," for it is the original nature of sentient beings. Sometimes it is named "the proper eye," for it makes visible all phenomena. At other times it is called "the sublime mind," for it is empty yet numinous, calm yet radiant. Sometimes it is named "the old master," for it has been the supervisor since time immemorial. Sometimes it is called "the bottomless bowl," for it can survive anywhere. Sometimes it is called "a stringless lute," for it is always in harmony. Sometimes it is called "an inextinguishable lamp," for it illuminates and disperses delusion and passion. Sometimes it is called "a rootless tree," for its roots and trunk are strong and firm. Sometimes it is referred to as "a sword which splits a wind-blown hair," for it severs the roots of the defilements. Sometimes it is called "the unconditioned kingdom," for the seas are calm there and the rivers clear. Sometimes it is named a "wish-fulfilling gem," for it benefits the poor and distressed. Sometimes it is called "a boltless lock," for it shuts the six sense-doors. It is also called "a clay ox," "a wooden horse," "moon of the mind," and "gem of the mind." It has such a variety of different names that I cannot record them all.[33]

If you penetrate to the true mind, you will fully comprehend all of these names; but if you remain dark to this true mind, all names are only a block. Consequently, you must be precise in your investigation of the true mind.

The Sublime Essence of the True Mind

Question: We have learned the names of the true mind, but what is its essence like?

Chinul: It states in the *Radiating Light Prajñā Sūtra: "Prajñā* is entirely free of signs. It has no signs of arising or ceasing."[34] In the *Awakening of Faith* it is said:

> The essence of true suchness itself neither increases nor decreases in any ordinary man, *śrāvaka, pratyekabuddha,* bodhisattva, or Buddha. It did not arise in an earlier age and will not be annihilated in a later age. Ultimately, it is constant and eternal. Since the beginning, its nature has been utterly complete in all meritorious qualities.[35]

According to this *sūtra* and *śāstra,* the original essence of the true mind transcends cause and effect. It connects past and present. It does not distinguish between ordinary and holy; it is free from all relativity; it pervades all places like the vastness of space. Its sublime essence is settled and calm; it transcends all conceptual proliferation. It neither arises nor ceases; it neither exists nor does not exist. It is unmoving and unshakable; it is still and constantly abiding. It is referred to as "the old master," "the awesome-voiced man on that bank," or "oneself prior to the kalpa of utter nothingness."[36] It is uniformly calm and still; it is free of the slightest flaw or obscuration. All the mountains and rivers of the great earth, the grasses, trees, and forest groves, all phenomena in creation, and all tainted and pure dharmas appear from within it. As the *Complete Enlightenment Sūtra* says, "Men of good family! The Supreme Dharma King has a great *dhāraṇī* called complete enlightenment. It issues forth from the complete purity of true suchness, *bodhi,* nirvana, and the *pāramitās* and is taught to the bodhisattvas."[37] Kuei-feng [Tsung-mi] said:

> The mind: it is vacuous, empty, sublime, and exquisite; it is clear, brilliant, numinous, and bright. It neither comes nor goes, for it permeates the three time periods. It is neither within nor without, for it pervades the ten directions. As it does not arise or cease, how could it be harmed by the four mountains? As it is separate from nature and characteristics how could it be blinded by the five sense-objects?[38]

Therefore, Yung-ming's *Secrets on Mind-Only* says:

> As for this mind, it assembles all wonders and all mysteries; it is the king of the myriads of dharmas. It is the hidden refuge of the three vehicles and the five natures. It is the mother of the thousands of saints. It alone is revered; it alone is honored. It is incomparable, unmatched, and certainly the fountainhead of the great path. It is the essential element of the true dharma.[39]

If we have faith in this, we should realize that all the bodhisattvas of the three time periods are studying the same thing—this mind. All the Buddhas of the three time periods have the same realization—the realization of this mind. The teachings elucidated in the *tripiṭaka* all elucidate this mind. The delusion of all sentient beings is delusion in regard to the mind. The awakening of all cultivators is the awakening to this mind. The transmission of all the patriarchs is the transmission of this mind. The search in which all the patchwork monks of this world are engaged is the search for this mind. If we penetrate to this mind, everything is just the way it should be and every material object is fully illuminated. But if we are deluded in regard to this mind, every place is inverted and all thoughts are mad. This essence is not only the Buddha-nature with which all sentient beings are innately endowed but also the basic source of creation of all worlds. When the World Honored One was momentarily silent at Vulture Peak, when Subhūti forgot all worlds below the cliff, when Bodhidharma sat in a small cell in wall contemplation, when Vimalakīrti kept silent in Vaiśālī—all displayed the mind's sublime essence.[40] Therefore, when we first enter the courtyard of the patriarchs' sect, we must understand the essence of this mind.

The Sublime Functioning of the True Mind

Question: We have now learned about the sublime essence of the true mind. But what is meant by its sublime functioning?

Chinul: The ancients said:

> The wind moves, but the mind shakes the tree.
> Clouds build up, but the nature raises the dust.
> If you are clear about the affairs of today,
> Then you are dark to the original man.

This poem alludes to the function which arises from the sublime essence. The sublime essence of the true mind is originally unmoving; it is peaceful and calm, true and eternal. The sublime function manifests from this true, eternal essence; it is unobstructed as it follows the flow and reaches the marvel. Therefore a patriarch's verse says:

> The mind whirls between the myriads of objects.
> In its whirling, its real power lies dormant.
> If one follows that flow and recognizes the nature,
> There is no joy and also no sorrow.[41]

At all times and in all activities—whether traveling eastward or westward; whether eating rice or donning clothes; whether lifting a spoon or handling chopsticks; whether looking left or glancing right—these are all manifestations of the sublime function of the true mind.

Ordinary men are deluded: when donning clothes they only understand that they are donning clothes; when eating they only understand that they are eating; in all their activities they are deceived by appearances. Hence they use the sublime function of the mind every day but do not realize it; it is right before their eyes but they are not aware of it. On the other hand, a man who is conscious of the nature has no further misunderstandings in any of his actions. As a patriarch said:

> In the womb it is called a fetus; on being born it is called a man. In the eye it is vision, in the ears it is hearing, in the nose it is smelling, in the mouth it is talking, in the hands it is grasping, in the feet it is running. When expanded, it contains all of the *dharmadhātu;* when contracted, it exists within one minute particle of dust. Those who are aware of it know that it is the Buddha-nature; those who are not call it soul or spirit.[42]

Master Tao-wu's dancing with his tablet, Master Shih-kung's aiming a bow, Master Mi-mo's holding a pair of tweezers, Master Chu-ti's raising a finger, Master Hsin-chou's striking the ground, Master Yün-yen's toy lion— all were displaying the great functioning of the mind.[43] If we are not deluded to its functioning each and every day, we will naturally be free from obstructions anywhere.

Similarities and Differences Between the True Mind's Essence and Function

Question: We are not yet clear about the essence and function of the true mind: are they the same or different?

Chinul: From the standpoint of their characteristic signs they are not the same. From the standpoint of their natures they are not different. Thus the essence and its function are neither the same nor different. How can we know this to be the case? I shall attempt to explain.

The sublime essence is unmoving; it is free of all relativity and separate from all signs. If we do not have the tallying-realization gained by penetrating to the nature, we cannot fathom this principle. The sublime function accords with conditions and responds to all kinds of events. It masquerades in mock signs and seems to possess shape and appearance. As the function has signs and the essence does not, they are not the same. Nevertheless, as the function is produced from the essence, the function is not separate from the essence; as the essence can give rise to the function, the essence is not separate from the function. Hence, considered from the standpoint of their mutual inseparability, they are not different. Take water for example: its essence is moisture, for this is the factor which is unalterable. But its waves are characterized by their alterability, for they build up because of the wind.

Since the nature of water is unalterable and the appearance of waves is alterable, they are not the same. Nevertheless, apart from the waves there is no water, and apart from water there are no waves. Since their nature, moisture, is the same, they are not different.[44] If you correlate the similarities and differences between the essence and function with this analogy, you should be able to understand.

The True Mind Amid Delusion

Question: If everyone is endowed with the essence and function of the true mind, how is it that saints and ordinary men are not the same?

Chinul: The true mind is originally the same in the saint and the ordinary man. But because the ordinary man endorses the reality of material things with the false mind, he loses his pure nature and becomes estranged from it. Therefore the true mind cannot appear. It is like a tree's shadow in darkness or a spring flowing underground: it exists, but it is not perceived. As a *sūtra* says:

> Men of good family! Take as analogy a pure *maṇi* gem which glows with the five colors according to the direction in which it shines. Fools think this *maṇi* gem really has five colors. Men of good family! It is exactly the same with the pure nature of complete enlightenment: it manifests in body and mind and adapts differently according to the object. Yet fools say the self-nature of that pure, complete enlightenment actually possesses those different bodies and minds.[45]

In Seng-chao's treatises it is written: "Between heaven and earth, and within the universe, is contained a jewel. It is concealed in the mountain of form."[46] This refers to the true mind amid entanglements. Furthermore, Tz'u-en said: "Ordinary men originally possess the *dharmakāya* which is identical with that of all the Buddhas. But as they are screened from it by falsity, they have it but do not recognize it. This innate *dharmakāya* which is present within the entanglements of defilement has been given the name *'tathāgatagarbha.'* "[47] P'ei Hsiu said: "Ordinary men are those who are fully enlightened the whole day long without ever knowing it."[48] Therefore we know that even amid the troubles of the dusty world, the true mind remains unaffected by those troubles. Like a piece of white jade which has been thrown in the mud, its color remains unchanged.

Extinguishing Delusion Concerning the True Mind

Question: When the true mind is beset by delusion, it becomes an ordinary man. How then can we escape from delusion and achieve sanctity?

Chinul: The ancients said, "When there is no place for the deluded mind, that is *bodhi. Saṃsāra* and nirvana are originally equal." The *Complete Enlightenment Sūtra* says:

As the illusory body of that sentient being vanishes, his illusory mind also vanishes. As his illusory mind vanishes, illusory sense-objects also vanish. As illusory sense-objects vanish, this illusory vanishing also vanishes. As this illusory vanishing vanishes, that which is not illusory does not vanish. It is like polishing a mirror: when the dirt is removed, its brightness appears.[49]

Moreover, Yung-chia said:

The mind is the sense-base, dharmas are the dusty objects.
These two are like a dirty streak on a mirror:
When the streak is removed, the mirror's brightness appears.
When mind and dharmas have both been forgotten, the nature is then true.[50]

This indeed is the removal of delusion and the accomplishment of truth.

Question: Chuang-tzu said, "The mind's heat is like blazing fire; its cold is like frozen ice. Its speed is such that it can pass beyond the four seas of the world in the twinkling of an eye. In repose it is like a deep pond; in movement it flies far into the sky. This indeed is the human mind."[51] This is Chuang-tzu's statement concerning the fact that the ordinary man's mind cannot be controlled or subdued. We are not yet clear, however, through which dharma method the Sŏn school proposes to gain control over the deluded mind.

Chinul: The deluded mind can be controlled through the dharma of no-mind.

Question: If people have no mind they are the same as grass or trees. Please give us some expedient descriptions so that we can understand this idea of no-mind.

Chinul: When I said no-mind, I did not mean that there is no mind-essence. It is only when there are no things in the mind that we use the term no-mind. It is like speaking of an empty bottle: we mean that there is no thing in the bottle, not that there is no bottle. We do not say that it is empty to express the idea that it is made of no material. A patriarch said, "If you have no concerns in your mind and no-mind in your concerns, then naturally your mind will be empty yet numinous, calm yet sublime."[52] It is mind in this sense that is meant here. Accordingly, we refer to the absence of the deluded mind, not to the absence of the true mind's sublime functioning. All the explanations of past patriarchs about the practice of no-mind are unique. Now, I will give a synopsis of these different techniques and briefly describe ten of them.

One: attention. This means that when we are practicing, we should always cut off thoughts and guard against their arising. As soon as a thought arises we destroy it through attention. Nevertheless, once deluded thoughts have been destroyed through attention and no subsequent thoughts occur, we should abandon this aware wisdom. When delusion and awareness are both forgotten, it is called no-mind. As a patriarch stated, "Do not fear the arising of thoughts; only be concerned lest your awareness of them be tardy."[53] A *gāthā* says, "There is no need to search for truth; you need only put all views to rest."[54] This is the method of extinguishing delusion through attention.

Two: rest. This means that when we are practicing, we do not think of either good or evil. As soon as any mental state arises, we rest; when we meet with conditions, we rest. The ancients said:

> Be like a strip of unbleached silk cloth,
> Be like cool, clear water,
> Be like an incense burner in an old shrine.
> Then you can cut through the spool of silk and leave behind all discrimination.
> Once you are like the stupid and senseless, you will have become partially united with it.[55]

This is the method of extinguishing delusion through resting.

Three: efface the mind but preserve objects. This means that when we are practicing, we extinguish deluded thoughts and do not concern ourselves with the external sense-spheres. We are only concerned with extinguishing the mind, for when the deluded mind is extinguished, what danger can sensual objects present? This is the teaching advocated by the ancients: "take away the man but leave the objects."[56] There is a saying which goes, "In this place there is fragrant grass. In the whole city there are no old friends." Layman P'ang said:

> You need only keep no-mind amid the myriads of things.
> Then how can you be hindered by the things which constantly surround you?[57]

This is the method of extinguishing delusion by effacing the mind but preserving objects.

Four: efface objects but preserve the mind. This means that when we are practicing, we contemplate all internal and external sense-spheres as being void and calm. We preserve only the one mind, signaling solitarily and standing alone. As the ancients said, "Don't be friends with the myriads of dharmas. Don't be partners with the world of dust."[58] If the mind is attached to the sense-spheres it becomes deluded. But if there are no sense-spheres, what delusion can there be? The true mind shines alone and is unobstructed in regard to the path. This is what the ancients called "take away the objects but leave the man." There is a saying which goes:

> In the upper garden the flowers have already withered,
> The carts and horses are still bustling and crowded.

It is also said:

> The three thousand swordsmen: where are they now?
> Chuang-tzu's private plan brought peace to the whole empire.[59]

This is the method of extinguishing delusion by effacing objects but preserving the mind.

Five: efface both mind and objects. This means that when we are practicing, we initially make the external sense-objects void and calm and then annihilate the internal—the mind. Since internal and external are both calmed, where can delusion arise? As Kuan-ch'i said, "In the ten directions there are no walls; at the four sides there are no gates. All is innocent, pure, and undefiled."[60] This is the patriarchs' teaching of "take away both man and objects." There is a saying:

> The clouds scatter, the river flows along.
> All is calm, heaven and earth are void.

It is also said:

> Both man and ox are not seen,
> This indeed is the time when the moon is bright.

This is the technique of extinguishing delusion by effacing both mind and objects.

Six: preserve both mind and objects. This means that when we are practicing, mind remains in its place and objects remain in their place. If there is a time when the mind and the objects come in contact with each other, then the mind does not grasp at the objects and the objects do not intrude upon the mind. If neither of them contacts the other, then, naturally, deluded thoughts will not arise and there will be no obstacles to the path. As a *sūtra* says, "As [mundane] dharmas abide in the place of the [supramundane] dharma, their worldly characteristics abide forever."[61] This is the patriarchs' teaching of "take away neither the man nor the objects." There is a saying in regard to this:

> One slice of moonlight appears on the sea,
> The members of a few families ascend the tower.[62]

It is also said:

> In the mountains covered with a million blossoms,
> A stroller has lost his way home.

This is the technique of extinguishing delusion by preserving both objects and mind.

Seven: internal and external are all the same essence. This means that when we are practicing, the mountains and rivers of the great earth, the sun, the moon, the stars, and the constellations, the internal body and the external world, as well as all dharmas, are all viewed as being the same essence of the true mind. That essence is clear, empty, and bright without a hair's breadth of differentiation. The world systems of the chiliocosm, as numerous as grains of sand, have fused into one whole: where would the deluded mind be able to arise? Dharma Master Seng-chao said, "Heaven and earth and I have the same root. The myriad things and I have the same essence."[63] This is the method of extinguishing delusion by recognizing that external and internal are all the same essence.

Eight: internal and external are all the same function. This means that when we are practicing, we take up all the dharmas of the physical universe —internal or external, mental or physical—as well as all motion and activity, and regard them all as the sublime functioning of the true mind. As soon as any thought or mental state arises, it is then the appearance of this sublime function. Since all things are this sublime functioning, where can the deluded mind stand? As Yung-chia said:

> The real nature of ignorance is the Buddha-nature.
> The phantom, void body is the dharma-body.[64]

Chih-kung said in his *Song of the Twelve Hours:*

> During the peaceful dawn, the hour of the Tiger:
> Inside the crazy mechanism hides a man of the path.[65]
> He doesn't know that, sitting or lying, it is originally the path.
> How busy he is bearing suffering and hardship![66]

This is the method of extinguishing delusion by recognizing that external and internal are all the same function.

Nine: substance and function are identical. This means that when we are practicing, although we conform with the true essence which has the single taste of void-calmness, numinous brightness is still concealed there. Hence essence is identical to function. As Yung-chia said, "The alertness of calmness is correct; the alertness of deluded thoughts is wrong. The calmness of alertness is correct; the calmness of blankness is wrong."[67] Since blankness is not present in calmness, and distracted thoughts are not engaged during alertness, how will any deluded thoughts be able to arise? This is the method of removing delusion by recognizing that essence and function are identical.

Ten: transcend essence and function. This means that when we are practicing, we do not divide the internal and the external. Nor do we discriminate north, south, east, and west. Rather, we take the four quarters and the eight directions and simply transform them all into a great gate to liberation. Clearly, then, essence and function are not divided. As there is not the slightest outflow, the entire body becomes fused into one whole. Where, then, would delusion be able to arise? The ancients said:

> The entire body is free of creases and cracks,
> Above and below are perfectly round and spherical.

This is the method of extirpating delusion by transcending essence and function.

You need not use all ten methods of practice. If you merely select one approach and perfect your work with it, delusion will vanish of itself and the true mind will instantly manifest. According to your faculties and background, choose whatever method appeals to you and train yourself in it. These practices are endeavorless endeavors which do not involve the applied power of the existent mind. Since these methods of bringing the deluded mind to rest are of vital importance, I have given a rather detailed explanation and am not merely being verbose.

The True Mind in the Four Postures

Question: In the explanation you just gave about extinguishing delusion, we are not yet clear whether these methods should be practiced only during sitting in meditation or whether they ought to be carried through into walking, standing, and all the other bodily postures as well.

Chinul: The *sūtras* and *śāstras* often talk about sitting practice because it is easier to obtain results that way. Nevertheless, the training should also be carried through into the other postures, and over a long period of time it will gradually mature. The *Awakening of Faith* says:

He who wants to cultivate tranquillity should find a quiet place and sit upright with proper attention. His attention should not be based upon the breath, nor upon any shape or form, nor upon voidness, nor upon earth, water, fire, and wind . . . nor upon seeing, hearing, sensing, and knowing. All thoughts should be discarded as they appear—even the thought of discarding should be banished. As all dharmas are originally free of thought, no thoughts arise and no thoughts cease. Moreover, he should try not to follow the mind; but if he does have thoughts which become involved externally with the sense-spheres, he should subsequently remove these thoughts mentally. If the mind is agitated and distracted, it must be collected and fixed in right thought. "Right thought" means that he should be aware that there is only mind and that the external sense-spheres are nonexistent. This mind is, furthermore, devoid of any distinctive signs of its own and thus can never be ascertained.

If he gets up from sitting, then at all times and during all activities, whether going, coming, moving, or being still, he should constantly be attentive to expedients which will enable him to adapt his contemplation to the situation at hand. After long training, the practice will mature and the mind will become stabilized. After the mind is stable, it gradually becomes sharper and, accordingly, will be able to enter the *samadhi* of true suchness and completely subdue the defilements. The mind of faith will grow and his practice will rapidly reach the stage of irreversibility. Only those who are skeptical, faithless, and slanderous, or have grave transgressions and karmic obstacles, or are proud and lazy, will be unable to enter.[68]

According to this passage, the practice should continue throughout the four postures.

It states in the *Complete Enlightenment Sutra:* "Initially he relies on the *śamatha* practice of the *tathāgata* and firmly keeps the prohibitions and precepts. He dwells alone in a peaceful place, or quietly sits in a still room."[69] This is the initial training. Yung-chia said:

> Walking is Sŏn, sitting is Sŏn.
> During speech, silence, action, and stillness, the essence is at peace.[70]

According to this passage also, the practice should continue throughout the four postures. But, generally speaking, if the efficacy of a person's practice is such that he cannot pacify the mind even while sitting, then how can he expect to do it while walking, standing, or otherwise? How will he ever be able to enter the path?

For someone whose practice has matured, even if a thousand saints appeared he would not be surprised; even if ten thousand *māras* and goblins showed up, he would not turn his head. Thus, in walking, standing, and sitting, how could he not maintain his practice? If a person wanted to take revenge on an enemy, he would not be able to forget it, whatever the time and whatever the action—whether walking, standing, sitting, reclining, eating, or drinking. If he is in love, it is the same too. Hatred and love are matters in which the mind plays an active role. If we can easily keep such things in mind even when the mind is active, why do we doubt that our present practice, in which no mind is involved, could not continue throughout the four postures? We need only fear that our faith is lacking or that we do not try; for if we exert ourselves in all the deportments and have faith, the path will never be lost.

The Abode of the True Mind

Question: When the deluded mind is extinguished, the true mind appears. Yet where are the essence and function of the true mind now?

Chinul: The sublime essence of the true mind pervades all places. Yung-chia said:

> It is not separate from this very spot and is constantly still.
> If you search for it then you should know that it cannot be found.[71]

The *sūtras* state, "It is of the nature of empty space; it is eternally immovable. In the *tathāgatagarbha* there is no arising or ceasing." Ta Fa-yen said, "Everywhere is the way to *bodhi*. Everything is a grove of meritorious qualities."[72] This indeed is the abode of the essence.

The sublime function of the true mind reacts to stimuli and manifests accordingly, like the echo in a valley. Fa-teng said:

> In past and present its response has been unfailing;
> It is clearly present before your eyes.
> A wisp of cloud appears in the valley at evening,
> A lone stork descends from the distant sky.[73]

Yüan, a Hua-yen master from Wei fu, said:

> The Buddha-dharma is present in all your daily activities. It is present during your walking, standing, sitting, and reclining, while drinking tea and eating rice, during conversation and dialogue, in whatever you do and perform. To stir up your mind and set thoughts in motion is indeed far from being correct.[74]

Hence we know that the essence pervades all places and always gives rise to function. But as the presence or absence of the appropriate causes and conditions for its manifestation is uncertain, this sublime functioning is not fixed: it is not that in some cases the sublime functioning is absent. If people who cultivate the mind want to enter the sea of the unconditioned and cross beyond all birth and death, they must not be confused about the abode of the true mind's essence and function.

The True Mind Beyond Death

Question: We have heard that men who have seen the nature transcend birth and death. However, all the patriarchs of the past had seen the nature; and yet they all were born and they all died. Nowadays, we see that those who are cultivating the path are born and will die too. How can we leave behind birth and death?

Chinul: Birth and death are originally nonexistent; they exist because of a false notion. It is like a person with diseased eyes who sees flowers in the sky. If a person without this disease says there are no flowers in the sky, the afflicted person will not believe it. But if his disease is cured, the flowers in the sky will vanish naturally and he can then accept that they were nonexistent. Although the flowers he sees have not yet vanished, they are, in fact, still void. It is only the sick man who takes them to be flowers; their essence does not really exist.

In the same way, people wrongly assume that birth and death exist. If a man free of birth and death tells them that birth and death are originally nonexistent, they will not believe him. But one morning, if delusion is put to rest, and birth and death are spontaneously abandoned, they will realize that birth and death are originally nonexistent. It is only when birth and death are not yet ended that, although they do not really exist, they seem to exist because of this false conceptualization. As a *sūtra* says:

> Men of good family! Since time immemorial all sentient beings have been subject to all kinds of inverted views. They are like people who have confused the four directions. They wrongly assume that the four elements are their own bodies. They regard the shadows conditioned by the six sense-objects as their own minds. This is like diseased eyes which see flowers in the sky. Yet even if all the flowers in the sky were to vanish from space, it still could not be said that they actually vanished. And why is this? Because they never came into existence in the first place. All sentient beings mistakenly perceive an arising and a ceasing within this nonarising state. For this reason, it is called the revolving wheel of birth and death.[75]

According to the text of this *sūtra,* we can be sure that if we have a penetrating awakening to the true mind of complete enlightenment, then, as originally, there is no birth or death.

We know now that there is no birth and death; but still we cannot liberate ourselves from birth and death because our practice is imperfect. As it says in the texts, Ambapāli once asked Mañjuśrī, "I can understand that birth is actually the unborn dharma, but why then am I still subject to the flow of birth and death?" Mañjuśrī answered, "It is because your power is still insufficient." The mountain master Chin asked the mountain master Hsiu, "I understand that birth is actually the unborn dharma, but why am I still subject to the flow of birth and death?" Hsiu replied, "Bamboo shoots eventually become bamboo. But can you use them now to make a raft?"[76] Accordingly, to know that there is no birth or death is not as good as to experience that there is no birth or death. To experience that there is no birth or death is not as good as to be in conformity with the birthless and the deathless. To be in conformity with the birthless and the deathless is not as good as to make use of the birthless and the deathless. People nowadays do not even know that there is no birth or death, let alone experience, be in conformity with, or make use of the birthless and the deathless. Is it not only natural, then, that people who assume there really is birth and death would not be able to believe in the birthless and deathless dharma?

The Primary Practice and Secondary Aids for Realizing the True Mind

Question: Once delusion is brought to rest as explained previously, the true mind will appear. But as long as delusion has not been extinguished, should we use only the no-mind practice to bring delusion to rest, or are there other methods to counteract all delusion?

Chinul: The primary practice and secondary aids are not the same. To extinguish delusion with no-mind is the primary practice; to train in all wholesome actions is the secondary aid. It is like a bright mirror which is covered with dust: even though we rub it with the hand, we still need a good polish to make it lustrous. Then and only then will its brightness manifest. The dust is defilement; the force of the polishing hand is the practice of no-mind; the polish is all the wholesome actions; the shine of the mirror is the true mind. As it is said in the *Awakening of Faith:*

> Furthermore, faith accomplishes the activation of the *bodhicitta*. What mind does it activate? Briefly, there are three kinds. What are the three? The first is the straight mind, which is right attention to the dharma of true suchness. The second is the deep mind, which accumulates all wholesome practices. The third is the mind of great compassion, which aims to eradicate the sufferings of all sentient beings.
>
> Question: You have explained the one sign of the *dharmadhātu* and the non-duality of the Buddha-essence. Why do we not simply recollect true suchness instead of contriving to train in all wholesome practices?
>
> Answer: The mind is like a large *maṇi* gem: its essential nature is luminous and transparent, but it is tainted by impurities of the ore. If a person merely imagines the essence of this gem but does not polish it in various ways with expedients, it will never become transparent. In the same way, the essential nature of the dharma of true suchness, which is inherent in sentient beings, is void and clear, but it is stained by incalculable defilements and impurities. If a person only imagines that true suchness but fails to develop his mind in various ways by training in expedients, it too will never get clean. As the impurities are incalculable and pervade all dharmas, he cultivates all wholesome practices in order to counteract them. If a person practices all wholesome dharmas, he will naturally return to harmony with the dharma of true suchness.[77]

According to this explanation, bringing the deluded mind to rest is the primary practice and cultivating all wholesome dharmas is the secondary aid.

When cultivating the good, if you accord with no-mind you will not be attached to cause and effect. If you cling to cause and effect, you will receive a karmic reward which falls within the sphere of ordinary men and gods, making it difficult to realize true suchness; you will be unable to liberate yourself from birth and death. But if you are united with no-mind, this will be the expedient needed to realize true suchness and the essential technique needed to free yourself from birth and death; simultaneously, you will receive the greatest of merits. The *Diamond Sūtra* says, "Subhūti! If bodhisattvas give without dwelling on signs, the merit of that giving will be inconceivable."[78] As soon as worldly men who practice meditation nowadays understand that they possess the original Buddha-nature, they rely solely on this impeccability and do not train in all the wholesome practices. How is it that their only mistake is that they will be incapable of penetrating to the true mind? To the contrary, in their laziness they will not even be able to avoid the evil bourns, let alone free themselves from birth and death. This view of theirs is a grave error!

The Meritorious Qualities of the True Mind

Question: We do not doubt that merit is produced when the mind plays an active role in cultivation. But how is any merit made from cultivating with no-mind?

Chinul: The cause of cultivation in which the mind plays an active role produces a conditioned result, but the cause of cultivating with no-mind reveals the meritorious qualities of the nature. We are originally in full possession of these meritorious qualities, but because we are enveloped in delusion they do not manifest. When delusion is removed, however, these meritorious qualities appear. As Yung-chia said:

> The three bodies and the four wisdoms are complete in the essence.
> The eight liberations and the six spiritual powers are stamped on the mind-ground.[79]

This is what is meant by the essence being fully endowed with the meritorious qualities of the nature. An ancient poem says:

> If a man sits in stillness for one instant,
> It is better than building seven-jeweled stupas as numerous as the sands of the Ganges.
> Those jeweled stupas will finally be reduced to dust,
> But one thought of purity of mind produces right enlightenment.[80]

Thus we see that the merit of no-mind surpasses that in which the mind plays an active role.

Once Master Shui-liao of Hung-chou went to see Ma-tsu and asked, "What is the real meaning of Bodhidharma's coming from the west?" Ma-tsu knocked him down and Shui-liao was instantly awakened. He stood up, rubbed his palms together, and laughed loudly, saying, "How wonderful! How wonderful! Hundreds of thousands of *samādhis* and immeasurable sublime meanings exist on the tip of one hair. In an instant I have recognized their source." He then prostrated and withdrew.[81] According to this passage, these meritorious qualities did not come from outside: they were originally complete in himself. The Fourth Patriarch said to Sŏn Master Fa-jung:

> The hundreds and thousands of approaches to dharma return together to this one square inch of the mind. Meritorious qualities as numerous as the sands of the Ganges are all present in the fountainhead of the mind. Every aspect of *śīla, samādhi,* and *prajñā,* as well as magic and miracles, are all complete there. They are not separate from your mind.[82]

According to the words of the patriarch, the meritorious qualities of no-mind are innumerable. It is merely those who prefer token merit who cannot allow themselves to give rise to faith in the meritorious qualities of no-mind.

Testing the True Mind's Operation

Question: When the true mind appears, how do we know that it has matured without obstructions?

Chinul: Although the true mind might manifest to those who are training on the path, if they have not yet eliminated their habit-energies they will occasionally lose their mindfulness when they encounter matured objects. It is like a herdsman who has trained his ox to follow obediently but still would not dare to lay down his whip or tether. He must wait until the ox's mind is fully trained and its pace steady, so that even if he guided it through a field of tender young rice sprouts it would not harm the paddy. Only then would he dare to loosen his grip. At that stage, even though he does not use the whip or tether, the ox would not injure the young sprouts.[83] It is the same for the man on the path. Even after he has realized the true mind he has to strive to maintain and nurture that realization in order to obtain great power and function; then and only then will he be able to benefit sentient beings.

If there comes a time when you want to test this true mind, you should take all the hateful and lustful situations you have encountered throughout your whole life and imagine that they are right before you. If a hateful or lustful state of mind arises as before, your mind of the path is immature. If hateful or lustful thoughts do not arise, your mind of the path is mature. Although your mind is matured to this extent, you should test it again if it is still not completely and naturally free from hate and lust in all circumstances. When hateful or lustful situations are encountered, thoughts of strong anger or desire ordinarily arise which cause one to cling to the objects of that anger or lust; but if such thoughts are not produced, the mind is unobstructed. It is like a white ox in a field which does not injure the young seedlings. Formerly, those masters who cursed the Buddhas or reviled the patriarchs accorded with this type of mind; but nowadays it is certainly premature for those who have just entered the patriarchs' school and have no perspective regarding the path to imitate cursing the Buddhas and reviling the patriarchs.

The Nescience of the True Mind

Question: When the true mind and the deluded mind are involved with the sense-spheres, how can we distinguish the true from the deluded?

Chinul: When the deluded mind is in contact with the sense-spheres it knows through discriminative awareness: it gives rise to greedy or hateful states of mind depending on whether pleasant or unpleasant objects are present; or else it gives rise to ignorant states of mind when neutral objects are encountered. Since the three poisons of greed, hatred, and delusion are produced because of these objects, it is easy to see that the mind is deluded. A patriarch said:

> The conflict between the adverse and the favorable,
> This is the sickness of the mind.[84]

Consequently, we know that it is the deluded mind which sustains the dichotomy between right and wrong.

As far as the true mind is concerned, it knows while knowing nothing; but because it is impartial, quiet, and utterly radiant, it is different from the nescience of grass and trees. Since it does not give rise to feelings of hatred or lust, it is different from the deluded mind. The mind which, when in contact with the sense-spheres, is empty and yet bright, neither hateful nor lustful, nescient and yet aware—this indeed is the true mind. As the *Treatises of Seng-chao* state:

> Since a saint's mind is sublime and signless, it is not right to assume that it exists. Nevertheless, however much he may use it, its reserves are never exhausted; so it is not right to assume that it does not exist. . . . Since it is nonexistent, it is aware and yet nescient; since it is not nonexistent, it is nescient and yet aware.[85]

Therefore, that nescience which is precisely awareness cannot be said to be different from the saint's mind.

When the deluded mind is present in existence, it is attached to existence; when it is present in nonexistence, it is attached to nonexistence. It is constantly caught in one of these two extremes and is never aware of the middle path. Yung-chia said:

> If you renounce the deluded mind but cling to the truth,
> The mind which clings and renounces becomes artificial and contrived.
> Students do not understand how to conduct their practice.
> In fact, they mistake a brigand for their son.[86]

The true mind dwells in existence and nonexistence but does not fall into either existence or nonexistence. It constantly abides in the middle path. A patriarch said:

> Do not follow the conditioned,
> Do not dwell in the recognizance of emptiness.
> When all is uniformly quiet,
> It is utterly extinguished of itself.[87]

The Treatises of Seng-chao state:

> Saints abide in existence but are nonexistent; they dwell in nonexistence but are not nonexistent. Although they cling neither to existence nor nonexistence, they do not reject existence or nonexistence. Therefore, their light blends harmoniously with the troubles of the dusty world. They pass between the five destinies, calmly going, suddenly coming. Tranquil, they do nothing and yet there is nothing they do not do.[88]

This passage explains that the saint opens his hands for the people; he passes between the five destinies and converts sentient beings. Nevertheless, although he comes and goes between those levels, he is still free of any sign of coming or going. This is not the case for the deluded mind. For this reason also, the true mind and the deluded mind are not the same. The true mind is the normal mind; the deluded mind is the abnormal mind.

Question: What is the normal mind?

Chinul: All men possess a point of numinous brightness which is still like space and pervades every region. When contrasted with mundane affairs, it is expediently called the noumenal nature. When contrasted with formations and consciousness, it is provisionally called the true mind. As it is without a hair's breadth of differentiation, when it encounters conditions it is unobscured and free from even one thought of clinging or rejection: whatever it encounters, it accepts. It does not follow after the myriads of objects. Even though it follows the flow and reaches the marvel, it never leaves the stillness of its abiding place. If you search for it, you should know that you will not be able to find it. This indeed is the true mind.

Question: What is the abnormal mind?

Chinul: The sense-spheres contain both the holy and the ordinary. The sense-spheres contain both the sullied and the pure. Annihilation and eternity, noumenon and phenomenon, arising and ceasing, motion and stillness, coming and going, beautiful and ugly, wholesome and unwholesome, cause and effect—all are contained in the sense-spheres too. If we were to discuss in detail everything contained in the sense-spheres, there would be myriads of differences and thousands of distinctions. The ten pairs of contrasting states I just mentioned refer to the abnormal sphere. The mind follows this abnormal sphere and arises; the mind follows this abnormal sphere and ceases. The mind which is involved in these abnormal sense-spheres can be contrasted with the normal, true mind mentioned previously. Consequently, it is called the abnormal, deluded mind. The true mind with which we are all originally endowed does not arise in relation to the abnormal sense-spheres and produce different distinctions. For this reason it is called the normal, true mind.

Question: Since the true mind is normal and devoid of all the different sorts of causes, how is it that the Buddha spoke of the laws of cause and effect and of good and bad karmic retribution?

Chinul: The deluded mind pursues all the diverse objects in the sense-spheres without understanding their true import. Accordingly, it gives rise to many kinds of mental states. The Buddha gave different examples of the law of cause and effect in order to subdue these various deluded mental states. But in the case of the true mind, these different sense-objects are not pursued and hence these various mental states do not arise. Since, from this standpoint, the Buddha would not need to speak of many different kinds of dharmas, how can there be any cause and effect?

Question: Does the true mind normally not arise?

Chinul: Although the true mind is sometimes activated, it does not arise in relation to external objects. Only its sublime functioning is at play; it is not that it is unclear about cause and effect.

The Destination of the True Mind

Question: Since people who have not yet penetrated to the true mind are confused about it, they create both good and evil causes. Due to the creation of good causes, they take birth in a good destiny; due to the creation of evil causes, they enter an evil bourn. According to their actions they receive a corresponding birth: there is no doubt about the validity of this principle. On the other hand, a person who has penetrated to the true mind has completely extinguished false passion; through his tallying-realization of the true mind, he no longer creates good and evil causes. After he passes away, where will his solitary spirit take refuge?

Chinul: Is it not usually said that it is better to have a refuge than not to have one? Furthermore, one who has no refuge is the same as a vagrant who drifts aimlessly among men. He resembles those lonely spirits of the ghost realms who have no master. But, to be specific, are you not actually seeking a refuge through this question?

Questioner: That is correct.

Chinul: After penetration to the nature, this refuge will no longer be necessary. Since all sentient beings are confused about the enlightened nature, they produce karma through false passions and craving thoughts. These actions are the cause for their being born into the six destinies where they receive both good and evil karmic retribution. If, for example, they perform actions commensurate with those of the devas, they will receive the corresponding result—rebirth in heaven. They receive the place of rebirth appropriate to their past action; there is no other reward they can expect. In all the destinies it is the same: it all depends on the karma. They are satisfied with the place in which they are reborn and would not be satisfied with any other birth. They consider their place of rebirth as their own personal refuge; they regard the places where they were not reborn as the refuge of others. Accordingly, if there are false passions then there are false causes. If there are false causes, then there are false results. If there are false results, then there is a refuge. If there is a refuge, then there is discrimination between here and there. And if there is discrimination between here and there, then there is right and wrong.

Now, those who penetrate to the true mind tally with the enlightened nature, which is not subject to arising and ceasing, and give rise to the sublime functioning, which is also not subject to arising and ceasing. Their sublime essence is real, eternal, and originally free of arising and ceasing, but their sublime functioning adapts to the environment and seems to display arising and ceasing. Nevertheless, since the function arises from the essence, function and essence are identical; thus how can there be any arising and ceasing? Because accomplished men have realized that true essence, could arising and ceasing intrude in any way? It is like water: moisture is its essence and waves are its function. Since the moist nature of water is forever unchanging, how can the moist nature within the waves change? But as waves cannot exist apart from that moist nature, they too are unchanging.[89] For this reason the ancients said, "The whole earth is the one proper eye of this *śramaṇa*. The whole earth is a *Saṃghārāma* [monastery]—a sanctuary for the man who has awakened to the noumenon."[90]

Once a person has penetrated to the true mind, the four kinds of birth and the six destinies instantly disappear. The mountains, the rivers, and the great earth are all discovered to be the true mind. Hence it is impossible that there could be any other refuge apart from this true mind. Since there are then no more false causes within the triple world, there can be no false results of rebirth in its six destinies. And if there are no false results, what refuge can be spoken of? There is no separate "this" or "that"; and since there is no "this" or "that," how can there be right and wrong? All the worlds in the ten directions are only this one true mind; the whole body is their reward—there is no refuge distinct from it.

In the teaching about the Buddhas' and bodhisattvas' exhibition of special skills and powers, it is explained that we may take rebirth at will without obstacles or hindrances. As it is stated in the *Transmission of the Lamp:*

> The presiding minister Wen-ts'ao asked Master Kuei-feng, "After men who have awakened to the noumenon complete this life, where is their refuge?"
>
> Kuei-feng answered, "There are no sentient beings who are not invested with the numinous and bright enlightened nature which is not different from that of all the Buddhas. If you can awaken to the fact that this nature is the *dharmakāya* and realize that originally you are unborn, then what need is there for a refuge? The numinous brightness is not obscured; it is clear and constantly aware. There is no place from which it came, and no place to which it will go. Only the void calmness can be considered to be your own essence; do not suppose that your essence is your physical body. The numinous awareness is your own mind; do not suppose that your mind is the deluded thoughts. If deluded thoughts arise, never follow them—then, when you are about to die, karma cannot bind you. Although you enter the intermediate state between rebirths, the direction you take is entirely up to you. Whether you go to the realm of gods or the realm of humans, you are free to take any refuge you want."[91]

This is the destination of the true mind after the dissolution of the body.

NOTES

1. The instruction given by Nan-ch'üan P'u-yüan (748–835) which brought Chao-chou Ts'ung-shen (778–897) to awakening; see *CTL* 10, p. 276c.

2. "Brahmacarya" chapter *(Fan-hsing p'in), HYC* 17, p. 89a; see also *HYCb* 8, p. 449c.

3. Te-shan Hsüan-chien (780–865), a fifth-generation successor in the T'ien-huang branch of the Ch'ing-yüan Hsing-ssu lineage and the teacher of Hsüeh-feng I-ts'un (822–908). For his "thirty blows" see *CTL* 15, p. 317c, and Suzuki, *Essays,* vol. 1, p. 276.

4. Lin-chi I-hsüan (?–866) was the founder of the Lin-chi school of the mature Ch'an tradition. For his four kinds of Ch'an shout (K. *kal;* C. *ho*) see *LCL,* p. 496c, and Suzuki, *Essays,* vol. 1, pp. 295–296.

5. "Groped for our heads": an allusion to the story of Yajñadatta *(Śūraṅgama*

Sūtra), who one day woke up thinking he had lost his head and went wildly around the city trying to find it. This is a simile for the ignorant person who has the enlightened nature but in his delusion assumes he has lost it. Even if he uses spiritual techniques and ascetic practices to recover that nature, he has never really lost it; he need only trace the light radiating from the mind back to its source until the nature is seen. For the simile, see *Leng-yen ching* 4, *T* 945.19.121b.

6. For a general survey of Japanese scholarship on the problems surrounding Aśvaghoṣa's reputed authorship of the text, see Paul Demiéville, "Sur l'Authenticité du Ta Tch'ing K'i Sin Louen;" and Sung-bae Park, "Wŏnhyo's Commentaries on the *Awakening of Faith in Mahāyāna*," pp. 7-19.

7. For a synopsis of the problems concerning Hui-neng (638-713) and his reputed authorship of the *Platform Sūtra* see Yampolsky, *Platform Sutra*, pp. 89-110. See also Carl Bielefeldt and Lewis Lancaster, "T'an Ching," especially pp. 200-201, which summarize three major theories concerning the text, and see the important works of Yanagida Seizan, "Daijō kaikyō toshite no *Rokuso dangyō*," and *Shoki Zenshū shisō no kenkyū*, pp. 148-212 and 253-278, where he presents his theory for a Niu-t'ou origin for the text.

8. Huang-mei is the respectful name for the Fifth Patriarch Hung-jen (601-674) after the mountain where he resided: Huang-mei shan, located in Huang-chou fu, Ch'i-chou, in Hupei province (*Chia-ch'ing i-t'ung-chih*, fasc. 340, Huang-chou fu 1.14). See Yampolsky, *Platform Sutra*, p. 3, n. 3, for references to Hung-jen's teaching as the "teaching of the East Mountain."

9. Mount Sumeru is here *Myogo pong* (Sublimely High Peak), the Chinese translation for the Sanskrit (as Li T'ung-hsüan notes in his *HHYCL* 22, p. 868c). Mount Sumeru was the center of the seven concentric iron mountain ranges which comprised the world according to ancient Indian cosmology. Indra, king of the gods, lived on its central peak, and the palaces of all the Gods of the Thirty-three *(Trāyas-trimśa-deva)* adorned its slopes (see Li's description in *HHYCL* 16, p. 826c).

In Hua-yen symbolism, Mt. Sumeru implies the unmoving *(avicala)* state and refers to the bodhisattva who has progressed beyond the ten stages of faith and has entered into the ten abidings. Consequently, it signifies the initial entrance into the five stages of the bodhisattva path proper (see *HHYCL* 16, p. 827a). In the *Avataṃsaka Sūtra*, the peak of Mt. Sumeru was where the lad Sudhana met Te-yün *bhikṣu* and was prompted into entering the ten abidings; see *Gaṇḍavyūha* chapter ("Entering the *Dharmadhātu*" chapter, *Ju fa-chieh p'in*), *HYC* 62, p. 334a. ff. Here Mt. Sumeru is used in contrast with the lower surrounding peaks of the seven ringed mountains to symbolize the distinction in level between noumenon and phenomenon, absolute and relative truth, and so forth.

10. In East Asia, long, bushy eyebrows indicated great wisdom; hence monks who use too many words and end up obfuscating the dharma will lose their eyebrows; see Kim Tal-chin, *Han'guk ŭi sasang*, p. 72, n. 1; and note *Pi-yen lu* 1, case 8, *T* 2003.48.148b.2, Cleary and Cleary, *Blue Cliff Record*, p. 53.

11. From the "Brahmacarya" chapter, *HYC* 14, p. 72b. This is a popular quote often cited in Ch'an works; see *THYL* 22, pp. 904c and 909b, and *THYL* 26, p. 924a-b.

12. Quoted by Tzu-hsüan (?–1038; *SSYN* 6.13b) in his *Ch'i-hsin lun shu pi hsüeh chi* 3, *T* 1848.44.313c.27.

13. Seng-ts'an (?–606), in his *Hsin-hsin ming, T* 2010.48.376b.

14. In his *Song of the Twelve Hours (Shih-erh shih sung), CTL* 29, p. 450b.5.

15. Yung-chia Hsüan-chüeh, in his *Song of Enlightenment, CTK*, p. 395c.

16. *TCCHL*, p. 583a–b; Hakeda, *Faith*, p.103.

17. See the *Diamond Sūtra, Chin-kang ching, T* 235.8.749b.

18. *Hsin-hsin ming, T* 2010.48.376b.

19. See especially the opening exchange between Ānanda and the Buddha concerning the nature of the mind in *Leng-yen ching* 1, *T* 945.19.106c–108b.

20. *Fan-wang ching, T* 1484.24.997b.14.

21. *Mo-ho po-jo po-lo-mi-t'o ching* 1, *T* 223.8.223c.17 et. passim.

22. *HYC* 6, p. 30a et. passim.

23. *Chin-kang ching, T* 235.8.749a.21–25 et. passim.

24. *Mo-ho po-jo po-lo-mi-t'o ching* 4, *T* 223.8.243b.25; *Chin-kang ching, T* 235.8.749a.8 et passim.

25. *Ho-pu Chin kuang-ming ching* 1, *T* 664.16.363a et. passim.

26. *Wei-mo-chieh so-shuo ching* 1, *T* 475.14.539c.1–9; *Shuo Wu-kou-ch'eng ching* 1, *T* 476.14.561a.10–21 et. passim.

27. *TCCHL*, p. 576a; Hakeda, *Faith*, pp. 31–33.

28. *Ta pan-nieh-p'an ching* 4, *T* 374.12.385b et. passim.

29. *YCC*, p. 913b.19.

30. *Sheng-man ching, T* 353.12.221b.11–14 et. passim.

31. *YCC*, p. 913c.4 et. passim. Chinul's analysis of true mind in this section is reminiscent of Tsung-mi's treatment of true nature in his *Preface*, see *CYCTH* 1, p. 399a.29–b.5.

32. *Wei-hsin chüeh, T* 2018.48.993c.

33. A few of these metaphors need explication. "A bottomless bowl": bowl here refers to the alms bowl which is traditionally the fourth of the six requisites of all monks. Before Buddhist monks became settled in monasteries, they followed an itinerant life-style, always on the move, going to the nearest village once a day to accept alms for their daily meal. Hence the bowl became a symbol for the mind which accompanies the person everywhere and is the guide and source of all thought and action. The fact that the bowl is "bottomless" indicates that it can never be filled. The mind is like the bottomless bowl because it is completely unlimited in function and adapts to any and all circumstances: "it can survive anywhere."

"A stringless lute": the spiritual qualities inherent in the mind-essence are like a melody played on the finest of lutes. This essence, however, requires no "strings" (conditioned dharmas) to sound its music. And because these qualities are always present in the mind, "at any time it is in harmony."

"A rootless tree": when the roots of a tree are strong and firm, they plunge deep into the earth and are invisible to the human eye; hence the tree is seemingly "rootless." Nevertheless, this invisible root system supports and nourishes the entire visible structure of the tree—its trunk, branches, leaves, and fruits. Similarly, the essence of the mind, though unmanifest in the conditioned sphere, supports the mind's function, which displays the mind's qualities in all their manifold aspects. Alternatively, by interpreting "root" as a pun on the Buddhist usage of the word to refer to the sense-faculties *(indriya)*, we could say that because the defiling activities undertaken through those sense-faculties are cut off through the counteractive measures of practice, the senses become rootless but the enlightened mind that remains is strong and firm.

"The unconditioned realm": the mind is originally calm and clear, referring to its innate void-calmness and numinous awareness; it is only because of the turbidity of defilements and the wind of passion that this original clarity is lost. In its fundamental unconditioned state, the mind is like a calm sea and a clear river.

"A boltless lock": when the mind has achieved a state of natural spontaneity and self-reliance, one can protect oneself from defilements and passion by guarding the six sense-doors; hence one's mind is "locked." But because it requires no external force or artificial device to perform this function, it has no "bolt."

"Clay ox": clay is essentially inert; an ox is dynamic. Clay, however, can be formed into something dynamic and powerful without losing its essentially passive nature. The mind too is passive in essence, but it can adapt to any conditions through its sublime function; it is, accordingly, also completely dynamic. Hence the mind is both clay and ox. "Wooden horse" should be understood in the same way. See Rhi Ki-yong, *Chinsim chiksŏl,* pp. 44–54.

34. *Pañcaviṃśatisāhasrikāprajñāpāramitā-sūtra;* see the *Fang-kuang po-jo ching* 16, *T* 221.8.112c. The quotation in the form given here is taken from the *Chao lun, T* 1858.45.153a.

35. *TCCHL,* p. 579a; Hakeda, *Faith,* pp. 64–65.

36. "Awesome-voiced man on that bank" (Skt., *Bhīṣmagarjita[nirghoṣa]svara-[rāja]*): the appellation of twenty thousand *koṭis* of Buddhas who previously taught the *Lotus Sūtra;* see *Miao-fa lien-hua ching* 6, *T* 264.9.184c ff. This Buddha's name also appears at *Leng-yen ching* 5, *T* 945.19.126a. In this case the Buddha is taken as a symbol of the original *dharmakāya.* "Awesome" implies form; "voice" indicates sound. "On that bank" refers to the unconditioned realm and is equivalent to the common Sŏn term "original face." Hence this appellation parallels the phrase "one's original face prior to the arising of form and sound" or "one's original face prior to the appearance of the ancient Buddhas." Similarly, "oneself prior to the kalpa of utter nothingness" should be understood as equivalent to the Sŏn question "What is your original face before your parents gave birth to you?" See Rhi Ki-yong, *Chinsim chiksŏl,* p. 65.

37. *YCC,* p. 913b.

38. Tsung-mi's *Preface to the Great Commentary to the Complete Enlightenment Sūtra, Yüan-chüeh ching ta shu,* ZZ 243b.9.323c. The "four mountains" *(sasan)* are the wrong views of a self, a being, a soul, and a person as found in the *Diamond Sūtra;* see *Chin-kang ching, T* 235.8.751c.25–26, and Conze, *Buddhist Wisdom Books,* pp. 33–34, for discussion.

39. *Wei-hsin chüeh, T* 2018.48.994b.

40. On Vulture Peak (Mt. Gṛdhrakūṭa), a mountain near the Indian city of Rā-jagṛha, many of the Mahāyāna *sūtras* were delivered. According to Ch'an legends,

the Buddha remained sitting in silence after a dharma assembly there and held up a flower for his audience to view—expressing thereby the wisdom innate in the enlightened mind which is beyond the ability of words to describe. Of his disciples, only Mahākāśyapa understood his meaning (and became the first patriarch recognized by the Ch'an tradition). For the scriptural antecedents for this story, see Miura and Sasaki, *Zen Dust,* pp. 151–152. This story appears as case 7 in the *Wu-men kuan, T* 2005.48.293c.12–16.

Subhūti, the interlocutor in most of the *Prajñāpāramitā* texts, was the disciple of the Buddha most renowned for dwelling alone in the forest, which came to symbolize "coursing in emptiness." Once when Subhūti was discussing dharma, he concluded with the words "I have never said one word . . ." and remained sitting in silence. This statement expressed the notion that no lecture is better than knowing the mind itself. See *Pi-yen lu 1, case 6, T* 2003.48.146c.29–147a.5; Cleary and Cleary, *Blue Cliff Record,* pp. 44–45.

According to Ch'an legends, when Bodhidharma was staying at the temple of Shao-lin ssu after his arrival in China, he sat for nine years facing the wall of his room rapt in concentration. This signifies that the enlightened mind is completely unaffected when facing a sense-object. See *CTL* 3, p. 219b, for the story; see Suzuki, *Essays,* vol. 1, pp. 181–186, for a discussion of the term "wall contemplation."

When the layman Vimalakīrti feigned illness at his home in Vaiśālī, a host of bodhisattvas and *śrāvakas* went to offer their condolences. The bodhisattva of wisdom, Mañjuśrī, who led the delegation, asked each member of the group to comment on the nondual dharma. After all had given their opinions, Vimalakīrti was asked to relate his views on the subject. He replied by keeping silence—indicating that, in the essence of the mind, the way of words and speech is cut off. See *Wei-mo-chieh so-shuo ching* 2, *T* 475.14.551c.22; the story is also case 84 in the *Blue Cliff Records* (see *Pi-yen lu* 9, *T* 2003.48.209b–210b).

41. The twenty-second Indian patriarch, Manorhita, quoted in *CTL* 2, p. 214a.

42. Bharati, in *CTL* 3, p. 218b; see *Secrets on Cultivating the Mind,* note 8, for information. "Fetus" *(t'ae)* reads "spirit" *(sin)* in Chinul's text, which I have corrected according to the *CTL* version and the quotation of this passage in *Secrets.*

43. Tao-wu Yüan-chih (769–835) was a disciple of Yüeh-shan Wei-yen (745–828) in the Ch'ing-yüan lineage. When he was asked about the dharma, he would simply take up his tablet and dance; see *Chodang chip* 19, p. 123a. The tablet (k. *hol;* C. *hu*), a hand-held accessory carried by monks, was equivalent in function to the *yŏui* (C. *ju-i*), which gave monks the authority to take the floor during doctrinal debates. See J. Le Roy Davidson, "The Origins and Early Use of the Ju-i," pp. 239–249 and especially p. 244. The *hol* was neither a "Zen stick" as Seo Kyung-bo translates ("A Study of Korean Zen Buddhism," p. 320) nor a drum as Rhi Ki-yong assumes (*Chin-sim chiksŏl,* p. 78).

Shih-kung Hui-tsang (n.d.), a disciple of Ma-tsu Tao-i, had originally been a hunter. After his enlightenment, whenever someone asked him about the dharma he would draw his bow and aim straight at the questioner; see *CTL* 6, p. 248b–c. This story is also case 81 in the *Blue Cliff Records, Pi-yen lu* 9, *T* 2003.48.207b.

Mi-mo-yen Ho-shang (817–888), also known as Ch'ang-yü, was a fifth-generation disciple in the Ma-tsu Tao-i lineage. For his biography and this story, see *CTL* 10, p. 280a.29–b.4. His "holding a pair of tweezers" *(kyŏngch'a)* has also caused problems in translation. Seo's "nutcracker" is arbitrary ("A Study of Korean Zen Buddhism," p. 321); Rhi's "pitchfork" *(samji ch'ang)* is also incorrect. I follow Kim T'an-hŏ and Kim Tal-chin. The *CTL* version reads "fork" *(ch'a);* see *CTL* 10, p. 280b.1.

Chin-hua Chu-ti (n.d.) was a disciple of Hang-chou T'ien-lung (n.d.) in the Ma-tsu lineage. Whenever he was asked a question, he merely held up one finger in reply. See *Chodang chip* 19, p. 123b; case 3 in *Wu-men kuan, T* 2005.48.293b.11; case 19 in *Pi-yen lu* 2, *T* 2003.48.159a–160a.

Hsin-chou Ta-ti (n.d.), also known as Tzu-hui, was a seventh-generation successor in the Ma-tsu lineage; Rhi's note that he was an immediate disciple of Ma-tsu is incorrect (*Chinsim chiksŏl,* p. 76). For his story see *CTL* 8, p. 261c.2–6.

Yün-yen T'an-sheng (782–841) was a disciple of Yüeh-shan and the younger brother of the Tao-wu mentioned above. Whenever students came to ask Yün-yen about the dharma, he would tease them with a toy lion carved out of wood. See *CTL* 14, p. 558a.25–26.

44. Chinul draws here from a popular simile in *TCCHL,* p. 576c; Hakeda, *Faith,* p. 41. It is also alluded to by Tsung-mi in *DCSPR* and by Fa-tsang in his *Ta-ch'eng fa-chieh wu ch'a-pieh lun shu, T* 1838.44.68b.16–20. Tzu-hsüan explains that water means the one mind; the nature of moisture refers to true suchness; the waves stand for birth and death (see *Ch'i-hsin lun shu pi hsüeh chi* 8, *T* 1848.44.327b.23–25).

45. *Complete Enlightenment Sūtra, YCC,* p. 914c.

46. From the *Pao-tsang lun, T* 1857.45.145b, attributed to Kumārajiva's assistant Seng-chao (374–414). Chinul mistakenly cites the *Chao lun* as the source of this quotation. This statement is a well-known *kongan* used in the Sŏn school; it appears as case 62 in the *Blue Cliff Records, Pi-yen lu* 7, *T* 2003.48.193c.

47. Tz'u-en K'uei-chi (632–682), assistant to the great Chinese translator Hsüan-tsang (ca. 596–664) and systematizer of the Fa-hsiang (Dharmalakṣaṇa) school in China. For the quotation see *Ch'eng wei-shih lun shu chi* 10b, *T* 1830.43.601a.29–601b.1.

48. The preface to Tsung-mi's *Great Commentary to the Complete Enlightenment Sūtra, Yüan-chüeh ching ta shu, ZZ* 243a.9.323a.

49. *YCC,* p. 914c.

50. *CTK,* p. 396b.

51. *Chuang-tzu* 3, Tsai-yu sec. 11, p. 59.

52. Te-shan Hsüan-chien; see *CTL* 15, p. 317c.

53. Yung-ming Yen-shou; *Tsung-ching lu* 38, *T* 2106.48.638a.

54. Seng-ts'an's *Hsin-hsin ming, T* 2010.48.376c.

55. By Chiu-feng Tao-ch'ien (n.d.), disciple of Shih-hsüang Ch'ing-chu (?–888) in the Ch'ing-yüan lineage; for the quotation see *Ch'an-lin seng-pao chuan* 5, *HTC* 1531.137.463b.13. This quotation appears also in *THYL* 17, p. 882b.

56. One of Lin-chi I-hsüan's four approaches to practice; see *LCL,* p. 497a, for this and the corresponding passages in the fourth, fifth, and sixth sections.

57. P'ang Yün (740?–808), a lay dharma-heir of Ma-tsu; for the quotation see *P'ang chü-shih yü-lu* 3, *HTC* 1318.120.78b.6.

58. P'ang Yün, *P'ang chü-shih yü-lu* 1, *HTC* 1318.120.55a.1.

59. See *Ku-tsun-su yü-lu* 34, *HTC* 1294.118.593b.5–6. "Chuang-tzu's private plan": Chao Wen-wang was fond of swordplay. His indulgence was rapidly bringing his kingdom to ruin as more and more men were killed in the events. The heir apparent hired Chuang-tzu to persuade the king to give up his sport, and Chuang-tzu succeeded by shaming the king with spiritual talk. For the story see *Chuang-tzu* 8, Shuo chien sec. 30, pp. 84–86.

60. Kuan-ch'i Chih-hsien (?–895) in the Lin-chi lineage; for his biography see *CTL* 12, p. 264b–c.

61. *Lotus Sūtra, Miao-fa lien-hua ching* 1, *T* 262.9.9b.10.

62. By the Ch'an master Shou-ning Shan-tzu (n.d.) of Kuei-chou; see *Hsü ch'uan-teng lu* 22, *T* 2077.51.619a.

63. *Chao lun, T* 1858.45.159b.

64. *CTK,* p. 395c.

65. "Hour of the Tiger": 3 to 5 A.M. "Crazy mechanism" *(kwanggi):* I follow the rendering of Rhi Ki-yong (*Chinsim chiksŏl*, p. 118) and Kim T'an-hŏ (*Pojo pŏbŏ,* fol. 75a). Rhi interprets the term as a metaphor for the impermanent physical body which is still subject to the play of the defilements.

66. *CTL* 29, p. 450a.

67. *Ch'an-tsung Yung-chia chi, T* 2013.48.389b–c.

68. *TCCHL,* p. 582a; Hakeda, *Faith,* p. 96.

69. *YCC,* p. 914b.

70. *CTK,* p. 396a.

71. *CTK,* p. 396b.

72. Ta Fa-yen is Fa-yen Wen-i (885–958), founder of the Fa-yen school of the mature Ch'an tradition.

73. Fa-teng is another name for Ch'ing-liang T'ai-ch'in (?–975), a disciple of Fa-yen Wen-i; for his biography see *CTL* 25, pp. 414c–415b.

74. Wei fu is the present Ta-ming hsien in Hopei province. During the T'ang dynasty it was known as Wei-chou; under the Sung, since the regional military headquarters *(chün-fu)* was located in the district, it was known as Wei fu (*Ta-ch'ing Chia-ch'ing ch'ung-hsiu i-t'ung-chih,* fasc. 35, Ta-ming fu 1.1 ff.). I have been unable to locate any information on this teacher. The passage, including the attribution, is taken verbatim from the *Shih-men Hung Chüeh-fan lin-chien lu* 1, *HTC* 1594.148.486a. This teacher's instruction has been added to the *Taishō* edition of the *tripiṭaka* (*CTL* 30, p. 466b.17–19) according to the Ming version (published in 1601) of the *CTL; CTL* 30, p. 466, collation n. 2.

75. *Complete Enlightenment Sūtra, YCC,* p. 913b–c.

76. The mountain master Hsiu is Lung-chi Shao-hsiu (n.d.), a disciple of Lo-han Kuei-ch'en (867–928) and friend of Fa-yen Wen-i. The mountain master Chin is Ch'ing-ch'i Hung-chin (n.d.), also in the lineage of Lo-han Kuei-ch'en.

77. *TCCHL,* p. 580c; Hakeda, *Faith,* p. 82.

78. *Chin-kang ching, T* 235.8.749a.

79. *CTK,* p. 395c.

80. In Shih Wu-chu's verse in the *Sung Biographies of Eminent Monks,* see *Secrets,* note 38.

81. Hung-chou Shui-liao (n.d.) was a disciple of Ma-tsu Tao-i. This dialogue appears in *CTL* 8, p. 262c.

82. Niu-t'ou Fa-jung (594–657), founder of the Niu-t'ou school of the early Ch'an tradition; see *CTL* 4, p. 227a, for the quote.

83. For this and the following references to the oxherding metaphors, see Tz'u-yüan's *Shih niu-t'u sung, HTC* 1254.113.917–921; Hu Wen-huan's *Shih niu-t'u sung, HTC* 1255.113.921–942; and Suzuki, *Essays,* vol. 1, pp. 363–376.

84. Seng-ts'an; *Hsin-hsin ming, T* 2010.48.376b.

85. *Chao lun, T* 1858.45.153c–154a.

86. *CTK,* p. 396a–b.

87. *Hsin-hsin ming, T* 2010.48.376b.

88. *Chao lun, T* 2010.48.154b.

89. For this simile from the *Awakening of Faith,* see note 44 above.

90. By Ch'ang-sha Ching-ts'en (n.d.), a disciple of Nan-ch'üan P'u-yüan; see *CTL* 10, p. 274a. Only the first line appears in the *CTL* selection.

91. From Tsung-mi's exchange with the presiding minister (K. *sangsŏ;* C. *shang-shu*) Wen-ts'ao; see *CTL* 13, pp. 307c–308a. A *shang-shu* directed each of the six ministries into which the T'ang bureaucracy was divided: civil service, finance, rites, army, justice, public works. As des Rotours describes, "A la tête de chacun de ces six ministères se trouvait un président de ministère *(chang-chou)* qui devait être un mandarin du troisième degré première classe" (*Le Traité des Examens,* p. 7). I have been unable to locate any information on this personage.

Excerpts from the Dharma Collection and Special Practice Record with Personal Notes: Selections

PŎPCHIP PYŎRHAENG NOK CHŎRYO PYŎNGIP SAGI

EXCERPTS FROM THE DHARMA COLLECTION and Special Practice Record with Personal Notes, Chinul's magnum opus, was written in 1209, one year before his death. A product of his mature thought and lifelong study, the work covers in detail most of the major themes prominent in the rest of his writings and, as such, is the best work through which to approach the entire range of his thought. The work was intended to serve as a handbook for Buddhist students under his tutelage; indeed, its treatment of the fundamentals of the Korean Buddhist tradition proved to be so influential that it came to be one of the basic texts used in the lecture halls of Korean monasteries and is still studied avidly today.

The text is structured around excerpts drawn from the *Dharma Collection and Special Practice Record* [*Pŏpchip pyŏrhaeng nok;* C. *Fa-chi pieh-hsing lu*] of the T'ang Buddhist scholiast Kuei-feng Tsung-mi, the fifth patriarch of both the Hua-yen scholastic sect and the Ho-tse school of Ch'an. The *Record* contains Tsung-mi's synopses of the views and practices of four representative schools of Middle Ch'an Buddhism and champions the Ho-tse school's approach of sudden awakening/gradual cultivation. These excerpts are an important source of information concerning both the formative period of Ch'an as well as Tsung-mi's own Ch'an thought.

Chinul's personal notes focus on a discussion of the different taxonomies of sudden and gradual approaches to enlightenment and practice as outlined by such important Chinese thinkers as Ch'eng-kuan in his *Chen-yüan Commentary* [*Hua-yen ching hsing-yüan p'in shu*], Yung-ming Yen-shou in his *Mirror of the Source Record* [*Tsung-ching lu*], and Tsung-mi again in his *Preface to the Fountainhead of Ch'an Collection* [*Ch'an-yüan chu-ch'üan chi tou-hsü*]. Virtually nothing of the writings of these seminal philosophers of medieval Chinese Buddhist thought has appeared in English, and Chinul's treatment of these thinkers should be of interest to scholars of the East Asian Buddhist tradition. Chinul's discussion is an excellent example of the scholarly writing produced by exegetes in the various Buddhist schools—including the Ch'an school, which has often been portrayed in the West as bibliophobic and antitheoretical. Chinul's exposition culminates in a detailed exegesis of the theory of sudden awakening/gradual cultivation, the approach to practice and enlightenment which, through the *DCSPR*'s influence, became the hallmark of Sŏn. While developing this central theme, Chinul discusses the simultaneous development of *samādhi* and *prajñā,* the cultivation of thoughtlessness, and the faith and understanding of the complete and sudden school of Hwaŏm thought. He concludes with selections from the writings of Ta-hui Tsung-kao, the systematizer of the *kung-an* (K. *kongan*) system of Ch'an practice, in order to elucidate the proper approach to *hwadu* meditation, a new type of practice first expounded in Korea by Chinul. As the most comprehensive of Chinul's works, *DCSPR* is well illustrative of the syncretic trend of his thought, in which the convergence of Sŏn teaching and scholastic doctrine is demonstrated.

Because of the technical nature of much of the material presented here, I have included detailed notes. These are drawn in the main from the subcommentaries of the Yi dynasty scholiasts Hoeam Chŏnghye (1685–1741) and Yŏndam Yuil (1720–1799); of the two, I have found Yuil's discussions to be particularly illuminating. To make the discussion easier to follow, I have added section headings, which were not included in the original text. I would like to acknowledge here my indebtedness to Yi Chi-gwan's explication of the text in the *Sajip sagi*—a compilation of the Haein sa lecture hall collected under his direction.

I. Chinul's Preface

Moguja said: Ho-tse Shen-hui was a master of our school known for his intellectual knowledge and conceptual interpretation.[1] Although he was not the formal dharma successor to Ts'ao-ch'i [the Sixth Patriarch Hui-neng][2] his awakened understanding was lofty and brilliant and his discernment was clear. Since Master Tsung-mi inherited his teachings, he has developed and explained them in this *Record* so that they could be understood clearly. Now, for the sake of those of you who can awaken to the mind through the aid of the scriptural teachings,[3] I have abbreviated its superfluous verbiage and extracted its essentials so that it can serve as a handbook for meditation.[4]

I have observed that people of the present time who are cultivating their minds do not depend on the guidance of the written teachings, but straightaway assume that the successive transmission of the esoteric idea [of Sŏn] is the path.[5] They then sit around dozing with their minds in a haze,[6] their labors all in vain, or else they lose their presence of mind in agitation and confusion during their practice of meditation. For these reasons, I feel you should follow words and teachings which were expounded in accordance with reality in order to determine the proper procedure in regard to awakening and cultivation. Once you mirror your own minds, you may contemplate with insight at all times, without wasting any of your efforts.

The entries in this *Record* were originally arranged with the schools of Shen-hsiu and the others at the beginning because the text progressed from the shallow schools toward the profound, clearly distinguishing each of their relative strengths and shortcomings. In the present condensation, I treat the school of Ho-tse first, primarily so that people who are practicing meditation will be able to awaken first to the fact that, whether deluded or awakened, their own minds are numinous, aware, and never dark and their nature is unchanging.[7] Subsequently, when the other schools are reviewed it will be apparent that their teachings also contain excellent expedients in regard to the aspect of "person."[8] If, at the beginning, you do not get to the source, you will be lured by the traces of the words used in the teachings of those schools and wrongly give rise to thoughts of either acceptance or rejection. Then how will it be possible for you to develop syncretic understanding and take refuge in your own minds?[9]

Furthermore, as I fear that meditators who are not yet able to forget the passions and keep their minds empty and bright might stagnate in theoretical interpretations, at the end of my exposition I briefly quote some statements by "original-share" masters of our school who followed the shortcut approach.[10] My purpose there is to remove the defects of conceptual understanding[11] so that you can find the living road which leads to salvation.[12]

In present times, people who propagate both Sŏn and the scholastic schools are preoccupied solely with scholastic understanding based on the letter of the scriptures; and yet they will never be able to settle their thoughts on transcending the world through meditation.[13] The style of practice in the Buddha-dharma may vary with the passage of time. Nevertheless, in the mind which is used daily by everyone and which is clear and capable of awareness, the nature of the defilements is void and the sublime functioning is self-reliant—this is according to rule and is simply the way it is. So what does it matter if the times change?[14] The Patriarch Aśvaghoṣa said, "The word 'dharma' means the mind of a sentient being."[15] Could he have been deceiving people? If your faith is firm and you are wholeheartedly devoted to insight and thereby accumulate pure karma, then even though you may not realize a penetrative awakening in this life, you will not lose the right cause for the achievement of Buddhahood.

When we think about it, for kalpas without beginning we have been submerged in birth and death and have endured immeasurable suffering. Now we have been fortunate enough to receive a human body; we have been fortunate enough to meet with the Buddha-dharma and to be free of worldly entanglements. But if we allow ourselves to backslide or indulge in indolence, and if we do not cultivate our meditation but spend our days idly, then following the instant when our lives end and we fall into evil realms, even though we might wish to listen to a phrase of the Buddha-dharma and would be willing to contemplate it with right mindfulness, how will it be possible? Consequently, I always admonish you, my friends on the path with whom I live, to practice meditation as much as you are able, and to vow to continue the living lineage of the Buddhas and patriarchs. I hope that all of you accomplished people will together attest to this.

II. Excerpts from the Dharma Collection and Special Practice Record

REVIEW OF THE FOUR SŎN SCHOOLS

The *Record* states:

> The essential focus of the Sŏn approach lies in looking inward. It can neither be described in writing nor expressed through words. Although words may not apply, we can still force the use of them; but where the pen's rendering does not apply, it is indeed hard to put down the words. I write now only because there is no other alternative. I hope that you will reflect on these words in your heart and will not stagnate in the letters.[16]

THE HO-TSE SCHOOL[17]

> All dharmas are like a dream:[18] this is what all the saints have taught. Consequently, deluded thoughts are originally calm and the sense-spheres are originally void. This void and calm mind is numinous, aware, and never dark.[19]
> This void and calm mind is precisely the pure mind which was transmitted by our predecessor, Bodhidharma. Whether deluded or awakened, the mind is fundamentally self-aware. It does not come into existence through dependence on conditions; it does not arise because of sense-objects. When deluded it is subject to the defilements, but this awareness is actually not those defilements. When awakened it can manifest magic and miracles, but this awareness is actually not that magic or those miracles.
> This one word "awareness" is the source of all wonders.[20] Because of delusion concerning this awareness, the marks of self arise. When it is assumed that there is "I" or "mine," liking and disliking automatically appear. According to these feelings of liking and disliking, good and bad actions are performed. As a result of these actions, a body within the six destinies is received.

Hence, generation after generation, life after life, the wandering in *saṃsāra* is never brought to an end.

If we happen to receive the instructions of a good friend and suddenly awaken to this void and calm awareness, the calm awareness becomes free of thought and formless. Who then would assume that there is "self" or "person"? Upon awakening to the fact that all signs are void, the mind naturally becomes free of thought. If we are aware of a thought at the moment it arises, then through that awareness it will vanish.[21] The sublime approach to practice lies only in this.

Consequently, even though we cultivate the manifold supplementary practices, they all have thoughtlessness as their core.[22] If we can only maintain thoughtlessness, liking and disliking will naturally fade away, and compassion and wisdom will naturally grow in brightness; wrong actions will naturally be halted, and meritorious deeds will naturally be augmented. As far as our understanding is concerned, we will perceive that all signs are signless; as far as practice is concerned, it will be called the cultivation whereby nothing is cultivated. When the defilements are finally extirpated, birth and death will be cut off. As arising and ceasing have ended, a calm radiance will manifest and our responsiveness will be unlimited.[23] This is called Buddhahood.

THE NORTHERN SCHOOL[24]

All sentient beings are inherently endowed with the nature of enlightenment in the same way that a mirror possesses the nature of brightness. When that nature is covered by defilements it cannot shine—just like a mirror obscured by dust. If we rely on the words of the teachings and cease all deluded thoughts, the nature of the mind will be awakened to when those thoughts have been ended and there will be nothing of which that mind is unaware. This process is exactly the same as polishing a mirror: once all the dust has been removed, the surface of the mirror will be bright and clean and there will be nothing which it cannot reflect.

Tsung-mi's Critique:
This school is characterized by its view that defiled and pure states arise from conditions. Its approach is to go against the stream [of defilements] and resist the residual habit-energies. Nevertheless, there is no awakening to the fact that deluded thoughts are originally nonexistent and the nature of the mind is originally pure. Since the awakening still lacks acumen, how can such cultivation be called true?

THE HUNG-CHOU SCHOOL[25]

The arising of mental states, the activity of thought, the snapping of the fingers, the shifting of the eyes, and indeed all actions and activities, are expressions of the functioning of the Buddha-nature's total essence. As there is no functioning which occurs apart from it, the total essences of greed, hatred, or delusion, the performance of good or bad actions, and the corresponding retribution of happiness or suffering are all the Buddha-nature. It is like flour: although a wide variety of foods can be prepared from it, each of these is still flour.[26]

To explain this perspective further: the four great elements which comprise this body of flesh and bones, together with the throat, the tongue, the teeth, the eyes, the ears, hands, and feet, are absolutely incapable of talking, seeing, listening, or acting by themselves. At the instant when life has ended and the body has not yet begun to decompose, the mouth cannot talk, the eyes cannot see, the ears cannot hear, the feet cannot walk anywhere, and the hands cannot do anything. Consequently, we know that what is capable of speech and activity must be the Buddha-nature. Moreover, if we examine carefully each of these four great elements which compose this body of flesh and bones, we see that none of them understands greed, hatred, or delusion. Hence greed, hatred, and all the defilements are also the Buddha-nature.

The essence of the Buddha-nature is devoid of differentiation, and yet it can produce the whole range of differentiation. That its essence is, however, free of differentiation means that this nature is neither profane nor holy, neither cause nor effect, neither good nor bad. It has neither form nor sign; it neither goes nor stays; and, finally, it is neither Buddha nor sentient being. But since it can produce all these different things, that nature is also the functioning of the essence. Consequently, it can manifest as profane or sacred, as cause or effect, as good or bad. It manifests forms and manifests signs; it can become either a Buddha or a sentient being; it can even display greed, hatred, delusion, and the other defilements.

If we closely examine the nature of that essence, we will see that ultimately it can neither be perceived nor realized—in the same way that the eye cannot see itself, and so on. If we extend our examination to its responsiveness, we will realize that all action and activity is the [functioning of the] Buddha-nature; there is no other dharma which can act as the realizer or as the realized. This idea is expressed in the *Laṅkāvatāra Sūtra:* "The *tathāgatagarbha* is the cause of both wholesome and unwholesome actions. It can produce all the [six] destinies and the [four kinds of] birth where the suffering or happiness which is received will be commensurate with the causes which were created."[27] In another passage it states: "The Buddhas say that the mind is the origin."[28] And finally: "Or there is a Buddha-realm where raising the eyebrows, shifting the eyes, laughing, yawning, coughing, and all other actions are all the activities of the Buddha."[29]

Since the principles realized through awakening are all impeccable and natural, the principles by which we cultivate should accord with them. We should not give rise to a mind which intends to excise evil and cultivate good, however, nor to a mind which wants to cultivate the path. The path is the mind; you cannot use the mind to cultivate the mind. Evil too is the mind; you cannot use the mind to excise the mind. One who neither excises evil nor cultivates good, one who is completely free and spontaneous in all situations: this is called a liberated man. There is no dharma which can bind, no Buddha which can be produced. The mind is like space which can be neither supplemented nor diminished. How can we presume to supplement it? And why is this? There is not one dharma which can be found outside the mind-nature; hence cultivation means simply to allow the mind to act spontaneously.

Tsung-mi's Critique:
The Hung-chou school and the [Northern] school discussed just prior to it are diametrically opposite. The previous school considered that, from morning to evening, all discriminative activities are false. This school considers that, from morning to evening, all discriminative activities are true.

THE NIU-T'OU SCHOOL[30]

All dharmas are like a dream; originally nothing is of any concern. The mind and the sense-spheres are originally calm; it is not now that they have become void. It is because we are deluded to this fact that we say they exist and we see various matters like flourishing and decay or nobility and ignobility. Since there are favorable and unfavorable aspects to all these matters, passions such as liking and disliking are produced—and when passions arise we become entangled in all manner of suffering. But when these are created in a dream and undergone in a dream, what gain or loss can there be? The wisdom which can comprehend this also derives from the mind in the dream. And finally, if there were a dharma which surpassed even nirvana, it too would be like a dream or an illusion.[31] If we penetrate to that original equanimity in which nothing is of any concern, this principle should enable us to surrender ourselves and relinquish our passions. When passions are relinquished, the causes of suffering are excised and we then transcend all suffering and distress.[32] Hence the practice of this school involves the relinquishment of passion.

Tsung-mi's Critique:
The previous school [Hung-chou] advocated that awakening means the awareness that all thoughts are completely true and cultivation means allowing the mind to act spontaneously. This school regards awakening as the equanimity in which nothing is of any concern and views cultivation as the relinquishing of passion.

CRITIQUE OF THE THREE "INFERIOR" SCHOOLS[33]

Consider the differences in the views and understanding of these three schools: the Northern school regards everything as false; the Hung-chou school regards everything as true; the Niu-t'ou school regards everything as nonexistent. Now consider their respective definitions of practice: the first defines practice as subduing the mind and eliminating falsity; the next defines it as having the faith to allow the nature of the passions [the mind] to act freely; the last defines it as pacifying the mind so that it does not arise.[34]

By nature, I, Tsung-mi, like to compare things. After examining each of these schools I have come to the conclusion that their doctrines are as set out above. But if I were to take these statements and ask students of these schools

about them, not one would accept my conclusions. If I asked in terms of existence, they would reply in terms of voidness; if I argued for voidness, they
would point to existence. Or else they might say that both alternatives are
wrong, or that everything is inexpressible, or that cultivation and noncultivation are the same, or other similar answers. They respond in this way because
they are always afraid of being trapped by words and letters; since they are
afraid of stagnating in what they have attained, they dismiss whatever you
advocate. Consequently, I would only give detailed instructions to students
willing to take refuge in their mind [and take the mind as their] master,[35] so
that they will be able to contemplate with insight at all times and mature their
practice and understanding.

CHINUL'S EXPOSITION

In a later section of this text, it is said:

> The Hung-chou school constantly advocates, "Greed, hatred, loving-kindness,
> and wholesome actions are all the Buddha-nature; how could they be differ-
> ent?" This statement is like that made by people who only observe that the
> moist nature of water never changes, but do not realize that the difference
> between the success of a boat which crosses over that water and the failure of
> a boat which capsizes on the way is immense.[36] Consequently, although this
> school is near the approach of sudden awakening, it does not quite reach it; as
> far as the approach of gradual cultivation is concerned, however, it is com-
> pletely off the mark. Since the Niu-t'ou school has already penetrated to [an
> understanding of] voidness, it halfway comprehends the approach of sudden
> awakening; since it advocates the relinquishment of passion, it has no short-
> comings in regard to the approach of gradual cultivation. Since the Northern
> school is devoted solely to gradual cultivation and is utterly devoid of sudden
> awakening, even its cultivation is incorrect. The Ho-tse school advocates that
> first there must be sudden awakening and that subsequently we should culti-
> vate while relying on this awakening.[37]

According to this section of the text, Hung-chou was near the approach
of sudden awakening but did not quite reach it, whereas Niu-t'ou only half
understood it. For this reason, it is implied that it is essential for ordinary
people who are cultivating the mind to have faith only in Ho-tse, and not in
the other schools.[38]

Although this may be the case, if we examine the ideas of the two schools
of Hung-chou and Niu-t'ou as they are recorded in this text, they can be
deep and wide-ranging, and extremely abstruse and arcane. They enable
people who are cultivating their minds to see clearly for themselves into
their own speech and activities. How could there be a more recondite purpose than this? I am not yet completely certain whether Master Tsung-mi's
intention was to deprecate the ideas of these two schools or to praise them!
Nevertheless, he did break the grasping at verbal explanations, which is all

too common among latter-day students of these schools, and prompted them toward a complete awakening to the knowledge and vision of the *tathāgatas;* hence he probably had no thoughts of either deprecation or praise toward the two schools.

How do we know this? In his *Preface to the Complete References to the Fountainhead of Ch'an Collection,* there appears a review of these three schools. Briefly, he states:

> The Northern school is the school which brings falsity to rest and cultivates the mind. The Niu-t'ou school is the school which teaches absolute annihilation. Those who have some vague knowledge of Sŏn would say that the words of Niu-t'ou—that all sacred and profane dharmas are like a dream or an illusion—are the ultimate; but they do not realize that this statement is not the only dharma of this school.[39]

Judging from this statement, how could Master Tsung-mi not have been aware that the path of Niu-t'ou was fully perfected? When he said that Niu-t'ou only half understood, it was because he wanted those who recognized only the void and calm principle as being the ultimate to know that it is only through the mind of numinous awareness—which is the original functioning of the self-nature—that one's understanding is complete.

> The Hung-chou and Ho-tse schools are the schools which teach the direct revelation of the mind-nature. They teach that all dharmas, whether existent or void, are only the true nature. This revelation of the mind-nature is of two types. First Hung-chou explains: "That which now enables us to have speech, action, greed, hatred, loving-kindness, forbearance, and so forth is precisely your Buddha-nature. If at all times and in all places we merely put to rest [karma-producing] actions, nurture the spirit, and mature the sacred embryo, then the natural, divine marvel will manifest." This is precisely true awakening, true cultivation, and true realization. Second, Ho-tse has said: "All dharmas are like a dream: this is what all the saints have taught. Consequently, deluded thoughts are originally calm and the sense-spheres are originally void. The void and calm mind is numinous, aware, and never dark. That is your true nature."[40] As these two schools both aim at the unity of all signs and the return to the nature, they are consequently the same school.
>
> The three schools just mentioned have many differences, but each is simply employing expedients in regard to the practice of the twofold benefit; hence there is no error involved in following their instructions as well. The principle on which they are all founded does not allow the existence of duality.[41]

For this reason, we should know that Master Tsung-mi was not unaware of the fact that Ma-tsu's explanations of dharma directly illuminated the mind-nature and certainly contained skillful expedients for the practice of the twofold benefit. When he said, "Although this school is near the approach of sudden awakening, it does not quite reach it," he meant only that he was afraid students would accept the reality of the words only and, trapped in the adaptable function, would never achieve an awakening to the calm awareness. For this reason, people who are cultivating the mind in this degenerate age of the dharma should first critically examine the nature and characteristics, as well as the essence and functioning, of their own minds according to the teachings presented by Ho-tse. They should not simply drop into the void-calmness or stagnate in adaptability.[42] After they have developed authentic understanding they should review the tenets of the two schools of Hung-chou and Niu-t'ou. If they understand how these two schools complement each other, how could they erroneously give rise to thoughts of grasping or rejection? Therefore it is said [in the *Preface*]: "If any of the three points [constituting the Siddham letter *i*] are out of place, the letter *i* cannot be constructed. If the three schools are in divergence, how can Buddhahood be achieved?"[43] This is what I mean here.

Previously it was said that "as far as the approach of gradual cultivation is concerned, however, [the Hung-chou school] is completely off the mark." But later it was added that it is "true cultivation and true realization." It would seem that these statements are contradictory. When this school is considered from its standpoint that the principles understood through awakening are impeccable and entirely natural, however, its approach is said to be completely mistaken because it assumes there is nothing which needs to be cultivated or counteracted. But if it is considered from the standpoint that it nurtures the spirit in all situations and manifests spiritually sublime practices, then it is said to be true cultivation. Consequently, both interpretations have their reasons and they are not mutually contradictory.

You who are cultivating the mind: do not give rise to thoughts of doubt! You should know that the primary purpose in looking into a mirror is to appraise the beauty or ugliness of your own face. How can you stagnate in the writings of others, spending your day in idle controversy, and neither examine your own minds nor cultivate right contemplation? The ancients said: "The value of Buddhism lies in putting it into practice, not in endless rhetoric."[44] Keep this in mind! Do keep this in mind!

THE DEGREE OF DEVELOPMENT IN EACH SCHOOL

Above I have given an exposition of each of the schools. Let us now assess their respective profundity and shallowness, together with their strengths and shortcomings.

The mind strings together the myriads of dharmas; the implications of this are limitless. All the different scholastic sects have elaborated and amplified the teachings; the Sŏn sect has condensed and summarized them. In regard to dharma, this abridgement has reduced them to the two aspects of immutability and adaptability; in regard to person, it has divided them into the two approaches of sudden awakening and gradual cultivation. When these two aspects are clear, we can know the central ideas of all the *sūtras* and *śāstras* in the whole *tripiṭaka*. When the two approaches are displayed, we can see the tracks of all the sages and saints. Herein lies the significance of the profound intent of Bodhidharma.

First I will discuss the immutability and adaptability of dharmas. As abstract principles are difficult to comprehend when expounded directly, however, I will give some similes as a means of comparison in order to specify the strengths and shortcomings of each school and to assess whether their perspectives toward the self-mind are true or false. On the first perusal, simply read through the similes once. When the general idea is clear, try to assess in detail the principle which is expressed by means of the comments accompanying each simile.

[The mind] is like a *maṇi* jewel which is perfectly round, pure, luminous, and untarnished by any shade of color.[45]

The monistic, numinous mind-nature is void, calm, and ever aware. It is originally free from any differentiation and any notion of good or evil.

As its substance is luminous, when it comes into contact with external objects it can reflect any color.

As its essence is aware, in any situation it can distinguish between the shades of right and wrong, good and evil, and can even produce or create all manner of mundane and supramundane phenomena. This is the meaning of adaptability.

These shades of color may have individual differences, but the luminous jewel is never altered.

Fool and wise, good and evil, each has individual differences. Sorrow and happiness, hatred and love, may arise and disappear. But the mind capable of awareness is never interrupted. This is the meaning of immutability.

Although there are hundreds and thousands of different colors which the jewel may reflect, let us consider the color black, which is diametrically opposed to the innate brilliance of the luminous jewel. This will serve to illustrate the fact that although the numinous and bright knowledge and vision is the exact opposite of the darkness of ignorance, it is nevertheless of the same single essence.
When the jewel reflects the color black, its entire substance becomes completely black; its luminosity is no longer visible. If ignorant children or country bumpkins then happened to see it, they would immediately think it was a black jewel.

When the mind of numinous awareness is present in an ordinary man, it is completely stupid, deluded, greedy, and lustful. Hence a deluded person simply assumes that he is definitely an ordinary man. This example is a simile for all the sentient beings in the six destinies.

If someone were to say, "This is a luminous jewel," you can be sure that they would not believe him. They might even get angry at him or accuse him of trying to deceive them. Even if he were to explain all his reasons, they would neither listen to nor consider his words.

I, Tsung-mi, have frequently encountered this type of person. If you tell them, "That which is clear and capable of awareness right now is your Buddha-mind," they evidently do not believe it. They are not even willing to consider it, saying simply, "I, so and so, am ungifted and really cannot comprehend this." This is the usual perspective among people who are attached to the characteristics of the dharma of the greater and lesser vehicles and those of the teaching of men and gods.

Chinul's Exposition: The understanding-awakening achieved by people who cultivate their minds refers to the fact that they have not been cowardly or timid in regard to this matter. Rather, by having firm faith in their own minds and relying on the practice of tracing back the light of the mind, they have come to appreciate for themselves the taste of dharma. There are those, however, who make no serious effort to trace back the mind's radiance but simply nod their heads affirmatively and say, "That which is clear and capable of awareness right now is your Buddha-mind"—such people have certainly not grasped the idea.[46]

THE VIEW OF THE NORTHERN SCHOOL

Even though they are willing to believe, as explained, that this is a luminous jewel, their eyes see that it is black and they say: "The jewel is enveloped and obscured by the black color; only after it has been cleaned and polished and the blackness removed will its luminosity finally manifest." Then and only then will they say that they see for themselves the luminous jewel. The view of the Northern school is parallel to this.

Chinul's Exposition: I hope that cultivators of the mind will examine this simile in detail so that they will not succumb to such a view.[47] You should not leave behind falsity in order to search for truth; nor should you assume that falsity is truth. Rather, if you understand that false thoughts arise from the nature, then their arising is precisely their nonarising and, at that point, they are calmed.[48] How could there then persist this view of a dichotomy between truth and falsity?[49]

THE VIEW OF THE HUNG-CHOU SCHOOL

There is another type of person who points out, "It is precisely this blackness itself which is the luminous jewel. The substance of that luminous jewel can never be seen;[50] so if you want to know what that substance is, it is precisely that blackness and precisely all the different colors like blue and yellow." Such a position will cause the fools who have firm faith in these words either to remember only that blackness or to recognize all the different shades as being the luminous jewel. At other times, if they should see the black kernel of a *bodhi* nut,[51] or blue beads made of rice gum,[52] or even beads of dark amber or creamy quartz, they would say that these are all *maṇi* jewels. Later on, if they see a genuine *maṇi* jewel when it is not reflecting any color and only its transparent, pure appearance is visible, they fail to recognize it. Since they do not see the colors they are able to recognize, they have doubts about the jewel's luminous transparency.

> The view of the Hung-chou school is parallel to this. "Fools" refers to later students of this school. "At other times, if they should see the black kernel of a *bodhi* nut" refers to the thoughts of greed, craving, hatred, and conceit which manifest in the mind when it is immersed in the mundane world and discriminates the objects in the coarse sense-spheres. "Amber and creamy quartz" refers to thoughts of friendliness, goodness, humility, and reverence. "When it is not reflecting a color" refers to the mental state which is devoid of all thoughts. "Only its transparent, pure appearance is visible" refers to the thoughtlessness which is clear and self-aware. "They have doubts" means they assume that to say the mind is only something which apprehends and knows is a misconception.

THE VIEW OF THE NIU-T'OU SCHOOL

Chinul's Exposition: If people who are cultivating the mind comprehend that the nature of both good and evil is void and utterly unascertainable, then even though they act all day long, they constantly maintain the state of no-mind and do not succumb to the view of these fools. On the other hand, at times when that thoughtlessness which is clear and self-aware has no contact with external conditions, if they give rise to any further intellectualization, the net of views will become even more tightly meshed.[53]

> There is another type of person who, if he hears that these different colors are false and utterly void to the very core of their essence, assumes that the jewel itself is also utterly void. He then says, "When you grasp at nothing you are an accomplished man; but if you still recognize even one dharma, you do not yet understand." Such people do not realize that at the point where all shades of color are void, there still exists the brilliant luminosity of the jewel which is not void.

> > The view of the Niu-t'ou school is parallel to this. When its adherents hear the explanation of voidness in the *Prajñāpāramitā sūtras,* they assume that the original enlightened nature is also void and unascertainable. Hence it is clarified here that voidness of the mind refers to the absence in the true mind of discriminative thoughts like greed, hatred, and so forth. It does not

mean that there is no mind. "No-mind" means only that we banish the defilements in the mind. Consequently, we know that Niu-t'ou only explicated the negative; he did not illuminate the positive.

Chinul's Exposition: Although this sort of explanation is given so that people who are cultivating the mind will not fall into dead voidness, what fault is there if it is explained that the nature of original enlightenment is also nothingness so that the blindness of the mind will be cured in those who still tend to grasp at verbal explanations? A simile illustrating Ho-tse's view follows.

THE VIEW OF THE HO-TSE SCHOOL

Why can it not be stated straight out that only the brilliant, pure, and full luminosity is the substance of the jewel?

The mind-essence is merely void and calm awareness. If only void-calmness is explained, without revealing awareness, how would this essence differ from empty space? It would be like a brilliant sphere of porcelain which, though clean, lacks luminosity. How could it be called a *maṇi* jewel capable of reflecting everything?

All the reflected colors—black as well as the shades of green, yellow, and so forth—are empty and false. Hence, at the moment when black is seen,[54] it is not really black which is seen after all: it is the transparent luminosity of the jewel. Blue is really not blue: it is only that same luminosity. Red, white, yellow, and so forth are exactly the same: they are only the jewel's luminosity. Therefore, if you regard each color as being merely that brilliant, pure, and full luminosity, you cannot be confused about the jewel.

Everything is void; only the mind is immutable. Even when the mind is deluded, it is still aware, for awareness is inherently undeluded. Even when thoughts arise, it is still aware, for awareness is inherently free of thoughts. For that matter, whether the mind is sad or happy, joyful or angry, loving or hateful, in each of these cases it is always aware. Since awareness is inherently void and calm, the mind is void and calm and yet aware. It is at that point that a person is clear and unconfused about the mind-nature. This description is considerably different from that of the other schools.[55]

If you are merely unconfused about the nature of the jewel, then black is not really black: black is actually the jewel itself. With all other colors it is exactly the same. At that point it no longer matters whether colors are present or not—for the luminosity of the jewel can freely adapt to either circumstance.

"Black is not really black" is the same as Niu-t'ou's approach. "Black is actually the jewel itself" is the same as Hung-chou's description. If one has seen for oneself the luminous jewel, the profound will perforce contain the shallow.[56]

CONCLUSION

If you do not realize that luminosity is the eternally unchanging essence of the jewel which is able to reflect all other colors, but insist that black and so forth are the jewel [Hung-chou's view], or that one should attempt to remove the black in order to find the jewel [the view of the Northern school], or that luminosity and blackness are both nonexistent [Niu-t'ou's view], then in all these cases you have not yet seen the jewel.

Chinul's Exposition: Previously the statement was made that "[Ho-tse's] awakened understanding was lofty and brilliant and his discernment was clear." This is exactly what is meant here.

WHY NUMINOUS AWARENESS IS DISCUSSED[57]

Question: According to the explanations of the noumenal nature given in all the *Mahāyāna sūtras,* in the teachings of all the schools of Sŏn both past and present, and even in Ho-tse's school, there is neither arising nor ceasing, creation nor sign, ordinary man nor saint, right nor wrong: truth is inexpressible and unattestable. Why not simply accept this standpoint? What need is there to discuss numinous awareness?

Answer: These are all examples of apophatic discourse;[58] they are not intended to expose the essence of the mind. If I did not point out that the clear, constant awareness which is present now, never interrupted and never obscured, is your own mind, what could I refer to as being uncreated and signless and so forth? For this reason, you must realize that all the various teachings explain only that it is this awareness which is neither arising nor ceasing and so forth. Consequently, Ho-tse pointed to the knowledge and vision which exist within the void and signless state so that men would recognize it; then they could comprehend that even though their minds pass from one life to another, the mind is eternally uninterrupted until the achievement of Buddhahood. Furthermore, Ho-tse gathered together various terms like uncreated, nonabiding, even inexpressible, and simply referred to them all as being the void and calm awareness which assimilates everything. Voidness means that it is devoid of all signs; it is still an apophatic term. Calm is the immutable, immovable aspect of the real nature; it is not the same as empty nothingness. Awareness refers to the manifestation of this very essence; it is not the same as discrimination. These three components alone comprise the fundamental essence of the true mind. Therefore, from the inital activation of the *bodhicitta* until the attainment of Buddhahood, there is only calmness and only awareness, unchanging and uninterrupted. It is only according to the respective position [on the bodhisattva path] that their designations and attributes are slightly different.[59]

HOW HUNG-CHOU AND HO-TSE DIFFER

Question: Hung-chou also referred to numinous attention, gleaming reflection, and so on.[60] How are they any different from awareness?

Answer: Suppose we try to display the one essence through its many different properties. Since the myriads of dharmas are all this one mind, how could we be limited solely to attention, reflection, and so on? But if we try to point directly to that fixed essence, then the mind-nature of the foolish and the wise, the good and the evil, all kinds of birds and animals, and so forth is, in all these cases, naturally clear, constantly aware, and accordingly different from trees and stones.

Such terms as attention and awareness are not all-inclusive. For instance, if we say that a person is deluded, it means that he is unenlightened; if we say that a person is foolish, it means that he has no wisdom. When the mind is blank,[61] it cannot be called gleaming, reflective, and the like. Hence how can these states be identical to the mind-nature which is constantly aware by nature? For this reason, the chief of the Hwaŏm commentators said in his *Epistle on the Essentials of the Mind:* "In the essence of the unabiding mind, the numinous awareness is never dark."[62] Although Hung-chou referred to numinous attention, he simply wished to indicate that sentient beings possess such a quality; it is as if he were to say that they all have the Buddha-nature. But this is not a precise indication. If we try to point it out, we can only say that this explains that which is capable of speech and so forth. If we try to ascertain exactly what that is, however, we will only be able to say, "All things are false appellations; there are no fixed dharmas."[63]

To sum up, the teachings include the two approaches of negation and revelation,[64] and if we try to ascertain their real import they refer respectively to true voidness and sublime existence. If we probe the original mind we find that it is complete in both essence and function. Now the Hung-chou and Niu-t'ou schools consider wiping all traces away to be the ultimate virtue; this involves only the style of apophatic discourse and the import of true voidness. Although this is complete as far as essence is concerned, their approach is deficient regarding the teachings of revelation and the import of sublime existence; they overlook the function.

THE HUNG-CHOU SCHOOL NEGLECTS THE INNATE FUNCTION

Question: Since Hung-chou revealed the mind-nature through its capacity for speech, action, and so forth, this corresponds to the revelation teaching. As this capacity is identical to the functioning of the mind-nature, what deficiency is there?

Answer: The original essence of the true mind contains two types of function. First, there is the innate function of the self-nature. Second, there is the function which adapts to conditions. These can be compared to a bronze mirror. The bronze itself corresponds to the essence of the self-nature. The brightness of the bronze corresponds to the function of the self-nature. The images reflected because of that brightness are the function which adapts to conditions. Under suitable conditions images can be reflected and manifest in thousands of different ways; but the brightness is ever bright. The "one taste" of this brightness is used as a simile for the constant calmness of the mind. This is the essence of the self-nature. The capacity of this awareness for speech, discrimination, and so on is the function which adapts to conditions. Now, when Hung-chou points to the capacity for speech and the like he only points out the function which responds to conditions; he overlooks the function of the self-nature.

The revelation teaching also employs the two approaches of revelation through inference and revelation through perception. Hung-chou notes, "The mind cannot be pointed out; it is through such properties as capacity for speech and so forth that we can prove its existence and become aware of the presence of the Buddha-nature." This is the approach of revelation through inference. Ho-tse says straightaway,[65] "Since the mind-essence is that which is capable of awareness, awareness is precisely the mind." To reveal the mind through its awareness is the approach of revelation through perception. I have now completed my narration of the two aspects of immutability and adaptability.

CHINUL'S EXPOSITION

In a letter of the Premier P'ei Hsiu addressed to Sŏn Master Tsung-mi it is written: "Adherents of the Sŏn school all have divergent opinions; they criticize and slander each other and are unwilling to come to any kind of accord."[66] Master Tsung-mi also said, " 'Fools' refers to later disciples of this school." Now it is clear that the adherents who discriminate between the virtues and shortcomings [of the different schools] have all wrongly inherited the teachings of Sŏn; they have lost its true import. In his *Forest Records,* Hung Chüeh-fan sharply criticizes the assessments of Master Tsung-mi and supports the approaches of Hung-chou and Niu-t'ou.[67] He fears that the shortcomings discussed by Master Tsung-mi, which seemed to implicate the founders of these schools, might confuse the minds of students in later generations. When teaching people of different capacities, every ancient master used skillful expedients; hence we cannot hold views in favor of this or that approach based solely on their words. We should rather use this bright mirror to illuminate our own minds. Discerning between right and wrong, let us cultivate *samādhi* and *prajñā* simultaneously, and quickly realize *bodhi.*[68]

SUDDEN AWAKENING AND GRADUAL CULTIVATION[69]

Here I will elaborate on the two approaches of sudden awakening and gradual cultivation. The principle of suchness is absent of even Buddhas and sentient beings, let alone a transmission from master to disciple. Nevertheless, since there has been a patriarchal succession starting from the Buddha we can know that there is still preserved an approach which people can follow through cultivation, realization, approach, and entry. If this approach is discussed in regard to the person, there is delusion and awakening, ordinary man and saint. Awakening from delusion is sudden; transforming an ordinary man into a saint is gradual.

Just what is sudden awakening? Due to beginningless delusion and inverted thinking, you consider the four great elements to be the body, deluded thoughts to be the mind, and these together to be the self. But if you come across a good friend who explains the significance of these concepts of immutability and adaptability, nature and characteristic, essence and function, you can abruptly awaken to the fact that the numinous, bright knowledge and vision are your own true mind. That mind is originally ever calm and devoid of nature or characteristic; it is indeed the *dharmakāya*. This nonduality of body and mind is the true I; there is not the slightest difference between it and all the Buddhas. Consequently, it is said that awakening is sudden.[70]

Suppose a high courtier dreams he is in prison, his body carrying the cangue and lock, suffering all kinds of anxiety and pain. While he is trying to think of a hundred different ways to escape, suppose that someone happens to call out and awaken him. Suddenly awakened, he would then see that he had always been at home, and that in his ease and happiness, wealth and rank, he is no different from any of the other magistrates at the imperial court.

The "high courtier" stands for the Buddha-nature, the "dream" for delusion, and the "prison" for the triple world. The "body" represents the *ālayavijñāna,* "the cangue and lock" stand for greed and attachment, and "suffering all kinds of anxiety and pain" refers to karmic retribution. "A hundred different ways to escape" corresponds to inquiries about dharma and eagerness in cultivation. "Someone happens to call out and awaken him" refers to good friends. "Suddenly awakened" corresponds to the mind which opens upon hearing dharma. "He would then see" refers to the true self, the *dharmakāya.* "Had always been at home" refers to the statement in the [*Vimalakīrtinirdeśa*] *sūtra* of the ultimate void and calm house.[71] "In his ease and happiness" is the happiness of nirvana. "Wealth and rank" means that the essence is originally endowed with meritorious qualities and sublime functions as numerous as the sands of the Ganges. "No different from any of the other magistrates at the imperial court" means that he has the same true nature as all the Buddhas.

Since each element in this dharma-analogy is clear, you can easily ascertain that although the body and mind during dreams are fundamentally identical to the body and mind during the waking state, when it comes to discussing their characteristics and functions there is a drastic difference between the distorted and the correct. Once the man in the analogy has awakened he will never return willingly to being the courtier in the dream. Hence the analogy shows that although the source of the mind is one, delusion and awakening are drastically different. Thus to be a grand minister[72] in a dream (to obtain through one's practice a rebirth as Mahābrahmā or other high states, while remaining deluded) is not as good as to become a superintendent of employees[73] in the waking state (to have entered the first level of the ten stages of faith after having awakened). To possess the seven jewels in a dream (to cultivate the innumerable meritorious actions while remaining deluded) is not as good as having a hundred coins in the waking state (to keep the five precepts and to develop the ten wholesome actions after having awakened). In all these cases one is illusory and the other is true; consequently, they cannot be compared. (This is what is meant in all the *sūtra* teachings when it is said, "To make offerings with all the seven jewels in the trichiliocosm is not as good as listening to one line of a *gāthā* [of dharma]."）[74] Now, since there has been a transmission from master to disciple, we must distinguish clearly the distorted and the correct.

I hope that all who are in search of the path will evaluate this approach of sudden awakening from every perspective. Since the dharma-simile is clear, confirm it for yourself anytime. If you have no awakening or understanding, how can you say that your cultivation is true?[75]

I have seen that students of the doctrine are trapped in the explanations of the provisional teachings. Grasping at the differentiation between true and false, they make themselves backslide. Others chat about the unimpeded [conditioned origination] of all phenomena but do not cultivate meditation. As they do not believe that there is a secret formula for awakening to their own minds,[76] when they hear about the Sŏn approach of seeing the nature and achieving Buddhahood, they think it refers to nothing more than the principle of leaving behind words as advocated in the sudden teachings.[77] Nor are they aware that in a complete awakening to the original mind, immutability and adaptability, nature and characteristics, essence and function, ease and happiness, as well as wealth and rank are the same as that of all the Buddhas. How can such people be considered wise?

I have also seen that some students of Sŏn believe only that people of outstanding capacity can directly ascend to the Buddha-*bhūmi* without having to progress through all the steps. They do not believe in the text of this *Record,* which teaches that after achieving awakened understanding one enters into the ten levels of faith. Consequently, even if they do develop their minds somewhat, they are unaware of the various degrees of understanding and practice, or of the arising and ceasing of tainted habits. They are full of conceit regarding dharma, and the words they utter exaggerate their achievement. The *Exposition of the Avataṃsaka Sūtra* states: "When, in the cause of faith, an ordinary man of great aspiration meshes without the slightest degree of error with all the qualities of the fruition of Buddhahood, then faith is achieved."[78] If we are aware of this fact, we will, without being self-denigrating or haughty,[79] know the meaning of cultivating the mind.

The explanation of gradual cultivation which follows refers to the gradualness of the complete teachings; reflect on it carefully.[80]

Now I will explain gradual cultivation. Even though you suddenly awaken to the fact that the true mind, the *dharmakāya,* is exactly the same in all the Buddhas, for many kalpas you have mistakenly grasped at the four great elements as being the self. Since your habits have become second nature, it is extremely difficult to abandon them suddenly. For this reason you must, while relying on your awakening, cultivate gradually. If after reducing [defilements] and reducing them again,[81] you have nothing left to reduce, this is called achieving Buddhahood. There is no Buddhahood which can be achieved outside this mind. Nevertheless, even though you must cultivate gradually, you have previously awakened to the fact that the defilements are originally void and the nature of the mind is originally pure. While excising the unwholesome, therefore, you excise without excising anything; while cultivating the wholesome, you cultivate without cultivating anything. This is true cultivation and excision.

Question: As to the cultivation which is undertaken after awakening: if this is related to the previous analogy of the dream, would it not be the same as if, after the courtier had been awakened, he were again to try to escape from prison and throw off the yoke?

Answer: That was only an analogy concerning the meaning of sudden awakening; it does not apply to gradual cultivation. Indeed, the dharma has an infinity of meanings; but mundane matters have only one.[82] Therefore, although the *Nirvāṇa Sūtra* discusses only the Buddha-nature, it presents eight hundred similes, each with its own application; they cannot be used at random.[83]

Here is a simile to explain gradual cultivation.[84] Suppose an expanse of water is disturbed by the wind and heaves with wave after wave: one is then in danger of drifting away or drowning. Or suppose the cold air freezes it into a sheet of ice: its capacity for irrigating or cleansing is then blocked. Nevertheless, the moist nature of water remains unchanged whether turbulent or placid, frozen or flowing.

"Water" is a simile for the true mind. "Wind" stands for ignorance and "waves" stand for the defilements. "Drifting away or drowning" stands for wandering between the six destinies. "Cold air" refers to habitual tendencies toward ignorance, craving, and sensuality. "Freezes it into a sheet of ice" stands for the tenacious clinging to [personal and impersonal forms of] the four great elements as being entirely distinct from one another.[85] "Its capacity for irrigating or cleansing is then blocked": "irrigating" is a simile for the expression "it rains a great rain of dharma" which benefits the masses of beings and nourishes the sprout which grows into the path;[86] "cleansing" refers to removing the defilements; and, as all this is impossible so long as delusion remains, it is "blocked." "Nevertheless, the moist nature of water remains unchanged whether turbulent or placid, frozen or flowing" means that when you are greedy or angry, you are aware; when you are compassionate and charitable, you are also aware; whatever your emotional state—

depression, joy, grief,[87] happiness—you are never unaware. Hence the word "unchanged."

Now, the sudden awakening to the constant awareness of the original mind is like recognizing the immutable moist nature of water. Since the mind is no longer deluded, there is no ignorance. It is as if the wind had suddenly stopped. After awakening, mental disturbances naturally come to a gradual halt like waves which gradually subside. By developing both body and mind in *śīla, samādhi,* and *prajñā,* you gradually become self-reliant until you are unhindered in displaying magic and miracles and can universally benefit all sentient beings. This is called Buddhahood. . . .

III. Chinul's Exposition

THE INSTANTANEOUS ATTAINMENT OF BUDDHAHOOD

Nowadays some people are unable to penetrate to the fact that, whether mundane or supramundane, all good and evil causes and effects derive from this one thought.[88] In their daily life they place only light supervision over their minds and do not understand the role of careful investigation. Although there are times when, by chance, they understand the meaning while reading *sūtras* or Sŏn *gāthās,* it is only momentary good fortune. Later they will lay this understanding aside lightly and fail to develop their discernment. Moreover, they will not give rise to the thought that this dharma is something which, in myriads of kalpas, is difficult to meet. As they follow after defiled conditions, thought after thought will flow on continuously. What hope is there that they will ever complete their work?

The Sŏn Master Tsung-mi issued some great words of warning: "Men who are training on the path treat cause lightly and effect importantly. I hope that those of you on the path will have deep faith in your own minds."[89] If we scrutinize these words, can we not but feel sad? I will attempt to discuss this point.

The discriminative thought processes of ordinary men nowadays derive from the conditioned arising of the true nature. Since that nature is originally pure, if we empty ourselves of passion and simply trace back the radiance of the mind, then with only one thought [we can return to that original state of purity] without wasting considerable effort. Although the power of *prajñā* might then be great, the power of ignorance is inconceivably greater. Consequently, it is difficult afterward to nurture our achievement constantly and remember to maintain it. Later, when our practice of looking back on the radiance of the mind is progressing satisfactorily and our faculty of faith is firm, if we then persist with ardor over a long period of time, how could we not succeed in our practice? But if we disregard the importance of this one thought and seek elsewhere for the supernatural powers and the power of the path which both result from seeing the nature, how will we ever gain repose?

The so-called one thought which is present now in all men is precisely the one dharma; consequently, it is said, "The word 'dharma' means the mind of the sentient being."[90] This mind is the source of the three greatnesses and its two aspects of suchness and arising/ceasing. For this reason, the essential nature of the mind plunges to the depths and embraces all vastness. It completely contains the myriads of phenomena, yet it adapts to conditions while remaining unmoved. Hence it is essence and function, person and dharma, false and true, phenomena and noumenon. Its aspects manifest in an infinity of ways, but it is always placid and ever calm, for it cuts off all plurality. For this reason, it is neither nature nor characteristic, neither noumenon nor phenomena, neither Buddha nor sentient being, and so on. The freedom and nonobstruction of comprehensive assimilation and radical analysis, mentioned before, is what is meant here.

Since the mind is so inconceivable, the masters of our school pointed directly to the one thought which is present now in all men and advocated achieving Buddhahood through seeing the nature. When we speak of nature here, it is the fundamental dharma-nature of the one mind—not the nature which stands in contradistinction to characteristics. Consequently, in the *Epistle on the Essentials of the Mind* by the chief of the Hwaŏm commentators [Ch'eng-kuan] it is said:

> The great path originates in the mind;
> The mind-dharma originates in nonabiding.
> In the essence of the unabiding mind the numinous awareness is never dark.
> Nature and characteristic are calm and embrace all meritorious functions.[91]

My hope is that those today who are suspicious of the Sŏn dharma will examine this excellent testimony and, resolving their doubts, will cultivate their minds.

Furthermore, the Great Master Yung-chia Chen-chüeh said, "One thought means the numinously aware thought of right enlightenment."[92] A poem by Master Pao-chih says:

> The great path is clearly before your eyes,
> But the ignorant who are deluded and confused cannot recognize it.
> It is in one thought of the mind,
> So why search for it elsewhere?[93]

Pointing only to this "one thought" is an abbreviation used in Sŏn *gāthās* to indicate the immediate crossing-over to liberation. Therefore we know that although this one thought was said to be the mind of sentient beings, it is clear that it is not limited to the arising/ceasing aspect of the two divisions of the mind or the characteristics aspect of the three greatnesses. Moreover, it is not the same as the principle in the inferior teachings which holds out the hope of achieving Buddhahood in one thought. Some people see the similarity in these statements and multiply their discriminations needlessly; they are thus unable to gain deep insight into the sublime truth.[94]

Sŏn Master Yen-shou, citing the *Avatamsaka Sūtra,* said: "The triple world contains no particularized dharmas; it is only a construct of the one mind."[95] Now this means that the triple world is only a construct of the mind which, in the period of one thought-moment, becomes ignorant and clings to signs. This is then the origin of the triple world's ailment of birth and death. If we realize our ignorance, do not give rise to [craving], clinging, and becoming, and finish with our old karma and make none anew, this will be the basic cause for curing the ailment. For this reason, we should know that the one thought of the mind, the origin of the ailment, is also the fountainhead of the path.[96]

Grasping at reality is an error; knowing voidness is faultless. Awakening takes place in a *kṣaṇa;* past and future then will no longer exist. For this reason, we should know that when our discernment becomes subtle and sublime, the absolute principle will be extremely near. Although we might be sentient beings of the degenerate age, if the measure of our mind is wide and spacious, we will be able to empty our hearts of passion, practice self-reflection, and have faith that not even one thought-moment of conditioned arising is produced. Even if we do not yet have personal realization, the mind will act as the foundation for entering the path. The *Complete Enlightenment Sūtra* says: "If the mind of a sentient being in the degenerate age does not give rise to falsity, the Buddhas would say that such a person is a bodhisattva who has appeared in the world."[97] If in the degenerate age there were no way to enter the path through faith and yet the Buddhas made this sort of statement, they would be lying. But the Buddhas speak truthfully and in accord with reality; thus how can we make ourselves backslide by not investigating? As it is said in the *Mirror of the Source Record:*[98]

Question: The seeds and the manifesting formations of sentient beings' karma and retribution have been developing over a number of kalpas; they are like glue or lacquer. How is it, then, that if we only know the one mind, they will be suddenly destroyed and Buddhahood will be achieved?

Answer: If you grasp at mind and objects as being real and at person and dharmas as being nonvoid, you will needlessly practice for an infinity of kalpas without ever realizing path-fruition. But if you suddenly recognize that there is no self and penetrate deeply to the emptiness of material things, subject and object will both be obliterated. What then will remain to be realized? It is as if a particle of dust were thrown into a fiercely howling wind or a light boat were to flow with a swift current. My only fear is that you will not believe in the one mind and will make difficulties for yourselves. If you enter the mirror of the source (the one mind is the source which reflects all dharmas like a mirror), where can you go where this realization will not follow you? It is like the bodhisattva Pradhānaśūra who transgressed the precept on sexual misconduct but still awakened to the unborn. It is also like the *bhikṣuṇī* Hsing who could practice no-mind and also realized path-fruition. If even they could achieve enlightenment, how much more possible is it for those who have faith and understanding in the one-vehicle dharma and who know their own minds to have full realization?[99]

Someone who had a doubt asked, "Why should we not excise the defilements?"

In explanation I answered, "You should only observe that killing, stealing, sexual misconduct, and lying all arise from the one mind. If they are calmed as soon as they arise, what further excision is necessary? Therefore, if you only know the one mind, then naturally the myriads of sense-objects will become like an illusion. Why is this? All dharmas arise illusorily from the mind; but, as the mind is formless, what sign can those dharmas have?"

According to the meaning of excising disturbances as explained in the [*Mirror of the Source*] *Record*—an explanation given from the standpoint of both nature and characteristics—the exciseless excision which excises while excising nothing is true excision.[100]

Nowadays Sŏn adepts say only that originally there are no defilements and that inherently those defilements are *bodhi;* but if they do not yet have the clarity which is produced by sudden awakening, this principle will still be difficult to comprehend when they are involved in killing, theft, sexual misconduct, or lying. The *Strategy of the Avataṃsaka Sūtra* says:

Perturbations have fundamentally no source; they arise abruptly because of delusion about the truth. If one is deluded but does not turn away from it, confusion will be boundless. It is like wisps of cloud covering the sky: though they have come from nowhere, they fill the sky in an instant and the six directions are darkened. But should a strong wind suddenly blow, the clouds scatter at once. Then not a trace of them remains for thousands of *li,* and the myriads of images all stand out clearly. In the same manner, when the wind of expedients arises and exposes the fact that the perturbations are without basis, then in the appearance of the voidness of the nature all qualities are originally complete. The eighty-four thousand defilements are all *pāramitās;* the delusory obstacles numerous as the sands of the Ganges are entirely suchness.[101]

This explanation is quite clear. Killing, stealing, sexual misconduct, and lying all arise from delusion; but if through expedient wisdom you expose the fact that the perturbations are without foundation and the voidness of the nature appears, then, as was said, from where do killing, stealing, sexual misconduct, and so forth arise?[102] But rather than saying merely[103] "exposes the fact that the perturbations are without basis," it is better to say "you should only observe that killing, stealing, sexual misconduct, and lying all arise from the one mind. . . . They are calmed immediately when they arise." Here both nature and characteristics are clarified. One who does not use his mind in contemplative wisdom will not understand this principle.

The last lines of the *Chart of the [Avataṃsaka's] One-Vehicle Dharmadhātu* say:

> As I sit upright on the seat of the middle way at the reality limit,
> What has been unmoving since of old is called Buddha.

> Question: Sentient beings who are completely bound have yet to excise the defilements or to achieve merit and wisdom. For what reason is it said that Buddhahood has already been achieved since of old?
>
> Answer: If defilements are not yet excised, it cannot be said that Buddhahood has been achieved; but once the defilements are utterly excised and merit and wisdom are brought to perfection, it is called the achievement of Buddhahood since of old.

> Question: What is the excising of defilements?
>
> Answer: The *Daśabhūmikasūtra-śāstra* explains that [defilements and counteractive expedients] do not exist in past, present, or future but are, nevertheless, operative in past, present, and future.[104]

> Question: How do you perform this excision?
>
> Answer: Like space: in such a manner should you excise. As long as you have not yet done any excision, it is not called excising. But once the excision has been completed it is called the excising which has been finished since of old. It is like awakening from a dream: sleeping and waking are not then the same. Hence, although we refer to achievement and nonachievement, excision and nonexcision, the real truth is that the sign of reality of all dharmas neither increases nor decreases and is originally unmoving.[105]

What Master Ŭisang meant by "the defilements are utterly excised and merit and wisdom are brought to perfection" is that the activation of the *bodhicitta* at the first level of the ten abidings is precisely the achievement of Buddhahood from the standpoint of perfect interfusion which incorporates the five stages [of the bodhisattva path]. This is possible because if one defilement is excised, all are excised; and if a portion of merit and wisdom is achieved, all are achieved. From that point on, as he follows the progressive approach, he can look forward to the ultimate fruition of Buddhahood. Since nature and characteristics, as explained in the complete teachings, are unimpeded, perfect interfusion does not impede progression. Since progression does not impede perfect interfusion, he does not use the perceptions of the affective consciousnesses to construct an understanding of the differences in the time factor.[106] "[Defilements and counteractive expedients] do not exist in past, present, or future" means that the object—the defilements which are revealed—is originally void, and the subject—the wisdom which reveals—is also calm. When the nature of both subject and object is abandoned, nothing is ascertainable because the signs of the three time limits are eliminated. Hence one must initially have faith and understanding which accords with the nature; then and only then can one practice.

"Operative in past, present, and future" means that if one uses nonexistent expedients and investigates accordingly, this wisdom operates throughout past, present, and future. Nevertheless, as this expedient wisdom is absolutely unascertainable, it acts and yet is nonacting, for nonaction is precisely action. Hence it was said: "Like space: in such a manner should you excise." Compare the *Mirror of the Source*'s statement: "You should only observe that killing, stealing, sexual misconduct, and lying all arise from the one mind. If they are calmed as soon as they arise, what further excision is necessary?" This is exactly what is meant here.

Ordinary students are not aware that the true cultivation and true excision of the nature school are like space—they are unascertainable. On the basis of their own sensual perceptions they wrongly assume that there really is something which excises and something which is excised, in the same way that light and darkness are in contradistinction. They argue vainly and do not look back on their minds. Hence when will they ever be able to practice correctly the true excision in which the defilements are seen to be originally nonexistent? If you understand this, you should be able to perceive the meaning of Dharma Master Ŭisang's idea that Buddhahood has been achieved since of old and excision has been accomplished since of old. Then you will also be able to harmonize easily with the sign of reality of all dharmas without falling into the extreme views that dharmas can either be augmented or diminished.

The *Essentials of the Hua-yen Teachings* says: "Since one who enters the *dharmadhātu* enters nowhere, there is nowhere he does not enter. Since one who cultivates the boundless qualities gained through practice actually gains nothing, there is nothing he does not gain."[107]

Master Chih-kung's *Gāthā in Praise of the Mahāyāna* says:

> *Śrāvakas* excise perturbations thought after thought,
> But the thought which does this excising is a brigand.
> If brigand after brigand is, in turn, trying to chase each other away,
> When will they be able to understand that originally speech is silence?

They do not understand the comprehensiveness of the Buddha-dharma,
And waste their efforts in following lines and counting drops of ink. . . .

The dharma-nature is originally ever calm,
Vast and without borders.
But if you settle the mind within, grasping or rejecting,
You will constantly alternate between these two.

Wearing a serious expression while he sits in meditation, he enters *dhyāna,*
He absorbs the sense-spheres and calms the mind's thoughts and imagina-
    tions,
But this is the cultivation of a mechanical, wooden man.[108]
When will he ever arrive at the other shore?

All dharmas are originally void and unattached.
Ultimately they are like floating clouds that form and scatter.
If one suddenly awakens to the inherent voidness of the original nature,
It will be the same as the sweating out of a fever.

Do not speak of this to men who lack wisdom,
Or else I will beat your body until it is scattered like stars.[109]

National Master Hui-chung said: "To excise the defilements is called the
two vehicles [the provisional teachings]; the nonarising of defilements is
called great nirvana."[110] The implication of this passage is not that *bodhi* is
gained by excising the defilements; most properly, it means to realize that
defilements are *bodhi.* This is then true cultivation and true excision. As a
former master said, "When bodhisattvas are deluded they assume that
bodhi is defilements. When bodhisattvas are awakened, they assume that
defilements are *bodhi.*" This is exactly what is meant here. It is like the person who asked the ancient master [Chih-wei], "The doctrine speaks of the
true nature's conditioned arising. What is this principle?" His attendant,
the future Ch'an master Hsüan-ting, answered, "O Great Venerable One!
Exactly at the time you gave rise to the thought to ask this question, the true
nature's conditioned arising was functioning."[111] Under the influence of
these words the monk experienced a great awakening.[112] Consequently, we
know that if those who are cultivating the mind nowadays do not contemplate deeply the fact that the conditioned arising which occurs in one
thought-moment is uncreated, they will never be able to avoid the suspicious argumentation engendered by their attitude—that the perturbations
are something concrete which must be excised. Furthermore, they will not
be aware of the meaning of the true excising which excises nothing. When
confronted by this type of person it is best to remain silent.

Now, when we say you must realize that defilements are *bodhi,* we mean
you must realize that the nature of the defilements is originally void. As it is
said in the *Commentary to the Complete Enlightenment Sūtra,* " 'Whether

thoughts are of a positive or negative nature, there are none which are not liberation.' Since those thoughts themselves are originally void and inherently thoughtless, deluded people say that, as defilements are originally nonexistent, *bodhi* is the attainment of what?"[113] This is said to be a person who understands the words but loses their meaning.

Another past saint said, "When bodhisattvas observe sentient beings, they give rise to three kinds of compassionate thoughts: first, the false suffering [of *samsāra*] is originally nonexistent, but they accept it without noticing it; second, the true bliss [of nirvana] originally exists, but they forgo it without caring; third, they can transpose the two previous attitudes at will."[114] Consequently, we know that if the false suffering of sentient beings really existed and true bliss did not, then whoever would enter the path must subdue this and excise that—just like a well digger who digs up the soil but finds nothing but empty space. How then could it be that, in the biographies of past and present masters, those who in one thought had complete and sudden awakening and understanding are too numerous to count? Hence we know that it is only because a person is narrow-minded and his character inferior that he falsely endeavors to excise the defilements and does not turn his thoughts back to the mind—the place where the ability to excise originates.[115]

The Great Master Yung-chia Chen-chüeh's *Song of Enlightenment* says:[116]

> Though the lion's roar is the speech of fearlessness,
> We should sigh deeply for the stupid and obstinate [who refuse to listen].
> They can only comprehend that transgression of the major precepts is an
>   obstacle to *bodhi,*
> And cannot see that the *tathāgata* is constantly disclosing his esoteric
>   formulas.
>
> There were two *bhikṣus:* one broke the precept on celibacy; the other,
>   the precept against killing.
> But Upāli's firefly wisdom only tightened the knot of wrongdoing.
> The mahāsattva Vimalakīrti instantly removed their doubts,
> Like the hot sun which melts both frost and snow.
>
> Due to their wrong spiritual family and their mistaken knowledge
>   and understanding,
> They do not understand the *tathāgata*'s complete and sudden system.
> The *Hīnayānists* are zealous but neglect the mind of the path;
> The heretics are clever but lack wisdom.[117]

From this passage it is clear that this approach of awakening and understanding in one thought-moment is not a gradual method which rejects falsity and grasps at truth. For this reason, it is called "the *tathāgata*'s esoteric formulas" and "the *tathāgata*'s complete and sudden system."[118] How then can the Hwaŏm sect alone be invested with the qualities of the complete and sudden approach? From the standpoint of its theoretical implications, the Hwaŏm doctrine is not deficient in any respect concerning completeness. But from the standpoint of gaining entrance to the path, the approach of the Sŏn sect involves a complete awakening to the nature and characteristics, as well as the essence and function of one's own mind.

The meaning of complete and sudden awakening and understanding implies no special expedients; it involves merely one thought of personal faith. If your faith is insufficient, you can make use of the power of many skillful means, but you will still end up creating difficulties for yourself. A *gāthā* of Sŏn Master Lung-men Fo-yen says:

> Delusion means to be deluded about awakening,
> Awakening means to be awakened to delusion.
> Delusion and awakening are the same essence—
> Once you awaken you will know this.

> In delusion you take the south for the north
> And grasp at this observation as being real.
> Actually north is originally the same as south—
> Upon awakening you will no longer doubt it.

> If you delve into the conditions of delusion,
> You cannot find the place where they arise.
> Should you suddenly awaken to the right direction,
> Where can delusion go?

> Delusion is just delusion,
> It is you yourself who wrongly assign value.
> Through the mistaken attention of the saṃsāric mind,
> You vainly accept doctrinal tenets.

> If you penetrate through delusion and falsity disappears,
> Your joy will be limitless.
> The slaying of the brigand, ignorance,
> Happens in an instant.
> Within that instant,
> You arcanely pervade the chiliocosm.

> If there is immediate cognition,
> The three time periods become an empty mystery.
> Since beginningless time,
> All things exist now today.
> For the rest of time,
> You need search no further.

> The present thought is thoughtless,
> The numinous light is brilliant.
> As the numinous brilliance shines ever bright,
> The mind's awareness is difficult to block.
>
> The numinous source reaches clear to the blue sky
> And enters all phenomena in creation.
> When ocean-seal *samādhi* manifests clearly,
> You will be unconcerned about activity or rest.[119]

I request all men of great virtue who are cultivating the mind to reflect deeply and carefully on this *gāthā*.

I will now make a humble attempt to review the implications of the process of initial awakening followed by subsequent cultivation. My purpose here is primarily to ensure that beginners will be neither self-denigrating nor haughty and, seeing these principles clearly for themselves, will never become confused.[120]

The text of this *Record* says:

> The sudden awakening to the constant awareness of the original mind is like recognizing the immutable moist nature of water. Since the mind is no longer deluded, there is no ignorance. It is as if the wind had suddenly stopped. After awakening, mental disturbances naturally come to a gradual halt like waves which gradually subside. By developing both body and mind in *śīla, samādhi,* and *prajñā,* you gradually become self-reliant until you are unhindered in displaying magic and miracles and can universally benefit all sentient beings. This is called Buddhahood.

If one contemplates the efficacy and benefit of such a method, it is seen to be vast and brilliant. It is readily understandable, sensible, and permits easy comprehension. It is the best mirror on the mind for those men of today who, while relying on the words of the teachings, have the capacity to enter the path through faith.

Question: When it is said that the void and calm, numinous awareness which has been awakened to by men cultivating the mind nowadays is indeed the mind which has been transmitted successively from the Buddha through the patriarchs, one who is not of superior faculties will be doubtful and confused. If you have valid substantiation of this identity, please give us some examples so that we can examine them and resolve our remaining doubts.

Answer: Although there is much valid evidence, there are special cases where it is clear in every detail and you will be able to see distinctly. As it is said in the *Preface to the Complete References to the Fountainhead of Ch'an Collection:*

It is only because men in China grasped at the texts while remaining deluded to the mind and considered that names were the essence [of the Buddha-dharma] that Bodhidharma used skillful means and rejected the texts while transmitting the mind. First he displayed its name (mind is its name) and silently pointed to its essence (awareness is its essence). He illustrated this through "wall contemplation" so that his student Hui-k'o would be able to eliminate all remaining conditions. Once he had brought his conditioning to an end, Bodhidharma asked, "Has it been extirpated yet or not?"

Hui-k'o answered, "Although all conditioning has been brought to an end, it was not extirpated."

"How will you prove your statement that it was not extirpated?"

"I myself am clearly aware of it; but words cannot express it."

The master then certified this and said, "This alone is the pure mind, your self-nature. Harbor no further doubts about it."

If that answer had not tallied with the truth, Bodhidharma would have pointed out his mistake to him and had him investigate further. At first he did not mention the word "awareness" to Hui-k'o, but merely waited for him to awaken to it for himself so that he would be able to verify the truth through his own personal realization of that essence. Afterward he was given certification and his remaining doubts were resolved. This is what is called "the silent transmission of the mind-seal." "Silent" refers only to keeping silent about the word "awareness"; it does not mean that he did not speak at all. Each transmission throughout the six generations of Chinese patriarchs was of this type.

At the time of Ho-tse, the different schools were competing in the propagation of their doctrines. Even if you wished to search for [enlightened masters who had come into] secret accordance with the truth, the opportunity never presented itself.

Furthermore, consider Bodhidharma's "hanging thread" prediction. Bodhidharma said, "After the sixth generation, my dharma lineage will be like a hanging thread." As Ho-tse feared that the tenets of the [Sŏn] school might be lost, he said that this one word "awareness" is the gate to all wonders. According to the relative profundity or shallowness in the awakening of his students, he resolved to ensure that the teachings of the school were not cut off. This was a decisive point in the fate of the great dharma in this kingdom. As monks and lay adherents both listen extensively to this dharma, the response of the Buddha should be forthcoming.

As other people could not know about the silent transmission, the *kāṣāya* robe was used as its symbol so that they could believe in it. The visible transmission could be easily examined by students; and it employed words and theory exclusively in order to remove doubts.[121]

Here Master Tsung-mi indicates that the one word "awareness" is the source of both the exoteric and the esoteric transmission from generation to generation of the Buddhas and patriarchs.[122] According to people's capacities and the profundity of their awakening in regard to this one word "awareness," those cultivating the mind should try to ensure that the teachings of the school will not be cut off but will continue to shine like a bright mirror. How can one entertain doubts about this?

Question: According to the import of this passage concerning the orthodox transmission,[123] the generations of patriarchs did not first explain the word "awareness" to others.[124] Rather, they waited for them to awaken to it for themselves so that they would be able to verify its truth through their own personal realization of that essence.[125] Afterward those people were given certification. We see that those who are cultivating the mind now initially develop discriminative understanding by means of this word "numinous awareness" and subsequently contemplate their own mind. This is only the approach of the exoteric transmission which uses words and theories to resolve doubts; it does not involve a personal realization of the essence. Hence how can we say such people have awakened to the mind?

Answer: Was this not answered previously? Recall this: "Those who make no serious effort to trace back the mind's radiance but simply nod their heads affirmatively and say, 'That which is clear and capable of awareness right now is your Buddha-mind'—such people have certainly not grasped the idea." How can you assume that the reflections you see before your eyes are the void and calm, numinous awareness? Can one who is unable to distinguish between true and false have awakened to the mind? You should know that when I refer to a man who has awakened to the mind, I do not mean only the removal of doubt through words and theories. Rather, I mean that the student has used the explanation of the void and calm, numinous awareness to develop the efficacy of his practice of looking back on the radiance of the mind. Because of his effort at looking back on the mind's radiance, he gains the essence of mind which is free from thought.

THE LIVE WORD: THE SHORTCUT APPROACH OF *HWADU* INVESTIGATION

The approach to dharma I have discussed so far has been designed to give a detailed assessment of the two aspects of dharma (adaptability and immutability) and the two approaches concerning person (sudden awakening and gradual cultivation) for students who can develop understanding, awakening, and entrance while relying on the teachings. Through these two aspects of dharma, they will be able to understand the doctrine to which all the *sūtras* and *śāstras* of the entire *Tripiṭaka* return: the nature and characteristics of one's own mind. Through the two approaches concerning person they will be able to see the tracks of all the sages and saints—which are the beginning and end of their own practice. This clear assessment of the process of practice will help them to free themselves from delusion, move from the provisional toward the real, and realize *bodhi* quickly.

If students develop understanding based solely on words, however, and remain indecisive about the road they should follow, then even though they investigate the whole day long, they will only end up being bound by intellectual understanding and will never gain tranquillity. Consequently, even though it was not advocated by Master Tsung-mi, for the sake of those patch-robed monks in the Sŏn lineage today who have the capacity to enter the path after leaving behind words, I will briefly cite some passages from the records of the patriarchs and masters. These shortcut expedients, used to inspire progress in their students, should allow accomplished meditators to know the one living road which leads to salvation.

Sŏn Master Ta-hui said:

> Kuei-feng referred to it as numinous awareness. Ho-tse said that the one word "awareness" is the gate to all wonders. Huang-lung Ssu-hsin Sou said, "The one word 'awareness' is the gate to all calamities." It is easy to recognize the intent of Kuei-feng and Ho-tse, but difficult to see that of Ssu-hsin. "Here" [in your mind] you must be endowed with eyes which transcend this world. You cannot make allusions to it; you cannot transmit it. For this reason Yün-men said, "The great majority of statements are like brandishing a sword before a doorway. But beneath the one word there is definitely a road which leads to salvation. If this were not the case, you would die beneath that word."[126]

The Sixth Patriarch addressed his assembly saying:

> "There is one thing which supports the heavens above and the earth below. It exists during all activity, but it is not confined to that activity. All of you! What do you call it?"
> Shen-hui came forward from the assembly and said, "It is the original source of all the Buddhas and Shen-hui's Buddha-nature."
> The patriarch said, "Even if I call it 'one thing' it still isn't correct. How dare you call it 'original source' or 'Buddha-nature'? From now on, even if you go and build a thatched hut to cover your head, you will only be a follower of the school of conceptual understanding."[127]

In the *Records of Master Fa-chen Shou-i* it is said:

> When Master Huai-jang went to see the Sixth Patriarch, the patriarch asked, "Where have you come from?"
> Huai-jang answered, "I came from National Master Sung-shan An's place."
> The patriarch asked, "What thing came in this manner?"
> Huai-jang was left resourceless. Only after acting as the patriarch's attendant for eight years did he understand what he meant. He then told the patriarch, "When I first came here, the master received me with, 'What thing came in this manner?' I have understood."
> The patriarch inquired, "What do you understand?"
> "Even if you allude to it as 'one thing' it does not strike the mark."

"Have you been able to cultivate and realize it, or not?"

"Though cultivation and realization are not absent, they can never be sullied."

"That which can never be sullied is precisely what all the Buddhas safeguard. I am like this and so are you."[128]

Sŏn Master Ta-hui said:

When Master Yüeh-shan first visited Shih-t'ou, he asked, "I have studied the three vehicles and the twelve divisions of the teachings somewhat, but I have heard that in the south of China they point directly to men's minds in order to see the nature and achieve Buddhahood. Since I am still confused about this matter, I beg the master to give me some instructions."

Shih-t'ou said, "This way you cannot get it, but that way you cannot get it either. Whether it is this way or not, you cannot get it." As Yüeh-shan did not understand, Shih-t'ou said, "Go to Kiangsi and ask Great Master Ma-tsu."

Yüeh-shan took his advice and went to Ma-tsu's place, where he asked the same question. Ma-tsu said, "Sometimes I teach people by raising my eyebrows and twinkling my eyes. At other times I do not teach people by raising my eyebrows or twinkling my eyes. The times when I raise my eyebrows and twinkle my eyes is correct; the time when I do not raise my eyebrows or twinkle my eyes is incorrect."

Under the influence of these words, Yüeh-shan had a great awakening; but, having nothing with which to show his gratitude, he merely lowered his head and bowed.

Ma-tsu asked, "What truth have you seen that makes you bow?"

Yüeh-shan said, "When I was at Shih-t'ou's place I was like a mosquito biting the back of an iron ox."

Ma-tsu sanctioned it.[129]

Sŏn Master Ta-hui said:

At first, the Second Patriarch Hui-k'o did not understand the skillful means used by Bodhidharma when he said, "Bring all conditioning to rest externally, and keep the mind without panting internally." In this wise Bodhidharma tried to discuss mind and nature, path and truth. But Hui-k'o quoted texts and thereby sought certification. For this reason, Bodhidharma rejected all his statements; finally, when there was no place left for Hui-k'o to use his mind, he was able to step back and see the mind itself. Hence we may surmise that words which suggested making the logical mind like a wall were not Bodhidharma's real teaching. Suddenly in front of the wall, all conditioning was instantly halted; immediately Hui-k'o saw the moon and forgot all about the finger pointing at it. He then said, "It is clear and constantly aware; words cannot describe it." This statement was only intended to show Bodhidharma that he understood; it was not the real dharma of the Second Patriarch.[130]

Ta-hui said further:

When you are reading the *sūtras* or the stories surrounding the entrance to the path of ancient masters and you do not understand them clearly, your mind will become puzzled, frustrated, and "tasteless"—just as if you were gnawing on an iron rod. When this occurs you should put forth all your energy. First, do not let go of your perplexity, for that is where the intellect cannot operate and thought cannot reach; it is the road through which discrimination is cut and theorizing is ended. Ordinarily, all theorizing and discrimination are aspects of the [sixth] sense-consciousness. You have always been mistaking a thief for your own son.[131] You must not be unclear about this!

Nowadays there is a group of shaven-headed heretics whose eyes are not clear. They only teach people to rest in a charnel ground. But even if a thousand Buddhas appeared in the world while resting in that way, you would not only be unable to rest but your mind would become deluded as well.

Other heretics teach people to forget all passion and maintain silent reflection. Reflecting here, reflecting there, maintaining here, maintaining there, you only become more deluded; you have no hope of gaining comprehension. They sabotage the expedients of the patriarchs and mislead others.

Still other heretics teach people to remain unconcerned about everything and try to "rest" as much as possible—for when you can "rest," passionate thoughts will not arise. Once that happens, you will not be dull and unaware but will immediately be alert and clear. But that sort of teaching is like blinding a man's eyes with poison; it is no small matter.

Even in the case of the old man [Yün-men], it is not that he did not teach people to sit in meditation and find a quiet place to practice; but this is like giving medicine to suit a specific illness: it is not really a proper way to instruct men. Didn't you see? Master Huang-p'o said, "Throughout its transmission, this Sŏn school of ours has never taught men to seek knowledge or understanding. It only says, 'Study the path.' "[132] But actually these are only words of guidance. The path cannot be studied; if you study the path while passions still exist, you will only become deluded to the path. The path which has neither direction nor position is called the Mahāyāna mind. This mind does not exist inside, outside, or in between; in reality, it has no direction or position. Thus it is of primary importance not to give rise to conceptual understanding about it. I want only to tell you that even though you consider your present feelings and thoughts to be the path, once these feelings and thoughts are finished, your mind will have no direction or position.

The path is impeccable. Originally it is nameless. It is only because worldly men do not recognize it and stupidly remain in sensuality that all the Buddhas appeared in the world to destroy that tendency. Fearing that you would not understand, they conventionally established the name "path." But you should not consider that name to be an ultimate and base your interpretations on it.

What I said before about a blind man misguiding others is similar to mistaking a fish-eye for a bright jewel. To make interpretations while remaining attached to names, or to teach people to maintain some sort of provisional practice all involve interpretations which are made while remaining attached to the awareness of the reflections before one's eyes.

To teach people that they must be absolutely intent on resting involves interpretations based solely on maintaining the void-calmness of indifference—that is, to teach people to rest until they attain a nescience wherein they are like earth, wood, tile, or rock. At such a time, to assume that such a state is not merely dull nescience is an interpretation which wrongly endorses words which are designed as expedients to free people from bondage.

To teach people to be attentive to their minds in all circumstances, telling them that they should not allow wrong attention to manifest, is another approach involving interpretation based on the misconception that the affective consciousnesses should be made void like a skull.

To teach people only to relax and let everything take care of itself shows a lack of concern for the arising of mental states or the activity of thoughts. The arising and vanishing of thoughts is originally devoid of any real essence. If you cling to them as being real, the mind which is subject to arising and ceasing will arise. This refers to a person who develops interpretations while assuming that maintaining a natural state is the ultimate dharma.[133]

These defects do not originate from students training on the path. They are all due to the erroneous instructions of blind masters of our school.[134]

Ta-hui said:

If you want to understand the principle of the shortcut, you must blanket the one thought and suddenly break through it—then and only then will you comprehend birth and death. This is called the access of awakening. You should not retain any thought which waits for that breakthrough to occur, however. If you retain a thought which simply waits for a breakthrough, then you will never break through for an eternity of kalpas. You need only lay down, all at once, the mind full of deluded thoughts and inverted thinking, the mind of logical discrimination, the mind which loves life and hates death, the mind of knowledge and views, interpretation and comprehension, and the mind which rejoices in stillness and turns from disturbance. Only when you have laid down everything should you look into the following *hwadu:*

A monk asked Chao-chou, "Does a dog have the Buddha-nature or not?" Chao-chou replied, "*Mu!* [No!]"

This one word is the weapon which smashes all types of wrong knowledge and wrong conceptualization. [1] You should not understand it to mean yes or no. [2] You should not consider it in relation to doctrinal theory. [3] You should not ponder over it logically at the consciousness-base. [4] When the master raises his eyebrows or twinkles his eyes, you should not think he is giving instructions about the meaning of the *hwadu*. [5] You should not make stratagems for solving the *hwadu* through the use of speech. [6] You should not busy yourself inside the tent of unconcern. [7] You should not consider it at the place where you raise the *hwadu* to your attention. [8] You should not look for evidence in the wording.[135]

Throughout the twelve periods and the four postures, try always to keep the question raised before you and centered in your attention. Does a dog have the

Buddha-nature or not? He said *mu.* Without neglecting your daily activities, try
to work in this manner.[136]

I, Moguja, said: This dharma-discourse only delineated eight defects. If
we examine its exposition from beginning to end, however, we must also
include these two defects: [9] taking it to be the *mu* of true nonexistence and
[10] grasping at a deluded state, simply waiting for awakening. Consequently, together they amount to ten defects.
   Ta-hui said further:

> Chao-chou's *hwadu,* "a dog has no Buddha-nature," must be kept raised before
> you regardless of whether you are joyful or angry, calm or disturbed. It is of
> prime importance not to set your mind on expecting an awakening—if you do,
> you are saying to yourself, "I am deluded now." If you grasp at delusion and wait
> for awakening, then even though you pass through kalpas as numerous as dust
> motes, you will never achieve it. When you raise the *hwadu,* you must put your
> spirits in good order and inquire: "What is the meaning of this?"[137]

CONCLUSION

Although the discussion to this point has been given in accordance with the
faculties of the readers, the meaning lies beyond the ken of the logical operation of the mind and consciousness. It will enable men to remove the nails
and pull out the pegs and to free themselves from the bridle and yoke.[138] If
you can attend carefully to your investigation, you will be able to cleanse
away the preceding defects of conceptual understanding concerning the
Buddha-dharma. Then you will reach the ultimate stage of peace and happiness.
   You must know that men who are cultivating the path in this present
degenerate age of the dharma should first, via conceptual understanding
which accords with reality, discern clearly the mind's true and false aspects,
its arising and ceasing, and its essential and secondary features. Next,
through a word which splits nails and cuts through iron, you should probe
closely and carefully. When a place appears at which your body can escape,
it will be like the saying "to put a desk on the ground and have its four legs
set firmly." Whether coming out into birth or entering into death, you will
have complete mastery of yourself.
   Through such a word or phrase which cuts through iron, you may reach a
stage where your only passion is to train in this method which sloughs off
cleansing knowledge and views; but if you have not yet gained authentic
awakening, your conduct and understanding will perforce be out of balance
and you will still have no mastery over the realm of birth and death. This is
precisely what the ancient masters used to warn against. But if you will only
awaken to the mystery in the word, you will be a pure patch-robed monk

whose mind is free of intellectual knowledge and opinionated views about the Buddha-dharma.

Even though this might finally happen, if knowledge and views still pressure you into acting, then your practice is still not correct. If you still have thoughts of liking and disliking, anger and joy, oneself and others, success and failure, it is because you have not awakened to the mystery in the essence. External to the mind the sense-spheres still exist; hence, although it seems that you are awakened when you speak, when you are in contact with those sense-spheres you are still deluded. For such a person, it is better to rely on the words and teachings of Master Tsung-mi, which accord with reality, and put all your effort into investigation. This will enable you to subdue the thoughts of liking and disliking, anger and joy, others and self, success and failure. Since it is only through this sort of knowledge and vision of the Buddha-dharma which accords with reality that you will find a way out of *saṃsāra,* the mystery in the mystery, and the other proposition which was established separately will naturally come to exist within that conceptual knowledge and vision. You should not employ the approaches to dharma of the three propositions and the three mysteries and investigate chaotically or get into controversial discussions.

If you are truly an outstanding person, you will not be pressured by words and speech or by intellectual knowledge and conceptual understanding. Then, throughout the twelve periods of the day, whether you are in contact with sense-objects or involved with conditions, you will neither disseminate mundane truths nor formulate theoretical notions about the Buddha-dharma. If you do find the living road, you will naturally see the mistakes of all the Buddhas of the three time periods, the mistakes of the six generations of patriarchs, and the mistakes of all the masters of this generation.[139] Afterward, if you will cart out the riches and treasures of your own home and offer them to all beings, the kindness of the sovereign and the kindness of the Buddha will, simultaneously, be completely requited.

Personal notes by Chinul, the Oxherder of Chogye Mountain, in the country of Haedong, on a day in the summer of the year of the Snake [1209][140]

NOTES

1. K. *chihae chongsa;* C. *chih-chieh tsung-shih.* Shen-hui used readily understandable intellectual symbols to present his teaching, in contrast to the radical methods developed in the Hung-chou lineage. These latter methods appealed to direct experience rather than theoretical understanding and, in the long run, proved to be the most popular method among Ch'an masters for awakening their students to the truths of Ch'an. Nevertheless, that the Southern school of Hui-

neng/Shen-hui was able to overtake and eventually supersede the Northern school of Shen-hsiu was, to no small degree, due to its vigorous dissemination by Shen-hui using his intellectual knowledge and conceptual interpretation.

2. "Formal dharma successor" (K. *chŏkcha;* C. *ti-tzu*): the son (especially first-born) of one's legal wife. This term came to be used in the Ch'an school to refer to the immediate successors in the legitimate lineage of a teacher (as in *Tung-shan yü-lu, T* 1986B.47.524c.3). It is interesting to note here that Chinul, writing nearly four hundred years after Tsung-mi, does not support the latter's contention that Shen-hui was the legitimate successor of Hui-neng. Tsung-mi had gone so far as to call Shen-hui the seventh patriarch of the school in a number of passages (*CHT,* p. 867b; *YCCTSC* 3b, p. 535a.6–7). The obvious success of the rival Nan-yüeh lineage in establishing Ch'an solidly in China, coupled with the extinction of the Ho-tse line following its brief respite under Tsung-mi's leadership, may explain Chinul's acceptance of the Hung-chou school's epistemological position and practice in later sections of his exposition.

3. Individuals of average and inferior capacity in spiritual matters require the help of scriptural instruction to guide them toward enlightenment. They should first use the theoretical descriptions of the Ho-tse school to assess the absolute and relative aspects of the mind and to outline the proper course and expected results of meditation. This is an expedient method of encouraging their practice. Once they are clear about the path of practice, they should abandon the relative descriptions of dharma found in such teachings and enter the living road: the path of *hwadu* practice. See *CYHJ,* p. 410.13–14; *CYKM,* fol. 1b.5–10.

4. "Handbook" (literally "tortoise-speculum"; K. *kugam,* C. *kuei-chien*): tortoise shells and speculums were both used as divination devices from earliest times in China. "To undertake a tortoise divination" (K. *chakku,* C. *tso-kuei;* see *Li-chi* 26, Chiao t'e sheng sec., fol. 4a.9, *Shih-san ching chu shu* 5, p. 498) and "to consult the tortoise" (K. *pokku,* C. *pu-kuei;* see *Shang-shu* 13.9b.8, *Shih-san ching chu shu* 1, p. 187a) are common expressions used in the early literature to refer to the practice of applying heat to a tortoise shell and then forecasting events according to the cracks in the shell. Speculums (K. *kam;* C. *chien*), magic mirrors, also appear early on in classical Chinese texts, conveying a sense of reflecting the true and essential, especially in conduct (cf. *Shang-shu* 19.24a.1, p. 299b). Moreover, the use of speculums as divination devices is implied in the secular literature as well—for example, "these were all previously *predicted* portents" (K. *cha kae chŏn'gam chi hŏm,* C. *tzu chieh ch'ien-chien chih yen;* see Hsün Tzu-ching's *Wei Shih Chung-jung yü Sun Hao shu, WH* 393.43.11a).

By the T'ang period, the two characters appear together as a compound implying a "guide (to conduct or practice)," "digest," "handbook"; see *T'ang shu* 140c.12a.11, *PNP* 20, p. 15695; and *Sung shih* 75.2b.2, *PNP* 29, p. 22928. From at least the late eighth century onward we find the compound turning up in Buddhist compositions: see, for example, Ch'eng-kuan's *Hua-yen ching hsing-yüan p'in shu* 2, *ZZ* 227.5.64a; *Pi-yen lu* 5, case 50, *T* 2003.48.185b.5; and the Korean master Hyujŏng's *Son'ga kugam, HTC* 1241.112.911a.

5. The "transmission of the esoteric idea" refers to the transmission of the mind from the Buddha to the patriarchs, claimed by the Sŏn sect to be a transmission entirely separate from the teachings of the scriptures. Therefore some Sŏn adepts criticize the *sūtras* as containing only the words—the relative descriptions of dharma—rather than the mind of the Buddha himself, which is transmitted by Sŏn. Actually, the Sŏn ideals presented in its "special message" were not intended to disparage the teachings of the *sūtras* or to incite students to ignore their doctrines. Rather, the Sŏn message was meant to point out that the truth lies beyond the relative descriptions found in words, thus encouraging the student toward direct realization of that truth. Chinul felt that abandoning the scriptures completely was as much a fault as clinging to them, and here tries to vindicate the utility of scriptural understanding in developing the process of meditation.

6. "Minds in a haze" is a relatively free rendering for K. *myŏnghaeng yŏn,* C. *ming-hsing jan,* which has a sense of vastness or diffuseness. See *Huai nan tzu* 8.5b.7, and *Chuang tzu* 3, T'ien-ti sec. 13, p. 619.

7. "Numinous, aware, and never dark" (K. *yŏngji pulmae;* C. *ling-chih pu-mei*): according to Tsung-mi (*Yüan-chüeh ching lüeh-shu* 1, *T* 1795.39.533c.7) this phrase appears in the *Fo-ting ching*—usually the abbreviation for the *Shou-leng-yen ching (Śūraṅgama Sūtra).* I have not been able to locate the quotation there, but the idea is clearly conveyed at *Leng-yen ching* 1, *T* 945.19.107a.29– 107b.1. The phrase is commonly used by both Tsung-mi and Ch'eng-kuan (see his *Hua-yen ching hsing-yüan p'in shu ch'ao* 1, *HTC* 200.7.801a.16; and *Hsin yao chien,* in *CTL* 30, p. 459b.23–24) and appears in Sŏn texts as well (see *Pi-yen lu* 10, case 99, *T* 2003.48.222c.24). See also note 19 below.

8. "The aspect of 'person' ": the approach of sudden awakening/gradual cultivation, the soteriological aspect of Sŏn. See Introduction and *DCSPR,* Part II, The Degree of Development in Each School.

9. "Syncretic understanding" (K. *yunghoe;* C. *jung-hui*) is an essential element in the whole array of Chinul's thought. By knowing the essence of the mind—the numinous awareness which is the source of all the relative descriptions of the absolute in the various teachings—one can recognize the value of all those teachings.

10. "Original-share masters of our school": teachers who have realized their "original share" in suchness; see *Pi-yen lu* 1, case 5, *T* 2003.48.145c.5.

11. See *DCSPR,* Part III, The Live Word.

12. "Living road which leads to salvation" (K. *ch'ulsin hwallo;* C. *ch'u-shen huo-lu*): "salvation" refers to the sphere of perfect freedom attained as a result of following the shortcut Sŏn approach; see *Yün-men kuang-lu* 1, *T* 1988.47.545c.19, and *Sŏn'ga kugam,* p. 38. "Living road" is a synonym for *hwadu* practice, which does not allow for any understanding along the way of words and letters; see *Pi-yen lu* 8, case 77, *T* 2003.48.204c. See also *Pi-yen lu* 7, case 70, *T* 2003.48.199c.5–6, which correlates the "road to salvation" with "investigating the live word."

13. Previously, Chinul had criticized the contempt of Sŏn students for the

scriptural teachings. Here he points out the hypocrisy of those who use the state ments in the Sŏn scriptures as an excuse to abandon all teachings but even then do not practice meditation. See *CYKM*, fol. 2a.2–4.

14. The question here refers to followers of the Pure Land school who assumed that because it was the degenerate age of the dharma, people were no longer able to cultivate traditional forms of Buddhist practice. Using this as an excuse to forgo direct work on the mind in the present life, they called on the name of Amit-ābha in the hopes of achieving rebirth in his pure land. There they expected conditions more favorable for formal practice.

15. The *Awakening of Faith*, *TCCHL*, p. 575c; Hakeda, *Faith*, p. 28.

16. For ease in comparing the text of the *PCPHN* with similar passages in other works of Tsung-mi, all parallel passages in the *Ch'an-men shih-tzu ch'eng-hsi t'u (CHT)*, *Yüan-chüeh ching ta shu ch'ao (YCCTSC)*, and *Ch'an-yüan chu-ch'üan chi tou-hsü (CYCTH)* will be noted. For this passage see *CHT*, p. 870a.1–4. For a discussion of the title's meaning, see the appendix.

17. *CHT*, pp. 871b.14–872a.9. The school of Ho-tse is the last of the seven schools of the Middle Ch'an period covered in the *YCCTSC;* the description there, however, differs considerably from what we have here. See also *CYCTH* 2, pp. 402c.27–403a.10.

18. A metaphor common especially to the *Prajñāpāramitā* texts; see *Mo-ho po-jo po-lo-mi-t'o ching* 1, *T* 223.8.217a.22, and *Chin-kang ching, T* 235.8.752b.27. Nāgārjuna explains:

Like a dream means that there is nothing real which can be called reality. When we awaken from a dream we know that there was nothing real and we only laugh. With men it is exactly the same. In the sleep of being bound by fetters, there is really nothing binding us. Likewise, when we attain the path and awaken, we can only laugh. For this reason, it is said to be like a dream. [*Ta-chih-tu lun* 6, *T* 1509.25.101c, 103b.29–c.1]

19. In the preface to *YCCTSC*, Tsung-mi says:

The mind is calm and yet aware. [Note:] Calmness is the real essence, which is firm, steady and immovable. It has the meaning of immutability. Awareness is the awareness and attentiveness of that essence itself which is bright and never obscured. It can neither be rejected nor clung to. It has the meaning of revealing the essence. [*YCCTSC*, p. 468a.16–20; and see *Yüan chüeh ching ta shu hsü, ZZ* 243a.9.323c]

20. Considerable controversy has surrounded the rendering in this passage for the word "awareness" (K. *chi;* C. *chih*). Hu Shih ("Ch'an (Zen) Buddhism in China," p. 15) translates it as "knowledge"; D. T. Suzuki ("Zen: A Reply to Hu Shih," p. 31 ff.) prefers the rendering "*prajñā*-intuition." More recently, Jan Yün-hua has entered the debate on the side of Hu (see his "Tsung-mi: His Analysis of Ch'an Buddhism," p. 40, n. 1). Both translations miss the point, and I have adopted the rendering "awareness" consistently throughout the texts. Awareness is a direct reference to the dynamic capacity of the void and calm mind-essence—the potential form of sen-

tience through which all mental qualities, be they "knowledge" or "*prajñā*-intuition," are able to manifest. This awareness is itself formless and free of thoughts and is consequently able to adapt without hindrance to the various inclinations of sentient beings. In other texts we find instead of "source" (K. *won;* C. *yüan*) the phrase "Awareness is the gateway (K. *mun;* C. *men*) to all wonders." (See *CYCTH* 2, p. 403a.2. This phrase is adapted from *Lao-tzu* 1; see Ch'eng-kuan's discussion at *Hua-yen ching sui-shu yen-i ch'ao* 1, *T* 1736.36.2b.) Both here and in the *CHT* reading (p. 871b.18) we find "source," which is an important difference: as the source, this awareness is essentially nondual but nevertheless dynamic enough to manifest in any dualistic form ("wonders").

21. This same passage appears later in the text, where a note is appended: "This is the vanishing which penetrates to a higher sphere of experience; it is not the vanishing of annihilation."

22. This phrase, the hallmark of the Southern school, appears in the Tun-huang edition of the *Liu-tsu t'an ching, T* 2007.48.338c.15–16; the Ming edition reads instead "have *samādhi* and *prajñā* as their core" (*LTTC,* p. 352c.13). See Yampolsky, *Platform Sutra,* p. 137, n. 69, for detailed references to thoughtlessness in canonical materials and the works of Shen-hui.

23. "Calm radiance" (K. *chŏkcho;* C. *chi-chao*): the essence of mind is characterized by calmness, its functioning or outward manifestation by radiance. This term could also be interpreted as "nirvana-illumination" as Jan Yün-hua has done in his translation from *CYCTH;* see Jan, "Tsung-mi," p. 40. His translation clarifies the fact that nirvana, often thought to be simply a state of extinction (the common Chinese translation for this term is "calm-extinction"; K. *chŏngmyŏl,* C. *chi-mieh*), is actually a fully dynamic state.

24. *CHT,* p. 870a.13–b.2; *YCCTSC,* 532c.21–533a.1 (where this is the first school covered); *CYCTH* 2, p. 402b.21–29.

25. *CHT,* pp. 870b.4–871a.11; *YCCTSC,* p. 543b.7–24 (where this is the fourth school covered). The critique is at *YCCTSC,* p. 543b.24–c.1, and *CYCTH* 2, p. 402c.20–27.

26. See the parallel in the *Awakening of Faith* using pottery and clay: *TCCHL,* p. 577a; Hakeda, *Faith,* p. 45. For the ultimate source of this simile see *Chāndogya Upaniṣad* 6.1.4 ff. (Hume, *Upanishads,* pp. 240–241).

27. *Leng-chia ching* 4, *T* 670.16.510b and 512b.

28. This quote does not appear as stated in any of the three Chinese translations of the *Laṅkāvatāra Sūtra.* In *CHT* the quotation appears as K. *u pul ŏ sin* (C. *yu fo yü hsin*), which appears in the chapter titles of the four-fascicle translation of Guṇabhadra (*T* 670.16.480a). In Ch'an literature, however, the quote is commonly cited as it appears here: see Ma-tsu, *CTL* 6, p. 246a; Yen-shou, *Tsung-ching lu* 57, *T* 2016.48.742c.

29. *Leng-chia ching* 2, *T* 670.16.493a–b (adapted).

30. *CHT,* p. 871a.14–871b.2–3; *YCCTSC,* p. 534c.11–16 (where this is the fifth school covered); *CYCTH* 2, p. 402c.3–10.

31. When it is seen that "various matters like flourishing and decay" are void, the individual can recognize that his mundane affairs are nothing more than the things

of dreams. When it is recognized that "the wisdom which can comprehend this also derives from the mind which exists in the dream," the illusoriness of supramundane states like nirvana or enlightenment, or indeed any supposed goal of practice, is demonstrated.

32. Adapted from the opening lines of the *Heart Sūtra; Po-jo hsin ching, T* 251.8.848c.7.

33. *CHT,* p. 871b.3–10.

34. Reading *hyu* ("pacifying") for *ch'e* ("experiencing"). The most commonly available edition of *DCSPR,* compiled by An Chin-ho and published by Pomnyun sa, contains a few serious misprints or misreadings which considerably alter the meaning of the text. (The latest edition of Kim Tal-chin follows An Chin-ho's readings.) These have been corrected on the basis of readings appearing in Yi dynasty woodblock editions by Pak Sang-guk in his study of the text, "*Pŏpchip pyŏrhaeng nok* yŏn'gu," pp. 14–24. Important corrections will be noted.

35. This passage is probably corrupt, though Pak Sang-guk notes no variant readings. *CHT,* p. 871b.9, reads *hakcha* for *sahak,* which makes for an easier rendering: "students who" would take refuge in their minds.

36. "A boat which crosses over" refers to the previous loving-kindness and wholesome actions, because good actions ferry one across to the bliss of the other shore of nirvana. "A boat which capsizes on the way" refers to greed and hatred which drown one in the sea of suffering.

37. *CHT,* p. 875a.18–b.6.

38. The conclusion that Tsung-mi intended to extol the approach of Ho-tse is the only logical one based on the text of *PCPHN.* Chinul, however, through his broad acquaintance with Tsung-mi's writings, sees a deeper purpose behind the conclusions drawn by Tsung-mi here and later quotes from another of his works, *CYCTH,* to indicate it. He has added detailed commentary on this section to show that Tsung-mi did not intend to slight the three other schools and extol only that of Ho-tse but, rather, simply employed skillful expedients to guide his readers, regardless of their sectarian persuasions, to a greater understanding of Sŏn.

39. *CYCTH* 2, p. 402b–c. For the Northern school, see p. 402b.18–402c.3; for the Niu-t'ou school, see p. 402c.3–15.

40. *CYCTH* 2, p. 402c.15–29. For the Hung-chou and Ho-tse schools, see pp. 402c.15–403a.11.

41. *CYCTH* 2, p. 403a.11–15.

42. Reading *t'a* ("to drop into") for *su* ("to follow").

43. *CYCTH* 1, p. 402b; the simile is taken from the *Nan-pen nieh-p'an ching* 2, *T* 375.12.616b. The Sanskrit Siddham letter for the high front vowel *i* was an arrangement of three dots in a triangular shape; hence if any point was out of place or missing, the letter was not formed properly. See Ch'eng-kuan's description in *Ta-fang-kuang Fo Hua-yen ching sui-shu yen-i ch'ao* 7, *T* 1736.36.47a–b. For an example of the orthography, see *Hsi-t'an tzu-chi, T* 1232.54.1187c.3.

44. Yung-ming Yen-shou, *Wan-shan t'ung-kuei chi* 3, *T* 2017.48.972b.

45. Here Tsung-mi borrows a metaphor from one of his favorite texts: the *Complete Enlightenment Sūtra, YCC,* "P'u-yen p'u-sa chang," p. 914c.6 ff. For a dis-

cussion of the same metaphor see Tsung-mi's *Yüan-chüeh ching lüeh-shu* 1, *T* 1795.39.541c; 2, p. 533b–c.

46. Here Chinul counters the misconception that the commonplace awareness present in any type of sense perception is the numinous awareness. While such ordinary awareness is obviously based in principle on the absolute numinous awareness, to forgo the practice which makes such understanding come alive is a grave mistake. Only by having faith "in this matter"—the reality of the mind which is alluded to in the simile—and by looking back on the radiance of the mind can the numinous awareness be known in fact as well as in theory. See *CYHJ,* p. 414.3–6, and *CYKM,* fol. 4b.3–5.

47. Reading *sang* ("in detail") for *p'yŏng* ("to criticize").

48. Chinul alludes to the standard definition for nature origination found in the works of the early Hua-yen patriarchs: for Chih-yen's (602–668) definition, see his *Hua-yen ching k'ung mu chang* 4, *T* 1870.45.580c.8; for Fa-tsang, see *Hua-yen ching i-hai po-men, T* 1875.45.632b.16, and *Hua-yen yu-hsin fa-chieh chi, T* 1877.45.649b.7. See discussion in Jae Ryong Shim, "The Philosophical Foundation of Korean Zen Buddhism," pp. 63–67.

49. To "leave behind falsity in order to search for truth" is the view of the Northern school. To "consider that falsity is truth" is the view of the Hung-chou school. Both approaches are incomplete. However, a combination of the views of Hung-chou ("false thoughts arise from the nature") and Niu-t'ou ("their arising is precisely nonarising") calms all deluded thought. Through this combination, the understanding of Ho-tse is achieved and all limited views, like those of the three inferior schools, drop away. See *CYKM,* fol. 4b.5–8.

50. Reading *kyŏn* ("to see") for *tŭk* ("to obtain").

51. "*Bodhi* nut" is the *Sapindus mukurosi,* which is used to make rosaries.

52. Since I am unable to make a precise identification for "rice gum" (K. *mich'wi;* C. *mi-ch'ui*), I follow Jan's rendering ("Tsung-mi," p. 52), which seems plausible.

53. The "fools" in the Hung-chou school whom Tsung-mi criticizes here were actually his contemporaries. Later Chinul reinterprets the line to apply to any students of Sŏn who praise their own school at the expense of others. Here Tsung-mi criticizes the Hung-chou approach for ignoring the numinous awareness itself in the development of their doctrine. However, Chinul shows that if one can maintain the state of no-mind, or nondifferentiation, through the Hung-chou school, then that approach is impeccable. ("If people who are cultivating the mind comprehend that the nature of both good and evil is void . . . , [they] do not fall into the view of these fools.") By the same token, if one grasps intellectually at the concept of numinous awareness, then the Ho-tse school is even less effective for inducing enlightenment than the ostensibly inferior approach of Hung-chou. Chinul shows here that, in his view, the ultimate in Sŏn is not the sudden awakening/gradual cultivation doctrine of Ho-tse but the no-mind approach. No-mind can of course be cultivated in the Hung-chou, Niu-t'ou, and Ho-tse schools, and it is the ultimate technique for inducing the syncretic vision. Explication will follow in Chinul's exposition. See *CYKM,* fol. 5a.1–5.

54. Reading *kyŏn* ("to see") for *si* ("to be").

55. Only the Ho-tse school teaches the need to realize the luminosity of the jewel: the eternal, immutable essence of the mind. Hence it is especially to be practiced. See *CYKM,* fol. 5a.10.

56. The luminous essence of the jewel ("the profound") can reflect ("contain") any shade of color ("the shallow"). Because the mind-essence (the essence of the luminous jewel) has been realized through the approach of Ho-tse, both the perspective of Niu-t'ou ("black is not really black") and that of Hung-chou ("black is actually that jewel itself") are incorporated into the view of Ho-tse. After knowing the luminous nature of the jewel, whether one accepts the existence of everything as Hung-chou did or rejects it as did Niu-t'ou, one can adapt freely to either perspective and is consequently free from all limitations. ("At that point it no longer matters whether colors are present or not—for the luminosity of the jewel can freely adapt to either circumstance.") As Tsung-mi says, when the other schools are considered from the standpoint of this school, they are all the same because they derive from the same calm and aware mind-essence. This is also why, in this rearrangement of the selections from *PCPHN,* Chinul placed Ho-tse at the beginning rather than leaving it at the end. From Chinul's standpoint, the purpose of *PCPHN* was not to extol the virtues of the Ho-tse school exclusively but to guide the student toward a comprehensive vision of the nondual reality to which all the schools converge. See *CYKM,* fol. 5a.9-12.

57. *CHT,* pp. 873b.7-874b.13.

58. Reading *ch'agyŏn* ("apophatic discourse") for *ch'agwa* ("to cover up mistakes").

59. An additional passage from *PCPHN* has been omitted from the excerpts because it had already been recorded in Chinul's *Encouragement to Practice.* The passage appears in my translation of that work, *The Korean Approach to Zen,* p. 111. According to Yuil (*CYKM,* fol. 6a.5-6), the first level ("at the moment of awakening") refers to the initial stage of the ten faiths, the preliminary stage before entering the path proper. The second level ("when one first activates the *bodhicitta* and begins to cultivate") refers to the three stages of worthiness: the ten abidings, ten practices, and ten transferences. The third level ("when the practice continues naturally in all situations") refers to the ten *bhūmis.* Finally, the fourth level ("when the defilements are completely extinguished and the consummation of meritorious practices has led to the attainment of Buddhahood") refers to the actual fruition of the path, or Buddhahood. This answer has exposed the main deficiency of the Niu-t'ou approach: its excessive emphasis on an apophatic description of the absolute. The Ho-tse school, on the other hand, gives a description which combines both apophatic and kataphatic perspectives. See also *CYHJ,* p. 414.16-17.

60. "Numinous attention" refers to the essence. "Gleaming reflection" refers to the function.

61. Tsung-mi explains (*YCCTSC,* p. 537a.21-22) that "blankness [K. *mugi;* C. *wu-chi*] is *samādhi* which is not [accompanied by] *prajñā.*"

62. The commentator is Ch'eng-kuan. *Hsin yao tieh (chien), CTL* 30, 459b.23-24. The first line, "in the essence of the unabiding mind," has been added according to the woodblocks and *CHT,* p. 874a.12.

63. Although numinous awareness and numinous attention seem nearly identical, their roles in the systems of Ho-tse and Hung-chou are slightly different. Numinous attention was intended only to point out that people possess a certain quality which enables them to be cognizant of sensory experiences. Ho-tse's numinous awareness, on the other hand, is a direct pointing to the mind-essence itself, not simply the manifestation of that essence in the relative sphere. Hence numinous awareness is a more precise interpretation than is numinous attention and, as such, has more utility than the term of Hung-chou. See *CYKM,* fol. 6a.6–10.

64. "Negation" and "revelation" refer to the second and third divisions of the Sŏn teaching in Tsung-mi's *CYCTH:* the school which teaches absolute annihilation (K. *minjŏl mugi chong,* C. *min-chüeh wu-chi tsung; CYCTH* 2, p. 402c.3–15; Jan, "Tsung-mi," pp. 28–29, 38–39) and the school of direct revelation (K. *chikhyŏn simsŏng chong,* C. *chih-hsien hsin-hsing tsung; CYCTH* 2, pp. 402c.15–403a.11; Jan, "Tsung-mi," pp. 29, 39–40). To teach through negation involves describing the absolute in exclusively negative terms—explaining what it is *not* until some idea of it gets across. This is the approach of the Mādhyamika school and the *Prajñāpāramitā* texts. Revelation—using positive descriptions of the qualities attributable to the absolute in order to awaken understanding—is common in the Hwaŏm school and is found in the *Vijñānavāda* texts. These two approaches correspond to the radical analysis and comprehensive assimilation approaches discussed later.

65. Reading *chik* ("straightaway") for *chŭk* ("precisely").

66. *CHT,* p. 866a. This is the opening question of *CHT,* which probably opened *PCPHN* as well. To preserve the continuity of his arrangement of the excerpts, however, Chinul apparently moved this question into his exposition rather than including it with the main text.

67. *Lin-chien lu,* by Chüeh-fan Hui-hung (1071–1128), a third-generation master in the Huang-lung lineage of the Lin-chi school and noted Sung Buddhist historian (see Jan Yün-hua, "Buddhist Historiography," pp. 367–368). The quotation:

[Tsung-mi] considered the path of Ma-tsu to be like the blackness of the jewel. This is absolutely incorrect. To explain that the true is the same as the false is simply an expedient description. Anyone who has only summary knowledge of the teaching vehicle can realize this. How else could Ma-tsu have been able to make such deep repentance to his holy teacher [that is, received transmission from his teacher Nan-yüeh Huai-jang] and become the master of the dharma in China? His lineage produced such disciples as Nan-ch'üan [P'u-yüan; 748–835], Po-chang [Huai-hai; 720–814], Ta-ta [Wu-ye; 760–821], and Kuei-tsung [Chih-ch'ang; n.d.], who are all extensively recorded in the *tripiṭaka.* He was fully matured in theories concerning truth and falsity. How could honored monks have revered him [if, as Tsung-mi says,] his path stopped merely at the blackness of the jewel?

Furthermore, [Tsung-mi] considered Niu-t'ou's path to be "Everything is a dream. True and false are both nonexistent." This is absolutely incorrect. If we examine [Fa-jung's] composition, *Inscription on the Mind-King,* it says:

The past is void;
Knowledge creates delusion about the source.
[The mind-nature] clearly shines over sense-objects,

But follow after that radiance and all becomes hazy.
Horizontally, vertically, there is no radiance—
This is most subtle and sublime.
To know the dharma takes no knowing,
Not knowing is to know what is important. . . .

All this cures the diseases of knowledge and view. And yet it can be seen that Ho-tse openly established superiority and inferiority in regard to knowledge and view. And still [Tsung-mi] said that [Niu-t'ou's] path was like a jewel in which neither light nor black existed! How could he not have been greatly deceiving us?

This passage is quoted from *Lin-chien lu* 1, *HTC* 1594.148.592b–593a; the quotation from the *Hsin [wang] ming* appears in *CTL* 30, p. 457b.27–28 and c. 1–2.

68. "We should rather use this bright mirror . . . discerning between right and wrong . . .": to inherit wrongly the teaching of Sŏn and not to distinguish the proper approach to practice from the improper is wrong. In such a case, the bright mirror of Tsung-mi's instructions should be used to counteract the mistake. However, to grasp wrongly at Tsung-mi's analysis and discriminate between the different Sŏn approaches, exalting some, renouncing others, is also wrong. In such a case, the bright mirror of Hui-hung's instructions should be used to counter the mistake. See *CYKM,* fol. 6b.7–10.

69. *CHT,* pp. 874b.14–875a.17. To this point, Tsung-mi has shown that the Ho-tse approach is superior to that of the other schools. In this final section of the text, he gives a detailed explanation of the hallmark of the school: sudden awakening/ gradual cultivation.

70. To "awaken abruptly" resolves beginningless delusion and inverted views. "The numinous and bright knowledge and vision" overcome the misconception that deluded thoughts are the mind. "The mind is originally . . . the *dharmakāya*" resolves the misconception that the four great elements are the body. "The nonduality of body and mind" counters the idea that this false body and mind are the true self. "There is not the slightest difference between it and all the Buddhas" reveals that enlightenment is the same for all beings. See *CYHJ,* p. 415.12–13; *CYKM,* fol. 7a.4–7.

71. *Wei-mo-chieh so-shuo ching* 2, *T* 475.14.544b.

72. K. *paesang* (C. *p'ai-hsiang*) is equivalent to the grand ministers (K. *chaesang;* C. *tsai-hsiang*) who directed the three departments of government during the T'ang dynasty. See des Rotours, *Traité des Examens,* pp. 3, 12–13.

73. K. *wi* (C. *wei*) were petty bureaucrats who directed the employees of a prefecture; des Rotours, *Traité des Fonctionnaires,* p. 735, n. 2.

74. *Diamond Sūtra, Chin-kang ching, T* 235.8.752b.

75. Chŏnghye explains (*CYHJ,* p. 415.15) that Chinul attempts here to encourage all students of both Sŏn and the scholastic schools to start out correctly on the path of practice through a proper understanding of sudden awakening/gradual cultivation. "From every perspective": literally, "progress, regress, think, examine." Yuil explains that this means "progressing" to think about the dharma of sudden awakening and "regressing" to examine the simile. "How can you say your cultivation is

true?": since students of the teachings do not believe in sudden awakening, they should be urged toward such an awakening. Since students of Sŏn have stagnated at the stage of sudden awakening, they should be urged to undertake gradual cultivation. See *CYKM,* fol. 7a.10–12.

76. See *Encouragement to Practice,* in *The Korean Approach to Zen,* p. 104, and note 12.

77. Chinul deals with this question at length in his *Complete and Sudden Attainment of Buddhahood.*

78. *HHYCL* 14, p. 809a.

79. Yuil explains that once he "meshes with . . . the fruition of Buddhahood," a student of a scholastic sect will not be self-denigrating—for example, assuming that it will take him three *asaṃkhyeya* kalpas to attain Buddhahood, while Sŏn practitioners gain enlightenment in one lifetime. Similarly, when a student of Sŏn "meshes" he will not be haughty, for he will have realized that he is no more special than any of the other Buddhas. See *CYKM,* fol. 7a.12–7b.2.

80. "Gradualness of the complete teachings": the Ch'ŏnt'ae school distinguishes four major divisions of sudden and gradual. First, the gradualness of the gradual teachings (K. *chŏmjŏm;* C. *chien-chien*) refers to gradual cultivation/gradual awakening. Second, completeness of the gradual teachings (K. *chŏmwŏn;* C. *chien-yüan*) refers to gradual cultivation/sudden awakening. Third, the gradualness of the complete teachings (K. *wŏnjŏm;* C. *yüan-chien*) refers to sudden awakening/gradual cultivation. Finally, the completeness of the complete teachings (K. *wŏnwŏn;* C. *yüan-yüan*) refers to sudden awakening/sudden cultivation. See *Mo-ho chih-kuan* 6, *T* 1911.46.33a ff., and Yen-shou's explanations in *Tsung-ching lu* 36, *T* 2016.48.627a ff.

81. An allusion to *Lao-tzu* 48.

82. "Mundane matters" refers to similes like the ones just offered. The dharma as immanent suchness is the essence of all particularities and, consequently, can manifest in an infinite variety of ways. Worldly things, meaning those particularities themselves, usually have only a limited number of characteristics and hence are limited to a specific role. Here the simile is simply a relative device, a "mundane matter," to explain one attribute of the dharma. Thus its utility cannot be extended to fields in which it does not apply.

83. *Mahāparinirvāṇa-sūtra, Ta-pan-nieh-p'an ching, T* 374.12.365a–603c. This *sūtra* is replete with similes; eight hundred is probably a conservative estimate.

84. Adapted from *TCCHL,* p. 576c; Hakeda, *Faith,* p. 41.

85. "Clinging to [personal and impersonal forms] of the four great elements as being entirely distinct from one another": the rendering here follows the commentary; literally, the passage would translate as "mutual incompatibility between different materials." This means that one considers the four great elements which make up one's own body to be distinct from the four great elements which make up the objects in the sense-spheres. See *CYHJ,* p. 415.18; *CYKM,* fol. 8a.3.

86. See the simile of the medicinal herbs in the *Lotus Sūtra* in which the sublime dharma that can benefit all sentient beings is likened to a great rain which nourishes all plants; *Fa-hua ching* 3, *T* 262.9.19a–20b; Leon Hurvitz, *Scripture of the Lotus Blossom of the Fine Dharma,* pp. 101–103. For this quotation see p. 24b.7.

87. Reading *ae* ("grief") for *ae* ("love").

88. Adding *ki* ("derive, arise").

89. "Cause" means mundane, conditionally arisen events. "Effect" refers to the supramundane fruition of Buddhahood. The "mind" unites them both.

90. *TCCHL,* p. 575c; Hakeda, *Faith,* p. 28.

91. *CTL* 29, p. 459b.23–24.

92. *Ch'an-tsung Yung-chia chi, T* 2013.48.390b.

93. *Shih-ssu k'o sung,* in *CTL* 29, p. 450b.

94. Sŏn is not the same as the "inferior teachings" (K. *hagyo;* C. *hsia-chiao*), a derogatory term used by the complete teachings to refer to the sudden teachings; *CYKM,* fol 24b.4. Its conceptions of nature and this one thought are entirely different. In the sudden teachings, one thought means the thought which impels one toward the eventual attainment of Buddhahood; in Sŏn this thought is the thought of right enlightenment itself. Although it was said that this one thought is the mind of the sentient being (as in the *Awakening of Faith* quotation below), Sŏn does not limit its conception of this thought to the nature which is in contrast with characteristics. It means, rather, the nature of the liberated mind itself. See *CYKM,* fol. 24b.1–4. See also Li T'ung-hsüan's description of attainment of Buddhahood in one thought, *HHYCL* 5, p. 752a.12–15; 7, p. 761b.13–17 et passim.

95. *Wei-hsin chüeh, T* 2018.48.998a. This famous quote appears in slightly altered form in both major translations of the *Avataṃsaka Sūtra: HYC* 37, p. 194a.14; *HYCb* 25, p. 558c.10. The quote as it appears here comes from Vasubandhu's *Daśabhūmikasūtra-śāstra, Shih-ti ching lun* 8, *T* 1522.26.169a; see also *TCCHL,* p. 577b.

96. "If we realize our ignorance . . . this will be the basic cause for curing the ailment": this sentence is rendered according to the subcommentary of Yuil which takes it as a description of the twelvefold chain of conditioned origination. If, for the period of only one thought-moment, the student sees through his ignorance, he can no longer sustain his deluded attachment to sensual experience, and the path is revealed. Hence this "one-thought mind" is the origin of both *saṃsāra* and path-fruition. Craving, clinging, and becoming refer to the seventh, eighth, and ninth links of the twelvefold chain—the active links in which passive sensual attachment in thought and mind are brought into play in the actual world, making new karma and further immersing the sufferer in *saṃsāra.* See *CYKM,* fol. 24b.9–11.

97. *YCC,* p. 817b.

98. *Tsung-ching lu* 18, *T* 2016.48.511c.

99. In this first exchange, the question was made from the standpoint of the appearance schools but the answer was made from that of the nature schools. The bodhisattva Pradhānaśūra (K. Yongsi posal; C. Yung-shih p'u-sa) was a *bhikṣu* in a past Buddha's dispensation who transgressed the precepts concerning chastity and killing. (He desired a young woman and plotted to kill her husband in order to consummate his lust.) Later he felt great remorse and, after confessing his transgressions and hearing the dharma, he became enlightened. For his story, see *Fo-shuo ching ye-chang ching, T* 1494.24.1098b–1099a. The *bhikṣūṇi* Hsing was the religious name of the courtesan Mātaṅgī, the woman in the *Śūraṅgama Sūtra* who tried to seduce Ānanda; *Leng-yen ching* 1, *T* 945.19.106c.9–16.

100. In this second exchange, Yen-shou describes the proper attitude toward defilements in which nature and characteristics are balanced. The explanation that all defilements arise from the one mind deals directly with characteristics; from this standpoint, they can be excised. See *CYKM,* fol. 23a.5. "The exciseless excision . . . is true excision": according to Chŏnghye, exciseless excision means that characteristics are identified with the nature. "Which excises while excising nothing" refers to the nature identified with characteristics. "True excision" refers to the realization of the mutual identity of nature and characteristics during one's practice of excising the defilements. See *CYHJ,* p. 427.15–16.

101. *Ta Hua-yen ching lüeh-ts'e, T* 1737.36.705a.

102. Reading *ki* ("arise") for *yu* ("to have").

103. Adding *tan* ("merely") and transposing "perturbations" and "exposes" *(hokcho)* to coincide with the previous quotation; both changes are according to the woodblock.

104. "Defilements and counteractive expedients": *Shih-ti-ching lun* 2, *T* 1522.26.133a.10 and 29; and 133b.1. In reality there are neither defilements to be excised nor counteractive methods to excise them. From a relative standpoint, however, excision must be carried out by using these expedients throughout all three time periods. Yuil explains that "do not exist in past, present, or future" refers to the nature which is never cut off. "Operative in past, present, and future" refers to the relative characteristics which can be excised. He explains through a metaphor that a candle is kept burning not simply by the initial application of the flame or its present or future burning; only when the flame is kept burning (remains "operative") throughout all these time periods will it remain lit. Thus Yuil seems to be taking the phrase to mean that in eliminating defilements one's efforts must be consistent throughout the three time periods. This does not, however, seem to correspond with Chinul's explanations given in the exposition which follows, and I have rendered the passage to follow his description; *CYKM,* fol. 25b.1–5.

105. *Hwaŏm ilsŭng pŏpkye to, T* 1887A.45.711a; the question/answer series appears at p. 714a–b.

106. Since his realization has revealed that his entrance onto the bodhisattva path and his final achievement of Buddhahood are identical, he continues to practice while remembering that essentially there is nothing remaining to practice. He always keeps foremost in his mind the idea that Buddhahood has already been achieved and does not conceive that he must pass through a certain period of time to perfect his practice. Nevertheless, he does not allow this understanding to develop into complacency which might cause him to neglect his cultivation. See *CYKM,* fol. 25b.6–10.

Chinul's account here recalls the treatment of these two approaches by Ch'eng-kuan:

These two do not obstruct each other. The progressive approach is the operation of the characteristics of the teachings. Perfect interfusion is the meritorious functioning of the noumenal nature. Characteristics are the characteristics of the nature: hence progression does not obstruct perfect interfusion. Nature is the nature of characteristics: hence perfect interfusion does not obstruct progression. As perfect interfusion does not obstruct progression, the one is unlimited. As progression does not obstruct perfect interfusion, the limitless is the one. [*Ta Hua-yen ching shu* 1, *T* 1735.35.504b.22–26]

107. Yuil (*CYKM,* fol. 25b.10) says that this text, the *Hua-yen tsung-yao,* is an alternate title for the *Hua-yen kang-yao,* which is apparently a short title for an eighty-fascicle work by Ch'eng-kuan, the *Ta-fang-kuang Fo Hua-yen ching kang-yao; HTC* 209.12.787.13–end.

108. K. *kigwan mogin* (C. *chi-kuan mu-jen*); see *Ta-chih-tu lun* 9, *T* 1509.25.281a; see also Yung-chia's *CTK,* p. 395c.18.

109. *Ta-ch'eng tsan,* in *CTL* 29, pp. 449b–450a; the stanzas have been transposed here.

110. Nan-yang Hui-chung (?–775), a disciple of the Sixth Patriarch Hui-neng; he should not be confused with the Niu-t'ou master of the same name. The quotation is from *CTL* 5, p. 244b.

111. This question was asked by an unidentified Hua-yen lecturer from the capital of Ch'ang-an to the Ch'an Master Chih-wei (646–722), the fifth patriarch of the Niu-t'ou school. Chih-wei remained silent and would not answer, so his attendant, the future Ch'an Master Hsüan-ting of An-kuo ssu (n.d.), answered; *CTL* 4, p. 229b.

112. Since defilements are all products of the conditioned arising of the true nature, and the essence of that true nature is identical to the wisdom of *bodhi,* defilements are *bodhi; CYKM,* fol. 26a.5–6.

113. *Yüan-chüeh ching ta-shu, ZZ* 243.9.388b. The *sūtra* passage Tsung-mi comments on is at *YCC,* p. 917b.

114. Yuil says (*CYKM,* fol. 26a.8) that this is a quotation from Vasubandhu in the *Daśabhūmikasūtra-śāstra;* I have been unable to locate the quotation.

115. The wisdom which is able to excise defilements derives from the true mind. But as this true mind is innately free from defilements (the objects of the excising techniques), the defilements are identical to the excising wisdom. Since there is no wisdom apart from the defilements and no defilements apart from the wisdom, how can a person endeavor to remove the defilements with that wisdom? See *CYKM,* fol. 26a.8–10.

116. *CTK,* p. 396c.

117. The "two *bhikṣus*" were named Pao-ching and Pao-ch'in. One day after Pao-ching had gone into the village for provisions, a girl found Pao-ch'in alone sleeping deeply in his hermitage. Her lust aroused, she had sexual relations with him and spent the night. The next morning, as she was returning to the village, she met Pao-ching, who asked where she had stayed the night. Replying that she had passed it at their hermitage, he feared that his friend must have broken his precepts, and killed her lest the story reach the village. Hence one transgressed the precept concerning celibacy and the other the precept against killing. When they went to confess their transgressions to Upāli, the master of *vinaya* (precepts) among the main disciples of the Buddha, Upāli replied that their sins were as great as Mount Sumeru and could not be forgiven. Unsatisfied, the monks sought out the renowned layman Vimalakīrti, who said that if they could show him their sins, he would accept their repentance. Hearing this, both monks realized that the essence of their sins was

void, and they were enlightened. See *Wei-mo-chieh ching* 1, *T* 474.14.523a; *CYHJ*, p. 428.15–17; *CYKM*, fol. 26b.3–8.

"Firefly wisdom" refers to the fact that wisdom is as bright as the sun, but in Upāli's case it was no brighter than the light of a firefly. "The Hīnayānists are zealous . . . but lack wisdom": although the Hīnayānists are vigorous in their investigation of dharmas, they neglect the path—the self-nature itself—from which all dharmas arise. They grasp at nirvana when, in fact, even nirvana itself must be abandoned before the mind of the path, meaning complete enlightenment, is gained. "The heretics" are often proficient in worldly knowledge but neglect the wisdom of dharma and hence only add to their discriminations.

Chinul has included these passages from Yung-chia's work to counter the accusations of the complete schools that Sŏn is nothing more than a sudden approach. In the following paragraph Chinul carries this argument even farther and points out that, from the standpoint of doctrinal theory, the Hwaŏm school might represent a complete and sudden approach; Sŏn, however, is a complete and sudden approach in actual practice as well and is consequently superior to mere theoretical suppositions. Although Hwaŏm discusses the unimpeded interpenetration of phenomena, Sŏn realizes it. See *CYKM*, fol. 26b.8–11.

118. Adding *kyŏl* ("formulas").

119. These verses express an idea central to Sŏn—that awakening and understanding can be realized fully within the period of one thought-moment. (That is, Sŏn is a complete and sudden approach.) The first stanza explains that delusion and awakening derive from the same basic source. The second and third stanzas explain this same equality. The fourth stanza gives a different explanation of the characteristics of delusion. The fifth stanza to the end explains the nature of enlightenment, meaning the results to be expected from the awakening experience. See *CYKM*, fol. 26b.12–27a.2.

120. "Self-denigrating" means that a person does not believe he has the capacity to achieve Buddhahood through sudden awakening. "Haughty" means that he thinks he can dispense with gradual cultivation after awakening. See *CYKM*, fol. 27b.2–3.

121. *CYCTH* 2, p. 405b.

122. Reading *mil* ("esoteric") for *chong* ("school").

123. Reading *chŏn* ("transmission") for *chŏn* ("text").

124. Reading *tae* ("generations") for *tae* ("big").

125. Reading *ki* ("its") for *chin* ("true").

126. *THYL* 16, p. 879b; the quotation from Yün-men does not appear there. Ta-hui Tsung-kao (1089–1163) was the main disciple of Yüan-wu K'o-ch'in (1063–1135) in the Yang-ch'i lineage of Lin-chi Ch'an. Huang-lung Ssu-hsin Sou (1071–1115), also known as Wu-hsin, was a disciple of Hui-t'ang Tsu-hsin (n.d.), a second-generation master in the Huang-lung lineage of Lin-chi.

"The one word 'awareness' is the gate to all calamities": if one grasps at the concept of awareness, there is no road to salvation and hence that word becomes the gate to continued subjection. This statement expresses the live word of Sŏn. See *CYKM*, fol. 28a.7.

127. *LTTC*, p. 359b–c. When Hui-neng referred to the mind as "one thing," he

was using the live word to prompt his listeners to a direct realization of the mind-nature. Shen-hui, however, grasped at that live word and tried to understand it intellectually, thereby stagnating in dead words. For this he was criticized by the Sixth Patriarch; *CYKM*, fol. 28a.7–9. "Even if you build a thatched hut to cover your head": here Hui-neng predicts that Shen-hui would become the type of master who uses a theoretical approach to dharma—which conceals the true mind-essence in conceptual veils rather than pointing directly to that essence with the live word.

128. Pen-chüeh Shou-i (n.d.), also known as Fa-chen, was a disciple of Hui-lin Tsung-pen (1020–1099) in the Yün-men school; for his biography see *Hsü ch'uan-teng lu* 14, *T* 2077.51.557c–558a. His records are not extant. For this quotation see *LTTC*, p. 357b.

Here it is demonstrated how investigation of the live word can lead to enlightenment. The "thing" which the Sixth Patriarch asks about is the "one thing" mentioned in the previous passage. Even though it would have been easy for Huai-jang to grasp at this question as Shen-hui did and answer that it was his Buddha-nature (or whatever), he did not allow himself to fall into shallow conceptual interpretations. Finally, after eight years of study, he had a direct realization of this "one thing." When he says that "even if you allude to it as 'one thing' it does not strike the mark," he makes clear that purely conceptual understanding about the "one thing" has been overcome; *CYKM*, fol. 28a.9–15. Nan-yüeh Huai-jang (677–744) was reputedly the main successor to the Sixth Patriarch Hui-neng and the teacher of Ma-tsu. Sung-shan An is Sung-yüeh Hui-an (582–709), one of the Fifth Patriarch Hung-jen's ten major disciples.

129. *THYL* 22, p. 904a. Yüeh-shan Wei-yen (745–828) was a disciple of Ma-tsu and Shih-t'ou Hsi-ch'ien.

130. *THYL* 27, p. 925b–c. "It is clear and constantly aware; words cannot describe it": although "clear and constantly aware" seems to parallel Ho-tse's statements about numinous awareness, Hui-k'o specifies that this state cannot be described in words and demonstrates that conceptualization has been transcended. Ta-hui says that this statement "was not the real dharma of the Second Patriarch" to emphasize that this statement was simply intended to show that he was free from any conceptualization which might have remained after awakening and was not meant to be a complete statement of his realization. Hence Hui-k'o's awakening was an awakening onto the path via the live word; it was not like the dead word understanding in which Ho-tse stagnated. See *CYKM*, fol. 28b.10–29a.1.

131. For this simile see *YCC*, p. 919c.

132. Huang-p'o Hsi-yün (d. 850?) was a disciple of Po-chang Huai-hai (720–788). This quotation is from his *Ch'uan-hsin fa-yao*, *T* 2012.48.382c.

133. "Maintaining the void-calmness of indifference": these students enter the noumenon by leaving behind words and cutting off the thought processes but are not yet clear about the conditioned phenomena in front of their eyes. "Maintaining a natural state": these students recognize the ordinary mind which is used every day as being the ultimate path and do not seek the sublime awakening. See *CYHJ*, p. 430.3–4; *CYKM*, fol. 29a.7–9.

134. *THYL* 19, p. 891a.

135. As some of these defects carry subtle nuances, I will paraphrase them. (3) This is the hindrance that arises when thinking about the *hwadu*—that is, trying to examine it with the logical mind. (4) This could also be interpreted to mean that one should not try to express one's own understanding through gestures like raising the eyebrows or other "wordless" answers with which Sŏn novices try to express "non-conceptual understanding." For the truly enlightened one, words are not a hindrance, and he should be able to express his understanding fluently. In Korea today, as I learned through too many personal experiences, responses through gestures are summarily rejected by most Sŏn masters—and an immediate demand is made for a verbal explanation of the student's state of mind. (5) By the same token, one cannot use words alone or sophistic argument to express one's understanding. Expression must be based on direct experience of the mind. (6) This is the defect which results if one tries to investigate *mu* via the "silent reflection" (K. *mukcho;* C. *mo-chao*) approach of Sŏn, the epitome of the Ts'ao-tung school. (7) Kusan Suryŏn of Song-gwang sa explained that this means one should not inquire into the *hwadu* at the place where the mind becomes aware of sensory objects—that is, the student should not transform the doubt which is developed through investigation of the live word into a doubt about the mind which is aware of sensory stimuli. This is the hindrance which arises during meditation. (8) One should not look for the meaning by analyzing the working of the *kongan* or any other literary hints or allusions. (10) This refers to people who grasp at the fact that the Buddha-nature is an inherent quality in themselves and assume that no practice is necessary except to remain "natural" and allow this innate Buddha-nature to manifest. One must always put forth effort in investigating the *hwadu*.

136. *THYL* 26, p. 921c. This passage has given a description of the live word in practice.

137. *THYL* 19, p. 891b–c.

138. To grasp at self or dharmas is like nails and pegs. To stagnate in intellectual knowledge and conceptual interpretation is like a bridle or yoke. See *CYKM,* fol. 29b.10–11.

139. Yuil explains that "mistakes" should be taken to mean the traces of the unconditioned realization of the Buddhas and patriarchs which were left behind in the conditioned sphere; the word should not be taken as "faults." See *CYKM,* fol. 30a.9.

140. Korea was known as Haedong, "East of the Sea," because it was located east of the kingdom of Po-hai (K. Parhae), the successor to the Koguryŏ kingdom which ruled in the Manchurian region from 699 to 926; see Peter Lee, *Lives of Eminent Korean Monks,* p. 26, n. 62, for references.

Bibliography

Works in Asian Languages

An Kye-hyŏn 安啓賢. "Paekche Pulgyo" 百濟佛教. In *Han'guk munhwa sa taegye* 6 韓國文化史大系, pp. 194–201.

———. "Wonhyo ŭi Mirŭk chŏngt'o wangsaeng sasang" 元曉의彌勒淨土往生思想. *Yŏksa hakpo* 歷史學報 17/18 (1962): 245–274.

Chang Won-gyu 張元圭. "Chogye chong ŭi sŏngnip kwa palchŏn e taehan koch'al" 曹溪宗의成立과發展에對한考察. *PGHP* 1(1963):311–351.

———. "Hwaŏm kyohak wansŏnggi ŭi sasang yŏn'gu" 華嚴教學完成期의思想研究. *PGHP* 11(1974):11–43.

———. "*Hwaŏm kyŏng* ŭi sasang ch'egye wa kŭ chŏn'gae" 華嚴経의思想体系와그展開. *PGHP* 7(1970):15–61.

Ch'en Yüan 陳垣. *Shih-shih i-nien lu* 釋氏疑年錄. Peking, 1939.

Cho Myŏng-gi 趙明基. *Koryŏ Taegak kuksa wa Ch'ŏnt'ae sasang* 高麗大覺國師와天台思想. Seoul, 1964.

———. "Silla Pulgyo ŭi kyohak" 新羅佛教의教學. In *PKC*, pp. 149–175.

———. "Taegak kuksa ŭi Ch'ŏnt'ae ŭi sasang kwa Sokchang ŭi ŏpchŏk" 大覺國師의天台의思想과續藏의業績. In *Paek Sŏng-uk paksa songsu kinyŏm: Pulgyohak nonmunjip*, pp. 891–931.

———. *Wonhyo taesa chŏnjip* 元曉大師全集. Seoul, 1978.

Ch'oe Sun-u 崔淳雨 and Chŏng Yang-mo 奠良謨. *Han'guk ŭi Pulgyo hoehwa: Songgwang sa* 韓國의佛教繪畫:松廣寺. Seoul, 1970.

Chōsen sōtokufu 朝鮮總督府. *Chōsen kinseki sōran* 朝鮮金石總覽. Seoul, 1919–1967.

Eda Toshio 江田俊雄. "Chōsen Zen no keisei: Fushōzen no seikaku ni tsuite" 朝鮮禪の形成:普照禪の性格について. *IBK* 5(1957):351–359.

Endō Kōjirō 遠藤孝次郎. "Kegon shōki ronkō" 華嚴性起論考. *IBK* 14(1965): 214–216; 15(1967):523–527.

Han Chong-man 韓鍾萬. "Yŏmal Sŏnch'o ŭi paebul hobul sasang" 麗末鮮初의排佛護佛思想. In *PKC*, pp. 717–751.

Han'guk Pulgyo yŏn'guwon 韓國佛教研究院. See Rhi Ki-yong and Hwang Su-yŏng (eds.).

Han Ki-du 韓基斗. *Han'guk Pulgyo sasang* 韓國佛教思想, Iri [Chŏlla pukto], 1973.

———. "Koryŏ hogi ŭi Sŏn sasang" 高麗後期의禪思想. In *PKC*, pp. 597–653.

———. "Koryŏ Pulgyo ŭi kyŏlsa undong" 高麗佛教의結社運動. In *PKC*, pp. 551–583.

———. *Silla sidae ŭi Sŏn sasang* 新羅時代의禪思想. Iri, 1974.

———. "Silla ŭi Son sasang" 新羅의禪思想. In *PKC*, pp. 339–382.

Hatani Ryōtai 羽溪了諦, and Ho Ch'ang-ch'ün 賀昌羣, trans. *Hsi-yü chih Fo-chiao* 西域之佛教. Shanghai, 1933. Translation of *Seiiki no Bukkyō* (Kyoto, 1914).

Hong Chŏng-sik 洪庭植. "Koryŏ Ch'ŏnt'ae chong kaerip kwa Ŭich'ŏn" 高麗天台宗開立과義天. In *PKC*, pp. 561–476.

Hong Yun-sik 洪潤植. "Paekche Pulgyo" 百済佛教. In *PKC*, pp. 75–88.

———. "Koryŏ Pulgyo ŭi sinang ŭirye" 高麗佛教의信仰儀禮. In *PKC*, pp. 655–698.

———. "Samguk sidae ŭi Pulgyo sinang ŭirye" 三國時代의佛教信仰儀禮. In *PKC*, pp. 133–146.

Hyosŏng Cho Myŏng-gi paksa hwagap kinyŏm: Pulgyo sahak nonch'ong 曉城趙明基博師華甲記念：佛教史學論叢. Seoul, 1965.

Hyŏn Sang-yun 玄相允. "Chosŏn sasang sa: chunggo p'yŏn" 朝鮮思想史：中古篇. *Asea yŏn'gu* 亞細亞研究 4–1 (1961): 299–355.

Ikeda Rosan 池田魯參. "Tannen igo ni okeru goji hakkyōron no tenkai" 湛然以後における五時八教論の展開. *Komazawa daigaku Bukkyōgakubu ronshū* 駒澤大學佛教學部論集 6(1975):38–60.

Im Ch'ang-sun 任昌淳. "Songgwang sa ŭi Koryŏ munsŏ" 松廣寺의高麗文書. *Paeksan hakpo* 白山學報 11(1971): 31–51.

Im Sŏk-chin 林. *Chogye san Songgwang sa sago* [Han'guk saji ch'ongsŏ 2] 曹溪山松廣寺史庫 [韓國寺誌叢書]. Seoul, 1977. Photolithographic reprint of the handwritten manuscript in the Songgwang sa archives, compiled in 1932 by the abbot Im Sŏk-chin. A massive collection of all extant documentation partaining to Songgwang sa gathered from around Korea. The reprint is of fairly poor quality.

———. *Taesŭng Sŏnjong Chogye san Songgwang sa chi* 大乘禪宗曹溪山松廣寺誌. Songgwang sa [Chŏlla namdo], 1965. The best popular history of the monastery; richer documentation and wider scope than the newer work of the *Han'guk Pulgyo yŏn'guwon*.

Ishikawa Rikizan 石川力山. "Baso kyōdan no tenkai to sono shijisha tachi" 馬祖教団の展開とその支持者達. *Komazawa daigaku Bukkyōgakubu ronshū* 2(1971): 160–173.

Jan Yün-hua 冉雲華. "Tsung-mi chu *Tao-su ch'ou-ta wen-chi* te yen-chiu" 宗密著道俗酬答文集的研究. *Hua-kang Fo-hsüeh hsüeh-pao* 華岡佛學學報 4(1980): 132–166.

Kamata Shigeo 鎌田茂雄. "Chōsen oyobi Nihon Bukkyō ni oyoboshita Shūmitsu no eikyō" 朝鮮および日本佛教に及ぼした宗密の影響. *Komazawa daigaku Bukkyōgakubu ronshū* 7(1976):28–37.

———. *Chūgoku Kegon shisōshi no kenkyū* 中國華嚴思想史の研究. Tokyo, 1965.

———. "Shōki shisō no seiritsu" 性起思想の成立. *IBK* 5(1957):195–198.

———. *Shūmitsu kyōgaku no shisōshi teki kenkyū* 宗密教學の思想史的研究. Tokyo, 1975.

Kim Chi-gyŏn 金知見. "*Hōjū betsugyō roku setsuyō heinyū shiki* ni tsuite" 法集別行錄節要並入私記について. *IBK* 18(2)(1970):513–519.

———. "*Kegon ichijō hokkaizu* ni tsuite" 華嚴一乘法界圖について. *IBK* 19(2)(1971):262–267.

———. "Silla Hwaŏmhak ŭi churyu ko" 新羅華嚴學의主流考. In *PKC*, pp. 257–275.

———. "Silla Hwaŏmhak ŭi kyebo wa sasang" 新羅華嚴學의系譜와思想. *Haksurwon nonmunjip* 學術院論文集 12(1973):31–65.

Kim Ch'ŏl-sun 金哲淳. "Han'guk misul ŭi kkaedarŭm kwa saengmyŏng" 韓國美術의깨달음과生命. *Konggan* 空間 12(13)(1977):39–46.

Kim Chŏng-bae 金貞培. "Pulgyo chŏllipchŏn ŭi Han'guk sangdae sahoesang" 佛教傳入前의韓國上代社會相. In *PKC*, pp. 11–21.

Kim Hang-bae 金恒培. "Sŭngnang ŭi hwa sasang" 僧朗의和思想. *PGHP* 15(1978):183–197.

Kim Hyŏng-hŭi 金炯熙. "Hyŏnjon ch'anso rŭl t'onghae pon Wonhyo ŭi *Hwaŏm kyŏng* kwan" 現存撰疏를通해본元曉의華嚴経観. M.A. thesis, Tongguk University, 1980.

Kim Ing-sŏk 金芿石. "Puril Pojo kuksa" 佛日普照國師. *PGHP* 2(1964):3–39.

———. *Hwaŏmhak kaeron* 華嚴學概論. Seoul, 1974.

Kim Sang-gi 金庠基. *Koryŏ sidae sa* 高麗時代史. Seoul, 1961.

Kim Tŏng-hwa 金東華. "Kudara jidai no Bukkyō shisō" 百済時代の佛教思想. *Chōsen kenkyū nempō* 朝鮮研究年報 5(1963):8–15.

———. "Koguryŏ sidae ŭi Pulgyo sasang" 高句麗時代의佛教思想. *Asea yŏn'gu* 亜細亜研究 2(1)(1959):1–46.

———. "Paekche sidae ŭi Pulgyo sasang" 百済時代의佛教思想. *Asea yŏn'gu* 5(1)(1962):57–85.

———. *Pulgyo ŭi hoguk sasang* 佛教의護國思想. Seoul, 1976.

———. "Silla sidae ŭi Pulgyo sasang" 新羅時代의佛教思想. *Asea yon'gu* 5(2)(1962):1–62.

———. "Silla sidae ŭi Pulgyo sasang" 新羅時代의佛教思想. *Asea yon'gu* 6(1)(1963):367–421; 6(2)(1963):127–168.

———. *Sŏnjong sasang sa* 禪宗思想史. Seoul, 1974.

Kim Un-hak 金雲學. "Wonhyo ŭi hwajaeng sasang" 元曉의和諍思想. *PGHP* 15(1978):173–182.

Kim Yong-su 金映遂. "Hwaŏm sasang ŭi yŏn'gu" 華嚴思想의研究. In *Paek Sŏng-uk paksa songsu kinyŏm: Pulgyohak nonmunjip*, pp. 1–27.

Kim Yŏng-t'ae 金英泰. "Han'guk Pulgyo chongp'a sŏngnip e taehan chaegoch'al" 韓國佛教宗派成立에대한再考察. *Taehan Pulgyo* 大韓佛教 768(3 December 1978):2.

———. "Koguryŏ Pulgyo sasang: ch'ojŏn sŏnggyŏk ŭl chungsim ŭro" 高句麗佛教思想：初傳性格을中心으로. In *PKC*, pp. 23–39.

Ko Ik-chin 高翊晋. "Wonhyo ŭi sasang ŭi silch'ŏn wolli" 元曉의思想의實踐原理. In *PKC*, pp. 225–255.

———. "Wonmyo Yose ŭi Paengnyŏn kyŏlsa wa kŭ sasangjŏk tonggi" 圓妙了世의白蓮結社와그思想의動機. *PGHP* 15(1978):109–120.

Kobayashi Jitsugen 小林實玄. "Kegonshū kangyō no tenkai ni tsuite" 華嚴宗觀行の展開について. *IBK* 15(1967):653–655.

Kwon Sang-no 權相老. "Han'guk Sŏnjong yaksa" 韓國禪宗略史. In *Paek Sŏng-uk Paksa songsu kinyŏm: Pulgyohak nonmunjip*, pp. 265–298.

Makita Tairyō 牧田諦亮. *Gikyō kenkyū* 疑経研究. Kyoto, 1976.

Matsunaga Yūkei 松長有慶. "Gokoku shisō no kigen" 護國思想の起源. *IBK* 15(1)(1966):69–78.

Minamoto Hiroyuki 源弘之. "Kōrai jidai ni okeru Jōdokyō no kenkyū: Chitotsu no *Nembutsu yōmon* ni tsuite" 高麗時代における淨土教の研究：知訥の念佛要門について. *Ryūkoku daigaku Bukkyō bunka kenkyūjo kiyō* 龍谷大學佛教文化研究所紀要 9(1970):90–94.

Mochizuki Shinkō 望月信亨. *Shina Jōdo kyōrishi* 支那淨土教理史. Kyoto, 1942.

Naba Toshisada 那波利貞. "Tōdai no shayū ni tsuite" 唐代の社邑に就いて. *Shirin* 史林 23(2)(1938), pp. 223–265; 23(3), pp. 495–534; 23(4), pp. 729–793.

Nakamura Hajime 中村元. *Bukkyōgo daijiten* 佛教語大辭典. Tokyo, 1975.

Nakamura Hajime and Kawada Kumatarō 川田熊太郎, eds. *Kegon shisō* 華嚴思想. Kyoto, 1960.

Nukariya Kaiten 忽滑谷快天 and Chŏng Ho-gyŏng 奠湖鏡, trans. *Chosŏn Sŏn'gyo sa* 朝鮮禪教史. Seoul, 1978. Translation of *Chōsen Zenkyōshi* (Tokyo, 1930).

Ono Gemmyō 小野玄妙. *Bukkyō no bijutsu to rekishi* 佛教の美術と歷史. Tokyo, 1943. Includes the Chinese text of the *Yŏmbul inyu kyŏng*.

Paek Sŏng-uk paksa songsu kinyŏm: Pulgyohak nonmunjip 白性郁博士頌壽記念：佛教學論文集. Seoul, 1957.

Pak Chong-hong 朴鍾鴻. *Han'guk sasang sa: Pulgyo sasang p'yŏn* 韓國思想史：佛教思想篇. Seoul, 1972.

Pak Sang-guk 朴相國. "Pojo ŭi Sŏn sasang yŏn'gu" 普照의禪思想研究. *Tongguk taehakkyo yŏn'gu ronjip* 東國大學校研究論集 6(1976):29–43.

———. "*Pŏpchip pyŏrhaeng nok chŏryo pyŏngip sagi* rŭl t'onghae pon Pojo ŭi Sŏn sasang yŏn'gu" 法集別行錄節要並入私記를通해본普照의禪思想研究. M.A. thesis, Tongguk University, 1975.

Park Sung-bae [Pak Sŏng-bae] 朴性焙. "Pojo: chŏnghye ssangsu ŭi kuhyŏn" 普照：定慧雙修의具現. In *Koryŏ, Chosŏn ŭi kosŭng sibil in* 高麗朝鮮의高僧11人, pp. 51–66. Seoul, 1976.

Pulgyo munhwa yŏn'guso 佛教文化研究所. *Han'guk Pulgyo ch'ansul munhŏn ch'ongnok* 韓國佛教撰述文獻總錄. Seoul, 1976.

Rhi Ki-yong [Yi Ki-yŏng] 李箕永, ed. "*Inwang panya kyŏng* kwa hoguk sasang" 仁王般若経과護國思想. *Tongyanghak* 東洋學 5(1975): 491–519.

———. *Segye sasang chŏnjip 11: Han'guk ŭi Pulgyo sasang* 世界思想全集 11：韓國의佛教思想. Seoul, 1977.

———. *Wonhyo sasang 1: segye kwan* 元曉思想 1：世界觀. Seoul, 1967–1976.

Rhi Ki-yong [Yi Ki-yŏng] 李箕永 and Hwang Su-yŏng 黃壽永, eds. *Hwaŏm sa* [Han'guk ŭi sach'al 8] 華嚴寺：韓國의寺刹 8. Seoul, 1976.

———. *Pŏpchu sa* [Han'guk ŭi sach'al 5] 法住寺. Seoul, 1975.

———. *Pusŏk sa* [Han'guk ŭi sach'al 9] 浮石寺. Seoul, 1976.

———. *Songgwang sa* [Han'guk ŭi sach'al 6] 松廣寺. Seoul, 1975.

Sakamoto Yukio 坂本幸男. "Shōki shisō to aku ni tsuite" 性起思想と悪について. *IBK* 5(1957):469–477.

Shibata Tōru 柴田泰. "Sōdai Jōdokyō no ichi dammen: Eimei Enju ni tsuite" 宋代淨土教の一断面（永明延壽について）. *IBK* 13(2)(1965):676–680.

Sŏ Kyŏng-su 徐景洙. "Koryŏ ŭi kŏsa Pulgyo" 高麗의居士佛教. In *PKC*, pp. 585–595.

Sŏ Yun-gil 徐閏吉. "Silla ŭi Mirŭk sasang" 新羅의彌勒思想. In *PKC*, pp. 287–304.

Sŏk Sŏngch'ŏl 釋性徹. *Han'guk Pulgyo ŭi pŏmmaek* 韓國佛教의法脈. Haein ch'ongnim [Kyŏngsang namdo], 1975. The definitive study of the Korea Chogye lineage.

Song Ch'ŏn-ŭn 宋天恩. "Chinul ŭi Sŏn sasang" 知訥의禪思想. In *PKC*, pp. 477–513.

Song Sŏk-ku 宋錫球. "Pojo ŭi hwa sasang" 普照의和思想. *PGHP* 15(1978):235–253.

Sungsan Pak Kil-chin paksa hwagap kinyŏm: Han'guk Pulgyo sasang sa 崇山朴吉真博士華甲紀念：韓國佛教思想史. Iri [Chŏlla pukto], 1975.

Suzuki Chūsei 鈴木中正. "Sōdai Bukkyō kessha no kenkyū" 宋代佛教結社の研究. *Shigaku zasshi* 史學雜誌 52(1941):65–98, 205–241, 303–333.

Takamine Ryōshū 高峰了州. *Kegon ronshū* 華嚴論集. Tokyo, 1976.

———. *Kegon shisōshi* 華嚴思想史. Kyoto, 1942–1963.

———. *Kegon to Zen to no tsūro* 華嚴と禪との通路. Nara, 1956.

Takasaki Jikidō 高崎直道. "Kegon kyōgaku to nyoraizō shisō" 華嚴教學と如來藏思想. In Nakamura Hajime and Kawada Kumatarō (eds.), *Kegon shisō*, pp. 275–322.

Tanaka Ryōshō 田中良昭. "Tonkōbon *Zengen shosenshū tojo* no zankan ni tsuite" 敦煌本禪源諸詮集都序の殘卷について. *IBK* 25(1)(1976):107–112.

T'ang Yung-t'ung 湯用彤. *Han Wei Liang-Chin Nan-Pei-ch'ao fo-chiao shih* 漢魏兩晋南北朝佛教史. Shanghai, 1938; Taipei, 1976.

Tsukamoto Zenryū 塚本善隆. *Hokuchō Bukkyōshi kenkyū* 北朝佛教史研究. Tokyo, 1974.

U Chŏng-sang 禹貞相. "Sŏsan taesa ŭi Sŏn'gyogwan e taehayŏ" 西山大師의禪教觀에對하여. In *Hyosŏng Cho Myŏng-gi paksa hwagap kinyŏm: Pulgyo sahak nonch'ong*, pp. 473–504.

Ui Hakuju 宇井伯壽. *Shaku Dōan kenkyū* 釋道安研究. Tokyo, 1956.

———. *Zenshūshi kenkyū 3* 禪宗史研究. Tokyo, 1943.

Yamazaki Hiroshi 山崎宏. *Shina chūsei bukkyō no tenkai* 支那中世佛教の展開. Tokyo, 1942.

Yanagida Seizan 柳田聖山. "Daijō kaikyō toshite no *Rokuso tankyō*" 大乘戒経としての六祖壇経. *IBK* 23(1974):65–77.

———. *Shoki Zenshū shisho no kenkyū* 初期禪宗史書の研究. Kyoto, 1967.

Yaotani Kōho 八百谷孝保. "Shiragi sō Gishō den kō" 新羅僧義湘傳考. *Shina Bukkyō shigaku* 3(1)(1939):79–94.

Yi Chae-ch'ang 李載昌. "Koryŏ Pulgyo ŭi sŭnggwa sŭngnoksa chedo" 高麗佛教의僧科·僧錄司制度. In *PKC*, pp. 429–443.

———. *Koryŏ sawon kyŏngje ŭi yŏn'gu* 高麗寺院経濟의研究. Seoul, 1976.

Yi Chae-ch'ang and Kim Yŏng-t'ae. *Pulgyo munhwa sa* 佛教文化史. Seoul, 1976.

Yi Chi-gwan 李智冠. *Chogye chong sa* 曹溪宗史. Seoul, 1976.

———. *Han'guk Pulgyo soŭi kyŏngjŏn yŏn'gu* 韓國佛教所依経典研究. Haein sa [Kyŏngsang namdo], 1969.

————. (ed.). *Sajip sagi* 四集私記. Haein sa, 1969.

————. "Yŏndam mit Inak ŭi sagi wa kŭ ŭi kyohakkwan" 蓮潭및仁嶽의私記와 그의教學觀. In *PKC*, pp. 999–1012.

Yi Chong-ik 李鍾益. "Chinul ŭi Hwaŏm sasang" 知訥의華嚴思想. In *PKC*, pp. 515–550.

————. *Chogye chonghak kaeron* 曹溪宗學槪論. Seoul, 1973.

————. "Chosasŏn e issŏsŏ ŭi musim sasang" 祖師에있어서의無心思想. *PGHP* 10(1973):239–267.

————. "Kōrai Fushō kokushi no kenkyū—sono shisō taikei to Fushōzen no tokushitsu" 高麗普照國師の研究—その思想体系と普照禪の特質. Ph.D. dissertation, Taishō University, 1974. Mimeographed reprint, Seoul, 1974.

————. "Ogyo Kusan ŭn Nadae e sŏngnip" 五教九山은麗代에成立. *Taehan Pulgyo* 769(10 Dec. 1978):2.

————. "Pojo kuksa ŭi sasang ch'egye" 普照國師의思想體系. In *Yi Chong-ik paksa hagwi kinyŏm nonmunjip: Tongbang sasang nonch'ong*, pp. 249–292.

————. "Pojo kuksa ŭi Sŏn'gyogwan" 普照國師의禪教觀. *PGHP* 9(1972):67–97.

————. "Silla Pulgyo wa Wonhyo sasang" 新羅佛教와元曉思想. In *Yi Chong-ik paksa hagwi kinyŏm nonmunjip: Tongbang sasang nonch'ong*, pp. 183–197.

————. *Taehan Pulgyo Chogye chong chunghŭng non* 大韓佛教曹溪宗中興論. Seoul, 1976. Although somewhat strident in tone, the work is packed with information pertaining to Chinul's life and thought. Yi tries to demonstrate the utility of Chinul's thought in revitalizing the modern Chogye Order.

————. *Wonhyo ŭi kŭnbon sasang: Simmun hwajaeng non yŏn'gu* 元曉의根本思想：十門和諍論研究. Seoul, 1977

————. "Wonhyo ŭi saengae wa sasang" 元曉의生涯와思想. In *Yi Chong-ik paksa hagwi kinyŏm nonmunjip: Tongbang sasang nonch'ong*, pp. 198–239.

Yi Chong-ik paksa hagwi kinyŏm nonmunjip: Tongbang sasang nonch'ong 李鍾益博士學位紀念論文集：東方思想論叢. Seoul, 1975.

Yi Ki-baek 李基白. *Kuksa sillon* 國史新論. Seoul, 1963.

————. "Samguk sidae Pulgyo chŏllae wa kŭ sahoejŏk songgyŏk" 三國時代佛教傳來와그社會的性格. *Yŏksa hakpo* 歷史學報 6(1954):128–205.

Yi Ki-yŏng. See Rhi Ki-yong.

Yi Nŭng-hwa 李能和. *Chosŏn Pulgyo t'ongsa* 朝鮮佛教通史. Seoul, 1918–1976.

Yi Pyŏng-do 李丙燾. *Han'guk sa II: Chungse p'yŏn* 韓國史：中世篇. Seoul, 1961.

Yi Pyŏng-do and Kim Chae-won 金載元. *Han'guk sa I:Kodae p'yŏn* 韓國史：古代篇. Seoul, 1959.

Yi Sang-baek 李相佰. *Han'guk sa III: Kŭnse chŏn'gi p'yŏn* 韓國史：近世前期篇. Seoul, 1962.

Yi Yŏng-ja 李永子. "Ŭich'ŏn ŭi Ch'ŏnt'ae hoet'ong sasang" 義天의天台會通思想. *PGHP* 15(1978):219–233.

Yu Kyo-sŏng 劉教聖. "Koryŏ sawon kyŏngje ŭi sŏnggyŏk" 高麗寺院経濟의性格. In *Paek Sŏng-uk paksa songsu kinyŏm: Pulgyohak nonmunjip*, pp. 607–626.

Yu Pyŏng-dŏk 柳炳德. "Sŭngnang kwa Samnon sasang" 僧朗과三論思想. In *PKC*, pp. 41–74.

Yutsugu Ryōei 湯次了榮. *Kegon taikei* 華嚴体系. Kyoto, 1915.

Zengaku daijiten hensansho 禪學大辭典編纂所. *Zengaku daijiten* 禪學大辭典. Tokyo, 1977.

Works in European Languages

Banerjee, Ankul C. *Sarvāstivāda Literature*, Calcutta, 1957.

Basham, A. L. *The Wonder That Was India*. New York, 1967.

Bielefeldt, Carl, and Lewis Lancaster. "T'an Ching (Platform Scripture)." *Philosophy East and West* 25(2)(1975):197–212.

Broughton, Jeffrey. "Kuei-feng Tsung-mi: The Convergence of Ch'an and the Teachings." Ph.D. dissertation, Columbia University, 1975.

Chan, Wing-tsit. *The Platform Scripture: The Basic Classic of Zen Buddhism*. New York, 1963.

Chang, Chung-yüan. *The Original Teachings of Ch'an Buddhism*. New York, 1969.

Chang, Fu-jui. *Les Fonctionnaires des Song: Index des Titres*. Paris, 1962.

Chang, Garma C. C. *The Buddhist Teaching of Totality: The Philosophy of Hwa Yen Buddhism*. University Park (Pennsylvania), 1971.

Chappell, David W. "Introduction to the *T'ien-t'ai ssu-chiao-i*." *Eastern Buddhist* 9–1 (May, 1976): 72–86.

Chavannes, Edouard. "Les Pays d'Occident d'après le *Heou Han Chou*." *T'oung Pao* 8(1907):149–234.

Ch'en, Kenneth. *Buddhism in China: A Historical Survey*. Princeton, 1964.

———. *The Chinese Transformation of Buddhism*. Princeton, 1973.

Cho, Myong-gi. "Prominent Buddhist Leaders and Their Doctrines." *KJ* 4(5) (May 1964):15–21.

Chou, Yi-liang. "Tantrism in China." *Harvard Journal of Asiatic Studies* 8(1945): 241–332.

Cleary, Thomas, and J. C. Cleary. *The Blue Cliff Record*. Boulder, 1978.

Coedès, G. *The Indianized States of Southeast Asia*. Edited by Walter F. Vella. Translated by Susan Brown Cowing. Honolulu, 1968.

Conze, Edward. *Buddhism: Its Essence and Development*. New York, 1959.

———. *Buddhist Thought in India*. Ann Arbor, 1973.

———. *Buddhist Wisdom Books*. London, 1958.

Cook, Francis. *Hua-yen Buddhism: The Jewel Net of Indra*. University Park (Pennsylvania), 1977.

Davidson, J. Le Roy. "The Origins and Early Use of the Ju-i." *Artibus Asiae* 13 (1950):239–249.

Dayal, Har. *The Bodhisattva Doctrine in Buddhist Sanskrit Literature*. Delhi, 1970.

De Bary, William Theodore (ed.). *Sources in Japanese Tradition*. New York, 1972.

Demiéville, Paul. "La Pénétration du Bouddhisme dans la Tradition Philosophique Chinoise." *Cahiers d'Histoire Mondiale* 3(1956):19–38.

———. "Sur l'Authenticité du *Ta Tch'ing K'i Sin Louen*." *Bulletin de la Maison Franco-Japonaise* 2(1929):1–78.

des Rotours, Robert. *Le Traité des Examens: Traduit de la Nouvelle Histoire des T'ang*. Paris, 1932.

———. *Traité des Fonctionnaires et Traité de l'Armée*. Leiden, 1947.

Dumoulin, Heinrich. *A History of Zen Buddhism.* Boston, 1963.

Durt, Hurbert. "La Biographie du Moine Coréen Ŭisang d'après le *Song Kao Seng Tchouan.*" In *Kim Chae-won paksa hoegap kinyŏm nonch'ong* 金載元博士回甲紀念論叢. pp. 411–422.

Dutt, Nalinaksha. *Buddhist Sects in India.* Delhi, 1978.

Edgerton, Franklin. *Buddhist Hybrid Sanskrit Dictionary.* New Haven, 1953.

Fontein, Jan. *The Pilgrimage of Sudhana.* La Haye, 1967.

Gard, Richard. "The Mādhyamika in Korea." In *Paek Sŏng-uk paksa songsu kinyŏm: Pulgyohak nonmunjip,* pp. 1155–1174.

Gimello, Robert M. "Apophatic and Kataphatic Discourse in Mahāyāna: A Chinese View." *Philosophy East and West* 26–6 (1976): 117–136.

Gregory, Peter N. "Sudden Enlightenment Followed by Gradual Cultivation: Tsung-mi's Analysis of Mind." Paper presented at the conference on "The Sudden/Gradual Polarity: A Recurrent Theme in Chinese Thought," held at the Institute for Transcultural Studies, Los Angeles, 22–24 May 1981.

———. "Tsung-mi's *Inquiry into the Origin of Man*: A Study of Chinese Buddhist Hermeneutics." Ph.D. dissertation, Harvard University, 1981.

Grousset, René. *The Empire of the Steppes: A History of Central Asia.* Translated by Naomi Walford. Brunswick (New Jersey), 1970.

Ha, Tae-hung and Grafton K. Mintz. *Samguk Yusa: Legends and History of the Three Kingdoms of Ancient Korea.* Seoul, 1972.

Hakeda, Yoshito, trans. *The Awakening of Faith.* New York, 1967.

Han, Woo-keun. *The History of Korea.* Edited by Grafton K. Mintz. Translated by Kyung-shik Lee. Honolulu, 1971.

Hatada, Takashi *A History of Korea.* Translated by Warren W. Smith and Benjamin H. Hazard. Santa Barbara, 1969.

Hong, Chŏng-sik. "The Thought and Life of Wonhyo." In Chun Shin-yong (ed.), *Buddhist Culture in Korea* (Korean Culture Series 3), pp. 15–30 (Korean version, pp. 163–181). Seoul, 1974.

Hsu, Sung-peng. *A Buddhist Leader in Ming China: The Life and Thought of Han-shan Te-ch'ing.* University Park (Pennsylvania), 1979.

Hu, Shih. "Ch'an (Zen) Buddhism in China: Its History and Method." *Philosophy East and West* 3(1)(1953): 3–24.

Hume, Robert. *The Thirteen Principal Upanishads.* London, 1921–1977.

Hurvitz, Leon. "Chih-I (538–597): An Introduction to the Life and Ideas of a Chinese Buddhist Monk." *Mélanges Chinois et Bouddhiques* 12(1962): 1–372.

———. *Scripture of the Lotus Blossom of the Fine Dharma.* New York, 1976.

Jaini, Padmanabh S. *Abhidharmadīpa with Vibhāṣāprabhāvṛtti.* Patna, 1960.

Jan, Yün-hua. "Antagonism Among the Religious Sects and the Problem of Buddhist Tolerance." *International Buddhist Forum Quarterly* 1(4)(1979):62–69.

———. "Buddhist Historiography in Sung China." *Zeitschrift der Deutschen Morgenländischen Gesellschaft* 114(1964):360–381.

———. "Conflict and Harmony in Ch'an and Buddhism." *Journal of Chinese Philosophy* 4(1977):287–302.

———. "*Fo-tsu t'ung-chi*: A Biographical and Bibliographical Study." *Oriens Extremus* 10(1963):61–82.

————. "*K'an Hui* or the 'Comparative Investigation': The Key Concept in Tsung-mi's Thought." In C. S. Yu (ed.), *Korean and Asian Religious Tradition*, pp. 12–24. Toronto, 1977.

————. "Tsung-mi: His Analysis of Ch'an Buddhism." *T'oung Pao* 58(1972):1–54.

————. "Tsung-mi's Questions Regarding the Confucian Absolute." *Philosophy East and West* 30(4)(1980):495–504.

————. "Two Problems Concerning Tsung-mi's Compilation of *Ch'an-tsang.*" *Transactions of the International Conference of Orientalists in Japan* 19(1974): 37–47.

Joshi, Lamani, *Studies in the Buddhist Culture of India.* Delhi, 1967.

Kamstra, J. H. *Encounter or Syncretism: The Early Growth of Japanese Buddhism.* Leiden, 1967.

Keel, Hee Sung. "Chinul: The Founder of the Korean Sŏn (Zen) Tradition." Ph.D. dissertation, Harvard University, 1977.

Kim, Chong-guk. "Some Notes on the Songgyun'gwan." *Transactions of the Korea Branch of the Royal Asiatic Society* 38(1961):69–91.

Kwon, Sang-no. "History of Korean Buddhism." *KJ* 4(5)(1964):8–14.

Lai, Whalen. "Chinese Buddhist Causation Theories: An Analysis of the Sinitic Mahāyāna Understanding of *Pratītya-samutpāda.*" *Philosophy East and West* 27(3)(1977):241–264.

Lancaster, Lewis. "An Analysis of the *Aṣṭasāhasrikāprajñāpāramitā-sūtra* from the Chinese Translations." Ph.D. dissertation, University of Wisconsin: Madison, 1968.

Lancaster, Lewis, and Sung-bae Park. *The Korean Buddhist Canon: A Descriptive Catalogue.* Berkeley and Los Angeles, 1979.

Lee, Peter H. "Fa-tsang and Ŭisang." *Journal of the American Oriental Society* 82(1)(1962):56–62.

————(trans.). *Lives of Eminent Korean Monks: The Haedong Kosŭng Chŏn.* Cambridge, 1969.

Legge, James. *The Chinese Classics.* Hong Kong, 1970.

Leverrier, Roger. "Buddhism and Ancestral Religious Beliefs in Korea." *KJ* 12 (5)(1972):37–42.

Liebenthal, Walter. *Chao Lun: The Treatises of Seng-chao.* Hong Kong, 1968.

————. "Notes on the Vajrasamādhi." *T'oung Pao* 44(1956):347–386.

Link, Arthur E. "The Biography of Shih Tao-an." *T'oung Pao* 46(1958):1–48.

Lu, Kuan Yü [Charles Luk]. *Ch'an and Zen Teachings.* Vol. 2. Berkeley, 1971.

McRae, John. "The Ox-head School of Ch'an Buddhism: From Early Ch'an to the Golden Age." In Robert Gimello and Peter Gregory (eds.), *Studies in Hua-yen and Ch'an Buddhism.* Honolulu, 1983.

Miura, Isshū, and Ruth Fuller Sasaki. *Zen Dust: The History of the Koan and Koan Study in Rinzai (Lin-chi) Zen.* New York, 1966.

————. *The Zen Koan: Its History and Use in Rinzai Zen.* New York, 1965.

Moon, Sang-hee. "A History Survey of Korean Religion." *KJ* 14(5)(1974):14–24.

Nakamura, Hajime. "A Critical Survey of Mahāyāna and Esoteric Buddhism Chiefly Based on Japanese Studies." *Acta Asiatica* 7(1964):36–42.

Ñāṇananda, Bhikkhu. *Concept and Reality in Early Buddhist Thought.* Kandy, 1971.

————. *The Magic of the Mind: An Exposition of the Kalākārāma Sutta.* Kandy, 1974.

Nishiyama, Kōsen and John Stevens (trans.). *Shōbōgenzō: The Eye and Treasury of the True Law.* Tokyo, 1975.

Park, Sung-bae. "Wonhyo's Commentaries on the *Awakening of Faith in Mahā-yāna.*" Ph.D. dissertation, University of California, Berkeley, 1979.

Prebish, Charles, and Janine Nattier. "*Mahāsāṃghika* Origins: The Beginnings of Buddhist Sectarianism." *History of Religions* 16(3)(1977): 237–272.

Pryzlyski, Jean. *La Légende de l'Empereur Aśoka (Aśokāvadāna) dans les Textes Indiens et Chinois.* Paris, 1923.

Pruden, Leo. "The *Ching-t'u Shih-i-lun.*" *Eastern Buddhist* 4–1 (1973): 126–157.

Reischauer, Edwin O. *Ennin's Diary.* New York, 1955.

Rhi, Ki-yong. "Wonhyo and His Thought." *KJ* 11(1)(1971):4–9.

Robinet, Isabelle. "Metamorphosis and Deliverance from the Corpse in Taoism." *History of Religions* 18(1979):37–70.

Rogers, Michael. *The Chronicle of Fu Chien: A Case of Exemplar History.* Chinese Dynastic Histories Translations 10. Berkeley and Los Angeles, 1968.

Saha, Kshanika. *Buddhism and Buddhist Literature in Central Asia.* Calcutta, 1970.

Sasaki, Ruth Fuller, Yoshitaka Iriya, and Dana R. Fraser. *A Man of Zen: The Recorded Sayings of Layman P'ang.* New York/Tokyo, 1976.

Schafer, Edward. *The Divine Women: Dragon Ladies and Rain Maidens in T'ang Literature.* Berkeley and Los Angeles, 1973.

Schreiber, Gerhard. "The History of the Former Yen Dynasty." *Monumenta Serica* 14(1949–1955):374–480; 15(1956):1–141.

Seo, Kyung-bo [Sŏ Kyŏng-bo]. "A Study of Korean Zen Buddhism Approached Through the Chodangjip." Ph.D. dissertation, Temple University, 1960; mimeographed reprint, Seoul, 1973.

Shim, Jae Ryong. "The Philosophical Foundation of Korean Zen Buddhism: The Integration of *Sŏn* and *Kyo* by Chinul (1158–1210)." Ph.D. dissertation, University of Hawaii, 1979.

Strickmann, Michel. "On the Alchemy of T'ao Hung-ching." In Holmes Welch and Anna Seidel (eds.), *Facets of Taoism: Essays in Chinese Religion,* pp. 123–192. New Haven, 1979.

Suh, Kyung-soo [Sŏ Kyŏng-su] and Kim Chol-jun [Kim Ch'ŏl-chun]. "Korean Buddhism: A Historical Perspective." In Chun Shin-yong (ed.), *Buddhist Culture in Korea,* pp. 119–134 (Korean text, pp. 275–289). Seoul, 1974.

Suzuki, Daisetsu. *Essays in Zen Buddhism.* 3 vols. London, 1970.

————. *Studies in Zen.* New York, 1955.

————. "Zen: A Reply to Hu Shih." *Philosophy East and West* 3(1)(1953):25–46.

————. *The Zen Doctrine of No-mind.* London, 1958.

Takakusu, Junjirō. *The Essentials of Buddhist Philosophy.* Honolulu, 1947.

Takasaki, Jikidō. *A Study on the Ratnagotravibhāga.* Serie Orientale Roma 33. Rome, 1966.

Tamura, Enchō. "The Influence of Silla Buddhism on Japan During the Asuka–Hakuho Period." In Chun Shin-yong (ed.), *Buddhist Culture in Korea,* pp. 55–79 (Japanese text, pp. 201–232). Seoul, 1974.

Unno, Taitetsu. "The Dimensions of Practice in Hua-yen Thought." In *Yūki kyōju shōju kinen: Bukkyō shisōshi ronshū* 結城教授頌壽記念：佛教思想史論集, pp. 51–78. Tokyo, 1964.

Ware, James R. *Alchemy, Medicine, and Religion in the China of 320 A.D.* Cambridge (Massachusetts), 1966.

Wright, Arthur F. *Buddhism in Chinese History.* Stanford, 1959.

——. "Fo-t'u-teng." *Harvard Journal of Asiatic Studies* 11(1948):312–371.

Wu, John C. H. *Lao Tzu Tao Teh Ching.* New York, 1961.

Yampolsky, Philip. *The Platform Sutra of the Sixth Patriarch.* New York, 1967.

Zeuschner, Robert. "An Analysis of the Philosophical Criticisms of Northern Ch'an Buddhism." Ph.D. dissertation, University of Hawaii, 1977.

Zürcher, E. *The Buddhist Conquest of China.* Leiden, 1959.

Index

Bharati, 100, 125
Bhīṣmagarjitanirghoṣasvara Buddha, 123, 145 n.36
Bhūmis, ten: in Hwaŏm teachings, 51, 52
Bibliophobia of Sŏn school, 16–17
Birth: four types of, 141–142, 155; is the unborn dharma, 134
Birth and death, 133–134
Blankness: as nescience, 118; as *samādhi* without *prajñā,* 109, 194 n.61
Bodhi: achieved through *samādhi* and *prajñā,* 112; characteristics of, 126–127, 133; as defilements, 176, 200 n.112; as enlightenment, 120, 121; transgression of precepts as obstacle to, 177; as true mind, 121, 200 n.112. *See also* Enlightenment
Bodhicitta, activation of: as achievement of Buddhahood, 174; as entrance to Bodhisattva path, 51, 66; follows ten faiths, 51, 135; through realization-awakening, 59
Bodhidharma: adages of, 16, 180; Buddhism in India during time of, 115 n.8; his coming from the West, 137; relations with disciples, 183; and sudden awakening/gradual cultivation, 107; his transmission of mind, 16, 153, 180; wall contemplation, 124, 146 n.40, 183
Bodhimaṇḍa as purity of mind, 114
Bodhi nut, 162
Bodhisattvas: responsive power of, 2. *See also names of individual bodhisattvas*
Bodhisattva path: fifty-two stages of, 51–52; as gradual cultivation, 41
Bodies: transformation, 122. *See also Dharmakāya*
Bourns, three evil, 113, 140–141
Brahmā, 167
Buddha: as seeing the nature, 100. *See also* Buddhas
Buddhahood: achievement of, in one thought, 54, 198 n.94; achievement of, over three *asaṃkhyeya* kalpas, 54; achievement of, Ŭisang's view on, 174–175; characteristics of, 169, 174; fruition of, as faith, 105; is the mind, 99; as radiance, 155; seed of, 113; Tsung-mi's definition of, 155
Buddha-nature: characteristics of, 125; in Hung-chou school, 44–45, 154–155; method of realizing, 41–43, 99; as nature of ignorance, 120; as sentience, 99–100; as true mind, 122; universality of, 58, 100, 154–155
Buddha of Unmoving Wisdom: as noumenon, 61–62; as omnipresent, 25, 51; realized through sudden awakening, 61–62

Buddhas: bodies of, 100–101; cursing of the, 138; life force of, 104; as mind, 24, 121; mistakes of, 187, 203 n.139; as originally sentient beings, 120; powers of, 2, 17, 52; secret formulas of, 177–178; spiritual family of, 62, 102, 121; wisdom-nature of, 51; worship of, 20. *See also names of individual Buddhas*
Buddha's names, recollection of. *See* Recollection of the Buddha
Buddhism: Central Asian, sectarian development in, 37; Chinese, 1–2, 37–38, 91 n.178; Ch'ing, influence of Li T'ung-hsüan on, 53; Indian, scholastic penchant of, 37, 91 n.178; Japanese, role of Paekche in developing, 6; Korean, characteristics of, 1–5; as ecumenical tradition, 1–2, 39, 91 n.178; monastic education in, 94 n.201; ties with India and Central Asia, 73 n.11; Koryŏ, 17–19, 53; Ming, influence of Li T'ung-hsüan on, 52–53; Northern Chinese, 3–5, 75 nn.20, 21; Three Kingdoms, 3–6, 76 n.37; Yi, persecutions during, 18, 83 n.93. *See also* National protection Buddhism

Calmness: leads to dullness, 65
Cause: and effect, 135, 140; of faith, 105, 168
Central domain. *See Dharmadhātu*
Ch'amgu, 69
Ch'amŭmi, 69
Ch'angbok sa tamsŏn pang (Yi Kyu-bo), 34, 87 n.133
Chang-ching Huai-hui, 13, 80 n.60
Ch'angp'yŏng, 22–23, 85 n.110
Ch'ang-sha Ching-ts'en, 141, 149 n.90; syncretism of, 91 n.175
Changsu Tamjin, 84 n.104
Changyŏn sa, 27, 87 n.126
Ch'ang-yü, 146 n.43
Ch'an-lin seng-pao chuan, 128
Ch'an school: adages of, 45, 54, 55; as Chinese adaptation of Buddhism, 37–38; five schools of, in mature tradition, 40; Middle Ch'an period, 40, 92 n.182; monks of, who advocated rapprochement with Hua-yen, 91 n.175; role of Korean monks in development of, 9. *See also* Sŏn school
Ch'an-tsung Yung-chia chi (Yung-chia), 130, 171
Ch'an-yüan chu-ch'üan chi (Tsung-mi), authenticity of, 92 n.185
Ch'an-yüan chu-ch'üan chi tou-hsü (Tsung-mi), 86 n.120, 106–107, 112, 157–159, 179–180
Chao-chou Ts'ung-shen, 31, 142 n.1; *mu hwadu,* 68–69, 185–186

Chao-lun (Seng-chao), 123, 126, 130, 139
Chao-yang. *See* Yün-men Wen-yen
Ch'egwan, 15, 80 n.70
Chen-chüeh. *See* Yung-chia Hsüan-chüeh
Ch'eng-kuan, 116 n.17; Pure Land scheme,
72; syncretism, 38; *Hsin-yao chien (tieh),*
165, 171; *Hua-yen tsung-yao,* 175, 200
n.107; *Ta-fang-kuang Fo Hua-yen ching
kang-yao,* 175–180, 200 n.107; *Ta-fang-
kuang Fo Hua-yen ching sui-shu yen-i
ch'ao,* 105; *Ta Hua-yen ching lüeh-ts'e,*
173
Ch'eng-tao ko (Yung-chia), 120, 127, 130,
132, 138, 139, 177
Ch'eng wei-shih lun shu chi (Tz'u-en), 126
Chief of Enlightenment Bodhisattva, three
realizations of, 25
chien (measurement), 86 n.125, 90 n.166
Chigwang, 77 n.37
Chih-i, 77 n.37; syncretism, 15, 38
Chih-kung. *See* Pao-chih
Ch'i-hsin lun shu pi hsüeh chi (Tzu-hsüan),
120
Chih-tun Tao-lin, 5, 75 n.24
Chih-wei, 200 n.111
Chih-yen, 7; interpretation of nature origina-
tion, 193 n.48
Chin, Mountain Master, 134, 148 n.76
Chin'gak, National Master. *See* Hyesim
Chin'gak kuksa si chip (Hyesim), 34–35, 90
n.167
Chin'gam, National Master. *See* Hyeso
Ch'ing-ch'i Hung-chin, 134, 148 n.76
Ch'ing-liang, National Master. *See* Ch'eng-
kuan
Ch'ing-liang T'ai-ch'in, 133, 148 n.73
Chin'gong. *See* Ch'ŏnjin
Ching-te ch'uan-teng lu: burned as spurious,
81 n.80; use of, in Saṃgha examinations,
82 n.88; quoted, 98, 100, 101, 103, 104,
107, 118, 120, 124, 125, 127, 133, 136–137,
142, 164–165, 171
Ch'ing-yüan Hsing-ssu: lineage, 9, 93 n.193,
142 n.3, 146 n.43, 147 n.55; in Middle
Ch'an period, 92 n.185
Chin-hua Chu-ti, 125, 147 n.43
Chinhŭng, King (Silla), 74 n.11
Chinsim chiksŏl (Chinul), 69, 127–131
Chinul
—life: birth and early years, 20–21; attempts
to reform Koryŏ Buddhism, 19–22; establishment of Samādhi and Prajñā Community, 21, 26–28; three awakening experiences, 22–29; hermitages around Susŏn sa,
30; passes successorship to Hyesim, 30–33;
death, 33–34; place in Kulsan sa lineage, 84

n.104; memorial stele, 89 n.160; criticisms
of, 92 n.180
—Hwaŏm thought: accommodating attitude
toward scholastic teachings, 39, 56, 189
n.5; Li T'ung-hsüan's influence, 24–25
—Sŏn thought: source of Korean Sŏn
thought, 92 n.180; syncretic approach to
Sŏn schools, 194 n.56; Ho-tse teachings'
influence, 49–50; Ta-hui's influence, 28–
29; Tsung-mi's influence, 49–50, 187; does
not acknowledge Shen-hui as successor of
Hui-neng, 151, 188 n.2; leniency toward
Hung-chou school, 45; Sŏn as a complete
and sudden approach, 200 n.117; description of process of sudden awakening, 181
—syncretism: as merging of Indian and
Chinese Buddhism, 91 n.178; development
of, 21, 23–25, 29; correlation of Sŏn and
Hwaŏm, 54, 151, 188 n.3
—methods of meditation: cultivation of
samādhi and *prajñā,* 62–65; faith and
understanding according to the complete
and sudden teachings, 66–67; shortcut
hwadu technique, 28–29, 67–70; *kongan*
exchanges, 31–32; thoughtlessness, 70–71,
162; Pure Land practice, 71–72
Chiri, Mount, 28, 31, 79 n.52, 88 n.136
Chisŏn Tohŏn, 9, 80 n.53
Chiu-feng Tao-ch'ien, 128, 147 n.55
Chiwon (Sŭngt'ong), 12–13
Cho Chong-jŏ, 87 n.134
Chodang chip, 99
Ch'oe Cha, 26, 86 n.124
Ch'oe Ch'i-won, 79 n.53
Ch'oe Ch'ung-hŏn, 20
Ch'oe Sŏn, 86 n.121
Ch'oe Ŭi, 20
Chogye Order: its formation of national
militia, 2; lineage of, 92 n.180
Chogye san, 30
*Chogye san cheise ko Tansok sa chuji Susŏn
saju chŭng si Chin'gak kuksa pimyŏng* (Yi
Kyu-bo), 32–33, 89 n.148
Chŏkch'wi am, 88 n.146
Ch'ŏnch'aek, 80 n.58
Ch'ŏnch'uk Nŭngin, 84 n.104
Chŏnghak Tojam, 84 n.104
Chŏnghye. *See* Hoeam Chŏnghye
Chŏnghye sa, 30, 88 n.144
Chonghwi, 20–21, 84 n.104
Chŏng Kwangu, 20
Ch'ŏngnyŏng kul, 86 n.122
Ch'ŏngwon sa, 22, 29, 85 n.110
Ch'ŏnjin, 28, 34, 87 n.133
chonsin techniques, 80 n.55
Ch'ŏnt'ae school: antipathy toward Sŏn, 16–

Production Notes

This book was designed by Roger Eggers. Composition was done on the Quadex Composing System and typesetting on the Compugraphic 8400 by the design and production staff of University of Hawaii Press.

The text and display typeface is Compugraphic Times Roman.

Offset presswork and binding were done by Malloy Lithographing, Inc. Text paper is Glatfelter Offset Vellum, basis 50.